MW00780913

Tino Sanandaji

Mass Challenge

The Socioeconomic Impact of Migration to a Scandinavian Welfare State

Tino Sanandaji
Institute for Economic and Business
History Research (EHFF)
Stockholm School of Economics
Stockholm, Sweden

Translation by
Jonas Vesterberg

Edited by
Pontus Tholin

ISBN 978-3-030-46807-1 ISBN 978-3-030-46808-8 (eBook)
https://doi.org/10.1007/978-3-030-46808-8

This Palgrave Macmillan imprint is published by the registered company Springer Nature Switzerland AG
The registered company address is: Gewerbestrasse 11, 6330 Cham, Switzerland

Preface

For we are conquered by overwhelming motives: honor, fear, and profit
—Thucydides, on the motives for human conflict, 5th century B.C.

In the early morning of Saturday, July 16, 2016, the Rosendal fire station in the city of Uppsala received a phone call. The alert concerned a suspected fire in Gottsunda. This high-rise neighborhood is located about a mile southwest of the city center and was built as a part of the Million Program in the 1960s. Gottsunda is a typical immigrant neighborhood characterized by social exclusion—one of the areas often portrayed in the news in connection with unrest.

Earlier during the night, violent disturbance had erupted in the district. Some thirty masked youths set fire to trash bins and threw rocks at rescue personnel. The fires escalate at midnight and create a riot-like atmosphere in the area. At 2 am, the fire station receives an alarm that someone has noticed smoke smell in the stairwell of Bandstolsvägen 38. The fire commander had earlier in the evening made the decision that the fire department was not allowed to go to Bandstolsvägen without a police escort. Therefore, the fire truck awaits the five or six police cars that are to escort the fire department to the address. When the convoy approaches, another delay occurs when the fire truck is forced to stop, so that the police can regroup and protect it on foot for the last few hundred yards. This evening, the distance of about two miles, which typically takes less than ten minutes to travel, took more than 25 minutes.

The above description is based on the accident investigation report that was produced by the Uppsala Fire Department (2016). I used the Freedom of Information Act to obtain a selection of the partly classified incident report, created by the Swedish Police Authority in Uppsala (2016), which is cited below:

19:46:52 Situation yellow, upset atmosphere
19:49:25 Meeting ambulance
19:55:57 Very bad atmosphere at [crossed out]
22:01:26 Call from bus traffic control, individuals have thrown something at the bus on its way towards Bandstolsvägen
22:02:05 They will stop buses to Gottsunda
22:03:08 [Crossed out] regarding that [crossed out] had an "incendiary bomb" thrown at his unit
22:04:23 [Crossed out] perceives that it's bottles that they're throwing which explode when they reach the ground
22:05:20 Now trash bins are burning at [crossed out]
22:06:48 [Crossed out] burning tires and trash bins
22:15:19 There's a fire in a dumpster at Bandstolsvägen and two dumpsters at Hugo Alfvéns
22:16:45 The gang that has set the fire was wearing masks in [crossed out]
23:20:31 Aggressive atmosphere Bandstolsvägen and trash bins thrown out into the road are burning
23:46:50 Have received information from [crossed out] that juveniles are going to throw rocks and eggs at police and emergency services
01:13:24 The objective of the operation is to restore order in Gottsunda. The operation must be carried out as safely as possible from a work environment perspective
02:02:02 Call from emergency services—public has called and reported the smell of smoke in the stairwell [crossed out]
02:25:28 Emergency services, they will now break down an apartment door
02:27:11: There's been a fire inside the apartment
02:27:28 Emergency services wants ambulance on scene
02:33:55 One individual deceased in apartment

The person found lifeless on the floor of the apartment was an elderly disabled man, whose life could not be saved. The direct cause of death appeared to be smoke inhalation, as a likely consequence of having left the stove on. While we cannot be sure, there are indications that the man's life could have been saved had the rescue operation not been delayed. The fire department report states: "Since there was unrest in the area during the evening, including arson of trash bins and rock-throwing at rescue personnel, the fire truck was escorted by police to Bandstolsvägen 38, which delayed arrival with about 13–15 minutes." Swedish tabloid *Aftonbladet* (2016a) interviewed a neighbor:

> Jawad Kerim, 33, lives in the same stairway as the deceased man, and he was in bed when his wife noticed the smell of smoke.
>
> "I checked our apartment first and found nothing, so I went out on the balcony and talked with the neighbor. Then I went out into the stairwell and the smell was very strong, and then I knocked on a lot of neighbors' doors, including his door. But he couldn't walk, he had a walker with him at all times," said

> Jawad Kerim. When the smell got even more intense in the stairwell, the neighbor called 112.
>
> "The fire department didn't get here immediately because of these idiots who burn things," said Jawad Kerim. He estimates that it took between 20 and 30 minutes before the fire brigade arrived—which is consistent with the fire brigade time logs.

The riots didn't stop after the tragic death, but continued for another three nights. It is not clear what prompted this particular incident, as is often the case with riots in Sweden today. The trigger may have been the police's attempt to arrest the driver of a stolen dirt bike. *Aftonbladet* (2016b) quotes the Uppsala police:

> The unrest in Gottsunda and Valsätra began on Friday evening. There has been unrest in these areas before. The inception of this event may have been that police arrested a man on a stolen dirt bike in Valsätra on Friday.
>
> "We don't rule out that it may be related in some way. Some that we've talked to claim that the police would be a reason for this. In cases where we've made arrests, it's due to crime," says Christer Nordström. Police spotted the man on the dirt bike and followed him, after which he skidded, overturned, and hurt himself. He suffered no serious injuries. But the event itself may, like earlier incidents, have caused a rumor to spread in the districts that the police acted unfairly.

Gottsunda and Valsätra are areas of social exclusion that have long experienced problems with antisocial behavior in the form of violent rioting, attacks against the authorities, torching of vehicles, and throwing of rocks. The district often receives visits from worried politicians and journalists. A recurring word in connection with these visits is "challenge." For instance, local politician Erik Pelling spoke of "turning around the social challenges that still exist in Gottsunda" (Swedish Public Radio 2016). A K9 officer with the Uppsala police, who witnessed the events, recounted his critical observations in the local daily *Upsala Nya Tidning* (2016):

> Already early on Saturday evening, we received information that a handful of people were preparing so-called Molotov cocktails and stocked up on paving stones. At this point, you could've gone in to remove the stones and Molotov cocktails, and in the best-case scenario arrest the people who were getting ready. But the police chose not to. Instead, dialogue police went up to Gottsunda and talked to some of the older juveniles; they're a number of multi-criminal young men with major influence on the youths in the area. They tried to persuade them to talk with the young people that they shouldn't set fires and so on. The counterclaim from the juveniles was, like so many times before, that the police should evacuate from Gottsunda. Now, things start to get crazy. Society, here represented by law enforcement, delegates the initiative of order and security

to a number of criminal young men, and accepts the demand for the police to leave the area. Had I been a criminal, I wouldn't want the cops in my neighborhood either.

I was in a police van two blocks from Bandstolsvägen, suited up in riot gear and with my police dog by my side. From there, I saw black columns of smoke from burning cars rise up into the sky, one after another. The city buses turned at Linrepevägen, which forced all the passengers to walk through entire Gottsunda to get home. It didn't feel right having to answer the elderly lady, who asked me how she was supposed to limp all the way home: I don't know.

Stockholm, Sweden Tino Sanandaji

References

Aftonbladet. 2016a. "Aftonbladet avslöjar: Så länge fördröjdes utryckningen när mannen dog" [Aftonbladet Reveals: This Is How Long the Emergency Reponse Was Delayed when the Man Died]. By Hans Österman and Niklas Svahn, July 18, 2016, updated July 19, 2016. https://www.aftonbladet.se/nyheter/a/1ky08X/aftonbladet-avslojar-sa-lange-fordrojdes-utryckningen-nar-mannen-dog.

———. 2016b. "Oroligheter fördröjde räddningsinsats—en dog" [Unrest Delayed the Rescue Efforts—One Died]. By Niklas Svahn and Oskar Forsberg, July 17, 2016, updated July 10, 2019. https://www.aftonbladet.se/nyheter/a/A2X5Q5/oroligheter-fordrojde-raddningsinsats--en-dog.

Swedish Police Authority in Uppsala. 2016. "Händelserapport" [Event Report]. Confidentiality-approved, August 26, 2016, Andrew Tomkinson, inspector. Uppsala: Polismyndigheten.

Swedish Public Radio. 2016. "Framtidens Gottsunda planeras" [The Gottsunda of the Future Is Being Planned]. By Tomas Magnusson, *P4 Uppland*, April 19, 2016. https://sverigesradio.se/sida/artikel.aspx?programid=114&artikel=6414856.

Upsala Nya Tidning. 2016. "Polisman dömer ut insatsen" [Policeman Condemns the Operation]. By Erik, K9 officer in Uppsala, July 20, 2016. https://www.unt.se/nyheter/uppsala/polisman-domer-ut-insatsen-4306461.aspx.

Uppsala Fire Department. 2016. "Olycksundersökning – rapport" [Acident Investigation—Report]. Administrative officer: Robert Johansson, fire inspector, July 25, 2016. Diarienummer RÄN-2016-0201. Uppsala: Brandförsvaret.

Acknowledgments

The book was translated from the Swedish by Jonas Vesterberg.

A warm thank you to Jan Ekberg, Manne Gerell, Mats Hammarstedt, Magnus Henrekson, Assar Lindbeck, Paulina Neuding, Nima Sanandaji, Christian Sandström, Amir Sariaslan, Kristina Sundquist, Göran Svensson, Björn Wallace, and Sabrine Wennberg for your valuable thoughts and comments.

Additionally, I would like to express my gratitude for the helpful advice and patience extended by Rachel Sangster and Sophia Siegler of Palgrave Macmillan.

Lastly, I would like to direct *a special thanks to my editor*, Pontus Tholin, whose friendly guidance elevated the quality as well as the joy of writing.

Contents

List of Figures

List of Tables

CHAPTER 1

Introduction

May Sweden remain a moral superpower.

—King Zog I of Albania, at a state visit to Sweden in 1939

The Swedish word for challenge is *utmaning*. Both words have long historic roots and roughly carry the same connotations in the two languages. The *Swedish Academy Glossary* defines the word as an "act that entails a call to struggle or competition" (Swedish Academy 2009), whereas Wiktionary's online dictionary states "something that requires substantial effort, but still attracts," and provides the example "It is a challenge to climb the Mount Everest." In the English language, the *Oxford Dictionary* (2010) similarly traces the word as far back as summons to a trial or contest in the middle ages.

In both languages, the word challenge has increasingly come to be used by politicians as a euphemism for tough social problems, in order to pretend they are in fact positive and rewarding trials in which we benefit to partake. Few would, however, sincerely argue that it is an "attractive effort" that fire trucks must have a police escort to enter certain neighborhoods. An editorial by Per Gudmundson in Swedish daily *Svenska Dagbladet* (2016), entitled "Increased Gross Domestic Challenge," discusses the inflated use of the term:

> While GDP has slowed and GDP per capita has been virtually stagnant for a decade, the amount of social problems—or challenges, as they're called when there are no solutions—has increased. Integration is a challenge, school is a challenge, long-term unemployment in vulnerable groups is a challenge, the demographic trend of an aging population is a challenge, the torching of cars in the social exclusion areas is a challenge, municipal finances are a challenge, police shortage is a challenge, burnout among social workers is a challenge, and so on. Citizens feel it, although that's not possible to include in the government's forecast. Perhaps GDP estimates should be supplemented, as economist

T. Sanandaji, *Mass Challenge*,
https://doi.org/10.1007/978-3-030-46808-8_1

> Tino Sanandaji recently expressed facetiously, with a measure of gross domestic challenge (GDC). In such case, one way to measure it would be to count how many times the term "challenge" occurs in parliamentary proceedings. During the 1970s, the average GDC was 17.6. The most recent parliamentary year showed a gross domestic challenge of 124—an increase of 14.8 percent from the prior year. The challenge economy is strong, I would say.

The concept is widely used in the media and by public agencies. The word challenge is found, for example, 215 times in the National Board of Health and Welfare's report "Healthcare and Dentalcare for Asylum Seekers and New Arrivals" (2016)—including nine times on the first page alone.

It seems that challenge is used for intractable social problems, where one cannot come up with suggestions for concrete measures, or even an effective spin to deflect the issue. Many have acted as if a shift in the discourse from problem to challenge is a magic wand, with which problems can be conjured away. However, magic tricks are only about illusions; they do not change the underlying reality—merely distracting the audience for a moment. Over time, the concept of challenge therefore morphed into a tired cliché. The word was gradually worn out when it was used to play down problems like social exclusion, segregation, inequality, homelessness, child poverty, unemployment, vandalism, riots, gang killings, extremism, child marriage, honor-based violence, car-torching, rock-throwing, and assaults with fireworks.

The truth is that what Sweden is facing are not challenges; Sweden is facing problems. A country long known as one of the world's most prosperous and idyllic is about to turn into an ethnic class society, where parts of the population feel like second-class citizens, and where assaults against firefighters are only reported in brief unless they lead to fatalities. The number of neighborhoods that are defined as social exclusion areas has increased from three in 1990 to 186 in 2012, while gang crime, bitterness, alienation, and multi-generational poverty have taken root in a short time. Sweden must deal with social problems that are not in the least inspiring, which are hard to paraphrase into something uplifting, and where there are not even any definite solutions. It is hard to have to face all this, but it is necessary; few social problems have been solved by being swept under the rug.

It is painful to admit the link between social problems and immigration. Most Swedes have great goodwill and tolerance toward immigrants, and wish that immigration would have been more successful. Sweden's experiment with large-scale immigration from the Third World to a welfare state has been unique in its scope, but is in many respects a failure. Today, Sweden's social problems are increasingly concentrated to the portion of the population with immigrant background. Foreign-born people account for about 19% of the population, and second-generation immigrants an additional 6%. Despite this, foreign-born represent 53% of individuals with long prison sentences, 58% of the unemployed, and receive 65% of social welfare expenditures; 77% of

Sweden's child poverty is present in households with a foreign background, while 90% of suspects in public shootings have immigrant backgrounds.

The increase in social problems is also driven in large part by immigration. Since the early 1990s, those with immigrant background have accounted for half of the increase in the proportion of low-income earners; more than half of the reduction in high school eligibility of students leaving primary school; about two-thirds of the increase in social welfare expenditure; and more than 100% of the increase in unemployment—which, consequently, has dropped among Swedish-born. Problems such as rioting and unrest are also highly concentrated in immigrant areas. We must develop concrete actions that give all immigrants Sweden has received a place in Swedish society. This, in turn, requires a frank and evidence-driven analysis of how Sweden ended up here and, more importantly, can move on.

Now, when the debate on "mass immigration" is over, Sweden must understand and address the, in many ways, more complex problems—including mass unemployment, mass riots, mass vandalism, and mass vehicle-burning. If problems are to be referred to as challenges, we must conclude that the combined issues Sweden is facing cannot be characterized as anything else but a mass challenge. For the benefit of those who prefer the term challenge instead of problem, I have thusly chosen the title *Mass Challenge*.

A Policy Perspective

Let us begin with a few words about myself, as well as about the structure of the book. I am of Kurdish origin and was born in 1980 in Iran. My family moved to Sweden in 1989, although—like many migrants—we were not refugees fleeing our lives, but rather left a safe life in Iran in order not to live under the oppression of the Islamic Republic. Like many immigrants—again—we were hardly poor, instead belonging to the affluent and secular layers of society. My father studied as a young man in California. He and my mother were among the many Iranians who prefer Western enlightenment values to the authoritarian theocracy established by Ayatollah Khomeini, which to this day imprisons the people of Iran in a grim, if ever-weakening, grip.

Ironically, I lived in Teheran during the eight-year Iran–Iraq war, and experienced many nights with aerial bombings—including one that shattered the windows of our home—but only left Iran one year after the war was over. We left Iran for ideological reasons, not due to any objective threat to our lives or material needs. Once Ayatollah Khomeini passed away, without the Islamic Republic falling, my father gave up hope and decided to move to Europe, in order for my mother not having to be forced to cover herself in a veil, as well as not being exposed to daily propaganda. At the time, he worked with—and later for—a Swedish forestry company involved in building a pulp plant in the forested areas around the Caspian Sea, which gave him a visa to Sweden.

My brother and I did not experience any cultural shock, as we were already reared in Iran's significant Western bubble. In general, Iranian immigrants to the West have a lower cultural distance compared to those of many other Middle Eastern countries, since the Iranian middle and upper classes for generations have been comparably Westernized. After taking my economics degree from the Stockholm School of Economics in 2004, I lived eight happy, brutally cold, and intellectually stimulating years in the Windy City—obtaining my Ph.D. in Public Policy from the University of Chicago as well as doing my postdoc.

I returned to Sweden in 2012 and have since then worked as a researcher, focusing on entrepreneurship, historical economics, and public economics. In order to avoid tainting results with false accusations of bias, I have deliberately chosen not to do research on immigration, but instead refer to the research of others. Contrasting the inhibited Swedish debate climate with the openness of the Norwegian, a *New York Times* article by Hugh Eakin (2014) noted that "In Sweden, closely patrolled pro-immigration 'consensus' has sustained extraordinarily liberal policies while placing a virtual taboo on questions about the social and economic costs."

As an academic economist, with immigrant background, and a firm believer in liberal enlightenment values as well as the scientific traditions of the University of Chicago, I saw my duty to stand firm where others were silent or silenced. For a time, I was one of the very few economists in Sweden who publicly cited negative facts, which refuted the public consensus that immigration did not have negative economic or social effects. This taboo is today, to some extent, broken in Sweden under the overwhelming pressure of empirical reality. The original Swedish version of this book was part of this debate and released in early 2017—and became the best-selling economics book in that year.

Since I wrote the book as an economist and public intellectual, I have to the best of my abilities attempted to make it empirically solid, balanced, and scientifically stringent. Although the book is largely about Sweden, it has the benefit of being unusually detailed regarding the socioeconomic effects of migration. With Sweden not only being the archetypal welfare state, but also the archetypal multicultural welfare state, it makes a suitable subject as a case study as many of the results apply to other countries—both as lessons and warnings.

Conversely, the problems in Sweden have been exploited and grossly exaggerated by the white supremacists, right-wing extremists, and opportunistic populists. Anecdotes and kernels of truth are used to create a cartoonish caricature of Sweden, as a country engulfed in civil war, or experiencing collapse due to hordes of foreigners pouring in. In some cases, inflammatory claims—such as Muslims mass-raping Swedish women, or a planned white genocide—are tied to anti-Semitic conspiracy theories and to the manifestos of extreme terrorists. There are also reports that foreign powers, particularly Russia, have systematically used propagandistic disinformation about Sweden in its information operations, with the aim of influencing Western public opinion and elections.

The Swedish immigration debate has receded in intensity, as the country is coming closer to a realistic consensus, but since the country—at least to some extent—is used and misused in the international immigration debate, I believe it to be important to write a reliable and in-depth book. Facts and social science research tend naturally to be moderating in an otherwise polarized era. Most importantly, however, I hope that this book may be of some value to economists and other social scientists. While there are seminal books about immigration by economists and political scientists (e.g., Borjas 2014; Collier 2013), they tend to have broad and macroeconomic perspectives. This book, by contrast, attempts to give a fine-grained empirical examination—indeed, dissection—of one country with a particular focus on the social and cultural consequences, not the least to understand the dynamics of antisocial behavior and conflict.

Some foreign analysts noted similarities between Sweden's migration politics and the strategy to deal with the COVID-19 crisis, where Sweden followed a unique strategy but suffered death rates far above neighboring countries. In both cases, the Swedish policy was characterized by overconfidence, dismissal of other nations, and an explicit or implicit assumption that Swedish exceptionalism would guarantee success where other nations failed. Also, in both cases, a strong and expectant consensus was eventually followed by doubts and shifts in public opinion under the force of statistics. During the consensus, critical articles in the domestic media were rare, whereas critical articles in leading international outlets were dismissed or even accused as being foreign campaigns to tarnish the image of Sweden.

Swedes that cited critical articles on their policy by the BBC or the Guardian could be accused of being disloyal. Chauvinist defensiveness, where attempts to improve national policies are equated with treachery against the nation, is common in populist authoritarian countries; yet clear signs could be noted in some quarters in liberal Sweden. Perhaps this in part reflects the stress caused by facts that in national hubris were followed by the shame of losing face, where Sweden has for generations been used to success and adoration in the international court of public opinion. Sweden continues to be successful and appreciated in domains such as environmentalism, welfare, innovation, and feminism—but the image is increasingly mixed with failures in other domains.

The article "A Very Swedish Sort of Failure: A Flawed Policy on Covid-19 Was Driven by the Country's Exceptionalism" in the *Financial Times*, by its chief foreign affairs columnist Gideon Rachman (2020), discussed the underlying reasons for Sweden's flawed policy on COVID-19—so intriguingly laid out as to be quoted at length:

> Paradoxically, it may be Sweden's very success as a nation that led to its apparent failure over the pandemic. A self-image as a country that is superrational and modern means that Sweden is confident and cohesive enough not to follow the international consensus. Instead, policymakers have chosen to trust their own judgment. But Swedish self-confidence may have shaded into an arrogance about the country's supposedly superior rationality, which then led to policy errors.
>
> Nicholas Aylott, a professor of politics at Södertörn University in Stockholm, draws a parallel between Sweden's pandemic policies and its handling of the refugee crisis in 2015. In both cases, the country stood out from the international crowd because of its distinctive and radical approach. But, in both cases, the Swedish exception did not work out very well.
>
> For a long period, Sweden offered automatic asylum to all Syrians—a policy more liberal even than Germany's. Ironically, Sweden's ultra-permissive policy attracted scorn from many of the same American rightwingers now praising it over Covid-19. Sweden's distinctive refugee policy was initially a source of national pride. But, eventually, the government conceded that it was unsustainable, and changed course.
>
> Something similar may now be happening over coronavirus. As Mr Aylott sees it: "In Sweden, there is often near national consensus for a long time, then suddenly a brick falls out of the wall and everything changes."

Mass Challenge is an interdisciplinary book that, in addition to discussing the economic effects of immigration, touches on such areas as criminology and sociology. Parts of the book are factual descriptions and reviews of existing research, while others are my own subjective policy recommendations.

The English translation was not done by me but by Jonas Vesterberg. In addition to updating the book, I have attempted to redraft it for the international audience. Many sections dealing parochially with the Swedish debate have been cut, whereas other have been expanded to make the discussion more universally relevant. Should there be any errors or loss of context in the translation, I apologize to the reader.

References

Borjas, George J. 2014. *Immigration Economics*. Cambridge, MA: Harvard University Press.

Collier, Paul. 2013. *Exodus: How Migration Is Changing Our World*. New York: Oxford University Press.

Eakin, Hugh. 2014. "Scandinavians Split Over Syrian Influx." *New York Times*, opinion, September 19, 2014. https://www.nytimes.com/2014/09/21/opinion/sunday/syrian-refugees-nordic-dilemma.html.

National Board of Health and Welfare. 2016. "Hälso- och sjukvård och tandvård till asylsökande och nyanlända: Slutrapport oktober 2016" [Healthcare and

Dentalcare for Asylum Seekers and New Arrivals: Final Report, October 2016]. Socialstyrelsen, Stockholm. https://www.socialstyrelsen.se/globalassets/share-point-dokument/artikelkatalog/ovrigt/2016-10-13.pdf.

Oxford Dictionary of English. 2010. 3rd ed. Edited by Angus Stevenson. Oxford: Oxford University Press.

Rachman, Gideon. 2020. "A Very Swedish Sort of Failure: A Flawed Policy on Covid-19 Was Driven by the Country's Exceptionalism." *Financial Times*, Opinion Sweden, June 15, 2020. https://www.ft.com/content/4f6ad356-9f61-4728-a9aa-3fa1f232035a.

Svenska Dagbladet. 2016. "Ökad bruttonationalutmaning" [Increased Gross Domestic Challenge]. Editorial by Per Gudmundson, August 25, 2016. https://www.svd.se/okad-bruttonationalutmaning.

Swedish Academy. 2009. *Svensk ordbok* [Swedish Academy Glossary], "utmaning." 1st ed. Stockholm: Norstedt.

CHAPTER 2

A Nation of Immigrants?

What is past is prologue.

—William Shakespeare, *The Tempest*, 1611

Sweden is not a nation of immigrants. Unlike the United States, geographically and culturally isolated Scandinavia remained one of the world's most homogeneous regions until the late twentieth century. Naturally, there has always been a certain degree of immigration to the Scandinavian countries, but historically this was rarely large in scale. At the start of the Second World War, roughly one percent of Sweden's population was born abroad, and only one in a thousand was born outside of Europe.

One could, of course, make the case that on a fundamental level all Swedes are immigrants, since we know that Sweden was uninhabited at the end of the last ice age some 10,000 years ago. It is, however, silly to label all of humanity as immigrants by conflating settlers, who move into uninhabited territories, with immigrants. The formal definition of an immigrant is a person who voluntary moves from one area to another, a definition that is only meaningful in the context of existing sovereign states. Consequently, the first people who moved into these virgin territories when the ice sheets melted and unveiled the land buried underneath were settlers—not immigrants. Likewise, moving into an area by means of war and conquest does not constitute immigration but invasion. Following a similar logic, we do not call the slaves forcibly taken from Africa to the Americas and the Arab world immigrants, as their movement was not undertaken voluntarily but as part of historical crimes against humanity.

The term immigration refers to non-coerced relocation between states, which often makes the concept misleading when applied to prehistorical population movements. Due to the lack of records, we often do not know the exact circumstances of these events. In some cases, it represented peaceful absorption of new members into existing populations. However, in many

T. Sanandaji, *Mass Challenge*,
https://doi.org/10.1007/978-3-030-46808-8_2

other cases, archeological evidence and other sources suggest that the movement involved conquest, colonization, or even the complete annihilation of existing cultures. In recent years, there has been a tendency to romanticize these kinds of events in order to reach the conclusion that "we are all immigrants." This represents an ahistorical distortion and indeed risks blurring the lines between immigration and genocide.

Historical Migration

It was until recently generally acknowledged that Sweden was a homogeneous country with little immigration. A comparison by sociologist Elina Haavio-Mannila (1983) with other European countries pointed out that "Sweden used to be a linguistically and culturally homogenous country. Only the small groups of Lapps and Tornedal Finns broke this unity. After the Second World War, however, Sweden became an immigration country."

Today, there is a tendency to exaggerate the extent of historical immigration using anecdotal examples, which are often vague regarding actual detail and the quantity of migration. To rewrite the past in order to portray Sweden as a nation of immigrants is thus a novel phenomenon that emerged as a response to xenophobia. This tendency is not unique for Sweden, even though it may be particularly pronounced in the characteristically extreme Swedish migration debate. In all Western European welfare states, there has been a similar effort to recompose the historical narrative and to varying extent portray the country as a nation of immigrants. This Americanization of the European past is also a prominent feature of the rhetoric of EU officials.

Few outside of Sweden have probably heard about the Walloon migration to Sweden in the seventeenth century. This historical migration has become mythologized in modern Swedish discourse, even though it remains an obscure historical event everywhere else—including in the Belgian province of Wallonia. As a typical example, the former Swedish Prime Minister Carl Bildt (2016) reminded the world about the virtues of open migration policies by highlighting this event: "Once upon a time Wallonia spearheaded globalisation. Came to Sweden and modernised us."

One example of this modern mythology draws parallels between the historical immigration of Walloons to Sweden and the immigration that populated the United States, Canada, and Australia. The Walloons, who moved to Sweden in the seventeenth century from present-day Belgium and France, made a strong impression but were few in number (Douhan 1982). This group was tiny relative to the population of the Swedish kingdom, which at the time had around one million inhabitants. Moreover, many of the Walloons returned to their home country after a few years, which was a common pattern in historic labor migrations. According to the source *Nationalencyklopedin* (n.d.): "Little is known about the Walloons who returned home, whereas the approximately 900 people who stayed in Sweden have been studied in some detail."

The inflow of one to two thousand Walloons corresponded to about one-tenth or two-tenths of one percent of the population, spread out across several decades. By comparison, in 2015 Sweden took in approximately 134,000 immigrants, according to Statistics Sweden. Immigration minus emigration is referred to as net immigration. Furthermore, some of the people who annually move in and out of Sweden are native-born—for instance, Swedes who lived in Norway for a few years and returned home—and should be excluded from the analysis. When comparing to historical migration, it is more useful to focus on the foreign-born and also to subtract the foreign-born who returned home. In 2015, Sweden had a net immigration of foreign-born individuals of around 82,000 people—or 0.84% of a population of nearly ten million.

Thus, even after considering that Sweden has a much larger population, today's immigration is on an annual basis nearly 200 times larger than the famous Walloon inflow in the seventeenth century. Another reason why the Walloon immigration cannot be used as a parallel to today's immigration is that most of the immigration to Sweden today is from poorer countries, whereas the Walloons were highly skilled laborers from a technologically more advanced country (Douhan 1982).

Naturally, the inflow of Walloons from present-day Belgium is not the only episode of historical immigration. A more important group that arrived over a far longer period of time were German migrants. Again, these were also immigrants who, thanks to unusual skill sets, made important contributions to Sweden despite being few in number.

In the Middle Ages, Germany was more advanced than Scandinavia. German migrants were what we today might refer to as high-skilled workers in trading hubs and mining towns (Heckscher 1954). German burghers periodically made up a significant proportion of the population in some of the largest and most important Swedish, Danish, and Norwegian towns of the time. This group played an important role in organizing trade and finance as well as in maintaining Scandinavia's ties with Germany. Again, the total number of migrants was not large, simply because cities and mining towns constituted a very small proportion of the medieval population when the overwhelming majority were peasants. In the rural areas, where most people lived, there was no German immigration to speak of.

While no systematic population records exist for this period, we still have enough data to make estimates possible. For instance, Sidén (2008) estimates the number of Germans in Swedish towns during the High Middle Ages and arrives at "a proportion of the population of normally 10–20%." At the time, only about five percent of Sweden's population lived in towns, which means that the total population share of Germans was between one half and one percent.

Sweden as well as the other Scandinavian countries experienced other waves of immigration during the early modern era. In addition to Germans and Walloons, these included Scots, Dutch, Balts, and other groups concentrated to the higher echelons of society—in particular, the nobility and military officers (Heckscher 1954). The influx of immigrants to the elite has contributed to an exaggerated perception of past immigration. Many Swedish noble houses have overseas origins and foreign-sounding names, although the nobility only constituted about half a percent of Sweden's population at the time. One economic sector that attracted migrants was mining and metallurgy, in which Sweden held and continues to hold prominence.

Recent studies also show that the traditional narrative of Germany's importance for the Swedish ironworks has been exaggerated, and that much of the technological development in the mining industry was in fact domestic. Berglund (2015) discusses new findings in the history of technology:

> In this book, sensational discoveries are presented that, among other things, show that mining operations began in the late 900s and the technology to safely use the blast furnace emerged as early as in the 1100s in Sweden; probably even earlier. As late as the 1970s, it was still assumed, supported by written sources, that the blast furnace came to Sweden from Germany in the 1300s. But through new scientific methods in the form of vegetation and pollen analyses, we can now show that it in fact was most likely a Swedish innovation.

These findings suggest that the blast furnace was developed in Sweden and from there reached Germany—not the other way around as was long assumed.

The reason why immigrants have always been prominently featured in Swedish historical narratives is because it was concentrated to the elite strata of society and since it was exotic—not because Sweden was viewed as a nation of immigrants. Over the years, most immigrants to Sweden have arrived from Finland, with which Sweden has a long, shared history, being part of the same kingdom until 1809. Migration from Finland made a demographic imprint on the population—but, again, nowhere near contemporary levels. Perhaps the most famous example is the arrival of the so-called Forest Finns, a group of slash-and-burn farmers who escaped famine by settling in sparsely populated parts of Sweden. This event is discussed by the seminal economic historian Eli Heckscher in his *Sweden's Economic History from Gustav Vasa* (1935–1949). Under the heading "Immigration of Finns in central Sweden and southern Norrland," he estimated that between 12,000 and 13,000 immigrants came to these areas: "It is obvious that this immigration did not, even with the inclusion of immigrants' descendants, represent a great migration wave in the modern sense of the concept."

Heckscher was among those scholars who shaped modern historical economics by augmenting historical analysis with quantitative methods. One important lesson we can draw from his work is that anecdotal descriptions do not suffice in economic history. The discipline also requires a scientific theory and systematic empirical evidence in order to draw causal conclusions. This is especially important when it comes to so-called counterfactual conclusions; that is, what we think would have happened if events had taken a different turn.

In the early nineteenth century, the largest construction project in Swedish history, Göta canal, was completed with the help of a number of British experts, including a celebrated Scottish engineer Thomas Telford. A small portion of the work of digging the canal was carried out by a company of Russian prisoners of war. It would be fallacious from this to conclude that the project would not have been realized without foreign labor. The reason for this is that we know that many other similar construction projects in both Sweden and other countries were conducted without the use of foreign experts and labor. There are many alternative ways of carrying out a project. If the Russian prisoners had not been there, someone else would have dug the canal instead, though perhaps at a marginally higher cost. Technology and expertise were imported in other ways—for example, through books, manuals, or by Swedes studying abroad. Even in the case of Göta canal, the overwhelming majority of the work was in fact carried out by 58,000 Swedish soldiers.

During the industrial revolution, small countries such as Sweden imported most of its technology from abroad. Then as today, no single nation would have been able to develop all these technologies on its own. However, we further know that immigration made a relatively small contribution to the flow of technology. Most of new knowledge arrived through the exchange of information between countries, not through the exchange of people. Openness to trade and foreign influences is a separate issue from immigration, contrary to the tendency to vaguely lump them together.

Indeed, the fact that countries can import vast and transformative amounts of ideas and cultural influences from abroad without significant migration is self-evident, once one stops and thinks about it. The most important country from which Scandinavia imports technology and cultural impressions is the United States, despite negligible immigration from Silicon Valley, Hollywood, or New York. The explanation is that information flows through different channels. Bill Gates and Steve Jobs were not forced to move to Stockholm for innovations from Microsoft and Apple to reach Sweden—just as Sweden became Lutheran without Martin Luther ever setting foot in the country.

It is, of course, true that some industries were founded in Sweden by immigrants, but most industries made use of foreign technology without immigration. Likewise, even the industries that were developed through contributions by immigrants evolved in other European countries without the help of immigration. Long-term comparisons of various industrialized nations clearly show that technology eventually trickles in somehow and is absorbed regardless of the exact channel, indicating very strong underlying forces unrelated to migration flows.

Hence, in order to correctly estimate the effect of immigration, it does not suffice to simply list what immigrants have done and then conclude that these things would not have happened were it not for immigration. While it is likely true that immigration increased the flow of technology to Sweden and similar European countries, it is unclear by how much. The fundamental question thus becomes what the alternative would have been, and how much the outcome would have differed from what actually happened in the counterfactual scenario without immigration. In recent years, there has developed a tendency to inordinately exaggerate the role of immigration for historical economic development—usually without actual numbers or even attempts at stringent analysis.

This state of affairs represents a qualitative decline compared to when Eli Heckscher, himself the son of an immigrant, analyzed immigration to Sweden before it had become a controversial political issue. Immigrants were appreciated for the contributions they made, but their contributions were described quantitatively and with a sense of proportion. This sober approach can be contrasted with today's polarized debate, where some blame immigrants for virtually all societal problems, whereas others mythologize the contribution of immigrants beyond reasonable limits. Moreover, since immigration was not the sole focus, economic historians avoided the mistake of downplaying more important causes of technological development. Heckscher (1935–1949), for example, writes about the industrialization of Sweden: "The Swedes commonly traveled abroad to study and to an increasing degree, literature also mediated the foreign experience; it is likely that it had a bigger impact than immigration."

Even in areas where foreign experts had the biggest imprint, deeper analysis often shows that their contribution was the acceleration of a process that would have occurred sooner or later anyway. Long periods of immigration were rarely required to transfer expertise. Boëthius (1951) writes of German blacksmiths in Bergslagen: "The Swedish blacksmiths have quickly enough acquired their art. Already in the 1630s, they felt independent of the masters."

Similarly, Åkesson (1998) explains that "Developments in mining and metallurgy would have occurred even without Germans and Walloons. But it would have been different, slower and with a delay of processing, export of inferior and cheaper iron closer to the raw material."

Scandinavia was a major exporter of iron by the Viking Age, and it is therefore unsurprising that some of the sector's technological development took place in this region. Another example is the famous shipbuilding technology of the Scandinavian Viking Age. There are also examples of important institutional innovations with probable origins in the Nordic countries. One example was the *things*, which were political assemblies for legislation and justice (Brink 2002). These and other Scandinavian institutions exerted a major impact on Anglo-Saxon legal and political developments, such as the jury system (Turner 1968; Plucknett [1956] 2010).

In the Middle Ages, just like today, Sweden and the other Nordic countries had small populations and were primarily importers of innovation, but that does not mean that they were primitive societies that never contributed anything of their own. Former Swedish Prime Minister Fredrik Reinfeldt gave an example of such prejudice in a speech to students with immigrant backgrounds (*Dagens Nyheter* 2006): "Merely barbarism is fundamentally Swedish. The rest of the development has come from outside."

This is a contemptuous and almost colonial view. It is ahistorical to imagine that any society can import, adapt, and absorb ideas from other countries without any domestic contribution. The blend of external and internal impressions that constitute culture is unique in every society. A useful parallel to understand how the cultures of countries can be unique, while sharing common components, is to compare them with languages. Human culture is an information set as opposed to an essence. English, German, Swedish, Farsi, Arabic, Swahili, and Yiddish all share some common words and structure, if to varying degrees. Often due to historical reasons, some cultures have more common traits, just as some language groups are more similar to one another. No human culture exists in complete isolation; simultaneously, no country in our world can be said to lack a distinct culture. Culture is a set of knowledge transmitted over time, including beliefs, values, symbols, and customs. Culture and language both consist of thousands of distinct elements that are to various degrees both shared and unique. A common logical error is to instead think of culture as having an essence rather than consisting of a continuous set of complex information.

Languages and cultures are often influenced by one another. The English language has borrowed many words from Norse languages, including the words *husband*, *sky*, and *thrift*. It would be ridiculous to claim that the English language does not exist since it shares elements with other languages—and equally ridiculous to claim that Swedish culture does not exist because the recipe for Swedish meatballs may have been originally inspired by Persian cuisine. To state that a culture does not exist if it has borrowed elements or partially overlaps with other cultures is, therefore, a straw man. Culture and language are powerful analytical concepts, since they are sufficiently coherent over time and distinct across groups to be conceptually meaningful and easily identifiable. In recent years, fallacies relying on the "no pure culture" argument have become common in the Scandinavian debate and are generally utilized to claim that Swedish, Danish, and Norwegian cultures do not exist—often by citing anecdotes about foreign influences on cultural symbols. This line of reasoning is often a reaction to xenophobic and isolationist rhetoric, but it is equally simplistic. During the romantic nationalism of the nineteenth century, it was common to shamelessly exaggerate and raise one's own country to the heavens. But it is just as unnuanced to, as an overreaction, go to the opposite extreme and reduce the history of an ancient country to romantic anecdotes about Walloons and German burghers.

Migration in the Modern Era

While historical migration levels are based on estimates, Statistics Sweden started compiling migration statistics in the late nineteenth century. Between 1871 and 1940, Sweden received an average of about 6000 immigrants per year. Many of those immigrants were Swedes who had moved to North America and were returning home. The rest were almost entirely migrants from other Western European countries. Hallberg (2001) writes that "In the 1800s, during the time of the great emigration, immigration was relatively minor and mainly consisted of returning Swedish-Americans."

It is interesting to note that the period when Sweden transformed into one of the world's wealthiest economies was characterized by limited immigration. Until modernization took off in the mid-nineteenth century, Sweden's GDP per capita was average in Europe—below the Western European mean but higher than that of Eastern Europe. In this period, Sweden rapidly developed through industrial capitalism and created many of its famous export companies including Volvo, Ericsson, Nobel Industries, and Electrolux. By the start of the Second World War, Sweden had managed to become the world's ninth wealthiest economy, a higher ranking than today (Maddison 2010). Consequently, it is difficult to claim that Sweden became rich due to high rates of immigration.

It is not really until the Second World War that Sweden experienced large-scale immigration. An estimated 150,000–170,000 refugees were taken in during the war, most importantly from Norway and Finland. Statistics Sweden (2004) explains: "The large number of refugees who arrived during the war years from the neighboring Nordic countries returned immediately after the end of the Second World War."

Thousands of refugees with Jewish backgrounds were rescued by Sweden during the Second World War, many of whom chose to remain in Sweden after the war (Borevi 2012). Unlike most other European countries, Sweden's manufacturing base was intact after the war. The country was already fully industrialized with a highly skilled labor force and advanced levels of research and engineering. Contrary to popular perception, the Swedish economic system was not and never became socialist, instead choosing to retain free-market capitalism and private ownership of enterprise. Sweden did not join NATO but generally sided with the Western block and chose to receive Marshall aid from the United States, which further helped Sweden increase its prosperity.

At the same time, Sweden as well as other Scandinavian countries pursued a policy of high taxes, strong labor unions, and strict market regulations aimed at redistributing income. This approach of combining capitalism with a large welfare state financed by high taxes was sometimes referred to as a middle way between socialist and laissez-faire policies. The decades following the Second World War were characterized by affluence, high annual growth, low unemployment, and the expansion of the famous welfare state. Income inequality fell rapidly, and Sweden by the early 1980s had one of the lowest levels of inequality ever observed. As we shall see later, this ideal was not to last as the Swedish economic engine started losing steam by the 1970s. In subsequent decades, unsatisfactory growth, fiscal crises, and changes in political ideology led to a leaner and less generous welfare state as well as a deregulation of the economy.

Immigration to Sweden took off during the postwar period in the form of labor migration from other European countries. In the 1950s to early 1970s, large-scale or modest guest worker and labor migrant programs were introduced also in West Germany, France, the Netherlands, Belgium, Norway, and Denmark (Borevi 2012). According to Statistics Sweden (2004), the number of foreign-born tripled in the space of 20 years—from 198,000 in 1950 to 538,000 in 1970. The report further states that labor immigration was "primarily a Nordic phenomenon, and secondly a European one." There is generally a tendency for refugees and their kin to remain in their destination country once they migrate, whereas labor migrants in fact tend to return to their home country after a number of years. This was also observed regarding the industrial labor migration to Sweden, as many of the workers eventually returned to their home country. Due to high return migration, the permanent demographic impact on Sweden of labor migration was limited.

The most important group was from Finland, which increased by nearly 200,000 between 1950 and 1970. Immigrants from European countries outside the Nordics, such as Italy, Greece, and Yugoslavia, grew by just under 100,000—fewer than many imagine today. Non-European migrants increased by nearly 20,000. Here, the main country was Turkey followed by the United States and Canada.

Today, immigration to Sweden from outside of Europe is associated with developing countries, but historically it mainly came from North America. Immigration is not a homogeneous phenomenon, which makes it important to analytically categorize immigrants. Important factors include human capital, the reason for immigration, the development level of the country of origin, and the cultural proximity of immigrants to the country of destination.

A common division of countries of origin is European versus non-European. Another and arguably more accurate division is Western versus non-Western. In this book, the West is defined as Western Europe, the rest of the European Union, the United States, Canada, Australia, and New Zealand. The difference between the West and Europe is that the West does not include the less developed Eastern European countries, but includes the United States, Canada, Australia, and New Zealand.

Figure 2.1 shows the proportion of immigrants in Sweden's population in 1945, broken down by Western and non-Western origin. The chart illustrates that Sweden had relatively high immigration during the first postwar decades, a bit lower in the 1970s and the first half of the 1980s, before accelerating to record levels in recent years. It also shows the striking differences in countries

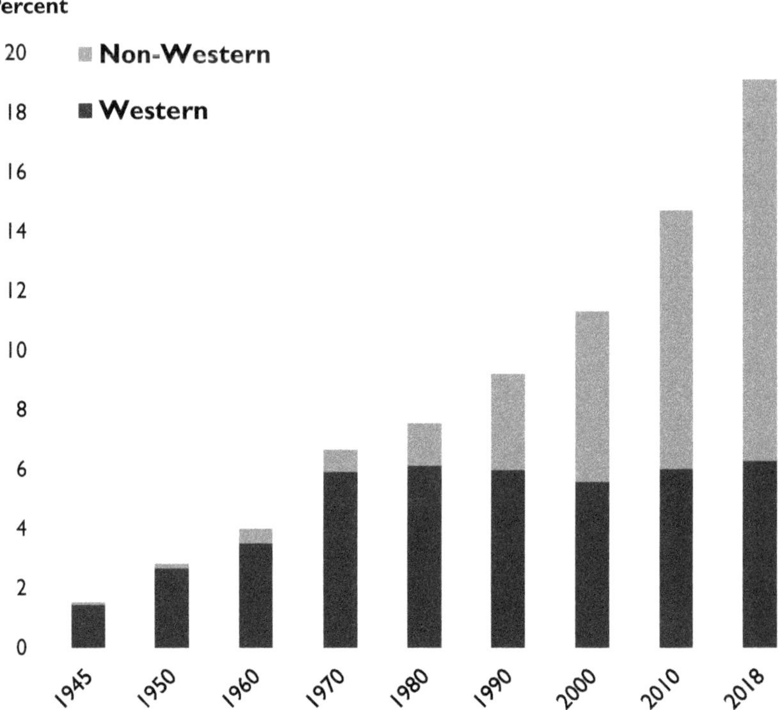

Fig. 2.1 Immigrants' proportion of the population, by origin (*Source* Statistics Sweden)

of origin. As late as 1980, the number of immigrants from non-Western countries in Sweden only made up just over one percent of the population, and the fraction from developing countries was tiny. The Western immigrant group as a proportion of the Swedish population has not increased since 1970, while the proportion of non-Western foreign-born has increased rapidly. Of course, Sweden has continued to have immigration from the Nordic countries and the rest of the West, but the proportion has been stable since many also return and as elderly immigrants eventually die.

The increase of non-Western immigrants is due to the fact that the labor migration era was eventually replaced by a shift toward refugees and their relatives (Borevi 2012). By the 1970s, an economic downturn and new policies led to a decrease in labor migration. A few years later, however, a new type of migration started to develop that eventually far surpassed labor migration in quantity. The creation of the Swedish Migration Board heralded a new age of refugee migration that in time turned the small country of Sweden into one of the world's primary destinations for refugees, and that in many ways was to transform the country.

Before citing figures, it would be valuable for the reader to familiarize herself with terminology. There are three related concepts that should not be confused, namely asylum seekers, refugee immigrants, and immigrants. Immigrants are defined as those who have either permanent or temporary residence permits. There are many types of immigrants such as family-based immigrants, workers, and students. Refugee immigrants are an important subcategory of immigrants: those immigrants who used to be asylum seekers. Asylum seekers are, however, not identical to refugee immigrants, since many asylum seekers are denied asylum or withdraw their application. Moreover, even for those asylum seekers who are granted asylum, there is usually a lag of one to two years before they officially become immigrants and registered residents. Asylum seekers who are granted asylum and stay become refugee immigrants after a few years. The distinction between asylum seeker and refugee immigrant is important to better interpret European data, especially since asylum seekers who have not yet been recategorized as refugee immigrants are often not counted as part of the official population. Additionally, the lag means that increases in the number of asylum seekers take some time to fully impact population statistics.

The Swedish Migration Agency reports the number of asylum seekers from 1984 onwards. A total of just over one million people applied for asylum between 1984 and 2015. Of these, about 515,000 were granted asylum as refugees or equivalent status. In addition, approximately 800,000 were granted family-based residence permits. Relatives who arrive directly in connection with refugees, or within two years of their arrival, are defined as relatives of refugees; those who arrive later from the same countries are instead counted as family-based immigrants. Historically, a little over 40% of asylum seekers were granted asylum in the first instance—a figure that has increased to about 50% in recent years. Additionally, some asylum seekers are granted residence permits by appeal or by changing their application.

As previously noted, immigrant workers and students tend to return home, while most refugees and their families tend to stay. Statistics Sweden (2011a) points out that more than half of labor migrants have returned after ten years, whereas 96% of those who arrive as refugees remain in Sweden ten years on. Kin migrants also tend to remain in Sweden.

Although some refugees return home or pass away, there are far more immigrants from the major refugee countries in Sweden than those who were granted asylum. This may appear strange but has a simple explanation. The reason is that asylum immigration is eventually followed by family-based immigration and chain migration. In addition to direct relatives, immigration also tends to lead to more people from the same country arriving in other ways, such as immigrant workers working in companies run by their friends or relatives. A significant proportion of what is formally defined as labor-based immigration is chain immigration, which is a social process whereby each immigrant leads to more immigrants from the same country.

Immigrants often assist their compatriots with information, employment, initial accommodation, and other factors that facilitate migration.

In total, immigrants from the 15 major refugee countries, including subsequent chain immigration, represent just over 60% of the increase in foreign-born since 1980. When countries from which Sweden has received a small number of refugees are included, the percentage is even higher. Thus, in recent decades, refugee immigration and accompanying chain immigration from these countries represent the lion's share of net immigration to Sweden.

Eurostat reports the number of asylum seekers to various European countries since 1985. During the period of 1985–2015, Sweden is at the top of the per capita table, with about four times as many asylum seekers in relation to the population as other Western European countries. More generally, asylum immigration in relation to the population is significantly higher in Western European welfare states than in Southern and Eastern Europe. The asylum immigration to Sweden of 2014 and 2015 in relation to the country's population is not only a record for Sweden, but is unique among industrialized nations. OECD (2016) writes: "in 2014–2015, Sweden saw the largest per-capita inflow of asylum seekers ever recorded in an OECD country." Today, according to Statistics Sweden, 19.1% of the population was born abroad in 2018. When second-generation immigrants who were born in Sweden with two foreign-born parents are added, 24.9% of the population has foreign background—a total of 2.5 million individuals.

Due to this rapid immigration, Sweden has experienced a population growth that is in line with developing countries like Bangladesh. In recent years, the population has grown at a rate of 1.0–1.5% per year, which is above normal levels for mature industrialized countries. One reason is that Sweden, apart from immigration, has unusually high birth rates for a wealthy nation, most likely due to generous parental leave, daycare, and child subsidies. In fact, with the exception of five years, Sweden has had more births than deaths every single year in the past two centuries. The number of people of Swedish origin—born in Sweden with one or two parents born in Sweden—has for some time been around 7.7 million, and is expected to remain stable going forward (Statistics Sweden 2011b). This differs from the situation in most other European countries.

The fertility rate, or the number of children per woman, must be just over 2 for a stable population. There are several different ways to measure fertility. A simple and often-quoted measure is total fertility, which in Sweden is about 1.9. The figure has sometimes been misunderstood, and many have come to the incorrect conclusion that Sweden without immigration would have a declining population. We know, however, that Sweden has a birth surplus in addition to net immigration.

This is due to the total fertility rate not taking into account that women are giving birth at older ages and during a longer period of their lives. The more refined measurement "Final number of children," or cohort fertility, which follows women over time, is more stable and has been fluctuating around 2.0. Statistics Sweden (2011b) writes in its analysis of different generations:

> Women born in 1930 have higher fertility rates in younger ages, while women born in 1960 have higher rates in older ages. However, if fertility rates are summed up across all ages, it turns out that both cohorts have ended up with the same average number of children, 2.01 children per woman.

As life expectancy increases and mortality among the elderly has fallen, this fertility would suffice for the population to slowly increase even without immigration.

The pattern is similar in Norway and Denmark, where cohort fertility is slightly above or slightly below two children per woman among the latest generations of mothers old enough to evaluate, namely those born in the 1970s and 1980s (Hellstrand et al. 2019; Jalovaara et al. 2019). The figure is somewhat lower in Finland and somewhat higher in Iceland. Across all Nordic countries, the snapshot figure in the form of total fertility rates have declined, although the more revealing cohort fertility rate has declined less as it is partially compensated by women having children in older ages. The Nordic fertility rates are similar to that of the United States, but substantially above those of Central European countries such as Germany, Italy, Spain, Portugal, and Austria where fertility rates are far lower—in many cases around 1.5 children per woman. France and the UK also have fertility rates that have remained more stable at slightly below the replacement rate.

Neither is it true that fertility only is maintained by immigrant women; women with Swedish origin also have high fertility. Sweden is one of the Western countries that stands out with the highest fertility rate among both women with Swedish and foreign background. It should, however, be noted that Sweden has experienced a gradual decline in recent years. If this trend continues, Sweden may come to resemble the patterns and long-term problems already observed in lower fertility European countries.

According to a demographic analysis that follows women over time, the final number of children is rather similar among foreign and native-born women: "A new report from Statistics Sweden on foreign-born childbearing—before and after immigration to Sweden—shows that native-born and foreign-born on average produce the same number of children" (Statistics Sweden 2014).

Far from being a nation of immigrants, for most of its history, Sweden was one of the most secluded kingdoms in the world. After the Second World War, Sweden opened up to the world and absorbed a moderate inflow of migrants, mostly from neighboring countries. Measured as a percentage of the population, between 1940 and 1990, Sweden had a net immigration of about 0.2% per year. This can be compared to the most memorable migration period in the emblematic nation of immigrants, where the United States at peak of the transatlantic migration in the 1880s reached a net immigration record of 0.67% per year.

Today, the migration flow to Sweden is remarkable, not only compared to Sweden'shistorical isolation, but also compared to other countries. Immigration further increased in the 1990s and accelerated in the new millennium. Astonishingly, Sweden overtook the American record already by 2009, and in 2016 shattered it with a net immigration relative to the population of 1.2%, before falling back to the current level of 0.8% in 2018. Given the historical context, it should surprise no one that immigration dominates national discourse in Sweden. In only one generation, Sweden shifted gears from a fairly homogenous and demographically stable society to one undergoing rapid demographic change. The flow of migration is swifter even than that of America in the Ellis Island era. There is, however, a striking difference between America in the age of migration and Sweden of today in that Sweden combines these voluminous immigration inflows with poor integration outcomes.

References

Åkesson, Åke. 1998. *Invandrare i Bergslagen: tyskar, finnar, valloner* [Immigrants in Bergslagen: Germans, Finns, Walloons]. Lindesberg: Blombergska bokhandeln.

Berglund, Bengt (ed.). 2015. *Järnet och Sveriges medeltida modernisering* [Iron and Sweden's Medieval Modernization]. Jernkontorets bergshistoriska skriftserie nr 48. Stockholm: Jernkontoret.

Bildt, Carl (@carlbildt). 2016. "Once Upon a Time Wallonia Spearheaded Globalisation." Twitter, October 24, 2016, 09:07 A.M. https://twitter.com/carlbildt/status/790630716694532097.

Boëthius, Bertil. 1951. *Gruvornas, hyttornas och hamrarnas folk: Bergshanteringens arbetare från medeltiden till gustavianska tiden* [The Peoples of the Mines, Cabins, and Hammers: The Workers of the Mining Industry from the Middle Ages to the Gustavian Times]. Stockholm: Tidens Förlag.

Borevi, Karin. 2012. "Sweden: The Flagship of Multiculturalism". In *Immigration Policy and the Scandinavian Welfare State 1945–2010*, edited by Grete Brochmann and Anniken Hagelund Jesch, 27–96. Basingstoke: Palgrave Macmillan.

Brink, Stefan. 2002. "Law and Legal Customs in Viking Age Scandinavia". In *The Scandinavians from the Vendel Period to the Tenth Century: An Ethnographic Perspective*, edited by Judith Jesch, 87–117. Woodbridge: The Boydell Press.

Dagens Nyheter. 2006. "Reinfeldt: Det ursvenska är blott barbari" [Reinfeldt: Merely barbarism is fundamentally Swedish]. By Owe Nilsson/TT, November 15, 2006. https://www.dn.se/nyheter/politik/reinfeldt-det-ursvenska-ar-blott-barbari.

Douhan, Bernt. 1982. "The Walloons in Sweden." *Swedish American Genealogist* 2, no. 1: 1–17.

Haavio-Mannila, Elina. 1983. "Level of Living of Immigrants in Sweden: A Comparison of Male and Female Immigrants from Finland and Yugoslavia with Swedes in Same Age and Occupational Groups." *International Migration* 21, no. 1: 15–38. https://doi.org/10.1111/j.1468-2435.1983.tb00075.x.

Hallberg, Lars. 2001. *Källor till invandringens historia i statliga myndigheters arkiv 1840–1990* [Sources of Immigration History in State Archives, 1840–1990]. Stockholm: Riksarkivet.

Heckscher, Eli F. 1935–1949. *Sveriges ekonomiska historia från Gustav Vasa* [Sweden's Economic History from Gustav Vasa]. Stockholm: Bonnier.

Heckscher, Eli F. 1954. *An Economic History of Sweden*. Cambridge: Harvard University Press.

Hellstrand, Julia, Jessica Nisén, and Mikko Myrskylä. 2019. "All-Time Low Period Fertility in Finland: Drivers, Tempo Effects, and Cohort Implications." MPIDR Working Paper WP 2019-006. Max Planck Institute for Demographic Research, Rostock. https://ideas.repec.org/p/dem/wpaper/wp-2019-006.html.

Jalovaara, Marika, Gerda Neyer, Gunnar Andersson, Johan Dahlberg, Lars Dommermuth, Peter Fallesen, and Trude Lappegård. 2019. "Education, Gender, and Cohort Fertility in the Nordic Countries." *European Journal of Population* 35, no. 3: 563–86. https://doi.org/10.1007/s10680-018-9492-2.

Maddison, Angus. 2010. *The Maddison Project: 2013 Version*. http://www.ggdc.net/maddison/maddison-project/home.htm.

Nationalencyklopedin. n.d. "valloner." https://www.ne.se/uppslagsverk/encyklopedi/lång/valloner.

OECD. 2016. "Sweden in a Strong Position to Integrate Refugees, but Support for the Low Skilled Needs to be Strengthened." Organisation for Economic Co-operation and Development (OECD), Employment, May 13, 2016. http://www.oecd.org/employment/sweden-in-a-strong-position-to-integrate-refugees-but-support-for-the-low-skilled-needs-to-be-strengthened.htm.

Plucknett, Theodore F. T. [1956] 2010. *A Concise History of the Common Law*. 5th ed. Indianapolis: Liberty Fund.

Sidén, Per Gunnar. 2008. "Hur tyska var de svenska städerna under högmedeltiden?" [How German Were the Swedish Cities During the High Middle Ages?]. Working Paper, Department of History, Stockholm University. https://www.historia.su.se/polopoly_fs/1.27755.1320939842!/SidenTyskaSvenskaStader.pdf.

Statistics Sweden. 2004. "Efterkrigstidens invandring och utvandring" [Immigration and Emigration in the Postwar Period]. By Åke Nilsson, Demografiska rapporter 2004:5, Statistiska centralbyrån (SCB), Enheten för demografisk analys och jämställdhet, Stockholm. http://share.scb.se/ov9993/data/publikationer/statistik/_publikationer/be0701_1950i02_br_be51st0405.pdf.

———. 2011a. "Återutvandring efter tid i Sverige" [Repatriation After Time in Sweden]. Bakgrundsmaterial om demografi, barn och familj 2011:1, Statistiska centralbyrån (SCB), Prognosinstitutet, Stockholm. https://www.scb.se/contentassets/cd880fda311f42389116264260f0b13b7/be0401_2011i60_br_be52br1101.pdf.

———. 2011b. "Olika generationers barnafödande" [Childbearing of Different Generations]. Demografiska rapporter 2011:3, Prognosinstitutet. Stockholm: Statistiska centralbyrån (SCB). http://share.scb.se/ov9993/data/publikationer/statistik/_publikationer/be0701_2011a01_br_be51br1103.pdf.

———. (2014). "Lika många barn för inrikes och utrikes födda" [Equal Number of Children for Native- and Foreign-Born]. Statistical news 2014:325, Prognosinstitutet. Stockholm: Statistiska centralbyrån (SCB).

Turner, Ralph V. 1968. "The Origins of the Medieval English Jury: Frankish, English, or Scandinavian?" *The Journal of British Studies* 7, no. 2: 1–10. https://doi.org/10.1086/385549.

CHAPTER 3

The Economics of Migration

> There is a wide difference between closing the door altogether and throwing it entirely open.
>
> —Alexander Hamilton, 1802

Historically, integration was not a problem in Sweden. The immigrants of the 1950s and 1960s had the qualifications required by the job market of the period and quickly got employment (Ekberg 2004; Borevi 2012). Often, they worked in industries that were running at full capacity and demanded foreign labor. Major Swedish companies such as Volvo, SKF, and Asea were at the time actively recruiting abroad. The situation was quite different from the Sweden of today. Language requirements in the job market were less stringent, and learning often took place at work. A large proportion of immigrants also came from linguistically and culturally similar countries. Another important difference from today's job market was that professions had fewer formal educational requirements.

Immigrants as late as in the mid-1970s, unlike today, had a higher or equal employment rate to the native-born (Ekberg and Hammarstedt 2002; Ekberg 2009). As the nature and composition of immigration changed, a gap in employment and earnings emerged and then widened as the foreign-born fell behind the native-born. This gap was fairly large by 1990 and has not closed since then. With the exception of business cycle fluctuations, the labor market gap has been relatively stable. During recessions, the gap tends to widen as immigrants are more sensitive to downturns. Conversely, the gap tends to shrink during upturns when tight labor markets make employers more likely to higher marginal workers. Jan Ekberg (2009) writes:

> During the 1950s and 1960s, as well as most of the 1970s, foreign-born had the same or periodically higher employment rate during working age than native-born. Towards the end of the 1970s, the picture changes.

T. Sanandaji, *Mass Challenge*,
https://doi.org/10.1007/978-3-030-46808-8_3

As labor migration transitioned into refugee and family-based migration, job market integration progressively deteriorated. Today, the foreign-born on average have significantly lower employment rates. At the same time, immigrants have fallen behind in salary growth. Compared to the native-born, foreign-born individuals are more often found in low-wage jobs and more often work part-time. This means that the average income of immigrants is significantly lower, which is particularly the case for non-European immigrants. The combination of a lower employment rate and lower wages means that large income gaps have opened up between the native- and foreign-born. As a consequence, many do not even enter the job market and lack the opportunity to contribute to the collectively financed welfare state.

Measuring Nonemployment

In official statistics, unemployment is defined as those who are actively seeking a job. Those without jobs who are instead on disability, sick leave, or live on social assistance and have given up on looking for work, are thus not counted as unemployed. Therefore, most people who are not working are not officially unemployed. The official unemployment rate is defined quite differently from what people normally mean by lacking a job; both in the United States and in most European countries, the number of people out of work is far larger than the official unemployment rate. This, in turn, means that unemployment is not a fully accurate metric for measuring the integration of immigrants. In the latest available figures for the second half of 2019, approximately 4% of native-born and about 17% of foreign-born individuals are defined as unemployed, which means that unemployment is around four times higher among immigrants in Sweden.

Another commonly used metric in job market statistics is the employment rate. This can be measured using either surveys or income statistics, which sometimes gives slightly different answers. Again, the official definition of employment does not fully correspond with what people ordinarily mean by jobs. This is because individuals can also be counted as employed if they are in government job market programs, or on sick leave. Moreover, the definition is very generous and includes those who only work an hour per week. The Swedish Ministry of Finance (2016) explains:

> A person is considered employed if he or she has undertaken paid work for at least 1 hour during the reference week or had a job that he or she was absent from. Persons who are absent from work due to, for example, illness or parental leave are thus considered to be employed.

The employment rate measures the share of the population who perform any kind of work, internship, or job-like tasks. The formal definition used for employment is not unique to Sweden, but is based on guidelines developed by international statistical agencies. Such guidelines may appear absurd—for instance, when someone who is on long-term sick leave, or who participates one hour per week in a government program, is counted as "employed." One reason for the current nomenclature is that each country differs, and that any definition would have its flaws. There is no perfect definition in international statistics that actually measures those who support themselves through real jobs. Hence, the importance of understanding the limits of the statistical measures to which we do have access.

One consequence of the generous definition of employment is that certain countries appear to consistently have stronger job markets than others, due to statistical artifacts. The Scandinavian countries have far more government programs as well as more generous sick leave and parental leave benefits than most other OECD countries. Additionally, it is more common for individuals to work part-time, in particular women and the elderly, in Scandinavian welfare states. In countries with other labor market institutions and cultural traditions, it is instead more common to work full-time, but to do so for fewer years—for instance, by retiring early or by having one-earner families.

The Scandinavian countries consistently have higher employment rates than virtually all other OCED countries, every year, for the time period covered by OECD data. Indeed, Sweden, Norway, and Denmark tend to have significantly higher employment rates than countries such as the United States, South Korea, and Japan, where we know that total hours worked is larger. This is not to say that the numbers are completely useless, or that the Lutheran work ethic is a myth. The Scandinavians tend to have shorter workdays and generous vacations, but compensate this by having most able-bodied natives work, and not least by having long work lives. Like the famously hard-working Americans, Scandinavians are more likely to continue working into their 60s and even 70s. Two countries stand out: tiny Iceland has among the highest number of hours worked in any OECD country by combining close to full employment, fairly long workdays, and a long work life that begins early and ends late; Norway, however, is characterized by few hours worked and a more leisurely lifestyle—in part due to the country's oil wealth.

Consequently, the exceptionally high employment rates in Scandinavia reflect healthy labor markets, which are additionally inflated by statistical measures that tend to exaggerate the amount of work carried out in such systems compared to other countries. It would be foolish to interpret the high Swedish employment rates as proof that Swedes work more than South Koreans and Americans, since common sense as well as statistics on aggregate hours worked show the opposite to be true. This is important to keep in mind when interpreting figures in this book and in the press. In particular, when the employment rate is used to measure how well immigrants perform in each country, it is necessary to compare them with natives within the same system. Comparing the employment rates of immigrants without taking into account the normal employment rate of each country is quite meaningless, since this is comparing apples to oranges.

When we wish to make cross-country comparisons of labor market integration, immigrants are first compared to others in the same country, after which the positive or negative differences can be compared between countries. This method gives us robust and consistent estimates, where the countries that do well in immigrant integration—using employment rates—also perform well when using other measures such as the unemployment rate or income. Comparing immigrants in different countries with one another, without first adjusting for the national normal, however, instead can produce nonsensical and confused results, where countries with high unemployment among immigrants can appear better integrated in terms of unemployment. To avoid this problem, this book will consistently report the gap between natives and immigrants when comparing across countries and over time.

The Gap

The most recent figures for gainful employment rates available from Statistics Sweden are for 2017. Gainful employment is defined using unusually accurate estimates from income records for the entire population. In 2017, 84.4% of native-born and 61.9% of foreign-born individuals aged 20–64 were gainfully employed. The figure is particularly low among foreign-born immigrants from outside of Europe, where only 56.3% were gainfully employed. The gap in the gainful employment rate between native- and foreign-born has remained at this level for a long time, if with some fluctuations. The proportion of those gainfully employed has increased both among foreign- and native-born, but since the increase has been about the same in both groups, the gap between these groups has not shrunk during the past 15 years. One reason for the increase is a recovery in the job market, whereas another explanation is that all workers are healthier and tend to remain in the labor market longer. Table 3.1 compares the figures for 1990, 2000, and 2017—while Fig. 3.1 shows the development throughout the period between 1990 and 2017.

Today, the job market situation for immigrants compared to the rest of the population is somewhat worse than it was in 1990, and almost identical to what it was in 2000. It is interesting to note that the integration of immigrants into the job market has neither improved nor worsened significantly

Table 3.1 Gainfully employed, ages 20–64

	1990 (%)	*2000 (%)*	*2017 (%)*
Native-born	86.1	78.5	84.4
Foreign-born	71.2	55.3	61.9
Born outside Europe	60.6	47.5	56.3
Gap between native- and foreign-born	14.9	23.3	22.5

Source Statistics Sweden

for 15 years. In other words, integration on the job market appears to have stabilized at a low level.

The proportion of immigrants who work increase with time spent in Sweden. After arrival, newcomers gradually learn Swedish and enter the job market. However, the process is slow. By the time earlier cohorts have become integrated, many new cohorts of immigrants have arrived, and after a sufficiently long time, those who have managed to get into work leave the job market (Statistics Sweden 2012a). For many years now, there has been an equilibrium where the foreign-born group as a whole has had a low and stable gainful employment rate, which has not improved. The low gainful employment rate among immigrants is, therefore, not a transitory phenomenon that will resolve itself over time.

Since 1997, Statistics Sweden also reports the relationship between arrival date and percentage employed for refugee immigrants. The rate of job market integration varies somewhat depending on the state of the economy and the composition of the cohorts, but it has been remarkably predictable. The rate of increase in the share of gainfully employed declines over time: after 15 years in Sweden, about 60% of refugees and family immigrants are employed, after which the rate levels out. The stability of this pattern is striking and probably reflects strong fundamental forces. The figures are only marginally better if we look at all immigrants, not just refugees.

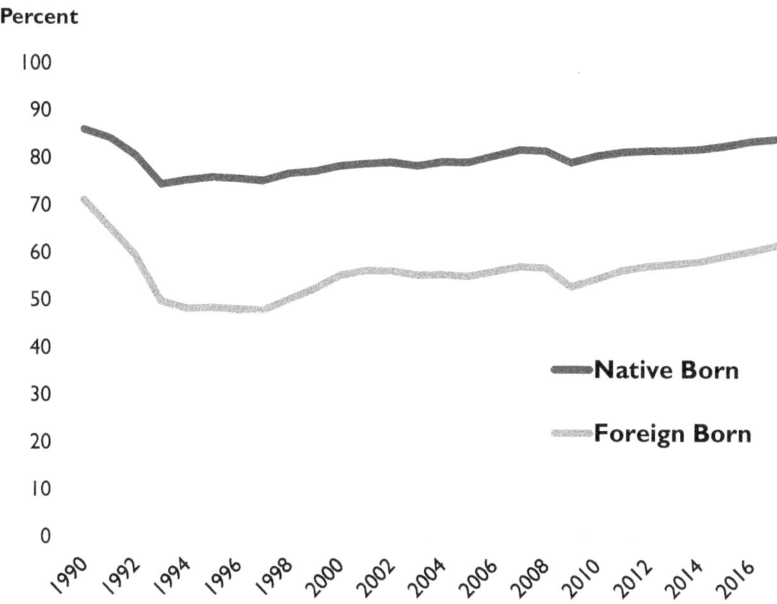

Fig. 3.1 Gainfully employed, ages 20–64 (1990–2017) (*Source* Statistics Sweden)

Even more important than employment is total earnings, where the picture is grimmer still. In 2017, the income per gainfully employed person of working age was approximately 10% lower among foreign-born than among native-born. The combination of the fact that a lower proportion of the group is working, and that those who do work have lower average incomes, means that foreign-born of working age have over 35% lower labor earnings than native-born. This gap is even greater among non-European immigrants of working age, who have 44% lower labor earnings than the native-born. The differences in the proportion of the population who work and average income are so large that they outweigh the immigrant group's advantage in terms of a more favorable age profile. This, in turn, means that foreign-born generate less income and pay less in taxes than the native-born, in spite of their oft-emphasized advantageous demographic profile. Even if we were to include the demographic advantage and look at the entire population, rather than just those of working age, non-Western immigrants earn 31% less than the native-born.

The main reason for the deterioration of the job market position of immigrants, compared to the early postwar period, is a compositional change in the foreign-born as a group: from labor immigrants from Europe to refugee and family-based immigrants from low-income countries. Immigrants from the Nordic countries and the rest of the Western world still do well in the job market, but today they make up an increasingly smaller percentage of the group foreign-born. The fact that refugee and family-based immigrants fare worse is primarily—or perhaps exclusively—due to them having lower average human capital.

Human capital refers to a person's overall skill level, including language skills, work experience, education level, and quality of education. While the demands of the job market have increased over time, an increasing proportion of new arrivals lack secondary school education. In addition to a lower share with formal degrees, there are also major differences in the length and content of the education, as well as great variation in the level of knowledge. The explanatory value of human capital for various outcomes is strengthened when more detailed measurements of knowledge are used.

One of the most detailed such analyses was made in the Swedish Ministry of Finance's 2015 Long-Term Survey using PIAAC—a knowledge test in language, math, and computer skills, given to a representative sample in various OECD countries. PIAAC is the adult version of the school test PISA. A striking result that emerged from the original OECD analyses was that immigrants and native Swedes, who had the same human capital, fared about equally well in the job market (Bussi and Pareliussen 2015). This was confirmed by the Long-Term Survey (SOU 2015:104):

> A positive result from the PIAAC survey is that there are no significant differences between foreign- and native-born when it comes to having a job, if taking into account the level of the individual's skills. The survey makes the assessment

> that the Swedish job market mainly looks to individuals' skills, and as a whole does not seem to be characterized by ethnic discrimination. The results from the PIAAC survey show that Sweden generally has a population with good human capital.... Just over 35 percent of foreign-born are showing insufficient skills in both reading and math, while the figure for those born in Sweden is about 5 percent.

In addition to skill levels, there is another potential explanation as to why immigrants have lost ground. At the same time as the relative skill levels of immigrants have deteriorated, skills have become even more important for job market success.

In recent decades, the economy has undergone technological and structural changes, which may have hampered the job market integration for many groups by increasing the demands on the workforce. The fact that technology and globalization have eroded the demand for simpler jobs makes it difficult for foreign-born individuals without specialist skills to gain a foothold in the Swedish job market, as well as in similar European economies (Calmfors and Sánchez Gassen 2019).

Most of the simple jobs in the manufacturing sector—which attracted guest workers to industrialized European economies such as Scandinavia, Germany, and the UK in the past—have disappeared. Instead, the types of occupations have replaced them are qualified specialist occupations that place higher demands on education, language skills, and know-how. Technology in the form of computers, robots, and automation has replaced routine jobs characterized by well-defined and repeated tasks. This along with globalization and trade with countries like China has reduced the number of simpler manufacturing jobs. There is, however, still a large number of low- and middle-skilled jobs in the service sector. Automation and trade have had less of an impact on routine service professions such as retail staff, taxi drivers, or security guards. But even for this category of occupations, the competition has become tougher.

As the opportunities to gain employment in existing companies have shrunk for many immigrant groups, self-employment has become a safety valve and a channel to integration. Self-employment offers immigrants the opportunity to circumvent discrimination and regulations. It should, however, be noted that most businesses started by immigrants tend to remain small and, in many cases, have no employees other than the business owner. This type of business activity is usually routine self-employment in activities such as corner shops, pizzerias, falafel stands, cafes, or hair salons—as opposed to high-tech startups that introduce new technology and have a high growth potential (Henrekson and Sanandaji 2014). Of course, most small businesses started by natives are also best described as small-scale self-employment rather than innovative entrepreneurship, but the discrepancy is often even larger among immigrants (Sanandaji 2014; Henrekson and Sanandaji 2020). Non-European business owners are particularly concentrated to the service sector—not least the retail, hotel, and restaurant industries (Andersson and

Hammarstedt 2011). According to Statistics Sweden (2012b), approximately 70% of the self-employed in the hotel and restaurant business in 2010 were born outside of Sweden.

It is true that in many countries such as the United States, the UK, and Canada, immigrant entrepreneurs have played an important role in creating new high-growth firms—in many sectors, disproportionally to their population share. This tendency is, however, not universal and is often exaggerated anecdotally even in the United States, where the vast majority of entrepreneurs are native-born. In many European welfare states, immigrants are underrepresented as successful entrepreneurs compared to their population share.

The Swedish Agency for Economic and Regional Growth's (2015) survey for the year 2014 measured the share of business activity in firms with ten employees or more. Merely 13% of these businesses were managed by first- or second-generation immigrants, who at the time constituted 21% of the population. This implies that those with a foreign background are underrepresented among business owners of firms with at least ten employees.

Fiscal Effects of Immigration

A much-debated issue in Sweden is the cost of immigration for the public sector. In principle, immigration does not need to be a fiscal cost. Historically, immigration generated an economic surplus, which in the early 1970s was estimated to be the equivalent of one percent of the gross domestic product of the time (Ekberg 1983, 2009). Later, immigration transitioned to become a net cost as the immigrants' position in the job market eroded, which meant that the group paid relatively less in taxes and generated significant costs in terms of subsidies and transfers. Research consistently shows that the effect of the foreign-born on public finances after the 1980s became a fiscal net cost (Ekberg 1999, 2009, 2011; Gustafsson and Österberg 2001; Storesletten 2003; Ruist 2015; Flood and Ruist 2015; Aldén and Hammarstedt 2016a, b, 2019). All of the cited reports are similar in terms of methods and results, but focus on different aspects of the issue.

Aldén and Hammarstedt (2016b) confirm that refugees' burden on the public sector is not only due to a high proportion of them being outside the job market, but also due to them having a low average income per worker: "This is probably explained partly by the fact that refugees often are employed in low-wage jobs, but also because a large proportion of the refugees who do receive employment often only become employed part-time." The estimates in Aldén and Hammarstedt (2016b, 2019) are close to those in Ruist (2015), which show a net cost of an average of $7000 per refugee and year.

An interesting conclusion in Ruist (2015) is that four-fifths of the net cost is driven by lower tax revenues, and only one-fifth by higher costs for subsidies and welfare. Greater costs for social assistance and other transfers for refugee immigrants are in part compensated by lower pension costs and a lower demand for elderly care.

Perhaps the most detailed research summary was produced by Professor Jan Ekberg, on behalf of the Expert Group for Studies in Public Finances (ESO) in 2009. Immigration always generates costs for welfare as well as revenues in the form of taxes and fees. The question is one of comparing revenues to costs. In practice, this is done by estimating how much immigration increases public sector revenues in the form of taxes and fees, and thereafter deducting additional expenses for welfare and subsidies. In addition to direct fiscal effects, immigration may also have broader impacts on the economy. Although immigration generates a deficit for public finances, it could in theory create socioeconomic surpluses that outweigh these fiscal costs. Such may involve direct gains through exchanges on the job market, or so-called dynamic effects, by increasing the rate of entrepreneurship or innovation. However, from a purely empirical point of view, no such socioeconomic surplus has been detectable in Sweden (Ekberg 2009).

Even in countries with more successful integration, like the United States, calculations suggest that the economic surplus for the domestic population generated by immigration in the job market is small—according to one study corresponding to 0.2% of GDP (Borjas 2013). In particular, studies in the United States have concluded that immigration contributes to long-term growth, since foreign-born are overrepresented among those who are granted patents. This creates so-called innovation spillovers—in other words, positive indirect effects on long-term economic development. In Sweden, however, the case is the opposite. Immigrants account for fewer patents than the native-born in relation to the group's population (Zheng and Ejermo 2015).

It is also possible that immigration carries negative indirect effects on the economy, such as crime or perceived deterioration in quality of life (Card et al. 2012). There are no estimates either for sizeable, indirect gains—nor for sizeable, indirect costs through spillovers and externalities. As will be argued in subsequent chapters, the historical experience of immigrant-heavy cities and neighborhoods, if anything, indicates that the overall indirect effect may be negative. While we lack precise numbers for indirect effects, the fiscal costs have been carefully calculated. Ekberg (2009) summarizes:

> In Sweden, there are a number of surveys on how the public sector during different periods has rebalanced revenues between immigrants and natives. In summary, the results show that the public sector until around 1980 re-allocated income from migrants to natives on an annual basis. During this period, immigrants had a good employment situation and from this perspective a favorable age structure. The annual net revenue appears to have peaked in the early 1970s, when it amounted to about 1 percent of gross domestic product (GDP). As the immigrants' employment situation weakened, the annual revenue decreased to reach a zero level in the mid-/late 1980s. In the 1990s, the

net revenue turned into a net cost, i.e. an income redistribution from natives to immigrants. By the mid-/late 1990s, the net annual cost for natives was 1.5 to 2 percent.

Another study by Flood and Ruist (2015) also discusses long-term fiscal effects of immigration. The calculation excludes initial reception costs for newly arrived refugees, instead focusing on costs and revenues arising after immigrants are registered as residents in Sweden. The conclusion is that immigration is a net expense, unless integration is significantly improved compared to the experience thus far. Both today's immigrants, who have already arrived, and future immigration are expected to generate a net cost. As in other studies, the cost is higher for immigration from low-income countries outside of Europe, while immigration from many parts of Europe is a net gain.

Contrary to what is sometimes expressed in popular discourse, immigration does not bolster the funding of future pensions, but instead adds to the burden. The reason is that immigrants, despite a more favorable age profile, do not generate enough revenue to fully fund their own pensions—let alone strengthen the Swedish pension system as a whole. One extensive calculation was made by the Swedish Pensions Agency (2016) for the period 2017 to 2100. Their conclusion was that 100,000 refugee immigrants in the beginning of the period until 2100 can be expected to generate approximately $7 billion in revenues and $15 billion in spending for the pension system, in net present value. Thus, the impact for the pension system will be a net cost of $8 billion—an average of $80,000 per refugee. The Swedish Pensions Agency's report confirms that refugee immigration does not mitigate the costs incurred by the aging Swedish population; rather, to the pension system, it is an additional burden.

In light of the great confusion that has characterized the debate, it may be worthwhile to elaborate a bit further on the demographic analysis, which in essence is easily quantifiable. As with most examples in this book, we use Sweden as a case, although the general framework can be applied to other European welfare states as well. The point is to show why the demographic advantage of immigration does not guarantee a profitable outcome when the group's income level is too low.

Just over half of the native-born population is of working age, here defined as 20–64 years of age. Since few young and old work, those of working age must support the rest of the population. The welfare state works because those of working age, who work collectively, pay enough tax to cover their own welfare and that of those of working age who are not working—as well as to generate a surplus large enough to finance the pensions and the welfare of children and the elderly. It should be stressed that the key objective of a welfare state is generating a surplus of tax revenue that can fund the welfare state, not merely increasing the number of inhabitants.

The notion that countries somehow run out of workers does not reflect reality. The popular imagination is that aging European countries risk running out of workers to take care of the elderly, unless they take in young bodies from abroad. This simplistic domestic analogy is, however, baseless since the share of the workforce that take care of the elderly is small. The expenses for elderly care account for about 3% of Sweden's GDP, and those who work with caring for the elderly make up less than 5% of the workforce. Even with extreme projections, no country risks running out of nurses and caretakers. As the share of old people increases, a few of the workers who would otherwise have worked in factories or department stores instead shift to this line of occupation.

Nor are there any high-skilled occupations that the education systems of European welfare states are unable to train. When structural shifts in the economy increase the demand for doctors, engineers, and programmers, and lower demand for typists, telephone operators, and manual archivists, the educational system and the economy are quite capable of redirecting resources—as has indeed been observed in the past centuries. Merely increasing the population does not improve welfare since there are then proportionally more people to take care of.

On the whole, the total population of countries is beside the point, as the standard of living is instead determined by average income per person and the distribution of resources. Otherwise, we would have observed that countries such as India, Indonesia, and Nigeria have higher standards of living and better welfare services than small countries such as Switzerland, Israel, or Singapore. The resource constraint for the welfare state is the amount of tax revenue available to fund services, such as health care, and benefits, such as pensions. What matters in particular is tax revenue per person. The reason immigrants may benefit the welfare state is that the group, in favorable circumstances, is younger or better skilled and thus generates a tax surplus, once their own costs have been covered. If immigrants instead generate too little tax revenue, immigration will make problems worse by increasing pressure on social services—without sufficiently covering its costs.

The reason an aging population presents a problem to welfare states is that tax revenue per person is reduced when the share of people in working age declines, whereas cost per person increases since a greater percentage of the population requires care and benefits. Once we understand this, it is clear that immigration of young but often unemployed low-skilled immigrants have similar effects. Just like an aging population, this reduces tax revenue per person, while increasing cost per person.

The empirical reality in Sweden is that immigrants, despite a more advantageous age distribution, have paid far too little in taxes to cover their own costs—let alone contributing to the welfare of elderly native-born. The age distribution cannot be considered in isolation and must be weighed against even greater disadvantages such as lower rates of employment, lower average incomes, less taxes paid, and higher costs generated in health care and other

Table 3.2 Age distribution and total earned income relative to native-born (2017)

	Native-born	*Foreign-born*	*Born outside Europe*
Percentage of population in working age 20–64 years old	54%	72%	76%
Immigrants relative to native-born[a]	1.0	1.35	1.41
Total earned income per person of all ages (dollars)	17,800	15,100	13,500
Immigrants relative to native-born[a]	1.0	0.85	0.76
Total earned income per person of working age (dollars)	33,100	20,900	17,800
Immigrants relative to native-born[a]	1.0	0.63	0.54

Source Statistics Sweden
Note [a]1.0 corresponds to the level for native-born

services. Immigration has therefore, on the contrary, reduced the resources available to finance an aging welfare state. This is summarized in Table 3.2, which contrasts the immigrant group's demographic advantage against its lower earned income for 2017.

The overall effect is that immigrants generate significantly less income despite a favorable age profile—especially those from outside Europe. It should, furthermore, be noted that long-term projections to, e.g., the year 2100 show that the Swedish welfare state is sustainable, as the gradual decrease in the share of the population in working ages is more than compensated by productivity growth and a greater tendency of the elderly to work. Similar projections show that the Norwegian and Danish systems are sustainable, and welfare states can remain generous in the future—as long as we sustain productivity growth and sufficient tax rates. Again, an aging population in itself does not guarantee the unsustainability of the welfare state, as long as those who work are productive and generate sufficient tax revenue.

Overall, fear of future labor shortages, making European welfare states unsustainable, is baseless. One reason this myth has spread is that many for ideological reasons would like to dismantle the welfare state, and for decades have prophesized it would soon become unsustainable. Another reason is that this has proven to be a convincing-sounding argument to justify immigration, since the public tends to have an unsophisticated understanding of the links between demographics and economics. Economist Nils Lundgren (2015) has written about these myths:

> One of the most common arguments for increased immigration to wealthy countries in Europe is that the proportion of older people is growing. We are too few who work and too many retirees. Our demographic structure must therefore be adjusted with the help of immigration of young people. Most things indicate that this is not true. Immigrants of working age have children and bring their parents here. It is not self-evident that immigration even temporarily increases the proportion of workers in the host country's population.

References

Aldén, Lina, and Mats Hammarstedt. 2016a. "Boende med konsekvens – en ESO-rapport om etnisk bostadssegregation och arbetsmarknad" [Housing with Consequences—An ESO Report on Ethnic Housing Segregation and the Labor Market]. Rapport till Expertgruppen för studier i offentlig ekonomi (ESO) 2016:1, Wolters Kluwer, Stockholm. https://eso.expertgrupp.se/wp-content/uploads/2016/02/Hela-2016_1-till-webben.pdf.

———. 2016b. "Flyktinginvandring: Sysselsättning, förvärvsinkomster och offentliga finanser" [Refugee Immigration: Employment, Employment Income, and Public Finances]. Rapport till Finanspolitiska rådet 2016/1, Finanspolitiska rådet, Stockholm. http://www.finanspolitiskaradet.se/download/18.21a8337f154abc1a5dd2876a/1463335875126/Underlagsrapport+2016+1+Aldén+och+Hammarstedt.pdf.

———. 2019. "Refugee Immigration and Public-Sector Finances: Evidence from Sweden." *FinanzArchiv* 75, no. 3: 297–322. https://doi.org/10.1628/fa-2019-0006.

Andersson, Lina, and Mats Hammarstedt. 2011. "Invandrares egenföretagande – trender, branscher, storlek och resultat" [Self-Employment of Immigrants—Trends, Industries, Size, and Results]. *Ekonomisk Debatt* 39, no. 2: 31–39. https://www.nationalekonomi.se/filer/pdf/39-2-lamh.pdf.

Borevi, Karin. 2012. "Sweden: The Flagship of Multiculturalism." In *Immigration Policy and the Scandinavian Welfare State 1945–2010*, edited by Grete Brochmann and Anniken Hagelund Jesch, 27–96. Basingstoke: Palgrave Macmillan.

Borjas, George J. 2013. "Immigration and the American Worker: A Review of the Academic Literature." Center for Immigration Studies, Washington, DC. https://cis.org/Report/Immigration-and-American-Worker.

Bussi, Margherita, and Jon Kristian Pareliussen. 2015. "Skills and Labour Market Performance in Sweden." OECD Economics Department Working Papers, no. 1233, OECD Publishing, Paris. https://doi.org/10.1787/5js0cqvnzx9v-en.

Calmfors, Lars, and Nora Sánchez Gassen, eds. 2019. *Integrating Immigrants into the Nordic Labour Markets.* Copenhagen: Nordic Council of Ministers. https://doi.org/10.6027/Nord2019-024.

Card, David, Christian Dustmann, and Ian Preston. 2012. "Immigration, Wages, and Compositional Amenities." *Journal of the European Economic Association* 10, no. 1: 78–119. https://doi.org/10.1111/j.1542-4774.2011.01051.x.

Ekberg, Jan. 1983. "Inkomsteffekter av invandring" [Income Effects of Immigration]. Diss., Lund Economic Studies no. 27, Lund University, Lund.

———. 1999. "Immigration and the Public Sector: Income Effects for the Native Population in Sweden." *Journal of Population Economics* 12, no. 3: 411–30. https://doi.org/10.1007/s001480050106.

———. 2004. "Immigrants in the Welfare State." In *Globalization and the Welfare State*, edited by Bo Södersten, 195–212. Basingstoke: Palgrave Macmillan. https://www.palgrave.com/gp/book/9781403918949.

———. 2009. "Invandringen och de offentliga finanserna" [Immigration and Public Finances]. Rapport till Expertgruppen för studier i offentlig ekonomi (ESO) 2009:3, Regeringskansliet, Finansdepartementet, Stockholm. https://eso.expertgrupp.se/wp-content/uploads/2013/08/2009_3-från-webb.pdf.

———. 2011. "Will Future Immigration to Sweden Make it Easier to Finance the Welfare System?." *European Journal of Population/Revue européenne de Démographie* 27, no. 1: 103–24. https://doi.org/10.1007/s10680-010-9227-5.

Ekberg, Jan, and Mats Hammarstedt. 2002. "20 år med allt sämre arbetsmarknadsintegrering för invandrare" [20 Years of Increasingly Poor Labor Market Integration for Immigrants]. *Ekonomisk Debatt* 30, no. 4: 343–53. https://www.nationalekonomi.se/filer/pdf/30-4-je-mh.pdf.

Flood, Lennart, and Joakim Ruist. 2015. "Migration, en åldrande befolkning och offentliga finanser" [Migration, an Aging Population, and Public Finances]. Bilaga 6 till Långtidsutredningen 2015, Statens offentliga utredningar (SOU) 2015:95, Wolters Kluwer, Stockholm. https://www.regeringen.se/contentassets/6a0373dacf97488d8aae6b5785e46583/migration-en-aldrande-befolkning-och-offentliga-finanser-sou-201595.

Gustafsson, Björn, and Torun Österberg. 2001. "Immigrants and the Public Sector Budget—Accounting Exercises for Sweden." *Journal of Population Economics* 14, no. 4: 689–708. https://doi.org/10.1007/s001480000043.

Henrekson, Magnus, and Tino Sanandaji. 2014. "Small Business Activity Does Not Measure Entrepreneurship." *Proceedings of the National Academy of Sciences* 111, no. 5: 1760–65. https://doi.org/10.1073/pnas.1307204111.

———. 2020. "Measuring Entrepreneurship: Do Established Metrics Capture Schumpeterian Entrepreneurship?" *Entrepreneurship Theory & Practice* 44, no. 4: 733–60. https://doi.org/10.1177/1042258719844500.

Lundgren, Nils. 2015. "Invandringen – vår tids största politiska fråga" [Immigration—The Biggest Political Issue of Our Time]. *Det goda samhället*, July 25, 2015. https://detgodasamhallet.com/2015/07/25/invandringen-var-tids-storsta-politiska-fraga.

Ruist, Joakim. 2015. "The Fiscal Cost of Refugee Immigration: The Example of Sweden." *Population and Development Review* 41, no. 4: 567–81. https://doi.org/10.1111/j.1728-4457.2015.00085.x.

Sanandaji, Tino. 2014. "The International Mobility of Billionaires." *Small Business Economics* 42, no. 2: 329–38. https://doi.org/10.1007/s11187-013-9481-0.

SOU 2015:104. "Långtidsutredningen 2015: Huvudbetänkande" [Long-Term Survey: Main Report]. Betänkande av Långtidsutredningen, Statens offentliga utredningar (SOU), Wolters Kluwer, Stockholm. https://www.regeringen.se/4ae55e/contentassets/86d73b72a97345feb2a8cbc8b6700fa7/sou-2015104-langtidsutredningen-2015-huvudbetankande.

Statistics Sweden. 2012a. "Tema: Arbetsmarknad. Sysselsättningen 2030 – kan dagens försörjningsbörda bibehållas?" [Theme: Labor Market. Employment 2030—Can the Current Dependency Burden Be Maintained?]. Temarapport 2012:4, Statistiska centralbyrån (SCB), Prognosinstitutet, Stockholm. https://www.scb.se/contentassets/05d59cd9c5334c208180e27177117552/uf0521_2011i30_br_a40br1204.pdf.

———. 2012b. "Utrikesfödda egenföretagare är mer välutbildade än inrikesfödda" [Foreign-Born Self-Employed Are More Well-Educated Than Native-Born]. By Susanne Gullberg Brännström, Article no. 2012:91, June 29, 2012. Stockholm: Statistiska centralbyrån (SCB).

Storesletten, Kjetil. 2003. "Fiscal Implications of Immigration—A Net Present Value Calculation." *The Scandinavian Journal of Economics* 105, no. 3: 487–506. https://doi.org/10.1111/1467-9442.t01-2-00009.

Swedish Agency for Economic and Regional Growth. 2015. "Mångfald i näringslivet: Företagens villkor och verklighet 2014" [Diversity in the Business Sector: The Conditions and Reality of Companies 2014]. Tillväxtverket, Stockholm. https://tillvaxtverket.se/download/18.a48a52e155169e594d35b1/1465388549038/info_0594.pdf.

Swedish Ministry of Finance. 2016. "Viktiga aspekter vid bedömning av åtgärder för lägre arbetslöshet" [Important Aspects When Assessing Measures for Lower Unemployment]. Promemoria 2016-02-11, Regeringskansliet, Finansdepartementet, Ekonomiska avdelningen, Enheten för arbetsmarknads- och utbildningsanalys, Stockholm.

Swedish Pensions Agency. 2016. "Asylinvandringens ekonomiska effekter på pensionssystemet" [The Economic Effects of Asylum Immigration on the Pension System]. Rapport PID148639, Pensionsmyndigheten, Stockholm. https://www.pensionsmyndigheten.se/nyheter-och-press/pressrum/ny-rapport-asylinvandring-stark-er-pensionssystemet-men-ger-lagre-pensionsokningar.

Zheng, Yannu, and Olof Ejermo. 2015. "How Do the Foreign-Born Perform in Inventive Activity? Evidence from Sweden." *Journal of Population Economics* 28, no. 3: 659–95. https://doi.org/10.1007/s00148-015-0551-2.

CHAPTER 4

A Moral Superpower

> His wits being quite gone, he hit upon the strangest notion that ever madman in this world hit upon ... righting every kind of wrong, and exposing himself to peril ... and so, led away by the intense enjoyment he found in these pleasant fancies, he set himself forthwith to put his scheme into execution.
>
> —Miguel de Cervantes, *Don Quixote*, 1605

Immigration is not a unitary phenomenon, and immigrants are not a homogeneous group. There is considerable variation in how well immigration succeeds in different societies, and we also often observe that some immigrant groups do better while some do worse within each country. Successful integration hinges both on the characteristics of the immigrants and of the host countries. It is therefore largely meaningless to talk about "immigration" as having positive or negative effects in general; the answer is simply: it depends. Or, in the words of Harvard professor George Borjas (1999), the world's perhaps leading expert on the economics of immigration: "The most important lesson of the research is that the economic impact of immigration will vary by time and place, and that immigration can be either beneficial or harmful."

Historically, successful examples of immigration include the transatlantic migration to the United States during the 1800s and early 1900s; the immigration to Sweden during the early postwar period; Jewish immigration to Israel from the Soviet Union after the fall of Communism; and more recently the employment-based immigration to Australia and Canada. In all of these cases, immigrants were absorbed into the fabrics of their new countries, caught up or even surpassed native-born in terms of socioeconomic success, and thereby contributed to advancing the country. Swedish refugee immigration, in stark contrast to these examples, has been far from successful.

Despite—or perhaps because of—this, Swedish refugee policy was until recently justified by pointing to historical and successful episodes of immigration like the ones above. However, the many less successful examples are

T. Sanandaji, *Mass Challenge*,
https://doi.org/10.1007/978-3-030-46808-8_4

rarely talked about, even when they represent experiences considerably closer to current Swedish conditions. Hence, it is still more common to talk about America in the nineteenth century or the Walloons in the seventeenth century than of refugee immigration to neighboring Nordic countries, immigration from former colonies to France, Belgium, and Holland in the twentieth century, or the immigration of Roma to Sweden. Contrary to popular belief, there is no guarantee that successful immigration episodes to other countries tell us anything about immigration to Sweden. This is particularly true when these success stories concern the immigration of highly skilled labor—in contrast to the reality of unskilled refugee immigration from the Third World to a welfare state.

An important ingredient of the Swedish self-image is that it is a country where everything is *lagom*—an expression that means "just right" or "in moderation." The term is a fitting description of the Swedish cultural ideal of temperament and behavior in everyday life. Interestingly, when it comes to immigration and integration, Sweden is an outlier that stands out in comparison to other countries—both in terms of the scope of immigration and the resulting difficulties. Sweden has combined exceptional rates of refugee immigration with some of the largest gaps between immigrants and the native-born in terms of employment, educational attainment, and poverty. The hierarchy of countries differs from year to year and across measures, but Sweden performs the worst in many outcomes and among the worst in nearly all.

This departure from *lagom* has had a transformative impact on Swedish society and made the country an outlier. There are differing accounts as to whether it was Sweden that deviated from the rest of Europe, or vice versa. The Director-General of the Swedish Migration Agency at the time, Anders Danielsson, memorably stated, "When I meet foreign colleagues, they tell me that Sweden is an odd country when it comes to asylum. No, I say, you're the ones who are odd. All of you" (Wager 2015).

Volumes

No comparable country has taken more refugees in relation to its population than Sweden. Eurostat reports the number of asylum seekers to various European countries since 1985. For the period 1985 to 2018, Sweden is at the top per capita, with about four times as much asylum immigration in relation to the population as the Western European average. Overall, population-adjusted asylum immigration is significantly higher among Northern European countries, as well as Switzerland and Austria, than for Southern and Eastern Europe. Although Sweden has been above the average for a long time, the intake of refugees increased sharply relative to the rest of Europe fairly recently.

Eurostat reports statistics for all EU countries since 2008. Figure 4.1 illustrates that Sweden received the most asylum seekers per capita, both before and during the 2015 refugee crisis. The red part of the bar shows the number

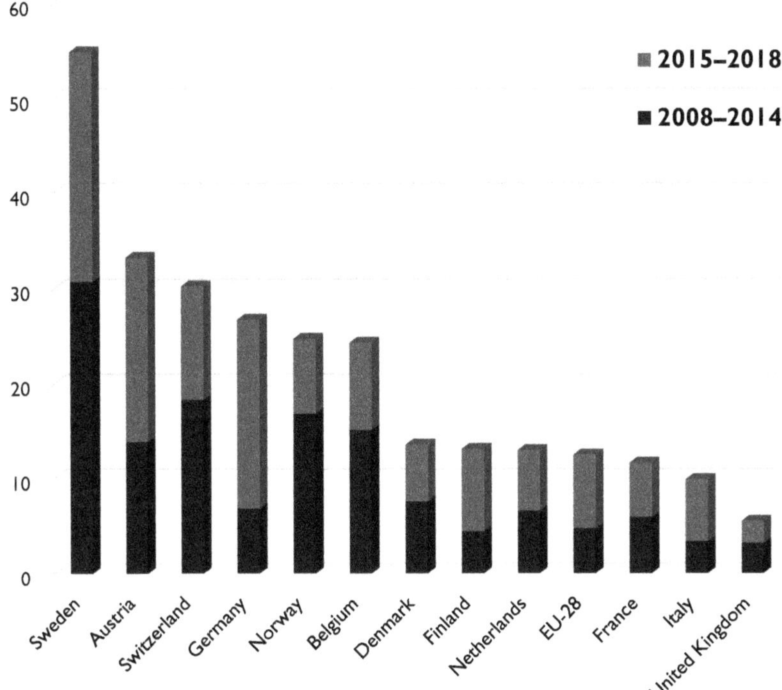

Fig. 4.1 Number of asylum seekers per thousand inhabitants in different European countries (*Source* Eurostat)

of asylum seekers since 2015, while the blue part is the total number of asylum seekers for the years 2008 to 2014. We see that for several countries, the number in 2015 is almost as high as for all the seven previous years combined. The asylum immigration to Sweden in 2014 and 2015 is in relation to the population not only a record for Sweden, but it is also unique in history (Eurostat 2016). Particularly, Sweden stands out when it comes to unaccompanied minors. Although Sweden has less than two percent of the EU's population, the country received 20% of unaccompanied minors who applied as refugees between 2008 and 2018, including 40% of those who arrived in 2015.

An obvious question to ask is why the number of asylum seekers has varied so much over time and between countries. A common misconception is that the explanation lies chiefly in external factors beyond the control of Sweden and other host countries. This assumption is however problematic, as migration flows are not merely caused by exogenous forces but also related to endogenous policy (Dustmann et al. 2017; Hatton 2017; Andersson and Jutvik 2019). A country with Sweden's geographical location actually has a lot of control over the number of asylum seekers. Instead, the increase in asylum seekers was primarily driven by political decisions that led to looser border control, which in turn made it easier to get inside Sweden and other EU countries in order to apply for asylum. Wars and the generosity of welfare programs, of course, also affect the number of asylum seekers, but these are of secondary importance. Thus, the fundamental factor in refugee policy is border controls.

While the EU plays an important role, asylum policy is mainly determined at the national level (Henrekson et al. 2019). EU countries that border with one another affect not only their own but also their neighbors' migration situation. This is because refugees have to pass through several borders to get to their destination. If the countries that border the Mediterranean or non-EU members have strict controls on the EU's external borders, asylum seekers will be unable to enter the interior countries using the land route. If neighboring countries, however, have weak or no border controls, the pressure on interior countries increases. At the same time, the interior countries also affect the policies of exterior ones. When the Scandinavian countries and Germany pursued generous migration policies, this increased the pressure on the exterior countries like Greece, as asylum seekers were trying to penetrate their borders in order to reach wealthier destinations. Additionally, EU countries, of course, influence each other through common policy, diplomatic pressure, and rhetoric.

The EU member states differ greatly in terms of asylum policy and migration rates. These differences in part reflect varying rates of economic development between Southern, Eastern, and Northern Europe, but there are also differences within wealthy member states. The variation in refugee flows is significantly larger than one would expect based merely on differences in economic characteristics. In relation to its population, Germany in the period 2008–2018 granted asylum to four times as many refugees as France and Italy, five times more than the UK, and over thirty times more than Spain. During this period, the number of asylum seekers that were granted asylum in Sweden was one hundred times greater than for similarly sized Portugal.

The reasons for this variation are complex. As expected, periods of conflict—such as the wars in the former Yugoslavia, Iraq, and Syria—give rise to greater flows of refugees to Europe. The member countries also differ with respect to pull factors that attract immigrants: geography, welfare rights, ease of being granted family reunification, the threshold for being granted status as a refugee, and the willingness to welcome refugees signaled by the country. This leads to stronger inflows of refugees to some countries and cross-country differences in the proportion of approved asylum applications.

Since Sweden and other Western countries have signed international treaties that oblige them to grant refugees protection under certain conditions, a member state does not fully control the number of refugees it will have to accept if they were to seek asylum. However, the right to be granted refugee status based on international refugee treaties only applies to those asylum seekers that make it into its territory. Countries who want refugees are free to let asylum seekers enter. This can for instance be done through the UNHCR resettlement problem, where, for instance, refugees who are in refugee camps, or urban areas of countries that neighbor conflict zones, are selected and settled in Europe. The number of such refugees that receiving countries accept is, however, limited and determined by the countries themselves. There are additionally millions of asylum seekers with legal right of protection, who would like to move to Western countries, but who cannot since they are denied the right to entry. This may be difficult to understand for many westerners, since they are used to being able to fly to most destinations using their passports without applying for entry visas. This is because most other countries have granted those who have American, Japanese, or Swedish passports the right to visit them temporarily, or even permanently, in order to encourage tourism and business.

However, this is not the case for individuals with passports from Iraq, Iran, Afghanistan, or Somalia. According to the Henley Passport Index, for instance, citizens of countries such as Japan, Switzerland, the United States, or Sweden—holding the most valuable passports—are allowed to visit 170 or more of the world's countries without having to apply for a visa. By contrast, citizens of Afghanistan, Iraq, Syria, and Somalia have some of the least powerful passports and are not allowed to enter most of world's countries—particularly no wealthy Western country—without applying for a visa, which is only granted in rare cases.

Asylum seekers unable to enter another country are not legally eligible to apply for asylum based on international refugee treaties such as the Geneva Convention. Taking advantage of this fact, Western countries regulate refugee inflows through border controls that make it difficult for asylum seekers to cross their borders in the first place. Countries are able to regulate the inflow of refugees since the treaties do not require countries to grant immigrants entry visas and only apply to those are able to travel there. Those who manage to cross the border into a Western country have the right to apply for asylum, but the country has some discretion in assessing whether the applicant's need of protection is sufficiently great to warrant asylum. In addition, member states can make it less attractive to apply for asylum by applying more austere economic policies toward refugees, such as high thresholds to qualify for financial assistance and social benefits, or by only granting temporary asylum, limiting family reunification, and other measures that are within the letter of the law.

The most important factor in refugee policy are border controls, and the reason for this is the way in which asylum immigration is controlled in practice. The international agreements that are in place, in particular the UN Refugee Convention, confers major rights to refugees with protection needs once they have crossed a border. Sweden admittedly has no obligation to give refugees permanent residence, but often does so for humanitarian reasons. The right to asylum, however, applies to refugees with protection needs, but only to those who have crossed the Swedish border. Therefore, globally, there are millions and millions who would have the right to asylum in Sweden if only they could cross its border. This is what makes border controls the most important factor in refugee and immigration policy.

At a first glance, Western countries have rules that are seemingly generous, but they have nonetheless managed to maintain a restrictive refugee policy. The key tricks needed to regulate immigration are thus, first, to not give asylum seekers entry visas and, second, to refuse to accept applications for asylum at embassies. Since Sweden is geographically isolated, refugees must either be smuggled across Europe or fly to Sweden on fake passports in order to be able to apply for asylum. These two options, however, have historically been difficult to implement, which has kept the number of asylum seekers down. Also, even many of those who managed to reach Sweden were not guaranteed asylum during the periods when the rules were strictly applied. These factors kept the application pressure relatively low.

As Sweden dismantled its border protection and went toward a more generous asylum policy, the number of asylum seekers increased, at the same time as the proportion who were allowed to stay also increased. This peaked in 2014 and 2015, when the EU's external border collapsed, and it became much easier to reach Sweden from the Middle East via land. At the beginning of the 2015 refugee crisis, the Swedish government refused to regulate immigration for political reasons. Ministers also incorrectly claimed that border controls would violate international law and would not really work anyway. After a few months, however, the government gave in and introduced stricter border protection and controls. This resulted in the number of asylum applications falling by about 95% in a very short period of time.

Sweden has since also introduced less generous rules regarding permanent residence and family-based immigration. The number of asylum seekers in 2019 was about 22,000 people—lower than in the past but still a relatively high number in a European context. If the goal is to reduce the number of asylum seekers, it would be easy to further tighten the rules, strengthen border security, improve checks of fake or stolen passports, and change the procedures of the Swedish Migration Agency. The international conventions that Sweden and most other countries have signed allow them great freedom to design their own asylum policies. The asylum application pressure that a country like Sweden is under is not exogenous or determined beyond its control; rather, it is essentially driven by its asylum policy.

There are many Third World countries that have received more refugees than Sweden, both in total numbers and in relation to their population. Lebanon and the region of Kurdistan have received over a million refugees each, and Jordan about half a million. Also, larger countries like Turkey, Iran, Pakistan, and Ethiopia have received larger numbers in absolute terms, but typically fewer than Sweden in relation to their population. Naturally, the pressure on surrounding countries to accept refugees has been much greater than that on Europe. The humanitarian benefits are the greatest when refugees flee to neighboring countries, as getting across the border to a neighboring country is what allows refugees to escape the conflict zone.

In contrast, the refugees who reach countries like Sweden are often refugees who are not escaping imminent danger. These are usually refugees who are coming from safe countries in neighboring areas, and who are traveling on to wealthier Western countries in order to boost their standards of living. One indication that immigrants are not necessarily under death threat in their country of origin is the significant share that travel back once they reside in the West. Based on Statistics Norway, *Aftenposten* (2018) cites the share of immigrants who vacation in the countries from which they have left, often as asylum seekers. 71% of Iraqis, 55% of Iranians, and 40% of Afghans have visited their country of origin. The most common reason to visit one's country of origin is vacation and seeing relatives.

The situation for neighboring countries is not fully comparable to that of Sweden, because the reception of refugees in these countries is mostly temporary, as refugees are expected to return after the conflict is over. Another difference with Sweden is that these countries receive support from the rest of the world to help fund and organize their reception of refugees.

That countries neighboring conflicts, like the one in Syria, have made huge humanitarian sacrifices should not be forgotten and they should receive considerably more support from the West. But when we analyze Swedish immigration and integration, it is more relevant to compare the situation in Sweden to that of other industrialized nations. For these countries, there are also often comparable data from the OECD and Eurostat. These data cover, among other things, the extent of immigration as well as many integration outcomes—allowing for comparisons across countries of how those with foreign background do relative to the rest of the population.

Looking at these data, it quickly becomes evident that Sweden stands out in comparison with other industrialized nations. Sweden combines the OECD's largest acceptance of refugees with the OECD's worst labor market integration. In 2018, no other country had a greater difference in employment between foreign- and native-born, as can be seen in Fig. 4.2. The exact numbers vary slightly from year to year, and some years Sweden has been ranked second after countries like the Netherlands and Finland; the rankings can also fluctuate across age groups. However, regardless of year and definition, Sweden competes for the bottom position and has in recent years often ended up last. Not only has Sweden the highest employment gap, but also the highest proportion of immigrant students who drop out of school, and it is placed second from the bottom in Eurostat's measures of the poverty gap and social exclusion. Swedish Public Television (2014) reported that "Sweden is the worst among industrialized countries when it comes to arranging jobs for immigrants."

As has already been mentioned, in addition to actual jobs, employment also includes government programs for the unemployed, sick, and parental leave as well as those who only work a few hours per week. Since the labor market institutions and definitions differ between different countries, the degree of employment integration is measured by comparing those with

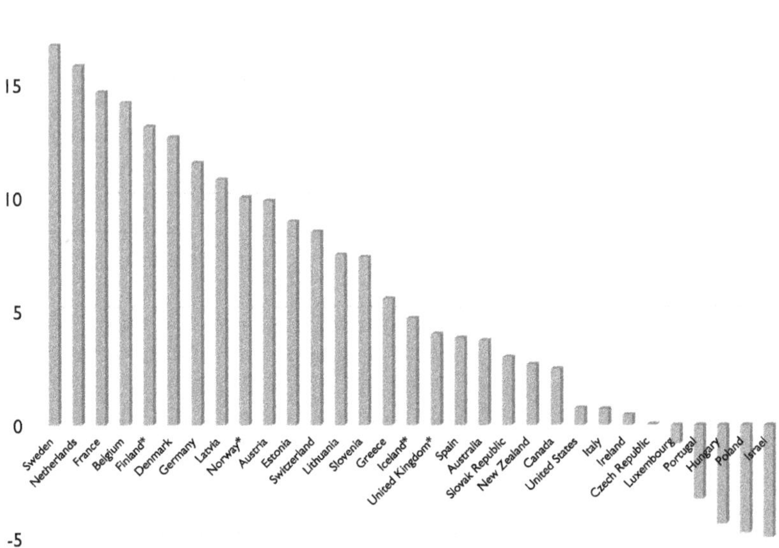

Fig. 4.2 The employment gap in various Western countries (2017) (*Source* OECD. *Note* The data for the UK, Norway, Finland, and Iceland are for 2015 since the 2017 figures were missing)

foreign background to others in the same country. Sweden has a high proportion of part-time workers, extensive employment policies in the form of government programs, and many women in the job market. Together with Switzerland, the Netherlands, and other Nordic countries, Sweden tends to have the highest employment rates in the OECD—even higher than countries like Japan, Australia, the United States, and Canada. This does not necessarily mean that Swedes work the most in the world. Total number of hours worked per person in Sweden is relatively high thanks to a well-functioning job market, cultural norms that support a strong work ethic, and more working women, but is still considerably lower than in the United States and several other countries. Consequently, the fact that Swedes have higher employment rates than, say, Americans does not mean that Swedes work more. It is, above all, an artifact driven of how employment is defined and measured.

Comparison of Outcomes

Sweden has a polarized job market. While Sweden's native-born population has an internationally very high employment rate, its foreign-born population is about average in the OECD. Compared to other countries, Sweden has a large employment gap for all education groups, but particularly among the low-skilled. OECD (2014) writes:

> In most countries in the OECD, migrants face more difficulties finding employment compared with their native-born peers—and Sweden is no exception in this regard and indeed, the gaps are larger than elsewhere. Indeed, across the educational distribution the large disparities in employment levels between immigrants and the native-born put Sweden among the worst performers in the OECD.
>
> ---
>
> These outcomes are certainly dependent, to some extent, on the composition of the migrant population: many refugees come from countries with failing education systems and lack even basic qualifications and skills; others with tertiary qualifications often acquired these in a very different context, raising issues about the transferability of their credentials. Alongside this, the discrepancy between employment levels among immigrants and native-born women is also particularly pronounced in Sweden.

It should be noted that the definition of "integration" of immigrants is a rather vague concept. Here, we use job market integration to measure integration overall. Different definitions that can be used in other contexts include problems related to cultural clashes, or the time it takes to establish oneself in the country. Job market integration, in turn, will be defined as differences in how immigrants fare relative to the rest of the population. The cause of this weak labor market integration is not exclusively, or even primarily, due to the Swedish job market being more closed than that of other countries. Rather, it is to be found in the unusually large differences in human capital and productivity between the foreign- and the native-born. On average, immigrants succeed better and integrate more rapidly in countries such as Canada and Switzerland, who admit many high-skilled immigrant workers (Brell et al. 2020). Sweden, on the other hand, stands out as most of the net immigration in recent years has consisted of refugees and immigrants from countries outside the West with low human capital.

Sweden is also a knowledge-based economy, where the existing workforce has a high average level of education and unusually few employees working in elementary occupations: "Norway, Sweden, Iceland and Finland belong to the five European countries with the lowest shares of such jobs: in the range of 3–6%. Hence, there is an obvious mismatch in these countries between the skills of many immigrants and the skill requirements on most jobs" (Calmfors and Sánchez Gassen 2019). This means that the productivity difference between the native- and the foreign-born workforce will be even greater in Sweden than in less demanding job markets, for example, in Southern Europe. The contrast with the lower skill and education levels of the Third World is even sharper in the knowledge-intensive Swedish economy, where low-productivity workers generate little or even zero benefit to employers, in contrast to the situation in less knowledge-intensive sectors in average-developed economies.

Not only does Sweden have the largest employment gap between native- and foreign-born, it also has the largest gap in human capital as measured by the knowledge test PIAAC. OECD (2016) writes: "Data from the OECD survey of Adult Skills suggests that the disparity between Sweden's foreign- and native-born adults with very basic literacy is the largest among surveyed countries." Sweden has, not unexpectedly, a large gap in terms of the proportion of foreign-born with formal education—not least since a high proportion of immigrants arrive here from countries with low education levels.

OECD (2016) further observes that Sweden receives an unusually high number of refugees and then points out: "As a result, the educational disparity in Sweden between foreign- and native-born individuals is among the largest in the OECD." According to the same report, the proportion of young people with immigrant backgrounds who do not complete their education is similarly very high—even the highest in the OECD:

> Across the OECD young immigrants—particularly those who arrive in their host country beyond the age of 15—are particularly likely to drop out of education, and no more is this true than in Sweden. In 2013 close to 38% of all those immigrants aged 15 to 24 who had arrived beyond the age of 15 were no longer in education. This represents the highest figure among the OECD countries for which this information was available.

The latest round of the PISA test (OECD 2019) estimated skill levels among 15-year-olds in the schools of 79 participating countries, and reports the average difference between native- and foreign-born individuals in most of these countries. The OECD itself cites the gap in reading, where Sweden had the largest gap among any participating country between immigrants and natives. If one instead calculates the average gap, including results in mathematics and science, Sweden has the second largest gap after Germany. Similarly, if one includes second-generation immigrants, the gap in Sweden is among the highest of all countries depending on the subtest and the exact definition of foreign origin. Finland, France, and the Netherlands also have very large gaps—in some cases larger than Sweden. It should also be noted that Sweden excludes an unusually large share of its immigrant population from the PISA test entirely, due to insufficient language skills.

An influential analysis led by Economics Professor Magnus Henrekson (Henrekson and Wennström 2019), which was subsequently both extended and popularized by the tabloid Expressen (2020), argued that the latest Swedish figures were inflated due to the practice of excluding the worst-performing pupils from taking the test. While all countries exclude some students, Sweden is suspected of abusing this practice in order to superficially improve its score, and has by far the highest share of excluded students in the entire OECD in the 2018 round of PISA—a full 11%. It is difficult to know exactly how much this has impacted Sweden's PISA result. According to Henrekson, though, the bias is potentially large enough to erase the country's entire gains from 2015 to 2018.

In addition, Sweden stands out with a considerable gap in poverty between foreign- and native-born. This is not about immigrants being more likely to live in poverty in Sweden than in other countries; Sweden generally has a low level of poverty, and even the poverty of immigrants is lower than the

European average. However, immigrant poverty in Sweden is high compared to the native-born population. Sweden also has the second largest gap in child poverty in Europe after Slovenia. Eurostat (2017) states: "The largest gaps between migrant children and children of nationals were recorded in Sweden, Denmark, Slovenia and Greece."

Statistics Denmark's report *Immigrants in Denmark 2016* contains—in addition to data on the situation for foreign-born in Denmark—an interesting comparison with Sweden and Norway. The employment rates for those aged 20–64 are compared across the countries, with data for women and men, as well as immigrants from the West and outside the West, reported separately. Sweden has the greatest gap in employment rates between immigrants and foreign-born for both men and women, and this is true for both Western and non-Western immigrants. Immigrants do somewhat better relative to the native-born in Norway, while the employment gap in Denmark is somewhere between that of Norway and Sweden. Statistics Denmark (2016) writes:

> The biggest difference in employment rates between native-born and foreign-born outside the West is thus in Sweden, where the difference is 24 percentage points. In Denmark, the difference is 23 percentage points, while it is 19 percent in Norway…. For the same reason, the difference in employment rates between native-born and foreign-born outside the West is also significantly higher among women in all countries. In Sweden, the difference is 30 percentage points, while the gap is 26 percentage points in Denmark, and 24 percentage points in Norway.

Statistics Denmark also presents age-standardized measures of employment rates, which are adjusted for native- and foreign-born having different age distributions in the three countries. This is an index that measures immigrant outcomes relative to the native-born, where a value of 100 means the same employment rate as native-born of the same sex and age. The report also calculates how the employment rate for the country as a whole among those of working age would have been affected if immigrants had achieved the same level as the native-born. In Norway and Denmark, the total employment rate would increase by three percentage points, while it would increase by five percentage points in Sweden. The figure is higher in Sweden relative to Denmark and Norway—both because the foreign-born do worse than the native-born and because immigrants constitute a larger proportion of the population. The overall job market in Sweden is, therefore, more sensitive to immigrants' outcomes than in Norway and Denmark.

Another interesting calculation that can be made is how many more would work if immigrants achieved full integration, in the sense of having the same employment outcomes as native-born. The effect is particularly significant in Sweden, again, by the combination of the employment gap being larger and because immigrants constitute a larger share of an already larger population. The report from Statistics Denmark (2016) concludes that total employment would increase by 300,000 in Sweden and 90,000 each in Norway and Denmark, if the employment rate of foreign-born would have been as high that of native-born.

Table 4.1 Age-standardized employment rate relative to native-born

	Sweden	*Norway*	*Denmark*
Western immigrants	78	93	85
Non-Western immigrants	66	71	66

Source Statistics Denmark
Note 100 corresponds to the level of native-born in each Scandinavian country, respectively

Table 4.2 Age-standardized employment rate relative to native-born

	Sweden	*Norway*	*Denmark*
Afghanistan	38	56	44
Bosnia	73	71	51
Iraq	47	47	37
Iran	63	60	47
Poland	67	77	71
Somalia	31	33	27
Thailand	59	68	68
Turkey	61	53	57

Source Statistics Denmark
Note 100 corresponds to the level of native-born in each Scandinavian country, respectively

In addition, Statistics Denmark presents the employment rate for various immigrant groups in the three Scandinavian countries—see Tables 4.1 and 4.2 for details. Overall, there are major similarities in how well groups of different origin do. Immigrants from Poland exhibit high figures in all three countries, while immigrants from Somalia exhibit low figures in all three countries.

The Second Generation

A decisive factor for the long run is how things turn out for second-generation immigrants, who are born and raised in Sweden. There are still only a few studies that reliably compare second-generation social mobility and outcomes for different countries, so it is difficult to comment on Sweden's position relative to other countries. It is also too early to start discussing third-generation immigrants—that is, children of second-generation immigrants. Non-Western immigration has not been going on long enough in Sweden for there to be a significant number of third-generation immigrants to draw conclusions from. As for the second-generation immigrants, we do know that the socioeconomic outcomes of children born in Sweden to immigrants converge partially toward those of the native population. The convergence that we observe is for most immigrant groups nevertheless far from the full convergence that would be needed for there to, in the long run, be no noticeable gaps between those with immigrant background and the rest of the population.

An in-depth analysis conducted by Statistics Sweden a few years ago showed that there are great differences between countries of origin when it comes to second-generation integration. Second-generation immigrants with parents from Europe have somewhat poorer job market outcomes than those of Swedish origin, while second-generation immigrants with parents from outside Europe on average do considerably worse. Statistics Sweden (2010) writes: “The employment rate of those with both parents from outside Europe in 2008 was 15–20 percentage points lower than for those with both parents born in Sweden.” In a recent newsflash, Statistics Sweden (2019) further concludes:

> The share of people who have a consistently low economic standard varies greatly between different groups within the population. Among the foreign-born, about 20 percent had a consistently low economic standard, while the proportion among individuals born in Sweden was 7 percent. If the foreign-born are divided according to countries of birth and continents, differences are likewise considerable. Around 33 percent of those born in Africa had a low economic standard.... Of foreign-born children who reside in Sweden, close to 40 percent had a low economic standard, compared to 6 percent of all Swedish-born children with two Swedish-born parents.

There is also considerable variation between different countries of origin in terms of educational choices. For example, when it comes to college-level education, second-generation immigrants with parents from Bosnia and Iran do at least as well as those of Swedish origin (Swedish Higher Education Authority 2016). A positive sign is that the proportion of young people with foreign background who start college-level education seems to have increased in recent years, even if all those entering college do not complete their studies. Overall, the proportion with tertiary education at age 30 was lower among second-generation immigrants than among those with Swedish origin (Statistics Sweden 2010).

Engdahl and Forslund (2015) show in a government report that the proportion of those who do not obtain secondary education is generally higher among both first- and second-generation immigrants. They compare individuals born in 1990 and conclude that “about 65 percent of young people with foreign background have a high school diploma, and just under 60 percent of the foreign-born. This can be compared with about 80 percent of young people with Swedish background.” The study further finds that individuals with foreign background were less likely to obtain academic degrees from colleges and universities. The fact that immigrants’ exclusion and social problems to a considerable extent are carried over to the second generation is an alarming trend for social development in the long run.

Although there are few studies on the third generation in Sweden, Danish data recently showed that integration comes to a halt in the second generation, so that third-generation immigrant children do just as badly in school as the second generation. Danish Minister for Immigration Inger Støjberg stated that “The development among second- and third-generation immigrants in Denmark is nothing short of disastrous” (*B.T.* 2017). She cites three tendencies: They perform worse in school than the average, are far more criminally active than ethnic Danes, and are also more criminally active than the generation before. The group was furthermore found to be more religious than both their parents and grandparents.

That Sweden has pursued a policy of large-scale refugee immigration despite having unusually significant challenges is probably linked to the country's distinctive culture. International comparisons of cultural differences and values show that Sweden and other Nordic countries are characterized by a high degree of tolerance and willingness to help others in need. Although there has long been a preponderance in public opinion to reduce the intake of refugees, this is not synonymous with intolerance toward immigrants. Sweden is the EU country with the most people who have positive emotional associations with immigration from outside the EU (European Commission 2015). In the World Values Survey, Sweden also ranks among the countries with the greatest tolerance for ethnic and sexual minorities. There are no signs that intolerance or racism would have increased in recent years; conversely, attitude studies suggest that this type of humanistic values remain strong in Sweden.

Sweden still maintains one of the highest levels of trust, although there are some signs in recent international surveys that trust has fallen. This is discussed in the article "Sweden's Unique Trust is Dropping: Can People be Trusted?" in the popular science magazine *Forskning & Framsteg* (2014):

> In most countries, people do not trust their fellow human beings. In the Nordic countries, this pattern is different since long ago. But now, the latest study shows that trust is decreasing in Sweden. Trust in other people is usually likened to a community's binding element. Countries with high trust usually have a stable democracy, strong economy, good public health, low corruption, low crime, and a high level of equity and equality. In the Nordic countries, trust is extremely high, but other countries in Western Europe also have high trust, while the bottom figures are found in the Middle East, Africa, and parts of Latin America.

Trust is usually highest in homogeneous societies and may decrease in multicultural societies, where integration is not working (Trägårdh et al. 2013). Immigrants have lower average trust, and in Sweden more diverse municipalities on average have lower trust. However, the relationship between immigration and reduced trust is not inevitable. When integration is successful, high-trust societies may produce high trust among immigrants, who find that a country like Sweden has well-functioning institutions and a generally trustworthy population. The article in *Forskning & Framsteg* (2014) cites Bo Rothstein, Professor of Political Science at Oxford, who argues that the impersonal Swedish trust is contagious by immigrants coming into contact with well-functioning institutions and receiving proper treatment from authorities:

> "Most people have no idea about whether they can trust their fellow human beings or not," he continues. "But a reasonable way to acquire an idea is to start from how the local teacher, doctor, police officer, judge, politician, and public official comport themselves. If they act corruptly and unjustly, it is a

perfectly reasonable conclusion that the world is corrupt and unjust. But if you can trust these people, it is reasonable to conclude that you also can trust people in general."

There is also evidence that the high level of trust in Swedish society, at least in part, is transferred to immigrants growing up in Sweden. Martin Ljunge (2014) studies the transfer of trust between generations among those with immigrant backgrounds, with a special focus on mothers and children. First-generation immigrants from countries with lower trust tend to have lower trust even after moving to high-trust countries. However, between the first and second generation, there is a partial convergence, so that the second generation approaches the trust level of the host country. In Sweden's case, the gap in trust is reduced by just over half between the first and second generation, so that the second-generation immigrants' level of trust is considerably closer to that of the native Swedes.

The Swedish Paradox

Many expected that the same high level of trust and tolerance that explain Sweden's large-scale refugee immigration would also more or less automatically deliver successful integration. This was not the case, though. As will be discussed later in the book, high trust and social capital can, paradoxically, be exclusionary to the extent that closely knitted groups are more difficult to gain access to for outsiders. The success factors behind Swedish society may instead have led to excessive self-confidence regarding how well integration would work—in turn, justifying an outsized refugee intake. The job market, school, and the rest of society's capacity to absorb new arrivals became overloaded. Sweden's attempt to adhere to an immigration policy that radically deviated from that of other countries failed dramatically and ended with a sharp policy turn. The stricter border controls and rules that were introduced in late 2015 resulted in a 95% drop in the flow of refugees in a short time, and a 99% reduction in the number of unaccompanied minors. Here, too, Sweden deviated from the average and closed its borders quicker than most other countries.

Today, Sweden has fallen into a situation where the general public simultaneously espouses conflicting values: extremely high tolerance for immigration is combined with the fact that many Swedes do not socialize with non-European immigrants. In addition, there is widespread pessimism about the possibility to achieve integration. The Swedish daily *Svenska Dagbladet* (2016) discusses this in an interview with Associate Professor Bi Puranen at the Institute for Future Studies:

> Three-quarters of the population believe that integration isn't working well. Meanwhile, four out of ten Swedes don't know any immigrants from a non-European country, according to new figures from SvD/Sifo. Yet, Sweden is seen as a moral superpower.

People who come here from outside of Europe have the toughest time entering society. Among the asylum seekers last year, most came from Syria, followed by Afghanistan and Iraq—the most remote countries from Sweden in terms of values and culture. This is something that Bi Puranen, Secretary-General of the global research network World Values Survey, which examines people's values, has studied in depth. She has established that Sweden is the world's most different country. Quite simply, we have made more progress than most in terms of democracy, equality, and tolerance for differences. Sweden is also the world's nicest country—"does more good than evil"—according to the UN's and the World Bank's index. It is of course something to be proud of, but risks creating problems in the encounter with new Swedes who have different values.

"Tolerance and trust are consistently high in the Nordic countries. They are deeply rooted, but naturally, this doesn't immunize us to populism in all its forms. Another risk scenario is about benevolent institutions that want to do good, but risk adding to prejudices by failing to ensure compliance with laws and regulations. Tolerance can, on a societal level, result in misguided 'niceism'," says Bi Puranen.

Professor Assar Lindbeck is often described as the nestor of Swedish economics. In an interview conducted by the Liberal current affairs magazine *Neo* (2013), he explained why Sweden is ill-equipped to integrate large numbers of low-skilled migrants:

"It's connected to our high starting salaries. We have high unemployment among low-skilled Swedes, and we have no functioning housing market since it's been ruined by rent control. So, immigrants arrive in municipalities where they can't get work or housing. And then you don't get the socioeconomic benefits that could be obtained from immigration. So, the conclusion is that in a welfare state of the Swedish type, with high starting salaries and a dysfunctional housing market—we can't manage unrestricted immigration without it leading to high unemployment and welfare dependency among immigrants."

How do you assess the current situation in that regard?

"60 percent of welfare assistance already goes to immigrants. Immigrants are five times more likely to live on welfare as a native. So, we already have problems. That means we need to have regulated immigration. We're a wealthy country with a welfare state, and we are nine million inhabitants in a world where three, four billion people would be considered totally impoverished. Clearly, such a country can't have unrestricted immigration.... This thing with unrestricted immigration, its champions, they make the assumption that wage levels should be dropped enough for people to get jobs. But that's not very much in line with Swedish society. You can't remake a country in any way you want, it has its values and its goals. The welfare state can't handle unlimited pressure. Should you then say that you should sacrifice wage levels for low-skilled Swedes? Are you supposed to do it in the way that the welfare state should be financed with dramatically increased tax rates? The supporters of unrestricted immigration don't seem to worry about that. But I do."

At a seminar in the same year, Lindbeck (2013) also pointed out that the conflict between welfare state ambitions and migration were acknowledged by the early Social Democratic intellectuals who designed the modern welfare state:

> A wealthy nation like Sweden, with nine million inhabitants in a world of billions of poor people, could not possibly have unrestricted immigration. It must have a restrictive immigration. And it must be very restrictive if one is to protect the wages and welfare systems of wealthy nations. This is absolutely inevitable. Even Gunnar Myrdal realized this many years ago when he wrote that the welfare state is a national project. With that, he believes that the benefits a nation manages to gain by successful economic development over a century cannot be offered the rest of the world without our system failing.

A similar analysis about welfare states has been made by prominent American economists, both on the right and the left. Milton Friedman famously stated, "It's just obvious that you can't have free immigration and a welfare state" (Brimelow 1998). This is one of the rare cases where Paul Krugman appears to be in agreement with Friedman and has similarly said that "open immigration can't coexist with a strong social safety net; if you're going to assure health care and a decent income to everyone, you can't make that offer global" (2010).

A True Moral Superpower

Sweden embraced the ambition of being a moral superpower, but failed to achieve this since humanism was not combined with evidence-driven analysis. When it comes to immigration-related issues, policy was mostly shaped as a reaction to xenophobia rather than being based on a well-thought-out strategy. Despite a several-years-long, intense, and divisive debate on refugee policy, there has been little discussion of how Sweden can develop a plan to help relieve the impact of refugee crises on the global arena. Instead, a false dichotomy has been painted where the choice is between extensive immigration to Sweden or not to help out at all. As a reaction to a relatively isolated group of xenophobes, who do not want to help in any way whatsoever, Sweden has maintained a policy characterized by irrational humanism, where the asylum pressure for a brief period of time reached historical record levels—only to be followed by sudden and sharp policy shift.

Sweden received a small fraction of the world's refugees, many of whom in fact did not arrive directly from war-torn countries. The enormous costs that this entailed were funded to a significant degree through cuts in humanitarian aid. In creating the Swedish refugee policy, there were few, if any, rational considerations regarding resource allocation. As an example, it has been estimated that Sweden's expenditure for the initial reception of unaccompanied minors in the years following the 2015 inflow would amount to about \$3.0–3.5 billion per year. To put this sum in perspective, it can be set against Afghanistan's total national budget in 2015, including revenues from international aid, of about \$4.5 billion for the country's roughly 30 million inhabitants.

If the costs of healthcare and other long-term expenses in addition to the reception costs are included, Sweden might have spent as much on a few thousand unaccompanied adolescents as the entire national budget of Afghanistan—the origin of most unaccompanied minors. It should also be noted that many unaccompanied adolescents with Afghani background are not actually fleeing from Afghanistan, but are moving to Sweden from countries like Iran, Pakistan, and the Gulf states, where many Afghans reside. It would be of far greater humanitarian benefit if Sweden improved living conditions in Afghanistan, as well as for the millions of Afghani immigrants living in poor conditions in neighboring countries, instead of spending vast resources on the small number of immigrants that made it to Sweden.

The fact that Sweden wants to be a humanitarian superpower is in itself admirable. That Sweden has been scorned for claiming to be a moral superpower is not because it is considered wrong to do good and to improve the world, but because Sweden has failed to do so. It is possible that Sweden has done more harm than good by cutting funding for valuable projects such as providing medicine, water, and HIV treatment in Africa. According to some estimates, these measures have saved tens of thousands of lives. Sweden has certainly raised the economic standard of living for hundreds of thousands of immigrants, but it is extremely doubtful if it has saved that many lives. In addition to cuts in foreign aid, the refugee policy of Europe and Sweden has led to thousands of unnecessary deaths on the Mediterranean Sea, as people have been lured to try to cross in an attempt to reach Europe from countries like Turkey.

All this could have been avoided if Sweden had attempted to maintain a more utilitarian policy focused on rational humanism, and it is still not too late to do so. In the European debate, it often sounds as if the refugee crisis is over. In fact, since 2015 the UN's estimate for the number of internal and external forcefully displaced people worldwide has continued to increase—from 60 million to around 80 million by mid-2020. The reason this is not perceptible in Sweden and other Western European welfare states anymore is because they have reinstated border controls and moved toward more restrictive immigration policies. From a global perspective, however, the problem is far from solved. Sweden's actions, thus, appear ill-conceived and self-centered, with refugees disappearing from the collective consciousness when they are not coming across the Öresund Bridge.

It is difficult to argue that refugee policy was motivated by a genuine desire to help when the calls for national mobilization fade some months after people stop sharing photos of refugees on social media—although the number of refugee children who need help has continued to increase. In the worst-case scenario, one could levy the charge against parts of the Swedish establishment that their declaration of humanism was insincere, and that it instead was driven by self-interest and opportunism. Many were willing to pay attention to the refugees in order to drum up votes, attract attention, and make money, but they have since fallen silent and switched their attention to more lucrative matters like the climate.

Sweden's chaotic refugee policy has not only created internal problems, but also helped to paralyze the EU. The fact that a country which many see as a role model has failed so miserably has impacted the debate in many other countries and, unfortunately, delegitimized assistance to refugees. Given the injury it has caused the world's refugees and the millions of people who depend on humanitarian aid from the West, Sweden may arguably have a moral obligation to live up to the high standards it has so loudly proclaimed. The refugee issue is far from resolved and, as we have seen, continues to expand. Any sincere and serious intellectual analysis and debate about how to best help refugees has been severely crippled by the emotional atmosphere that has surrounded the issue.

The most pivotal, but oft-forgotten, fact about the refugee crisis is the magnitude of potential refugee flows. There are already some 80 million displaced refugees in the world, and in addition to that, further tens of millions could flee if borders were opened. The number of people in the Third World who potentially would move to the West if they could amount to hundreds of millions, according to estimates by Gallup (Collier 2013). A considerable share of them have grounds for asylum in the West, or right to family-based immigration. Refugee policy must therefore be based on all who are fleeing, as well as the even greater number who would move if they could—not just the few who at any given time are on their way to Sweden and the rest of Western Europe. When borders are opened, the number of people seeking to enter is drawn from a pool of potential migrants in the Third World which is almost inexhaustible in relation to Western Europe's capacity to receive them.

The reception of the equivalent of 0.3% of the world's displaced refugees caused a national crisis in Sweden in 2015, without having any discernable impact on the global refugee crisis; neither did Western Europe's combined reception of asylum seekers, which totaled only a few percent of those fleeing. The reason is not that Sweden and other Western European countries are cheap or unwilling to make sacrifices. Rather, it is down to the combination of the size of their populations relative to the Third World, and the cost of receiving refugees in welfare states. In fact, Western Europe accounts for the majority of the money spent on global asylum assistance, and in addition to this it paid a high price for its chaotic refugee policy of 2015. However, these costs did not really lead to any significant relief of the refugee crisis or the mass death on the Mediterranean—on the contrary, they were arguably exacerbated. The decisive factor in resolving a global crisis is not moralistic arguments about how much the receiving countries suffer, but how well-conceived and effective the solution is.

There is an extensive and protracted debate on temporary refugee camps in war-torn countries and neighboring areas. These camps are underfunded in relation to how many they receive and should therefore be allocated more resources. However, a longer-term solution is to enable countries to receive refugees permanently. Nothing says that these countries must be located in the neighboring area. The amounts that wealthy countries in the West spend on refugees correspond to several times the national budget of many major developing countries. Using subsidies, the West would be able to support refugees and compensate countries which receive them. Potential candidates include Brazil, India, Indonesia, Argentina, Thailand, Turkey, Morocco, Tunisia, Peru, the Philippines, Vietnam, Mexico, and Malaysia. These are middle-income countries with, in many cases, large populations which without difficulties could absorb millions of refugees *en masse* in a way that Sweden cannot. Providing subsidies that correspond to what Sweden and the rest of the West today spend on refugee reception would be a significant contribution to these economies—and also make accepting refugees a potentially profitable deal for those countries that are interested.

The annual cost to receive one refugee in the Swedish welfare state would in many cases help dozens more to safety. Middle-income countries that combined have billions of inhabitants would, with enough financial support from the West, be able to absorb all 80 million current refugees, and more, in a relatively short time. The job market and skill levels in these countries are much closer to those of countries such as Syria, Afghanistan, and Iraq. The mismatch in productivity that occurs in high-tech knowledge economies would be avoided. Depending on origin, many refugee countries have similar language, religion, and culture as the potential recipient nation. Notwithstanding financial costs, small countries like Sweden, Norway, or Denmark cannot realistically receive millions of immigrants due to limited access to housing, infrastructure, health care, and education.

From a humanitarian utilitarian perspective, financial support to countries with lower cost levels would be the obvious solution in order to help as many refugees as possible. The huge resources already being spent on refugees in the West would be enough to fund this. It would also be worthwhile for the West to put even more money down to avoid the even greater long-term indirect costs—such as alienation, parallel societies, and antisocial behavior. There are many practical difficulties to sort out with the solution proposed here, but it is fully applicable and basically an expansion of already existing if heavily underfunded programs.

Even after the return to a strictly regulated immigration, the costs only for Sweden's initial reception of new arrivals are significant. In the Swedish budget proposition in the years following the 2015 inflow, the itemized costs for migration, integration of new arrivals, and budget increases for municipalities amount to about $6–8 billion per year—before taking into account long-term net costs of welfare benefits, subsidies, and public services. By 2020, due to reduced inflows, the costs for newly arrived refugees are expected to decline to slightly above $2 billion per year, though this figure, again, does not include the far larger long-terms costs—which, as previously explained, amount to additional billions of dollars.

These numbers can be compared to the UN refugee agency UNHCR's total funding that year of about $3 billion for all displaced worldwide. The UNHCR's formal budget is actually twice as large, but only half of the amount requested was funded; in "Needs and Funding Requirements" (2015), it is stated:

> By the end of 2015, the Office anticipates being able to cover only 47 per cent of its comprehensive budget. Thus, more than half of the needs of populations of concern will remain unaddressed, further exacerbating their vulnerability; contributing towards onward displacement; and undermining the potential stabilization of crises and the ever more challenging search for sustainable solutions.

The billions spent by Sweden alone can also be contrasted to the world's total humanitarian aid for food assistance, emergency aid, refugee programs, medical aid, etc., of an estimated $20–30 billion per year.

The most important thing that wealthy Europe can do for the tens of millions who are fleeing their home countries, and the upwards of hundreds of millions in affected countries, is of course to send resources—not to receive a few hundred thousands of those who are living in or around the countries affected by war, while neglecting the rest. In September 2015, during the ongoing refugee crisis in Europe, the *Guardian* published an article under the headline "UN Agencies 'Broke and Failing' in Face of Ever-Growing Refugee Crisis." The article describes how underfunded the UN's refugee agency is. Organizations who provide healthcare and food assistance are also in desperate need of resources. The effect of the lack of resources is that necessary care cannot be provided, and that the budget for food to refugees in some cases is as low as $13 per month. The *Guardian* (2015) article says:

> The Syria regional refugee response plan is only funded to 35% of the $1.3bn needed to support refugees, both in the camps and by providing resilience funding for the countries hosting them. In Africa, where the crises in the Central African Republic and South Sudan do not often make international headlines, many funding appeals are less than 15% full.
>
> – – –
>
> "People haven't been vaccinated, they suffer from malnutrition, they have mental health issues because of the conflict. We are setting countries back decades." Gayer said the decision to cut services was hugely difficult.
>
> "We are never 100% funded so we are always having to prioritise, but it breaks your heart when you end services for 3 million people. There will be no access for trauma like shrapnel wounds, no access for children's health or reproductive

health. There will be no surveillance of things like cholera. A generation of children will be unvaccinated."

– – –

Another major crisis for the UN is feeding refugees, not only those recently displaced but people who are still unable to return home years after leaving. This year the World Food Programme cut rations to 1.6 million Syrian refugees. The most vulnerable living in Lebanon now only have $13 to spend on food each month, a figure that the WFP warned would leave refugees vulnerable to recruitment by extremist groups.

Today, immigration and integration are among the policy issues that are ranked as the most important by Swedish voters. The image of Sweden as a well-functioning utopia has cracked—both to the outside world and to the Swedes themselves. In other countries, Sweden's experiment with a radical immigration policy is increasingly portrayed as a sign of hubris. Sweden thought itself to be above the basic laws of economics, and the country's failure is today used as a warning.

Also, there is a widespread pessimism among Swedes about the challenges facing their country. In the article "The People's Verdict: Sweden is Heading in the Wrong Direction," the results from a survey made on behalf of the tabloid *Aftonbladet* (2016) are presented. Strikingly, six out of ten respondents in the survey stated that Sweden is on the wrong track, whereas only two out of ten say that the country is on the right track. The level of dissatisfaction remained similarly high as of 2019 (*Aftonbladet* 2020). The share of the population saying their country is headed in the right direction is strikingly lower in Sweden even than in the United States, whose level of pessimism in recent years has received much attention.

Sweden's problems are self-inflicted, but obvious solutions are difficult to identify. Many Swedes expect, or rather hope, that in the long run the problems will solve themselves. The next chapter puts this expectation into perspective by portraying the development to date in those parts of the country that have already had several decades of immigration from less developed countries.

References

Aftenposten. 2018. "Flyktninger reiser hjem på besøk" [Refugees Travel Home for Visit]. By Olga Stokke and Thomas Olsen, December 31, 2018. https://www.pressreader.com/norway/aftenposten/20181231/281771335315408.

———. 2020. "Sex av tio väljare tycker att Sverige är på väg åt fel håll" [Six Out of Ten Voters Think Sweden Is Heading in the Wrong Direction]. By Lena Mellin, January 10, 2020. https://www.aftonbladet.se/nyheter/kolumnister/a/m6oMLE/sex-av-tio-tycker-att-sverige-ar-pa-fel-vag.

Aftonbladet. 2016. "Folkets dom: Sverige är på väg åt fel håll" [The People's Verdict: Sweden Is Heading in the Wrong Direction]. By Lena Mellin, September 20,

2016. https://www.aftonbladet.se/nyheter/kolumnister/a/ngBeLJ/folkets-dom-sverige-ar-pa-vag-at-fel-hall.

Andersson, Henrik, and Kristoffer Jutvik. 2019. "Do Asylum-Seekers Respond to Policy Changes? Evidence from the Swedish-Syrian Case." APSA Preprints. https://doi.org/10.33774/apsa-2019-6f46m.

Borjas, George J. 1999. "Immigration." The National Bureau of Economic Research (NBER). http://www.nber.org/reporter/fall99/borjas.html.

Brimelow, Peter. 1998. "Milton Friedman, Soothsayer." *Hoover Digest*, April 30, 1998. https://vdare.com/articles/milton-friedman-soothsayer-hoover-digest-1998-no-2.

Brell, Courtney, Christian Dustmann, and Ian Preston. 2020. "The Labor Market Integration of Refugee Migrants in High-Income Countries." *Journal of Economic Perspectives* 34, no. 1: 94–121. https://doi.org/10.1257/jep.34.1.94.

B.T. 2017. "Chok-tal om indvandrere går stik imod det, politikerne troede: 'Det er en katastrofe'" [Immigrant Shock Figures Go Against What Politicians Thought: "It's a Disaster"]. By Andreas Karker and Susanne Johansson, Berlingske Media, July 16, 2017. https://www.bt.dk/politik/chok-tal-om-indvandrere-gaar-stik-imod-det-politikerne-troede-det-er-en-katastrofe.

Calmfors, Lars, and Nora Sánchez Gassen. 2019. "Integrating Immigrants into the Nordic Labour Markets: Background, Summary and Policy Conclusions." In *Integrating Immigrants into the Nordic Labour Markets*, edited by Lars Calmfors and Nora Sánchez Gassen, 27–96. Copenhagen: Nordic Council of Ministers. https://doi.org/10.6027/Nord2019-024.

Collier, Paul. 2013. *Exodus: How Migration Is Changing Our World*. New York: Oxford University Press.

Dustmann, Christian, Francesco Fasani, Tommaso Frattini, Luigi Minale, and Uta Schönberg. 2017. "On the Economics and Politics of Refugee Migration." *Economic Policy* 32, no. 91: 497–550. https://doi.org/10.1093/epolic/eix008.

Engdahl, Mattias, and Anders Forslund. 2015. "En förlorad generation?: En ESO-rapport om ungas etablering på arbetsmarknaden" [A Lost Generation?: An ESO Report on Young People's Establishment in the Labor Market]. Rapport 2015:3 till Expertgruppen för studier i offentlig ekonomi (ESO), Regeringskansliet, Finansdepartementet, Stockholm. https://eso.expertgrupp.se/wp-content/uploads/2013/10/ESO-2015_3-till-webben.pdf.

European Commission 2015. "Public Opinion in the European Union: First Results." Standard Eurobarometer 83, Spring 2015. Survey conducted by TNS opinion & social at the request of the European Commission, Directorate-General for Communication. https://ec.europa.eu/commfrontoffice/publicopinion/archives/eb/eb83/eb83_first_en.pdf.

Eurostat. 2016. "Almost 90,000 Unaccompanied Minors Among Asylum Seekers Registered in the EU in 2015." Press release, 87/2016, May 2, 2016. Eurostat Press Office, Luxembourg. https://ec.europa.eu/eurostat/documents/2995521/7244677/3-02052016-AP-EN.pdf/19cfd8d1-330b-4080-8ff3-72ac7b7b67f6.

———. 2017. "Migration Integration: 2017 Edition." Statistical books, Publications Office of the European Union, Luxembourg. https://ec.europa.eu/eurostat/documents/3217494/8787947/KS-05-17-100-EN-N.pdf/f6c45af2-6c4f-4ca0-b547-d25e6ef9c359.

Expressen. 2020. "Sveriges PISA-framgång bygger på falska siffror" [Sweden's PISA Success Is Based on False Figures]. By Ludde Hellberg, June 2, 2020. https://www.expressen.se/nyheter/qs/sveriges-pisa-framgang-bygger-pa-falska-siffror.

Forskning & Framsteg. 2014. "Sveriges unika tillit sjunker: Kan man lita på folk?" [Sweden's Unique Trust Drops: Can You Trust People?]. By Henrik Höjer, September 4, 2014. https://fof.se/tidning/2014/8/artikel/sveriges-unika-tillit-sjunker-kan-man-lita-pa-folk.

Guardian. 2015. "UN Agencies 'Broke and Failing' in Face of Ever-Growing Refugee Crisis." By Harriet Grant, September 6, 2015. https://www.theguardian.com/world/2015/sep/06/refugee-crisis-un-agencies-broke-failing.

Hatton, Timothy J. 2017. "Refugees and Asylum Seekers, the Crisis in Europe and the Future of Policy." *Economic Policy* 32, no. 91: 449–96. https://doi.org/10.1093/epolic/eix009.

Henrekson, Magnus, and Johan Wennström. 2019. "Därför kan vi inte längre lita på Pisa" [Therefore, We Can No Longer Trust Pisa]. *Kvartal*, December 17, 2019. https://kvartal.se/artiklar/darfor-kan-vi-inte-langre-lita-pa-pisa.

Henrekson, Magnus, Tino Sanandaji, and Özge Öner. 2019. "Flyktingkrisen och nationalstatens återkomst: Bör EU ha en gemensam flyktingpolitik?" [The Refugee Crisis and the Return of the Nation State: Should the EU Have a Common Refugee Policy?]. In *EU och nationalstatens återkomst: Europaperspektiv 2019*, edited by Antonia Bakardjieva Engelbrekt, Anna Michalski, and Lars Oxelheim, 93–124. Stockholm: Santérus Förlag. https://santerus.se/eu-och-nationalstatens-aterkomst-bok-186.html.

Krugman, Paul. 2010. "The Curious Politics of Immigration." *New York Times*, April 26, 2010. https://krugman.blogs.nytimes.com/2010/04/26/the-curious-politics-of-immigration.

Lindbeck, Assar. 2013. "Hur kan vi förhindra att Sverige blir ett insider-outsider-land?" [How Can We Prevent Sweden from Becoming an Insider-Outsider Country?]. Center Party economic seminar, Swedish Parliament, Stockholm. Broadcasted in full by Swedish Public Television on October 28, 2013. http://www.svt.se/nyheter/svtforum/hur-ska-fler-fa-jobb-och-bostad.

Ljunge, Martin. 2014. "Trust Issues: Evidence on the Intergenerational Trust Transmission Among Children of Immigrants". *Journal of Economic Behavior & Organization* 106, 175–96. https://doi.org/10.1016/j.jebo.2014.07.001.

Neo. 2013. "Assar Lindbeck: Vinstfrågan är ett sidospår" [Assar Lindbeck: The Question of Profits Is a Side Track]. By Paulina Neuding, no. 3, 2013. http://magasinetneo.se/artiklar/vinstfragan-ar-ett-sidospar.

OECD. 2014. "Finding the Way: A Discussion of the Swedish Migrant Integration System." Organisation for Economic Co-operation and Development (OECD), International Migration Division, July 2014. https://www.oecd.org/migration/swedish-migrant-intergation-system.pdf.

———. 2016. "Working Together: Skills and Labour Market Integration of Immigrants and Their Children in Sweden." Organisation for Economic Co-operation and Development (OECD), OECD Publishing, Paris. https://doi.org/10.1787/9789264257382-en.

———. 2019. "Skills Matter: Additional Results from the Survey of Adult Skills." Skills Studies, Organisation for Economic Co-operation and Development (OECD), OECD Publishing, Paris. https://doi.org/10.1787/1f029d8f-en.

Statistics Denmark. 2016. "Indvandrere i Danmark 2016" [Immigrants in Denmark 2016]. Danmarks Statistik, Copenhagen. https://www.dst.dk/da/Statistik/Publikationer/VisPub?cid=29446.

Statistics Sweden. 2010. "Födda i Sverige – ändå olika? Betydelsen av föräldrarnas födelseland" [Born in Sweden—Yet Different? The Importance of Parents' Country of Birth]. Demografiska rapporter 2010:2, Statistiska centralbyrån (SCB), Prognosinstitutet, Stockholm. http://share.scb.se/ov9993/data/publikationer/statistik/_publikationer/be0701_2010a01_br_be51br1002.pdf.

———. 2019. "Varaktigt låg inkomst vanligt bland utrikes födda" [Lasting Low Income Is Common Among Foreign-Born]. Statistical news, April 29, 2019. Enheten för statistik om befolkning och ekonomisk välfärd, Statistiska centralbyrån (SCB), Örebro. https://www.scb.se/hitta-statistik/statistik-efter-amne/hushallens-ekonomi/inkomster-och-inkomstfordelning/inkomster-och-skatter/pong/statistiknyhet/inkomster-och-skatter-inkomstrorlighet3.

Svenska Dagbladet. 2016. "Integrationen i Sverige: 'Vi svenskar ser oss som en moralisk stormakt'" [Integration in Sweden: "We Swedes See Ourselves as a Moral Superpower"]. By Erica Treijs, July 23, 2016. https://www.svd.se/vi-svenskar-ser-oss-som-en-moralisk-stormakt-start.

Swedish Higher Education Authority. 2016. "Universitet och högskolor: Svensk och utländsk bakgrund för studenter och doktorander 2014/15" [Universities and Colleges: Swedish and Foreign Background Among Students and Doctoral Students in Higher Education 2014/15]. Statistiska meddelanden UF 19 SM 1601, Universitetskanslersämbetet, Stockholm. https://www.uka.se/download/18.12f25798156a345894e4a55/1487841855915/SM1601-svensk-och-utlandsk-bakgrund-studenter-o-doktorander-2014-15.pdf.

Swedish Public Television. 2014. "Sverige sämst på integration" [Sweden Is the Worst at Integration]. By Ulf Mattmar, Maria Holmin, and Diana Olofsson, *SVT Nyheter*, March 9, 2014. https://www.svt.se/nyheter/inrikes/sverige-samst-pa-integration.

Trägårdh, Lars, Susanne Wallman Lundåsen, Dag Wollebæk, and Lars Svedberg. 2013. "Den svala svenska tilliten: förutsättningar och utmaningar" [The Coolness of Swedish Trust: Conditions and Challenges]. Stockholm: SNS Förlag. https://www.sns.se/artiklar/den-svala-svenska-tilliten-forutsattningar-och-utmaningar.

UNHCR. 2015. "Needs and Funding Requirements: UNHCR Global Appeal 2016–2017." UNHCR, the UN Refugee Agency, Genève. http://www.unhcr.org/564da0e20.pdf.

Wager, Merit. 2015. "Migrationsverkets generaldirektör: 'När jag träffar utländska kolleger säger de att Sverige är ett udda land i asylfrågor. Nej, säger jag då, det är ni som är udda. Ni alla'" [Director-General of the Swedish Migration Agency: "When I Meet Foreign Colleagues, They Tell Me That Sweden Is an Odd Country When It Comes to Asylum. No, I Say, You're the Ones Who Are Odd. All of You"]. March 3, 2015. https://meritwager.nu/allmant/migrationsverkets-generaldirektor-nar-jag-traffar-utlandska-kolleger-sager-de-att-sverige-ar-ett-udda-land-i-asylfragor-nej-sager-jag-da-det-ar-ni-som-ar-udda-ni-alla.

CHAPTER 5

The Long Run

It's the duty of the individual to subordinate himself to society, or to be more precise, to the municipal authority in charge of our civic welfare!

—Henrik Ibsen, *An Enemy of the People*, 1882

Just as in many other countries, there was a consensus in the Swedish policy debate until recently that refugee migration was at the very least profitable, and perhaps even necessary for preserving the welfare state. Similar arguments have been echoed by the press and politicians in all Western European countries, whereas the opposite view has often been tarnished as populist or even racist. It is also common for international organizations such as the UN, the World Bank, the IMF, and the OECD to emphasize the economic benefits of refugee migration while deemphasizing costs.

It would be fair to say that public institutions as well as the public debate in the West have preferred a positive bias on the issue of migration. It is possible that they believe that the public already has a negative bias toward migration, and that the role of established organizations is to balance this out by emphasizing the benefits. For instance, the UN Global Impact for Migration (IOM 2018) states that "We also must provide all our citizens with access to objective, evidence-based, clear information about the benefits and challenges of migration, with a view to dispelling misleading narratives that generate negative perceptions of migrants."

It would be virtually impossible to imagine a UN compact that obliged countries to inform their citizens about the costs of migration. Similar types of explicit or implicit mission statements on migration permeate the reporting of many leading news agencies, as well as influential organizations like the European Union or the World Economic Forum. Given the history of xenophobia and irrational hostility toward foreigners that has long plagued Europe, it is understandable that there is a temptation to communicate that immigration—like trade—is almost always beneficial. This position is,

T. Sanandaji, *Mass Challenge*,
https://doi.org/10.1007/978-3-030-46808-8_5

however, not supported by research or by the historical experience, which instead indicates that immigration is sometimes profitable and sometimes not.

Another related claim is that immigration might impose short-term challenges, but is almost always beneficial in the long run—as though by some natural law. This assumption is also mistaken: there is nothing in the nature of immigration that guarantees that it is going to be beneficial, or that long-run gains will compensate for short-term costs (Storesletten 2000, 2003; Rowthorn 2008). In many instances, immigration is advantageous for the host country in the short run and even more advantageous in the long run. In other circumstances, it may take immigrants some time to adapt and initial costs will eventually be recovered. In other instances, however, immigration can be a short-term gain and a long-run cost, or a short-run cost and an even greater long-run cost.

There are several reasons why the latter might be the case. First-generation immigrants tend to arrive when they are already in their adulthood, so that the receiving country avoids the costs of rearing children. This creates a demographic advantage that the second and third generations lack. Moreover, social problems sometimes emerge over time. In some countries (prominently the United States), first-generation immigrants are more law-abiding than natives, whereas problems linked to gang activity tend to develop among second-generation immigrants. Similarly, it has been observed in some instances that religious extremism and hostility toward the host country's culture ripen among the children of immigrants.

We often observe assimilation and convergence of outcomes toward native levels across generations. It is, however, important to emphasize that there is nothing deterministic in this process; there are no economic nor moral laws that guarantee an auspicious outcome. It would be plausible to argue that the majority of modern immigration flows have been successful, not least because countries regulate migration and are less likely to intentionally open up for migration that is expected to have negative consequences. At the same time, it would not be hard to provide examples of less successful waves of immigration—both in the short and long run. The diverse experience of host countries as well as immigrant groups verifies the theoretical conclusion that the effect signs of immigration can be either plus or minus, and that the long-run impact can both amplify positive trends and deepening negative ones.

The academic result that immigration is non-deterministic has been known for decades and has never been controversial among leading experts. Nevertheless, a plainly different view became dominant in Western political debate. The notion that any type and any quantity of immigration was good suited the ideological views of both libertarians, yearning for greater freedom from state control, and the egalitarian preferences of the progressive left. As this conviction strengthened among politely enlightened society, it became socially costly—or even taboo—to bring up negative aspects of immigration.

Even in academic journals, there are cases were reviews of scientifically solid books by leading scholars, which point to the negative effects of immigration, have received unfairly hostile reviews (e.g., Card and Peri 2016). There are strong norms in economics to avoid normative rather than scientific arguments, but the charged issue of immigration is one of the areas where there is a degree of politicization and bias rather than mere adherence of evidence. Something to this effect appears to have happened in the migration debate in all Western European countries, but the politically correct consensus was undoubtedly unusually strong in Sweden. At its height, it was considered self-evidently racist to believe that migration could ever be a cost.

Many prominent commentators and policymakers took this argument to its logical conclusion and declared that Sweden should have open borders. Thus, a vision of a future with free immigration in a world without borders was adopted in the idea platforms of several Swedish political parties, both on the left and to the right. This consensus was ironclad while it lasted, but also brittle in that it rapidly broke when stressed by the inescapable consequences. Relaxing immigration restrictions eventually led to a surge of migrants that changed public opinion and made it more socially acceptable to discuss the costs of migration. Following the 2015 refugee crisis, the position of the Swedish government became more pessimistic and instead shifted toward the stance that immigration is a so-called "challenge."

While the focus of the debate has shifted, this does not mean that the most enthusiastic proponents of open borders have entirely changed their minds. Many instead retreated to an intermediate position, which holds that immigration may be costly in the short run but will become profitable in the long run. The argument goes that refugee migration is an investment that will eventually generate surpluses, as immigrants and their children enter the labor market.

The supply of low-skilled immigrants could, according to the theory, benefit high-income earners by making services dramatically cheaper. According to this theory, immigration generates gains for the economy despite the fact that immigrants themselves join the underclass. It is further argued that immigration leads to a more open and dynamic society, and increases the pace of innovation, but that these positive effects are not easily captured by standard statistical measures. Sometimes, prosperous clusters such as New York, Singapore, Zurich, and Silicon Valley are held up as evidence that a high proportion of inhabitants with immigrant backgrounds automatically generates innovativeness.

This type of argument is well worth entertaining, although it should be observed that many other cities are multicultural and poor, without being creative hotbeds. Immigration is a policy that is hard to reverse, and negative effects can take generations to fix. Therefore, in accordance with the precautionary principle, important decisions should be as well informed as possible. And although all forecasts of the future are by nature uncertain, it is still important to evaluate the long-term effects of immigration as carefully as possible. In this chapter, we try to see what we can learn from the experiences to date of the most multicultural Swedish cities.

Multicultural Cities

An interesting case study—which may provide clues about the effects of immigration on a country—is the development in areas that have already undergone a demographic change toward greater ethnic and linguistic diversity. We will here focus on cities and administrative areas referred to as *kommuner*, which are similar in size to areas that other countries refer to as municipalities or counties. The large-scale influx of immigrants started earlier in some parts of Sweden than others—often due to historical chance and factors such as the availability of housing and proximity to refugee camps. Therefore, the development of cities that have already moved toward greater ethnic diversity can give us hints of the probable long-term outcomes in the rest of Sweden as well as other European welfare states.

Overall, just over 25% of Sweden's population are of foreign origin, of which 19% points are foreign-born and 6% points second-generation immigrants. Of the foreign-born, in turn, about 11% points are non-Western. The city of Malmö, which is Sweden's third largest in population, surpassed these levels already a generation ago, as Malmö was a Scandinavian pioneer in multiculturalism. In addition to Malmö, the two large Swedish municipalities that stand out in terms of a high immigrant share are Botkyrka and Södertälje—both in the Stockholm Metropolitan Area.

The lakeside town of Södertälje was once known as the hometown of tennis legend Björn Borg and is today profiled for its large Assyrian and Arab-Christian communities. In 2008, NBC News highlighted neighborhoods with nicknames such as "Little Baghdad," and pointed out the stunning fact that this middling-sized Swedish town had alone taken in more Iraqi refugees than the entire United States. The municipality of Botkyrka is a large suburb halfway between Stockholm and Södertälje, named after the Christian missionary Saint Botvid. Botkyrka was similarly characterized by industrial activity that attracted guest workers.

The historical reason for why municipalities like Malmö, Botkyrka, and Södertälje have a large immigrant-origin population is that they took in substantial numbers of migrants during the 1950s through 1970s, not least industrial workers. Later, as migrants continued to arrive in Sweden, many of them naturally moved to neighborhoods that already housed their co-ethnics—particularly, if there was readily available housing. Due to this tendency—which can also be observed in the United States and other European countries—migration can snowball so that cities that take in a few thousand immigrants a generation or two later can become significantly more multiethnic than otherwise similar neighboring cities. Malmö, Botkyrka, and Södertälje are today atypical, but started out as being relatively average in terms of income and socioeconomic outcomes prior to the initiation of large-scale immigration. Hence, the influx of immigrants to these towns does not seem to have been caused by reverse causality—that is to say, attracting migrants because they were already low-income prior to immigration.

If we go back a few decades—before Malmö, Södertälje, and Botkyrka had been reshaped by large-scale immigration—these cities were relatively prosperous. This makes "early" multicultural cities interesting as case studies for understanding the effects of large-scale immigration, particularly regarding hypothetical spillover effects. As noted above, a popular theory among economic libertarians is that immigration renders positive but difficult-to-measure dynamic gains, which elevate the entire economy. If this theory was true, we would expect that these benefits would by now have materialized, at least in cities where nearly a majority of the population is of immigrant origin.

It should not be underestimated how important the notion of positive spillovers and productivity gains from immigration has been in the economic literature and in the policy debate. Few dispute that high-skilled immigrants, such as researchers or investors, generate indirect economic benefits for the host country. In theoretical economic models, however, even low-skilled immigrants generate benefits for natives such as lower cost of services. Since low-skilled immigration is the most politically controversial type, the magnitude of these gains and how they relate to various costs of immigration are central to the policy debate.

We do know that low-skilled migrants have low incomes and tend to push down average income levels in host countries. The argument put forward by libertarians, and by economists with a favorable view on the economics of immigration, is that low observed income is not a decisive problem. This is motivated by the belief that low-skilled immigrants significantly improve the economic prosperity of the rest of society—in spite of being poor themselves. Other economists argue that the gains from exchange are meager, and that low-skilled immigrants provide low-productive labor to produce standard goods and services, which the host country could have produced anyway at a marginally higher cost.

In some standard economic models, the surplus from low-skilled immigration is miniscule, because much of the benefit for consumers and capitalists from low-skilled labor, which pushes down prices, comes at the expense of existing workers. One estimate by a prominent economist is that the surplus for natives generated in the labor market by immigrants amounted to 0.2 percent of GDP for the United States in 2010 (Borjas 2013). In this type of estimate, low-skilled native workers are financially harmed by the labor-market effects of immigration.

It should be noted that the labor market competition is only one of the mechanisms through which immigration can impact low-skilled natives, and perhaps not the most important one. In other cases, natives are instead impaired by the fiscal costs and by negative social spillovers such as crime. Hence, the existence or non-existence of significant intangible benefits from low-skilled immigration becomes a critical issue. One mechanism for the presence of such positive spillovers is the theory that migrants substantially stimulate the productivity of native workers.

An increasingly popular claim is that low-skilled immigration benefits all natives, including unskilled native workers in local labor markets that experience unskilled immigration. At the empirical level, however, these claims about indirect effects and productivity spillovers are hard to evaluate. Studies that review the literature on the effects of immigration on the earnings of natives vary widely from negative to positive (Dustmann et al. 2016).

Calculating the effect is also complicated by the fact that immigration does not only affect workers but also consumers, property owners, and others. Estimates are in many cases not a question of direct measurement, but of using mathematical models to interpret the data—which are indeed very sensitive to the assumptions underpinning the models. This type of numerical exercise has in a few cases produced very large gains from low-skilled immigration (e.g., Foged and Peri 2016).

Both estimates in the pessimistic and optimistic ranges, respectively, have been criticized by scholars in different camps, and the supposed labor-market-gains effects of low-skilled immigration remains one of the most contentious areas in economics with several hitherto unresolved disputes. These debates tend to be technical and esoteric, since much of the discussion revolves around theoretical assumptions in mathematical and statistical models—which makes them inaccessible not only to the general public but even to economists, who are not specialized in this particular subfield of the economics of immigration.

Moreover, there is a disproportional focus in the academic debate on the United States. This debate has centered on a few cases, such as the 1980 Mariel boatlift, where 125,000 Cuban migrants arrived in Miami of which around half ultimately settled. These intense and academic debates further focus on fairly narrow topics, such as wages for particular groups of workers, and remain unresolved in part due to lack of sufficiently detailed and unambiguous data.

Economists have recognized the need for broadened horizons as well as to study other historical episodes in other countries—attempting to capture exogenous events on labor market outcomes as well as using model-based structural estimates (cf. Edo 2019). Examples include the repatriation of Algerian French to France (Hunt 1992; Edo 2017), Portuguese repatriates from Angola and Mozambique (Carrington and de Lima 1996; Mäkelä 2017), Soviet Jewish migration to Israel (Friedberg 2001; Borjas and Monras 2017), ethnic Turks from Bulgaria to Turkey (Aydemir and Kırdar 2017), internal refugees in Columbia (Calderón-Mejía and Ibáñez 2016), Syrian refugees to Turkey (Tumen 2016), refugees from Rwanda and Burundia to Tanzania (Ruiz and Vargas-Silva 2015), and inflow of Czech commuters to Germany (Dustmann et al. 2017).

There is, in addition, great value in tracing the historical development of cities that experienced long-term demographic transformation due to long periods of high immigration. The fact that the purported substantial gains from immigration are intangible makes them difficult to capture at the microlevel, but implies that they should be readily observable at the macrolevel. As long as labor markets are partially determined by local factors, cities such as Malmö provide us with an invaluable natural laboratory to set an upper bound on the gains from unskilled immigration. If taking in a large number of immigrants from low-income countries would have generated vast dynamic gains for natives, these should by now be detectible in the aggregate numbers in Malmö—without the need for abstract mathematical models, where the assumptions drive any number of possible results.

In a situation where we have model uncertainty, it is indeed more scientific to ground our analysis in overall historical trends, observable to the naked eye, when evaluating hypotheses. As will be shown below, Malmö and similar cities have not experienced any boom due to immigration, neither for natives nor the existing migrant population. On the contrary, it is difficult to find a plausible reason other than immigration for why this city, which was until recently fairly typical, has experienced worsening social and economic outcomes as the immigrant population has grown. Contrary to the predictions of optimistic models, we do not observe that native unskilled workers—or indeed any category of native or non-native workers—are prospering in cities with large inflows of migrants. This simple yet powerful result severely undermines any theoretical model predicting that low-skilled immigration generates productivity spillovers for natives.

Comparing different cities over time alone is, of course, not sufficient as a scientific method of establishing causality. Cities are not experimental objects, and there are no cities that are otherwise identical to Malmö, Södertälje, or Botkyrka, and thus can be used as control groups. Excluding the heavily Finnish municipality of Haparanda on the Finnish border, Botkyrka, Södertälje, and Malmö have the highest proportion of inhabitants with immigrant origin among Sweden's 290 municipalities. The proportion of inhabitants with a foreign origin is 59% in Botkyrka, 54% in Södertälje, and 46% in Malmö. Most of these are first-generation immigrants, of which non-Western migrants constitute the lion's share.

The effects of a high immigrant share on socioeconomic outcomes are clearly visible in these towns at an aggregate level—in other words, in outcomes as a whole. Similar patterns can be observed at the neighborhood and individual levels in parts of Sweden, where the proportion of immigrants is still too low for that group's outcomes to dominate aggregate trends. Even in the hypothetical extreme scenario where no immigrants work, immigration will not drive up unemployment statistics noticeably if immigrants are only, say, 1% of the population. It is therefore only in places where the proportion of those with immigrant background has grown large enough that effects become clearly visible in aggregate outcomes such as unemployment and tax base. This is obvious when pointed out, but often neglected in media reporting, where problems among the immigrant minority are dismissed based on the flawed reasoning that the city or country as a whole is doing well.

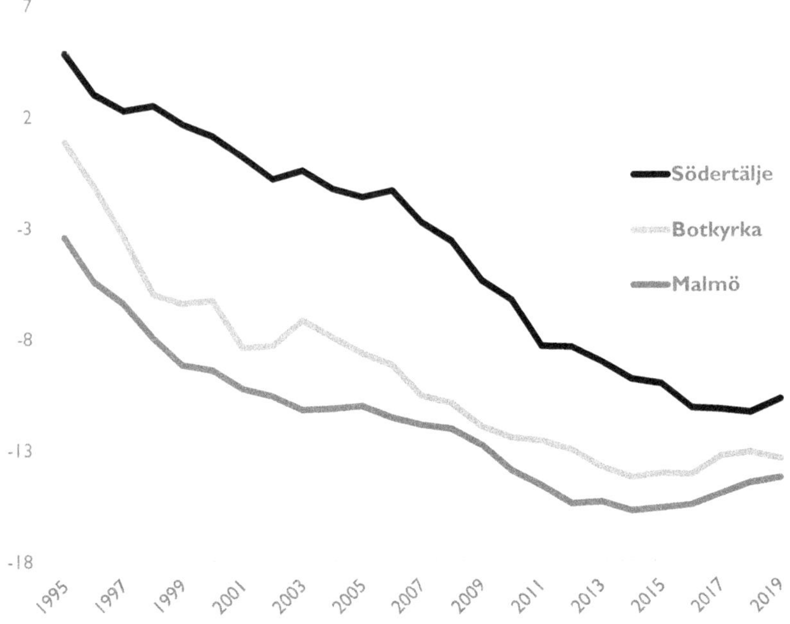

Fig. 5.1 Average income per resident relative to the national average (*Source* Statistics Sweden)

Statistics Sweden reports total earned income per resident since 1991, which is a measure of the tax base. In municipalities with low incomes, it is difficult to generate adequate revenue to fund welfare services. In Fig. 5.1, average income in Malmö, Botkyrka, and Södertälje is compared with the national average. The negative trend that is observed in the figure is not unique to these three municipalities, but can be seen also in other Swedish multicultural municipalities.

As the tax base in these three cities has eroded relative to the national average, they are increasingly dependent on subsidies from the rest of Sweden to fund welfare services. Today, Malmö, Botkyrka, and Södertälje receive almost $1 billion per year in municipal equalization funds, and much more through various other support programs. Since their finances are supported by other cities, the local welfare state still functions. However, had these three cities been on their own, their finances would have collapsed a long time ago.

The Challenges of Malmö

Malmö is a particularly interesting case, not only because of its large immigrant population, but also because it is Sweden's third largest city and the cradle of Swedish social democracy. Regardless of what measures we use, Malmö's challenges shine through among Sweden's 290 municipalities. The rate of child poverty is the highest in the nation at 25% (Save the Children 2018). In some immigrant neighborhoods, the majority of children lives in poverty—compared a child poverty rate of 3% nationally for ethnically Swedish children. Malmö is also unique in welfare support payments; almost one out of ten residents receive social assistance—the highest share in any Swedish municipality.

Statistics Sweden's figures for the period 1991–2017 show that real income per capita grew at an average rate of 1.9% per year for the entire country. In Malmö, Botkyrka, and Södertälje, growth was only 1.3% per year—which puts all three municipalities among the bottom five out of Sweden's 290 municipalities. The lowest growth rate was found in Burlöv, an immigrant-heavy suburb of Malmö. Similar patterns can be cited for virtually all socioeconomic outcomes. Malmö and other multicultural cities tend to be ranked close to the bottom when it comes to income inequality, unemployment, school performance, social assistance, child poverty, crime, health outcomes, and other social outcomes—for which Scandinavia as a whole tends to perform well.

In Malmö, homelessness has recently remerged as a major problem. Few other Scandinavian cities have such pronounced problems with unemployment, social exclusion, segregation, or violence. Of course, parts of Malmö still remain charming and well-functioning, and roughly half the population that is of Swedish origin perform around the national average. This means that Malmö is best described as a dual economy. One half of the city consists of fairly average Swedes and integrated immigrants, and remains a typical Scandinavian city. This well-functioning half abides wall-to-wall with the half of Malmö that consists mostly of socially deprived, high-crime neighborhoods, and a stagnating economy.

The city's challenges have in recent years made Malmö famous—not only as the birthplace of soccer star Zlatan Ibrahimović, but also for rates of gang violence comparable to that observed in the mafia regions of Sicily and Naples. Reporters from around the world have been drawn to Malmö, where the sounds of hand grenades, machine guns, police helicopters, and detonations in residential areas are now part of the city's natural soundscape.

The gang violence in Malmö has spilled over to the neighboring Danish capital of Copenhagen, where hired assassins and demolition experts cross over the bridge, so that Denmark in 2019 took the remarkable decision to enact border controls—citing safety reasons. During the Second World War, Malmö and neighboring regions became a safe haven for the Jewish population of Denmark. In 1943, the Danish resistance movement in a daring operation smuggled over seven thousand Danes of Jewish ancestry to Sweden by sea, saving virtually all Danish Jews from the Holocaust. In recent years, a less heroic image of Malmö has been reported around the world, in the form of anti-Semitic harassment and assaults on Malmö's small Jewish population. Some of this hostility comes from Swedish neo-Nazis, but much of it emanates from the city's Middle Eastern and Muslim population. In some schools, teachers are afraid to wear Jewish symbols—a far cry from the city's historical ideals.

These and other glaring problems have not prevented politicians from spinning and attempting to convey a positive image of Malmö as a role model. In this rhetoric, it is common to blame Malmö's problems on external factors, or to dismiss them outright as a populist smear campaign. Swedish Prime Minister Stefan Löfven declared the following in a 2013 speech:

> It feels good to come here to Malmö. Like you, Katrin, said recently: "The city is young. The city is global." In just a few years, you in Malmö have stepped up and shown that this is a city at the forefront of culture and development. And I think that it's the sense of confidence in the future that makes the city grow. … Malmö's pluralism is also part of the city's strength. With 280,000 people originating from 170 different countries, with 140 different languages, you're ready to take your place in the global economy.

Malmö's challenges have, however, grown so much that they have become increasingly difficult to deny. The city's daily newspaper *Sydsvenskan* (2016a) has investigated the negative development in the article "How Malmö Became One of Sweden's Poorest Cities." The article describes how the city's manufacturing jobs have disappeared: "Malmö has in forty years gone from prosperous working-class city to one of the country's poorest municipalities. Sky-high unemployment. Large immigration. Expanding gaps. Social unrest. 'The city is a pressure cooker,' says Professor Tapio Salonen."

Economic projections paint a gloomy picture of Malmö's future finances, as the population growth of low-income inhabitants causes welfare needs to grow without generating sufficient tax revenue to fund them. *Sydsvenskan*'s article (2016b) discusses a related problem, namely that an increasing number of Malmö's residents are too poor to afford their own housing. Since so many residents rely on public assistance to put a roof over their heads, the social service office has become one of the city's largest landlords.

Municipal budgets do not tend to be exciting reading material, but Malmö's is a notable exception. The city's own tax revenue is far from sufficient to fund spending. In 2019, Malmö projects some $2 billion in net costs, of which roughly $1.4 billion are financed with taxes and a staggering $0.6 billion come from subsidies. Malmö's deficit is small, but only because the rest of Sweden covers the shortfall in its budget.

The Long Run Arrives

Malmö's economic deterioration was not a priori obvious. Many had expected that Malmö would flourish after its university was opened in 1998, and the Öresund Bridge connected it to Denmark in 2000. The city boasts Sweden's perhaps best geographical location next to the European mainland, as well as other advantages in a period when urbanization has benefited other cities, and when the rest of the region close to Malmö has prospered.

Malmö's politicians have, over the years, produced countless excuses for the city's problems, but few that are convincing. The fundamental explanation of Malmö's development is large-scale immigration combined with failed integration. This conclusion is clear both in the macrodata and, more importantly, at the microlevel. When we decompose the various demographic groups in Malmö, it becomes clear that its Swedish population has performed fairly close the national average, and that the decline is driven by the growing immigrant population.

One statistical problem when analyzing Malmö is dealing with inhabitants who work in Denmark. An estimate by Statistics Sweden (2010) from a number of years back, which adjusted for this issue, showed that 79% of Malmö's Swedish-born population of working age are gainfully employed, which was close to the national average. Among the foreign-born population in Malmö, only 54% were working. The foreign-born who were working also have lower average incomes and hence pay less in taxes. In other words, if Malmö had had the same demographic distribution as the rest of the country, its economy would in general be similar to that of the national average.

Sydsvenskan (2016c) ordered data from Statistics Sweden on job market entry in Malmö for newly arrived migrants, stretching from 1997 until 2014. The numbers are low, even compared with the weak integration in the rest of Sweden: "Our inquiry shows that it is much more difficult for refugees in Malmö to get jobs compared to the rest of the country. Of those who arrived ten years ago, only 36 percent had jobs in 2014." Also second-generation immigrants in multicultural cities perform weak economically. As second-generation immigrants are becoming a larger share of the population, their incomplete integration exacerbates the financial problems caused by first-generation immigrants.

Södertälje has had a similar experience, going from being a prosperous industrial city to a city that competes with Malmö over the bottom rankings in unemployment and dependence on social assistance. Just as Malmö, Södertälje has a dual economy that includes prosperous areas with many high-tech industries, alongside large poor areas. In recent years, Södertälje has even witnessed a slight recovery driven by the economic boom in the Stockholm region—although it remains to be seen whether it will be persistent.

The picture that emerges from cities that are further ahead in the demographic transformation is not hopeful. While many immigrants integrate and even prosper, the overall picture is quite dismal. For immigration to work, immigrants must converge to, or preferably surpass, native outcomes within a few years—or at least by the second generation. If convergence stops after reaching say halfway, an increased immigration share will drag down the average. Regardless of the fact that one can anecdotally point to many successful individuals, this pattern is consistent with what we can observe in the case studies in this chapter from Malmö, Botkyrka, and Södertälje.

There is an understandable expectation by the proponents of current migration policy that the initial problems are temporary, and that we will in the long run realize the true gains from immigration. After all, many nativists were pessimistic about nineteenth-century immigration to the United States, which turned out to be successful overall. There is, however, no guarantee that history replays itself, or that short-run problems turn out to be long-term gains.

Moreover, the notion that, for instance, Irish, or Italian immigrants to the United States struggled with similar problems in the beginning is simply not accurate. Historical research shows that the Elis Island migrants in fact started working and generating economic gains swiftly, and that the negative view held by the nativists of the day was largely myths (Abramitzky and Boustan 2017).

The case of Scandinavian welfare states is different, both since immigrants integrate worse in the short term, and since there is insufficient long-run convergence. This may be claimed with a fair degree of confidence, since cities such as Malmö have had close to two generations of experience with large-scale immigration, resembling the recent refugee inflow in nature. Due to the stability of these patterns, it is reasonable to expect that the 2015 episode will not in the long run differ much from the dynamics that we can already observe in Malmö's past.

Thanks to such cities, we do not need to speculate about the future, but can observe the long run by learning from the past and examining the present. It is difficult to find signs of positive dynamic effects or intangible gains from today's large-scale immigration. On the contrary, the problems associated with immigration—such as crime and poverty—have not faded in the long run, but rather can be more clearly observed, as the immigrant population exerts an increasing effect on aggregate outcomes.

References

Abramitzky, Ran, and Leah Boustan. 2017. "Immigration in American Economic History." *Journal of Economic Literature* 55, no. 4: 1311–45. https://doi.org/10.1257/jel.20151189.

Aydemir, Abdurrahman B., and Murat G. Kırdar. 2017. "Quasi-Experimental Impact Estimates of Immigrant Labor Supply Shocks: The Role of Treatment and Comparison Group Matching and Relative Skill Composition." *European Economic Review* 98: 282–315. https://doi.org/10.1016/j.euroecorev.2017.07.005.

Borjas, George J. 2013. "Immigration and the American Worker: A Review of the Academic Literature." Center for Immigration Studies, Washington, DC. https://cis.org/Report/Immigration-and-American-Worker.

Borjas, George J., and Joan Monras. 2017. "The Labour Market Consequences of Refugee Supply Shocks." *Economic Policy* 32, no. 91: 361–413. https://doi.org/10.1093/epolic/eix007.

Calderón-Mejía, Valentina, and Ana María Ibáñez. 2016. "Labour Market Effects of Migration-Related Supply Shocks: Evidence from Internal Refugees in Colombia." *Journal of Economic Geography* 16, no. 3: 695–713. https://doi.org/10.1093/jeg/lbv030.

Card, David, and Giovanni Peri. 2016. "*Immigration Economics* by George J. Borjas: A Review Essay." *Journal of Economic Literature* 54, no. 4: 1333–49. https://doi.org/10.1257/jel.20151248.

Carrington, William J., and Pedro J. F. De Lima. 1996. "The Impact of 1970s Repatriates from Africa on the Portuguese Labor Market." *Industrial and Labor Relations Review* 49, no. 2: 330–47. https://doi.org/10.1177/001979399604900210.

Dustmann, Christian, Uta Schönberg, and Jan Stuhler. 2016. "The Impact of Immigration: Why Do Studies Reach such Different Results?" *Journal of Economic Perspectives* 30, no. 4: 31–56. https://doi.org/10.1257/jep.30.4.31.

———. 2017. "Labor Supply Shocks, Native Wages, and the Adjustment of Local Employment." *The Quarterly Journal of Economics* 132, no. 1: 435–83. https://doi.org/10.1093/qje/qjw032.

Edo, Anthony. 2017. "The Impact of Immigration on Wage Dynamics: Evidence from the Algerian Independence War." CESifo Working Paper Series no. 6595. https://ssrn.com/abstract=3025278.

———. 2019. "The Impact of Immigration on the Labor Market." *Journal of Economic Surveys* 33, no. 3: 922–48. https://doi.org/10.1111/joes.12300.

Foged, Mette, and Giovanni Peri. 2016. "Immigrants' Effect on Native Workers: New Analysis on Longitudinal Data." *American Economic Journal: Applied Economics* 8, no. 2: 1–34. https://doi.org/10.1257/app.20150114.

Friedberg, Rachel M. 2001. "The Impact of Mass Migration on the Israeli Labor Market." *The Quarterly Journal of Economics* 116, no. 4: 1373–1408. https://doi.org/10.1162/003355301753265606.

Hunt, Jennifer. 1992. "The Impact of the 1962 Repatriates from Algeria on the French Labor Market." *Industrial and Labor Relations Review* 45, no. 3: 556–72. https://doi.org/10.1177/001979399204500310.

IOM. 2018. "Global Compact for Safe, Orderly and Regular Migration." Draft Rev. 3, June 29, 2018. International Organization for Migration, UN Migration, Global Impact for Migration, Grand-Saconnex. https://www.un.org/pga/72/wp-content/uploads/sites/51/2018/06/PGA-Letter-Transmission-of-Draft-Rev-3-Global-Compact-Migration.pdf.

Löfven, Stefan. 2013. "Jobb & framtidstro för en global generation – tal av Stefan Löfven i Malmö 1 maj 2013" [Jobs & Faith for a Global Generation—Speech by Stefan Löfven in Malmö May 1, 2013]. Socialdemokraterna, Stockholm. https://www.socialdemokraterna.se/vart-parti/vara-politiker/tal/forsta-maj---tal-2013.

Mäkelä, Erik. 2017. "The Effect of Mass Influx on Labor Markets: Portuguese 1974 Evidence Revisited." *European Economic Review* 98: 240–63. https://doi.org/10.1016/j.euroecorev.2017.06.016.

NBC News. 2008. "'Little Baghdad' Thrives in Sweden." June 19, 2008. http://www.nbcnews.com/id/25004140/ns/world_news-europe/t/little-baghdad-thrives-sweden/#.XiyocrfQguR.

Rowthorn, Robert. 2008. "The Fiscal Impact of Immigration on the Advanced Economies." *Oxford Review of Economic Policy* 24, no. 3: 560–80. https://doi.org/10.1093/oxrep/grn025.

Ruiz, Isabel, and Carlos Vargas-Silva. 2015. "The Labor Market Impacts of Forced Migration." *American Economic Review* 105, no. 5: 581–86. https://doi.org/10.1257/aer.p20151110.

Save the Children. 2018. "Barnfattigdom i Sverige: Rapport 2018" [Child Poverty in Sweden: Report 2018]. Research and Analysis by Tapio Salonen. Rädda Barnen, Stockholm. https://resourcecentre.savethechildren.net/node/14233/pdf/rb_rapport_2018_final.pdf.

Statistics Sweden. 2010. "Integration – ett regionalt perspektiv" [Integration—A Regional Perspective]. Integration: Rapport 3, Statistiska centralbyrån (SCB), Prognosinstitutet, Stockholm. https://www.scb.se/contentassets/6dea477232504a3fabca50115ae5b18b/le0105_2010a01_br_be57br1001.pdf.

Storesletten, Kjetil. 2000. "Sustaining Fiscal Policy Through Immigration." *Journal of Political Economy* 108, no. 2: 300–23. https://doi.org/10.1086/262120.

———. 2003. "Fiscal Implications of Immigration—A Net Present Value Calculation." *The Scandinavian Journal of Economics* 105, no. 3: 487–506. https://doi.org/10.1111/1467-9442.t01-2-00009.

Sydsvenskan. 2016a. "Så blev Malmö en av Sveriges fattigaste städer" [Thusly Malmö Became One of Sweden's Poorest Cities]. By Olle Lönnaeus, Elin Fjellman, Erik Magnusson, Sara Johari, Peter Frennesson, and Krister Cronqvist, June 26, 2016. https://www.sydsvenskan.se/2016-06-26/sa-blev-malmo-fattigast-i-sverige.

———. 2016b. "Allt fler Malmöbor är för fattiga för ett eget hem" [Increasingly More Malmö Residents Are Too Poor for an Own Home]. By Elin Fjellman, Erik Magnusson, and Olle Lönnaeus, June 27, 2016. https://www.sydsvenskan.se/2016-06-27/allt-fler-malmobor-for-fattiga-for-ett-eget-hem.

———. 2016c. "Unika siffror: Svårare för flyktingar att få jobb i Malmö" [Unique Figures: More Difficult for Refugees to Get Jobs in Malmö]. By Jessica Ziegerer, Andreas Persson, and Sandra Pandevski, February 19, 2016. https://www.sydsvenskan.se/2016-02-19/unika-siffror-svarare-for-flyktingar-att-fa-jobb-i-malmo.

Tumen, Semih. 2016. "The Economic Impact of Syrian Refugees on Host Countries: Quasi-Experimental Evidence from Turkey." *American Economic Review* 106, no. 5: 456–60. https://doi.org/10.1257/aer.p20161065.

CHAPTER 6

Smoldering Concrete

Do not ignite fires you cannot extinguish.

—Swedish proverb

In 2005, France was shaken by violent riots triggered by the tragic deaths of two boys. Three teens of North African origin were on their way home from a soccer game for the evening meal during the fast of Ramadan. The teens happened upon a police car on its way to investigate a reported burglary in an immigrant-heavy suburb north of Paris. The boys had nothing to do with the break-in, but instinctively started running from the police, which led to a pursuit. The teens made the mistake of hiding in an electricity substation, where two of them later died of electric shock and the third suffered burns. There was already significant distrust of the police, and the anger over this event was the spark that caused the powder keg to explode. Clashes and car fires spread to other French suburbs and continued for several weeks.

The Paris riots received worldwide attention. Suburban riots have since lost their news value in Sweden, but when we look back to 2005, the events were depicted as something alien. In Sweden, large-scale arson of cars was seen as strange, scary, and above all distant. The Swedish tabloid *Aftonbladet* (2005) portrayed the events:

> Burning cars and buildings lit up the night sky around Paris on Saturday, when thousands of police officers unsuccessfully tried to curb the worst rioting France has experienced since the student revolt of 1968. About a hundred people were evacuated from two buildings when at least 20 cars burned in an underground garage in a suburb north of Paris. Two textile warehouses and an auto showroom were burning in an area northeast of the city, and at least 560 vehicles were destroyed by fire in the Paris area. A firebomb was thrown at a synagogue in Pierrefitte-sur-Seine north of the city, police said. Similar scenes were

T. Sanandaji, *Mass Challenge*,
https://doi.org/10.1007/978-3-030-46808-8_6

> reported from the towns of Lille in northern France, Rennes in the west, and Toulouse in the southwest. At least 200 persons were arrested during the night, among them a group of minors with firebombs. According to police, a total of over 750 vehicles were set on fire during the night, a quarter of which outside the Paris region.

In its analysis, Swedish media did not focus on the risk that similar problems could reach Sweden, but rather highlighted Swedish integration as a positive role model for France. The daily *Svenska Dagbladet* (2005a) proudly declared:

> "Rinkeby, a Swedish model for the suburbs." That's what French right-wing newspaper Le Figaro wrote yesterday. In the shadow of the French suburban riots, the paper's correspondent went to see the Swedish integration model in order to report on neighborhoods where buildings are never more than five stories tall, where books in forty languages are available at the library, and where kind-hearted, female police officers take their time to understand the old, African men who lack in Swedish-speaking skills. Rinkeby is described as "a neighborhood populated by immigrants, where order prevails and where life is pleasant to live."

Looking back, we can note that the situation in the French suburbs as late as 2005 was still seen as distant from Swedish conditions. But some warned that Sweden was moving in the same direction. In an *Aftonbladet* op-ed, the author Kurdo Baksi (2005) called on journalists to ask themselves "do I have any responsibility to ensure that the situation in Rinkeby and Rosengård will never become like the one in Clichy-sous-Bois? Were the Ronna riots only a prelude to the major riots that may take place in our country in the next few years?" There were also others who raised red flags—often immigrants familiar with developments in the streets of Swedish suburbs. In a parliamentary debate in connection with the passing of more generous asylum policies, Mauricio Rojas (2005) of the Swedish Liberal Party touched on the French experience in a speech that in hindsight appears prophetic:

> Madam Speaker, let me now turn my eyes to the future, towards the consequences of the decisions that will be made today. The question that the public ask themselves is: What will happen to those who now gain the right to live in Sweden? Will they end up in unemployment and social exclusion? Will it make their already very difficult situation in vulnerable suburbs even more vulnerable? Will the already troubling segregation become even deeper and more troubling? And we must now, in this chamber, dare to ask the question we all have asked ourselves during the past two weeks: How do we prevent social exclusion from derailing and becoming like in France? These are the questions that we must now have the courage to ask, and we must have a convincing answer. The Swedish people have a right to demand it. However, we must unfortunately conclude that it is precisely these questions that have been neglected and

> mismanaged for years. The failure of integration is clear. The country is drifting apart, and the government shows a complete lack of ideas and proposals on how to stop the grim spiral of social exclusion.

At the time, Rojas's comparison with France led to furious criticism. Today, it is easy to forget that in Sweden at the time, immigration was considered to have little to do with integration. To make an explicit link between immigration policy and integration outcomes was considered to be aiding and abetting xenophobia—and was thus both socially and politically taboo. The Left Party (2005) was so incensed by Mauricio Rojas's speech that the party's executive committee issued a statement, in which they denounced the Liberal Party as "racist" for "stigmatizing immigrants."

The debate on the French riots in Sweden back in 2005 is illustrative of the changes that Swedish public debate has since underwent, and for conveying the political atmosphere that for a long time made it personally costly to question immigration policy. Today, the Left Party's denunciation may appear extreme, but in 2005 it was rather Mauricio Rojas's comparison of Sweden with France that was considered deviant. However, this change in Swedish discourse did not come about painlessly, but only after the country experiencing repeated violent riots and social unrest. This might have been avoided if the realization that Sweden was on a similar path to France had been acknowledged before the problems had fully materialized.

This historical lesson may also be valuable for countries such as Norway and Finland, where similar problems are still small in scale. There is no guarantee that other countries will follow the same path, but it is also a mistake to overconfidently assume that your country is immune to these problems, simply because they have not yet emerged. Some socioeconomic outcomes, such as unemployment, appear to be fairly straightforward to predict in that the number of unemployed immigrants is roughly proportional to the immigrant population share. This type of problem is easy to forecast since it is visible early. The Swedish immigrant unemployment rate was about the same a generation ago, and the problem has simply scaled up at a linear rate as the group's share of the population has grown. Other problems such as social unrest, religious extremism, and gang crime have more nonlinear dynamics characterized by learning, contagion, and tipping points.

For a long time, the immigrant population in Sweden grew slowly without clear symptoms of social problems visible in riots or attacks against the police. Once these problems ignited, however, they grew rapidly since the underlying conditions had slowly built up in the preceding years. It may be difficult to predict when the tipping point arrives, and it may indeed never arrive. However, when this type of social problem escalates, it may be nearly impossible to reverse—whereas it could have been possible to prevent in the first place. For this reason, it is important to be on the watch for early warning signs and avoid the temptation to believe that your own society is charmed from the ills that have afflicted your neighbors.

Burning Automobiles

Today, Mauricio Rojas's warning in the wake of the French riots in 2005 seems clairvoyant rather than controversial. Sweden would soon experience car fires on a scale comparable to France—including in Malmö in 2009, and in Stockholm in 2013. By then, the image of Sweden as a peaceful utopia had been frayed at the edges. When French media, in turn, reported on the suburbs of Stockholm, they were no longer represented as role models, but as neighborhoods plagued by similar troubles as Paris. For example, the Swedish daily *Metro* (2013) wrote:

> This week, the riots in Husby and many other suburbs of Stockholm have dominated Swedish media. But the events have also created great attention in foreign media. In France, parallels are drawn to the suburban riots in Paris in 2005. France 24 has spoken with Jenny Andersson, a researcher at the Center for International Studies in Paris, who says that the image of the perfect and equal Swedish welfare state has become "severely eroded."

Deprived neighborhoods in France are known as *banlieues*. The word simply means suburb of a major city but has—in the same way as in Sweden—over time come to be associated with poor, segregated suburbs. Large-scale immigration from outside of the West began earlier in France than in Sweden, and multicultural crime-plagued neighborhoods also emerged decades earlier. Swedish primary school textbooks in the 1990s highlighted social problems and ethnic conflicts in the French *banlieues* as a remote problem that Sweden was spared from.

In depth and scope, the problems in Sweden have not yet reached the levels of the French *banlieues*. However, the comparison is now merely a matter of degree. Many phenomena that were first observed in France have now reached Sweden. In some cases, there have even been direct cultural imports from French as well as from American ghettos. In the press reporting on the Swedish car fires, there were speculations that the increase in car torching in Sweden was influenced by the televised events in Paris 2005.

This type of arson is not just a spontaneous form of vandalism, but rather a learned ritual with profound symbolism. In both France and Sweden, it is common for car fires to become contagious, in the sense that arson in one suburb inspires arson in suburbs in other parts of the country. By the late 1970s, vehicle arson had evolved into a symbolic act of protest in French suburbs.

Although the first car fires in the suburbs were spontaneous acts of vandalism against easy targets, the concept of car torching has over time developed ceremonial characteristics. Car arson is now a default action when protests erupt against the police—in France as well as on New Year's Eve. Chaos and disorder have developed into a carefully orchestrated tradition. Normally, about a thousand cars are torched every New Year's Eve. Around the New

Year, *Time Magazine* (2009) published the article "France's New Year's Tradition: Car-Burning:"

> For much of the world, they became iconic of France's worst social ills: the burned-out carcasses of thousands of cars set ablaze during nearly three weeks of nationwide rioting in 2005. But as yet another orgy of automobile arson on Wednesday demonstrated, the torching of cars in France has not only become an everyday event; it's also now a regular form of expression for disenfranchised suburban youths wanting to make sure the rest of the country doesn't forget they exist. And their fiery presence is never felt so strongly as it is each New Year's Eve—the day of France's unofficial festival of car-burning.
>
> ---
>
> But while annual figures may fluctuate, they've generally swelled since the late 1970s, when French suburban youths first started burning cars as a way to get the attention of society, the media and politicians. Later the practice became an ambush tactic to draw law and fire authorities to the scene—where they'd then be attacked by gangs. Now the act works as a manner of daily protest against alienation, discrimination and the indifference of more affluent French society.

There are of course many different parallel motives to the arson of vehicles. These include insurance fraud, pyromania, attempts to distract the police, or personal vengeance against the vehicle owner. However, there tends to be an underlying message when it comes to mass fires taking place night after night in the same area. Although this vandalism rarely involves carefully articulated political manifestos, it expresses rebellious feelings of discontent and indignation. Car arson is often an ideological act.

Both the youths in the suburbs who start the fires and the rest of society who watches the images of burning cars are aware of what the protest symbolizes. Car fires lead to extensive material damage and generate spectacular television images, while being simple to implement in practical terms. The youths who ignite these fires know that the media is likely to report their actions, thus sharing their act of dissatisfaction with a wider audience.

Interestingly, car arson is a violent act that rarely takes lives. Other than in exceptional circumstances, setting fire to parked cars causes only material and psychological damage, without running the risk of killing someone. In this regard, there is a certain restraint in the violence that car fires represent.

Quantifying Vehicle Arson

Sweden has not yet reached a quantity of vehicle arson equal to France's worst riots. Yet, the increase has been dramatic, and the worst riots in Sweden are now comparable to those of France—taking into account the differences in population.

Fire departments have collected data on vehicle arson since 1998, which have been compiled by the Swedish Civil Contingencies Agency. Similar data exist from the equivalent Finnish and Norwegian agencies. These statistics specify the number of times the fire brigade has responded to fires, where each response may involve several scorched vehicles. In connection with riots, it is common that many vehicles are set on fire in the same area, so that the number of burnt cars is greater than the number of rescue operations in the data.

Naturally, all car fires are not arson, and many are the results of accidents. The statistics distinguish between different types of fires, and the figures presented here refer to fires classified as arson. In interpreting the numbers, note that in addition to cars, they also include other types of vehicles such as buses, trucks, and—in rare cases—trailers and trains. Car fires constitute roughly nine-tenths of vehicle fires, and the two categories show similar trends.

Sometimes car fires are due to the owner willfully destroying the vehicle as part of insurance fraud. This is, though, exaggerated—in part because statistics on the share of car fires that constitutes insurance fraud is based on suspected cases of fraud rather than total cases of arson. Statements by Swedish police indicate that insurance fraud is not the main explanation for the rise of car arson in socially deprived areas. *Sydsvenskan* (2016a) explains: "Even the police rules out that this is about insurance fraud. Almost all cars that have been set on fire in Malmö during the summer are fifteen to twenty years old." Similarly, *Aftonbladet* (2016) reported that in the areas where car fires typically occur, many car owners lack insurance coverage for burnt cars. Between 1998 and 2017, the number of emergency callouts in connection with vehicle arson increased from around 400 to 1600—declining after a record of 1900 in 2016.

Figure 6.1 compares the situation in Sweden with Finland and Norway, starting in 1998. The graph shows vehicle arson per 100,000 inhabitants, as recorded by each country's fire and rescue services. To date, Norway has been relatively spared from mass torching. In the early 2000s, Sweden and Finland were close, but since then vehicle arson has dropped off slightly in Finland, while the phenomenon has increased sharply in Sweden. Data for Denmark are only available for later years, and thus do not enable a comparison over time, but Denmark also has significant problems with car arson in immigrant-heavy areas in connection with social unrest. In 2014, vehicle arson was at 9.1 per 100,000 inhabitants in Denmark—that is to say, well below Sweden, but significantly above the levels in Norway and Finland.

Various explanations have been given for car arson. These include—in addition to arson specifically targeting cars and other vehicles—the arson of nearby dumpsters, residences, schools, recreation centers, and other buildings. Researcher Manne Gerell (2013) has pointed to feelings of social exclusion and alienation in urban neighborhoods with multiple nationalities. Another theory links this to social control and the collective capacity of the community to keep crime and vandalism in check. Examples of social control may be that in response to behavior that the community deems undesirable, the

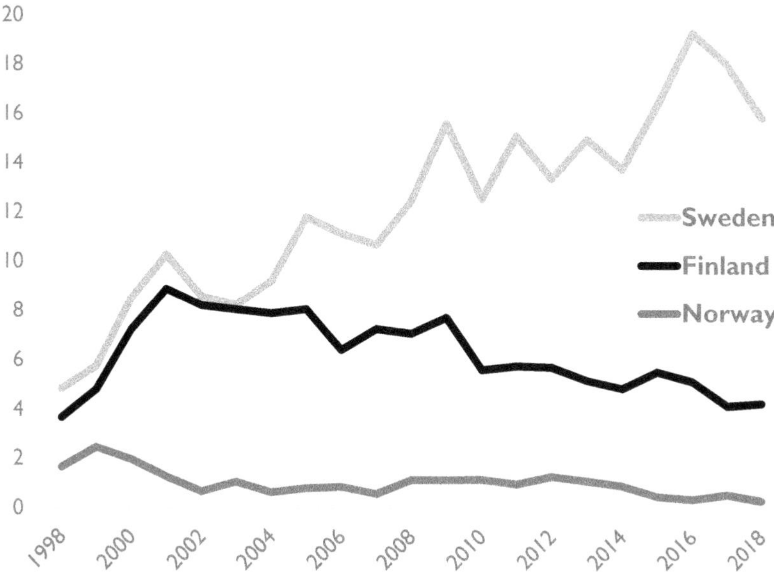

Fig. 6.1 Vehicle arson per 100,000 inhabitants in Sweden, Finland, and Norway (*Source* Swedish Civil Contingencies Agency; Norwegian Directorate for Civil Protection; Finnish Rescue Services)

perpetrator is chided, reported to the authorities, threatened by violence, or simply loses reputation and status.

Regardless of the risk of being arrested, or what their own conscience tells them, most young people in middle-class environments would not set their neighbor's car on fire for fear of what parents, friends, classmates, and other people around them would think. In subcultures where antisocial behavior is rewarded, or where the social ties that keep potential criminals in check are weak, the risk of crime is higher. In addition to social control, collective capacity is also impacted by physical crime prevention measures such as streetlights.

Fires tend to be more common in areas close to schools, sports fields, bars, and central squares, where young people hang out. Gerell (2013) ties the motivations for arson to thrill-seeking, combined with resentment against authorities, further explaining:

> These types of events are most common in areas where alienation and low confidence in the future lead to a strong mistrust of society, which can be expressed in violent statements against police in particular, but also emergency services and where arson is part of the course of conflict. It can be related to the theory "justified vandalism," where people who feel disadvantaged by society and at the same time have a low level of personal control take out their frustrations on public property.

Crime and social unrest have always occurred in all societies, but with tremendous variation in frequency and degree of intensity. Those who attempt to dismiss the increase in problems often exaggerate how bad the situation was in the past in order to normalize current levels. It is also easy to distort historical events that most people are unfamiliar with. For example, using some creativity, isolated incidents of youth unrest in 1950s Scandinavia can be presented as equivalent to today's violent riots.

Happy Days

In connection with the riots in recent years, it has become common for news reports to convey the picture that these are unremarkable, and that Swedish history is full of similar events. The Swedish daily *Dagens Nyheter* (2013) commented on the riots in the suburbs of Stockholm: "Rock-throwing is timeless and the riots in Husby are far from the first in Stockholm's history. For centuries, the city's inhabitants have clashed with power in more or less chaotic ways."

The reporting of the Swedish Public Television (2013) also followed the same narrative that "young people fight the police and what they see as oppressive power is not a modern thing. Stockholm has a long history of youth riots." Violent riots in 2013 were often compared by the press to events that took place 1951 in Berzelii Park in central Stockholm. The same article further explained that in the summer of 1951, "for a few days, riots occurred in Berzelii Park. Here, young people gathered after they had been out partying. The fights with the police got worse for each day. Finally, police from five different cities plus military police was deployed against 3000 civilians."

Youth violence has undoubtedly occurred in the past, with dynamics that in many ways resemble the riots we see today. But it is misleading to use historical anecdotes to portray today's unrest as equal to that of the past in terms of intensity. The youth brawls of the 1950s in Sweden aroused astonishment and are remembered exactly because they were a rarity, without being particularly violent. Today, clashes between young people and police have become more frequent and violent. Comparing these youth protests to the vicious riots of today is like comparing Arthur "Fonzie" Fonzarelli to a hardened member of MS-13, reasoning that they are after all both on the wrong side of the law. Indeed, youth mischief in 1950s and 1960s Scandinavia was directly influenced by the same American culture that produced Henry Winkler's TV character Fonzie in *Happy Days* and Marlon Brando's *Rebel Without a Cause*.

The youth brawl in Berzelii Park or later greaser brawls were in fact mild compared to the battles in Swedish streets of today, which involve firebombs, mass-torching of cars, and shootings against rescue personnel. The Swedish Civil Contingencies Agency's (2011) report finds that juvenile brawls have become more frequent, and that the trend over the last four decades shows a markedly more brutal use of violence in riots: “And it is not only the police who are seen as opponents, but also fire and rescue services, or other people who are considered to represent society, such as school bureaucrats or social services.” The report further explains that there have been other changes in today’s youth brawls compared to those which have historically occurred in Sweden:

> A third change is that there seems to be no barrier that prevents perpetrators from attacking police, and for example try to free friends who have been arrested, or attack police stations. When the police refuses to back away and take on the challenge, perpetrators instead attack other public personnel such as the rescue service, ambulances, and fire trucks. There is a widespread mistrust of society’s representatives and authorities in general. In the brawls that struck Rosengård, there also seems to have been a certain “contagious effect” that causes unrest to spread to other places. The most obvious examples of this are the riots in the Stockholm suburbs of Akalla and Husby in 2009, where some of the brawling youths referred to the unrest as being “in sympathy with our brothers in Rosengård.” A new feature was that they, through setting small fires and calling in fake emergencies, attempted to attract emergency services and police into the residential area and then expose them to rock-throwing.

Normalizing the Abnormal

In 2005, violent riots erupted in Södertälje. In retaliation against perceived provocations by law enforcement, the police headquarters in Södertälje was attacked with automatic gunfire. The shooting forced the police to take cover on the floor. The daily *Svenska Dagbladet* (2005b) cited Oslo Police Academy Professor Johannes Knutsson: “There have been other shootings and attempts to blow up police stations, but never like this where people shoot with automatic weapons.”

Today, shootings directed at police stations are no longer exceptional events and have occurred in a number of Swedish cities, often repeatedly. After a shooting at the police station in Malmö in the summer of 2016, *Sydsvenskan* (2016b) wrote: “Including Saturday’s shooting, there have been seven attacks with firearms or explosives against police buildings in Malmö since 2011.”

In 2009, the Swedish Civil Contingencies Agency published a report on the incipient violence against rescue personnel. The attacks that rescue personnel have been exposed to include ambush, attacks with fireworks, Molotov cocktails, and rock-pelting:

> Behaviors have changed, now we have experienced actual ambushes. At one point, perpetrators had rolled a car into a pedestrian underpass, set it on fire, and waited for fire and rescue service. When we arrived, they started firing at us with firecrackers and fireworks aimed at firefighters. We have noted an increased intent regarding planned ambushes against fire and rescue services.

It is common for attacks on the fire brigade to take place when criminals are fighting the police, who are the real target. The fire department is attacked by upset youths because they accompany the police into the impacted areas, but also because youths in the absence of the police attack other vehicles that are perceived as symbols of authority: "That it was a fire truck, we don't think it helped here—had it been the ice cream truck or the mail truck or a bus, they would also have been attacked in the area."

Hallin et al. (2010) investigated the riots in the notorious Rosengård neighborhood in Malmö. The fieldwork includes interesting interviews with the youths, the police, and the fire and rescue personnel. The spiral of violence is described in the following way from a typical sequence of events:

> In the evening, someone sets fire to a dumpster or a garbage collection building, and emergency services receive a call that there's a fire. When the fire and rescue service arrives at the scene, firefighters are attacked with rocks or eggs. They pull back and await the arrival of the police. When the police gets there, they are also attacked. ... Many people from the neighborhood flock to the scene as spectators. Later in the evening, police arrest some young people suspected of having started the fire. A bit later, the youths are released but claim that they have been mistreated by the police. The next day, after a chain of text messages, a larger group of young people gather at one of the stores. They set fire to a dumpster, fire and rescue services and the police are alerted, and the media arrives once again.

The study further describes in detail the sequence of events that may lead to a situation that deteriorates into riots:

> At the Rosengård school, I spoke with two guys of high-school age. They said the events occurred because the police had brought dogs into the cellar mosque. That's humiliating, and people are angry about it all over Rosengård. They said that their classmates are in the riots because they're really upset. I asked why they didn't participate themselves with their friends over there, and then they only smiled at me. As the police drove away, one of the guys told me: "The cops are scared of us; do you see how they're taking off?" ... I spotted several other young people who took large stone slabs from the walkways inside the courtyards and crushed them against the ground to make the rocks smaller. They then took the rocks (which were still very large) in their hands and went towards the police. They talked to each other and organized so that everyone simultaneously headed towards the police. Approximately 50 people had joined. They started throwing rocks at the police, and then the police got in the car and drove fast towards the youths. The group began to scatter, and everyone ran fast in different directions. Since I was standing on the same side of the street as the youths, I had to run along with them. As I ran, I heard many youngsters laugh. It felt like they thought it was fun.

A respondent explains that the police is viewed as harassing and needlessly beating the youth:

> I've been asked several times by the same young people if I also hate the police. It seems that they can't understand how people can like the police. The youths' different epithets for the police are: "Filth, pigs, disgusting, hobos, their mother is a whore." Their argument against the police is that the police beat the youths from Rosengård. The police are always after the youths of Rosengård, and that they are aggressive in their behavior towards the young people from Rosengård.

It should be noted that there is very little evidence that the police targets these young people. The perception of being persecuted most likely reflects antagonism of criminals against law enforcement's response to misconduct. Regarding the underlying reasons for riots, the combination of boredom and thrill-seeking also contributes:

> Another common motive mentioned by the young people is idleness and excitement. Without me even asking, he said, "Yeah, exactly, and the same thing about starting fires. It's fun, man. Nothing more than that. We're a bunch of friends hanging out, have nothing to do and then say: 'Hey, let's go burn something up.' Just so that something happens. Exactly the same thing with throwing rocks."
>
> – – –
>
> S. said that he and many others from school gathered in front of the convenience store, as they usually do. "We were bored. Then we saw that there was a bunch of junk in front of the waste collection buildings. So we thought we should set it on fire."
>
> – – –
>
> He began to tell a story of him participating in throwing rocks at the police during the events in December. He didn't think there was any particular reason. "I can only say for myself that the only reason I threw rocks was because it was fun. Exciting. You get a kick, man. Adrenaline."

Hence, the field interviews indicate that the pursuit of excitement and entertainment are important elements, where many participants experience the riots as fun and amusing. Nevertheless, the risk of being arrested or the family finding out are given as reasons for stopping:

> I asked why the riots ended. I added that many believe it ended because the parents and residents in the area organized. "No, he said, it wasn't because of that at all. People don't want to be arrested. Do you know how many cops were there? Thousands. Everybody was afraid of being arrested. Then the family finds out and everyone hates that. Then you get a lot of trouble at home."

Torching Utopia

One of the more major events of unrest in recent years, which can be used as an illustrative example, is the weeklong riots that erupted a few years back in the suburbs of Stockholm. On May 13, 2013, Stockholm police received calls from the immigrant-heavy suburb of Husby. After a confused deadlock surrounding a domestic disturbance, a 69-year-old Portuguese immigrant—armed with a machete—was shot and killed by police.

A week after this tragedy, the police was once again called to Husby. This time, residents told of masked men burning cars with gasoline-soaked rags and Molotov cocktails. When police and firefighters arrived, they were met by a barrage of rocks. Every morning the following week, Sweden woke up to new images of arson and riots. Rumors of racism and police brutality ignited riots in other immigrant suburbs with previously rampant resentment against Swedish society. The police managed to quell the riots only after having called up reinforcements from other cities.

The extent of material damage was approximately 200 burned cars, in addition to a number of burned-out schools and cultural centers. Unemployment among immigrants has long been high, but the unrest during spring 2013 can hardly be explained by austerity. Husby is a district that for many years has been a recipient of public investments, regeneration programs, integration projects, youth recreation centers, and job market projects. The year before the riots, all junior high school students in the municipal schools received a new iPad.

As in many similar areas, radical Islamism is certainly a growing problem in Husby, but not directly related to the social turmoil. According to the reporting, most troublemakers seemed to be secular, or even atheists; some were Assyrian Christians. Something that many with a Swedish background may fail to notice is that the vast majority of young people with an immigrant background and roots in Muslim countries do not care very much about Islam. A large proportion of immigrants from Muslim countries are not Muslims at all, but Christians, atheists, agnostics, or part of a religious minority such as Yazidis.

Many others have a formal Muslim background but have de facto been secularized. One important reason is that Islam is a demanding religion that limits alcohol consumption, diet, clothing, everyday actions, and not least opportunities to party and date—which are components in other young people's lifestyle in Sweden, and which are attractive to young people in the suburbs. American gangster rap and popular culture have a significantly stronger influence on Swedish ghettos than Islam.

The reason for the riots is probably based on feelings of bitterness and alienation. That this is not about radical Islamist social disorder, or a well-thought-out political rebellion, but a spontaneous and juvenile reaction, can be illustrated by how the Husby riots came to an end. One factor was the mobilization of adults in the surrounding area to exert social control. Another strategy through which the weeklong riots were quelled was by bribing the participants with snacks. The tabloid *Aftonbladet* (2013) reported:

> Yesterday, the rocks stopped falling over Husby. And the only thing that burned was the fire from barbecues.

"We're doing this to spread love," said Husby resident Zakaria. At midnight, the embers have died out in the barbecue by the Tempo store in central Husby. There was no organization behind the grilling, just the people in Husby, says Zakaria.

"First we bought the hot dogs and the buns, but then the stores gave us what we needed for free," he says. Next to the barbecues was a sign: "Leave a rock, pick up a hot dog."

References

Aftonbladet. 2005. "Värsta kravallerna i Frankrike sedan 1968" [Worst Riots in France Since 1968]. By TT, November 5, 2005, updated March 8, 2011. https://www.aftonbladet.se/nyheter/a/rLPeya/varsta-kravallerna-i-frankrike-sedan-1968.

———. 2013. "Kvällen när stenarna slutade att falla över Husby" [The Evening When the Stones Stopped Falling over Husby]. By Kenan Habul, May 25, 2013. https://www.aftonbladet.se/nyheter/a/e1qV3g/kvallen-nar-stenarna-slutade-att-falla-over-husby.

———. 2016. "Branddrabbade kan sakna försäkring" [Fire Victims May Lack Insurance]. By TT, August 20, 2016. https://www.aftonbladet.se/senastenytt/ttnyheter/inrikes/a/5VyqGW/branddrabbade-kan-sakna-forsakring.

Baksi, Kurdo. 2005. "Förortskrigen" [Suburban Wars]. *Aftonbladet*, op-ed, November 4, 2005, updated March 8, 2011. https://www.aftonbladet.se/debatt/a/KvMl1E/forortskrigen.

Dagens Nyheter. 2013. "Upplopp i Stockholm – en gammal historia" [Riots in Stockholm—An Old Story]. By Rebecca Haimi, May 24, 2013. https://www.dn.se/sthlm/upplopp-i-stockholm-en-gammal-historia.

Gerell, Manne. 2013. "Forskning kring anlagda bränder" [Research on Set Fires]. In *Stadens bränder: Del 2 Fördjupning*, by Helena Bohman, Manne Gerell, Jonas Lundsten, and Mona Tykesson, 8–22. Malmö Publikationer i Urbana Studier, MAPIUS 10, Institutionen för urbana studier. Malmö: Malmö högskola. http://muep.mau.se/bitstream/handle/2043/15506/SB_del2.pdf.

Hallin, Per Olof, Alban Jashari, Carina Listerborn, and Margareta Popoola. 2010. "Det är inte stenarna som gör ont: Röster från Herrgården, Rosengård – om konflikter och erkännande" [It Is Not the Stones That Hurt: Voices from Herrgården, Rosengård—About Conflicts and Recognition]. Malmö Publikationer i Urbana Studier, MAPIUS 5, Institutionen för urbana studier. Malmö: Malmö högskola. http://muep.mau.se/bitstream/handle/2043/10977/MAPIUS%205%20Det%20är%20inte%20stenarna%20som%20gör%20ont.pdf.

Left Party (Sweden). 2005. "Leijonkungen vilse i förortsdjungeln" [The Lion King Lost in the Suburban Jungle]. Vänsterpartiets verkställande utskott 2005-11-11. Uddevalla: Vänsterpartiet. http://uddevalla.vansterpartiet.se/2005/11/11/leijonkungen-vilse-i-forortsdjungeln.

Metro. 2013. "Franska medier: Det är som Parisupploppen" [French Media: It's Like the Paris Riots]. By Jenny Sköld, May 23, 2013. http://80.72.1.78/artikel/franska-medier-det-är-som-parisupploppen-xr.

Rojas, Mauricio. 2005. "Anf. 2 Maurico Rojas (fp)". Riksdagens protokoll 2005/06:26, onsdagen den 9 november kl. 09:00–17:14, Sveriges Riksdag,

Stockholm. https://www.riksdagen.se/sv/dokument-lagar/dokument/protokoll/riksdagens-protokoll-20050626-onsdagen-den-9_GT0926/html.

Svenska Dagbladet. 2005a. "Rinkeby franskt foredome" [Rinkeby, French Example]. By Torun Börtz/TT, November 13, 2005. https://www.svd.se/rinkeby-franskt-foredome.

———. 2005b. "Ingen gripen för skotten mot polisen" [No Arrest for the Shots Against the Police]. By Bosse Brink, September 14, 2005. https://www.svd.se/ingen-gripen-for-skotten-mot-polisen.

Swedish Civil Contingencies Agency. 2009. "Observatörsrapport: Anlagda bränder och hot/våld mot räddningstjänsten" [Observer Report: Incited Fires and Threats/Violence Against the Rescue Services]. Publikationsnummer MSB 0169-10, Enheten för lärande av olyckor och kriser, Myndigheten för samhällsskydd och beredskap (MSB), Karlstad. https://rib.msb.se/filer/pdf/25367.pdf.

———. 2011. "Våldsamma upplopp i Sverige – från avvikelse till normalitet" [Violent Riots in Sweden—From Deviation to Normality]. By Torbjörn Nilsson and Anders Ivarsson Westerberg. Publikationsnummer MSB222, Enheten för lärande av olyckor och kriser, Myndigheten för samhällsskydd och beredskap (MSB), Karlstad. https://rib.msb.se/filer/pdf/26016.pdf.

Swedish Public Television. 2013. "Kravaller i Stockholm inget nytt" [Riots in Stockholm Nothing New]. By Danielle Langert, *SVT Nyheter*, May 24, 2013. https://www.svt.se/nyheter/lokalt/stockholm/kravaller-i-stockholm-inget-nytt.

Sydsvenskan. 2016a. "Så hanterar försäkringsbolagen uppeldade bilar" [This Is How Insurance Companies Handle Arsoned Cars]. By Lena Stadler and Lovisa Höök, August 12, 2016. https://www.sydsvenskan.se/2016-08-13/sa-hanterar-forsakringsbolagen-uppeldade-bilar.

———. 2016b. "Polisen: 'Vi uppfattar det som ett hot'" [Police: "We See It as a Threat"]. By Mikael Funke, July 25, 2016. https://www.sydsvenskan.se/2016-07-25/polisen-vi-uppfattar-det-som-ett-hot.

Time Magazine. 2009. "France's New Year's Tradition: Car-Burning." By Bruce Crumley, January 2, 2009. http://content.time.com/time/world/article/0,8599,1869392,00.html.

CHAPTER 7

Inequality

> Empty words do not fill empty stomachs
>
> —Kurdish proverb

Although not the focus of this book, it is worth briefly describing the economic setting to provide the reader with context. Following widespread international convention, Finland is in this book included as one of the Scandinavian countries, even if many locals strictly reserve this only for Sweden, Norway, and Denmark, instead using term *Nordic countries* when including Finland and Iceland. Contrary to common perception in Sweden, the term Scandinavia lacks a clear definition, which makes both classifications acceptable.

Sweden is internationally renowned as a country with a relatively equal income distribution. When the income distribution was at its most equal during the 1970s and 1980s, the income share of top earners in Sweden was among the lowest ever recorded. The World Wealth and Income Database has compiled historical data on the share of total income going to the top of the income distribution. In Sweden and Finland, the top 1 percent received less than 4% of total income in the 1980s; according to some methods of measuring, this is the lowest figure ever recorded in any Western country—at any point in time.

During the postwar period, these countries achieved an income equality historically unparalleled among capitalist market economies, and was comparable to the available estimates for communist economies. In addition, this refers to income largely before redistribution through taxes and the welfare state, which makes the distribution of disposable income even more equal.

The Scandinavian countries are somewhat loosely described as socialist, since the term lacks a strict definition. The term socialist is often used by

T. Sanandaji, *Mass Challenge*,
https://doi.org/10.1007/978-3-030-46808-8_7

different people to refer to different concepts, which creates confusion. These countries have in the modern era always been capitalist market economies, where private property and free exchange were the essential defining characteristics of the economy. However, the Scandinavian model combined this with unusually large welfare states that redistribute income (Esping-Andersen 1990).

In such economies, the government's control of production can amount to 20–30% of GDP—including healthcare and schools—whereas tax rates are 50–60% of GDP. This is because much of government activity does not consist of engaging in command and control, but rather of paying out social insurance and pensions, while leaving spending and production decisions to households and markets. This means that the Scandinavian countries in practice have freer economies than is sometimes perceived based on superficial impressions. The four countries are fairly similar, although Norway is wealthier and has a more generous welfare state, whereas Finland is somewhat poorer than the others. (Iceland also has a capitalistic welfare state, but including this tiny country in a matter that would grant its fascinating particularities justice would require too great of a digression for this book.)

Since the Scandinavian countries combine private ownership of industry with high taxes, these countries are unusual in some aspects of economic equality. Typically, countries with an even income distribution have an even wealth distribution. Income refers to annual earnings, such as wages and capital income, whereas wealth refers to ownership of assets. A complex and often neglected feature of the Scandinavian countries is that they have had a high concentration of wealth even during periods when the income distribution was compressed. In some measures, the top concentration of wealth in Sweden and Denmark is not far from that of the United States, and, indeed, both countries have an unusually high number of billionaires and multimillionaires in relation to the population. This clearly shows that these countries are not socialist if we follow a traditional definition, since a defining feature of socialism was abolishing private ownership of wealth. In classic socialist economies—such as the Soviet Union, East Germany, or North Korea—it is meaningless to discuss the distribution of wealth, as almost all wealth is owned by the state.

This detour has no direct relationship to the issue of immigration; yet, it may be useful to help the reader in better understanding the economic system in the Scandinavian countries as well as their social history. Contrary to the mythological perceptions about "socialist Scandinavia," these countries combine an egalitarian social state with views on work and wealth that are not far from that which prevails in the UK or in the United States. Healthy individuals are expected to work, and those who are successful in their job or business activity have far more purchasing power and social status than those who live off public benefits. In recent decades, the economic system in these countries has come to resemble the Anglo-Saxon economies even more—as the former have reduced the size of government, while the latter have generally expanded their welfare states. While there are thus only small differences in the essence of how production is organized, there are some major differences in how redistribution works—particularly in comparison with the United States.

The Scandinavian countries guarantee all inhabitants tax-funded healthcare, university education, and daycare (Pedersen and Kuhnle 2017). People who do not work are furthermore provided with rather generous welfare payments and housing benefits. For a single adult, welfare benefits are rarely enough for an affluent life. For families, however, and in particular large families, welfare can amount to levels that surprise outsiders, and which can make low-paying manual labor economically futile. In Sweden, a family of two adults and two children can—depending on the circumstances—receive $2500 per month after tax, and a family with four children $3300 (*Dagens industri* 2016). These amounts are the same regardless of background, in contrast to the common myth that immigrants are given more generous welfare. Welfare recipients can, in addition, receive an allowance for public transportation as well as free healthcare, dentalcare, and cost of medicine. The purchasing power of a large family on welfare is, consequently, not far from middle-class Swedes—although significantly below high-earners.

The cost of providing welfare should not be exaggerated since most immigrants do not live on welfare. Nevertheless, the generosity of the system causes controversy and moral dilemmas. On the one hand, it would violate the egalitarian principles of the Scandinavian countries to deprive immigrants from the safety net—in particular children and the elderly. On the other hand, the system can cause perverse incentives that keep people out of work. It can also be exploited, for instance, by those who return to their home country without reporting it in order to continue collecting benefits—or by criminals who supplement illicit income with government-provided housing and welfare cheques in order to enjoy a luxurious lifestyle unobtainable for ordinary workers.

This generous system was originally designed as a last resort and temporary cushion in societies where virtually all able-bodied adults were assumed to participate in the job market. Due to the culture of Lutheran Scandinavia, with a strong work ethic, it was not expected that many would exploit the system or willingly accept the social stigma of not working. In the early welfare state, freeriding on public benefits was rare. Over time, norms evolved and at least some subcultures in Scandinavia became more likely to habitually exploit welfare, sick leave, and other public benefits—which subsequently led to a tightening of the rules.

The biggest challenge for the system was, however, the immigration of large numbers of people without the skillset required to obtain high-paying jobs, and without strong norms against living off public welfare. These culture clashes are perhaps most pronounced for groups that immigrate from countries with preindustrial cultures. An anecdotal observation by a Somali interpreter is worth citing in order to illustrate how customs adapted for a vastly different economic setting can clash with more modern systems (*Göteborgs-Posten* 2007):

> "When it rains and is green and the camels give milk, the nomads do not have to make the effort. They discuss and talk, and at night you play games. But when the drought comes, the nomads work harder than any Swedish farmer and make sure the camels and cows and goats survive in the desert. When the same people come to Sweden, it rains all the time—social assistance, child support, housing allowance, and all other grants. So, it becomes like the nomad life when it rains and is green, people take it easy. And here in Sweden, you can take it easy all year, sit in a cafe and talk. When life is so good, why should you work?"
>
> "But," he says, "put the same people in England or the United States, then the nomadic system kicks in and they become very enterprising."

It should, again, be emphasized that work culture is not likely the primary reason for the low employment rate among immigrants, and that most migrants culturally integrate; cultural differences are, however, likely contributing. There are also other more problematic cultural differences that complicate the smooth functioning of welfare systems. One such factor is patriarchal culture and the associated traditional gender roles, which limit women's entry to the job market and tie them to the home—financed by the welfare state. The most extreme cases of such cultural practices can appear outrageous, and even more so when they come into contact with the welfare state. For instance, Sweden used to recognize child marriage as long as the marriage occurred prior to migration, and as a consequence a family was entitled to child support for wives that themselves were children.

Another cultural practice that was not anticipated by the Scandinavian welfare state is polygamy. Again, Sweden recognizes preexisting polygamous marriages, with about 300 polygamous families officially registered by tax authorities. These households can receive provocatively high levels of welfare. One example publicized by Swedish press was a 57-year-old refugee who moved to Sweden from Syria, with three wives and 16 children.

According to the local newspaper *Nacka Värmdö Posten* (2017), the wealthy municipality of Nacka experienced housing shortage when placing new arrivals. The city therefore bought three lakeside condominiums in an exclusive area at $1.4 million for the polygamous family. The apartments are still owned by the municipality, but were bought by public funds in the private housing market—a practice that tends to drive up prices for regular homebuyers. This unusually large family was given about $10,000 per month in welfare. The Syrian man's unorthodox family constitution has been referred to as Sweden's first tax-financed harem. While this particular example is quite extreme, many Swedish taxpayers find it and similar anecdotes offensive. This is both because of the violation of modern gender norms, and because said taxpayers are made to pay for housing that they themselves could not afford.

In addition to these developments, readers should also note that income inequality in Scandinavia has increased in recent years, both due to immigration and as the consequence of completely unrelated trends. Even if the distribution still is among the more egalitarian globally, Scandinavia is now less exceptional in this regard. The growth in inequality has in fact been unusually rapid in Sweden, although being part of a global trend. In his acclaimed book, *Capital in the Twenty-First Century* (2014), French economist Thomas Piketty stated that the concentration of income and wealth has increased internationally in recent decades, a conclusion that few disputes—although there is disagreement about the underlying driving forces.

There are several dimensions to economic inequality, and countries may have different degrees of inequality across these. In general terms, "income inequality" refers to the distribution of the income generated annually in the economy. In addition, this income can be measured in several different ways. Below, four common measures or dimensions of economic inequality are presented.

Income Distribution

The factor distribution of income can be broadly be divided into income from employment, income from capital, and income from self-employment. After appropriate adjustments, for instance for depreciation, a rule of thumb is that about a third to a quarter of total income in the economy goes to owners of capital and the rest to wage earners. In turn, the wage share consists of both the wages of ordinary workers and the income of high-income earners such as lawyers, doctors, and managers. Income from self-employment is also, in practice, often income from work, reflecting the owner's efforts in the enterprise (Henrekson and Sanandaji 2011).

The share that goes to capital seems to have increased somewhat in recent decades, but the division between capital and labor is generally very stable over time. Instead the increase in inequality that we observe is more likely driven by the fact that the share of employment income that goes to the top earners has risen dramatically. This is reinforced by the fact that many high-earners and self-employed for various reasons, such as taxation, tend to declare income from work as return on capital. One way to summarize the degree of inequality in society is to measure how much of the income that goes to the top 1 percent. Figure 7.1 shows the development of top income earners' share of total income in Sweden from 1920, according to the World Top Incomes Database. Older estimates are uncertain, but they indicate that income inequality in Sweden was relatively high at the beginning of the twentieth century, and then declined until the 1970s, when the trend toward greater equality reversed.

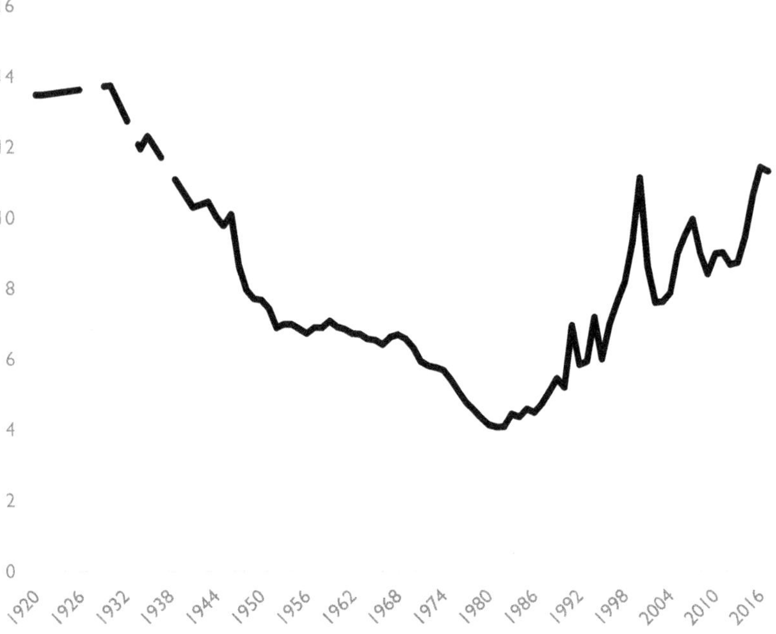

Fig. 7.1 Top 1 percent income earners' share of total income since 1920 (*Source* World Inequality Database)

Wealth Disparity

The second measure, concentration of wealth, describes who owns existing assets. Wealth and capital are funds saved from prior years that have not been consumed. In countries such as Sweden, aggregate national wealth or total capital assets in the form of shares, real estate, small businesses, and other assets usually amount to between three and five times the annual national income. Since a few wealthy people own a large share of all capital, wealth is much more unevenly distributed than income. Sweden has historically distinguished itself as a country with an even income distribution, but not by having a particularly even wealth distribution. An unusually high share of the total capital in business and the real estate market has been owned by the richest families. One reason is, paradoxically, that the generous pension and social security systems of *Folkhemmet* (the People's Home) have made it less important for the middle class to build up their own savings.

As can be seen in Fig. 7.1, the percentage of the population with the highest income earned about 9% of the total annual income in the latest estimates. Wealth is even less equally distributed. Estimates suggest that the wealthiest percentage of the population owns between 20 and 30% of the total wealth, depending on whether Swedes' assets abroad are included or not (Roine and Waldenström 2015).

Relative Poverty

A third measure of inequality is relative poverty, which is defined by income in relation to others in society. A common way to define relative poverty is the proportion of a country's population who earn less than 60% of the median income, where the median income is the income level of the person exactly in the middle of the income distribution. It is common to adjust for household size in order to take the larger income requirements of larger families into account when calculating relative poverty. When correcting for household size, the distribution is reported in terms of so-called consumption units. Often, it is disposable income that is measured—that is to say, income after taxes and government subsidies.

In rich countries like Sweden, those who are in relative poverty are usually not so vulnerable that their situation can be described in terms of absolute or material poverty. Today, single households with a disposable income of just below $1200 per month—after taxes but including government assistance—are defined as living in relative poverty. As Sweden becomes richer, the bar for relative poverty is raised. Relative poverty is not a measure of material deprivation, but it is still an important measure since social position is influenced by how much you earn in comparison with others in the same country.

In recent years, relative poverty has increased rapidly in Sweden—at a faster rate than in any comparable country. The OECD (2015) writes: "The growth in inequality between 1985 and the early 2010s was the largest among all OECD countries, increasing by one third." There are several reasons behind this increase. One is cuts in the social safety net, such as lower unemployment benefits and sick pay. Another reason is a general increase in the pay gap, which has occurred both in Sweden and in other countries. The situation among those with an immigrant background is another major driver behind increased income gaps in Sweden. This is partly since immigrants have experienced poorer income growth, and partly because the number of poor immigrants in Sweden has increased due to extended immigration. Statistics Sweden (2016) writes:

> The proportion with low economic standard is significantly higher among foreign-born than among Swedish-born, and the difference has been increasing steadily since 1991. Among foreign-born, the proportion was just over 10 percent in the early 1990s and around the turn of the century at just over 15 percent. In 2014, it had increased to 28 percent.

Additionally, Statistics Sweden (2018) writes about widening income differences:

> In 2016, the foreign-born enjoyed an economic standard corresponding to 77 percent of the economic standard for persons born in Sweden. The proportion has, though, remained largely unchanged since 2010. In 1991, the equivalent rate was 90 percent, which means that the gap has widened between foreign-born and Swedish-born individuals.

When the foreign-born increase their share of the population, at the same time as gaps stay the same compared to the native-born, immigration mechanically leads to increased income inequality. The Swedish Ministry of Finance's annual report *Distribution Policy Statement*, which is a supplement to the Spring Fiscal Policy Bill spring (Prop. 2014/15:100), describes the growing gaps:

> The position of foreign-born in income distribution has deteriorated between 1995 and 2013. One reason for this is that immigration structure has changed over time. From having almost entirely been dominated by employment-based immigration, refugee and family-based immigration have since the 1990s come to constitute an increasingly larger share of immigration.

In addition to these direct effects, immigration may indirectly increase poverty by sharpening wage competition, while the increase in the number of poor will tighten competition for public resources. However, these indirect effects are difficult to estimate and will, therefore, be excluded in what follows.

In addition, this exposition does not consider that immigration changes the bar for what counts as relative poverty. On the other hand, so-called mechanical or direct effects are easy to present by simply splitting the group with low income into those with and without immigrant background. Poverty, or low income, here follows Statistics Sweden's definition, classifying those having a disposable income per consumption unit below 60% of the median as poor. Note that immigrant origin in these data includes both those with one or two parents born abroad.

Between 1991 and 2013, the proportion of relative poverty in Sweden increased from 7.3 to 14.1%; in other words, it nearly doubled. Just over half of the increase of the proportion in relative poverty can be attributed to the group that has immigrant background, which is a striking figure. If foreign-born and second-generation migrants are excluded from the analysis, and we only study those of Swedish origin, the increase in the proportion of low-income earners was half as large—from 6.4 to 9.8%. By 2013, the proportion in relative poverty was about 20% among second-generation immigrants, about 30% among all foreign-born, and 40% among those born outside of Europe. Figure 7.2 shows the development of the proportion in relative poverty among those with Swedish background and immigrants born outside of Europe.

Immigration and the situation among those with foreign backgrounds are not the only driving forces, though, as the proportion of poor among those of Swedish origin has also increased—although much more modestly. The already high level of poverty among non-European immigrants is, on the other hand, increasing sharply. In addition to immigrants being more likely to be low-income earners, this group is increasing rapidly in size, which further increases the number of low-income earners in Sweden. Figure 7.3 shows this development from 1995 to 2013, by outlining the absolute number in

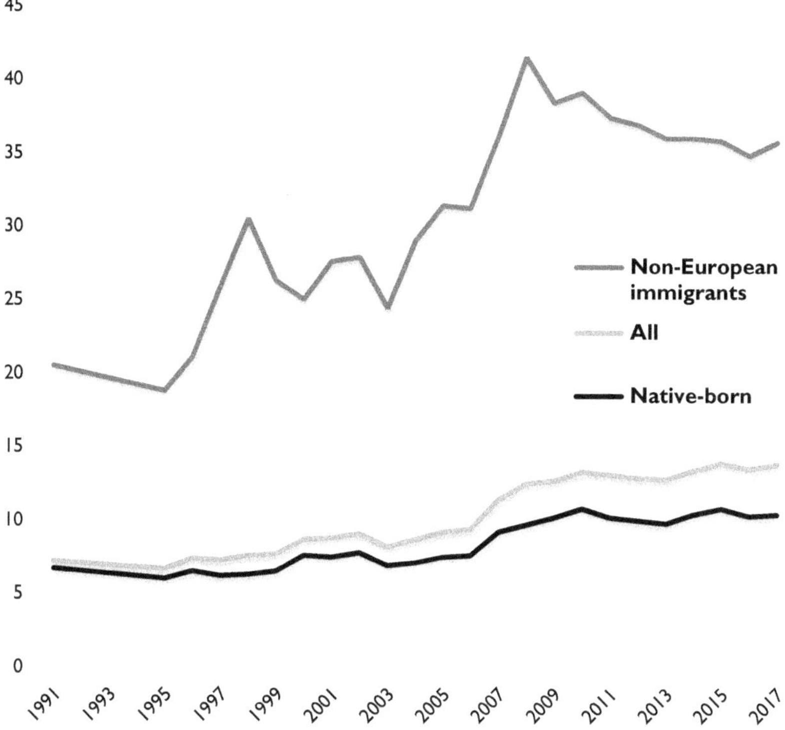

Fig. 7.2 Proportion in relative poverty among different groups (1991–2017) (*Source* Statistics Sweden)

relative poverty among those with Swedish and foreign backgrounds separately. The absolute number of poor individuals has increased slightly among those of Swedish origin, but the total has risen by much more in the immigrant category, since the absolute number of those with an immigrant background has grown substantially over time.

Absolute Poverty

A fourth measure of inequality is absolute poverty—that is, those who are not only poor in relation to others in their society, but poor enough to be unable to meet their basic needs. Since Sweden is a wealthy nation with a strong social safety net, the proportion living in deep material poverty remains among the lowest in the world. Inequality has increased at the top, but the social safety net is still strong enough to ensure a reasonably high material standard, at least compared to other countries. Eurostat compares different measurements of absolute and relative poverty in Europe. "Severe material deprivation" is defined as being unable to afford ordinary expenses. Statistics Sweden (2019) explains:

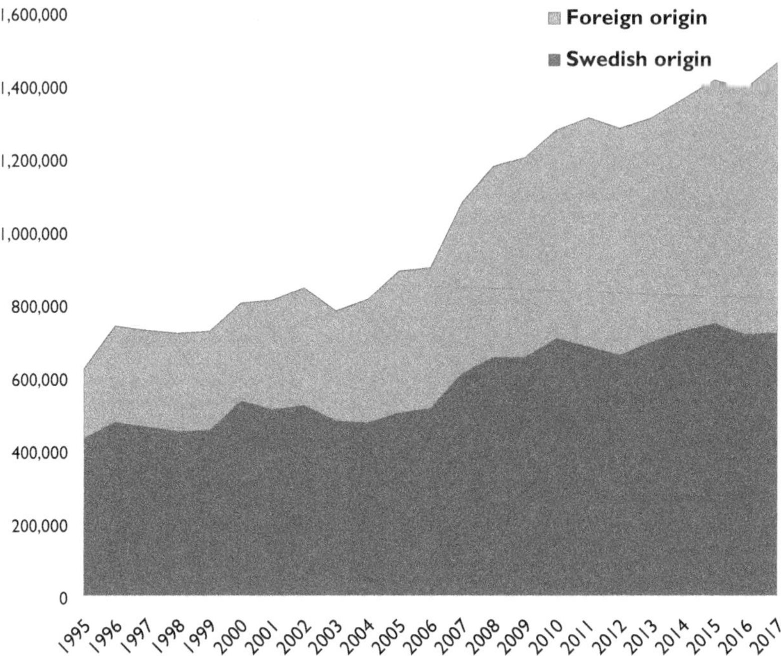

Fig. 7.3 Total number of people in relative poverty (1995–2017) (*Source* Statistics Sweden)

> This is measured by investigating whether people can pay unforeseen expenses, can afford a week's vacation per year, can afford a meal with meat, chicken or fish every other day, have sufficient heating of the home, have capital goods such as washing machine, color TV, telephone, or car, and can pay debts.

Looking at the 2014 data, Sweden was the country in Europe with the lowest proportion in severe material deprivation: merely 0.7% compared to 9% for the EU as a whole and, e.g., 55% in Turkey. According to the most recent numbers, however, Sweden's figure has increased to 2%, whereas the EU average decreased to 6% (Statistics Sweden 2019). Conversely, good material standard is defined as households that can afford all expense items. Even when it comes to this measure, Sweden is at the top in the EU, and second best in Europe overall after Norway. Statistics Sweden (2015) writes:

> Within the EU, Sweden has the highest proportion of the population with good financial and material standard. According to the above definition, about three out of four households in Sweden, 77 percent, have a good standard of living. In Norway, on the other hand, about 83 percent of the population have a good financial and material standard.

Although Sweden lacks the degree of poverty which characterizes the poor in most other countries, there are those who live close to poverty. This applies not least to the growing number of poor retirees, many of whom depend on charity to supplement the social safety net. According to the Swedish Pensions Agency (2016), the number of poor retirees has increased in recent years, so that in 2016 there were 231,500 elderly in households below the relative poverty line—the majority of them women. In Sweden, the income-based pension reflects total life income. Foreign-born individuals tend to have lower average income and work fewer years before retirement, and therefore have a lower pension. This applies not the least to those from outside Europe. Their pension is often supplemented by elderly income assistance, housing subsidies, and other forms of public support. *Dagens Nyheter*'s (2016) article "Not Enough Time for Foreign-Born to Earn a Pension" states:

> Many foreign-born have low income and don't have time to save up for a decent pension. Now, their children are fearing that they must support their aging parents. ... Over time, the pensions of immigrant groups have changed, since those foreign-born who received pensions in the 1980s to a greater extent were employment-based immigrants. Since the 1970s, Sweden instead has an increased immigration of refugees, who have a tougher time entering the job market, leading to lower pensions.

According to Eurostat, the proportion of poor retirees increased from 13 to 17% among the native-born between 2004 and 2015, and from 22 to 29% among the foreign-born. Although the proportion in poverty is higher among the foreign-born, poor retirees is a group where poverty is not concentrated to immigrants, and which also has many members with a Swedish background. An important explanation is that many native-born women, who have been away from the job market for long periods of time, have low pensions.

Over time, pensions and elderly care have become less generous, which means that many elderly people have rather small margins after expenses for healthcare, drugs, and other care. Many elderly people are forced to seek assistance from charity organizations, which Swedish Public Television (2016) describes in the article entitled "Retirees Can't Afford to Buy Food:"

> Meatballs, mashed potatoes, lingonberry jam, and green peas. Twenty crowns [$2], and that includes coffee after the meal. Elisabet Servaeus is one of all the retirees visiting the charity Stadsmissionen's elderly center in Stockholm today in order to get a meal. She's also one of the country's more than 231,000 retirees who today live below the poverty line.
>
> "You can go to Stadsmissionen where you can eat for 20 crowns. Otherwise I wouldn't survive. I wouldn't have," says Elisabeth Servaeus. The EU poverty line is 60 percent of the country's average (median) disposable income. In Sweden, this corresponds to just under SEK 11,000 [$1100] per month. When the rent and the bills have been paid, many retirees only have a few hundred crowns left. Now, non-profit organizations in Stockholm report that the situation

> has become so severe that many elderly can't even afford to eat. At Stadsmissionen's elderly center in Stockholm, the number of annual visitors has increased from just over 3,000 to over 11,000 retirees in just three years.
>
> "The food we offer may be the only cooked meal the elderly receive during the day," says Marika Hjelm Siegwald at Stockholm's Stadsmissionen. According to a forecast from the Swedish Pensions Agency released before the summer, the number of poor retirees has almost doubled since 2006.

In other words, Sweden is still able to guarantee almost all a minimum material standard, but the number of people living close to material poverty is increasing. The poverty that the so-called People's Home eliminated over decades of hard work has gradually returned—but in new guises. Poverty is increasingly concentrated to those with a foreign background, and in addition to a lack of money it is often combined with being in a state of social exclusion. This modern type of exclusion is not easy to explain with traditional theories of destitution and is difficult to solve with traditional anti-poverty measures.

The next chapter discusses how the return of poverty and other problems can be understood, and how these phenomena are linked to immigration.

References

Dagens industri. 2016. "M:s förslag förtjänar respekt" [The Moderate Party's Proposal Deserves Respect]. Editorial by PM Nilsson, September 4, 2016, updated September 5, 2016. https://www.di.se/artiklar/2016/9/4/ledare-ms-forslag-fortjanar-respekt.

Dagens Nyheter. 2016. "Utrikesfödda hinner inte få ihop pension" [Not Enough Time for Foreign-Born to Earn a Pension]. By Anna Gustafsson, May 2, 2016. https://www.dn.se/sthlm/utrikesfodda-hinner-inte-fa-ihop-pension.

Esping-Andersen, Gøsta. 1990. *The Three Worlds of Welfare Capitalism*. Cambridge: Polity Press.

Göteborgs-Posten. 2007. "Göteborgs somalier – ett folk i kris" [Gothenburg Somalis—A People in Crisis]. By Christer Lövkvist, October 28, 2007. https://www.gp.se/nyheter/göteborg/28-10-07-göteborgs-somalier-ett-folk-i-kris-1.1179853.

Henrekson, Magnus, and Tino Sanandaji. 2011. "Entrepreneurship and the Theory of Taxation." *Small Business Economics* 37, no. 2: 167–85. https://doi.org/10.1007/s11187-009-9242-2.

Nacka Värmdö Posten. 2017. "Ilska efter nyhet om kontroversiellt bostadsköp" [Anger for News of Controversial Housing Purchases]. By Erik Ljones, September 19, 2017. https://www.nvp.se/Arkiv/Artiklar/2017/09/ilska-efter-nyhet-om-bostadskop-till-man-med-tre-fruar.

OECD. 2015. "OECD Income Inequality Data Update: Sweden." Income Inequality and Poverty, Organisation for Economic Co-operation and Development (OECD), Paris. https://www.oecd.org/sweden/OECD-Income-Inequality-Sweden.pdf.

Pedersen, Axel W., and Stein Kuhnle. 2017. "The Nordic Welfare State Model." In *The Nordic Models in Political Science*, edited by Oddbjørn Knutsen, 219–38. Bergen: Fagbogforlaget.

Piketty, Thomas. 2014. *Capital in the Twenty-First Century*. Cambridge, MA: Harvard University Press.

Prop. 2014/15:100. "Bilaga 2: Fördelningspolitisk redogörelse" [Appendix 2: Distribution Policy Report]. In *2015 års ekonomiska vårproposition: Förslag till riktlinjer* [2015 Economic Spring Bill: Proposal for Guidelines], Finansdepartementet, Regeringskansliet, Stockholm. https://www.regeringen.se/49c85a/contentassets/16577670d2c147cb9db90a39e70a549f/bilaga-2-fordelningspolitisk-redogorelse.

Roine, Jesper, and Daniel Waldenström. 2015. "Long-Run Trends in the Distribution of Income and Wealth." In *Handbook of Income Distribution*, vol. 2A, edited by Anthony B. Atkinson and François Bourguignon, 469–592. Amsterdam: North-Holland. https://doi.org/10.1016/B978-0-444-59428-0.00008-4.

Statistics Sweden. 2015. "Sverige lever gott men risken för fattigdom ökar" [Sweden Lives Well But the Risk of Poverty Increases]. Statistical news, no. 2015: 85, Enheten för social välfärdsstatistik. Stockholm: Statistiska centralbyrån (SCB).

———. 2016. "Inkomstrapport 2014 – individer och hushåll" [Income Report 2014—Individuals and Households]. Ekonomisk välfärdsstatistik 2016:1, Statistiska centralbyrån (SCB), Avdelningen för befolkning och välfärd, Stockholm. https://www.scb.se/contentassets/3173557a55504ae391a04e7513d01308/he0110_2014a01_br_he50st1601.pdf.

———. 2018. "Skillnaderna i inkomst fortsätter att öka" [The Differences in Income Continue to Increase]. Statistical news, July 29, 2018. Enheten för statistik om befolkning och ekonomisk välfärd, Statistiska centralbyrån (SCB), Örebro. https://www.scb.se/hitta-statistik/statistik-efter-amne/hushallens-ekonomi/inkomster-och-inkomstfordelning/inkomster-och-skatter/pong/statistiknyhet/inkomstrapport-2016-individer-och-hushall.

———. 2019. "Sverige har lägre materiell fattigdom än de flesta andra länder i EU" [Sweden Has Lower Material Poverty Than Most Other Countries in the EU]. Statistical news, October 16, 2019. Enheten för social välfärdsstatistik, Statistiska centralbyrån (SCB), Stockholm. https://www.scb.se/hitta-statistik/statistik-efter-amne/levnadsforhallanden/levnadsforhallanden/undersokningarna-av-levnadsforhallanden-ulf-silc/pong/statistiknyhet/namnlos.

Swedish Pensions Agency. 2016. "Äldreförsörjningsstödets utveckling över tid" [The Development of Elderly Care Support over Time]. By Stefan Granbom and Tommy Lowén. Rapport PID151268, Dnr/ref. VER 2016-121, Pensionsmyndigheten, Stockholm. https://www.pensionsmyndigheten.se/content/dam/pensionsmyndigheten/blanketter---broschyrer---faktablad/publikationer/svar-p%C3%A5-regeringsuppdrag/2016/%C3%84ldref%C3%B6rs%C3%B6rjningsst%C3%B6dets%20utveckling%20%C3%B6ver%20tid.pdf.

Swedish Public Television. 2016. "Pensionärer har inte råd att köpa mat" [Retirees Cannot Afford to Buy Food]. By Rasmus Ejneberg, *SVT Nyheter*, July 21, 2016, updated July 23, 2016. https://www.svt.se/nyheter/lokalt/stockholm/pensionarer-har-inte-rad-att-kopa-mat.

CHAPTER 8

Parallel Societies

> The good home knows no privileged nor disenfranchised, no favorites nor step-children. There, one doesn't look down on another. There, no one attempts to gain advantages at the expense of others; the strong does not push down and plunder the weak. In the good home, there is equality, consideration, cooperation, and helpfulness.
>
> —Former Swedish Prime Minister, Per Albin Hansson, 1928, speech on *Folkhemmet*—the People's Home

The Malmö neighborhood of Rosengård is a remarkable example of a segregated area. The local school Rosengårdsskolan, which has about 300 students, is located only about a mile from the center of Malmö. The extent of segregation is apparent in an article published by Swedish Public Television (2016a):

> At Rosengårdsskolan in Malmö, there are no students who have Swedish as their first language, and this has been the case for the past 14 years.
>
> "It would be fun to meet Swedes so that I learn the language. Here, I mostly hear Afghan and Arabic languages," says Haia Abo Qarah at Rosengårdsskolan in Malmö.

The central problem of segregation is that it forces those with a weak social position to live in close proximity to others who are in a similar situation. Since geographical proximity is important for social interaction, there is a risk of segregation reinforcing socioeconomic problems. Social networks, schoolmates, and the like are often locally based. Immigrants would also often prefer to live in prosperous areas if they could afford to move, but are instead left to live near other low-earners.

Children with immigrant background, who grow up in deprived areas, often stay on as adults. About two-thirds of minorities, who at the age of

T. Sanandaji, *Mass Challenge*,
https://doi.org/10.1007/978-3-030-46808-8_8

16 lived in a low-income area in 1990, lived in a low-income area as adults (Gustafsson et al. 2017). A perhaps surprising result is that the mobility of children with immigrant background in Sweden is almost as low as among the African-American population in the United States. The percentage of people who start in the poorest decile when young and remain in it as adults is 48% in Sweden and 55% in the United States. Regarding the comparison between Sweden and the United States, Gustafsson et al. (2017) write:

> Measured by the intergenerational income correlation, as well as by mobility matrices, the intergenerational persistency in a spatial context appears to be lower in metropolitan Sweden than in the US. However, there is also a similarity between the two countries. The probability of leaving the decile of neighbourhoods with the lowest average incomes is nearly as low for visible minorities in Sweden as it is for African-American people in the US.

In Swedish Public Television (2016b), one of the study's authors says: "We see that the trend in Sweden is approaching the American picture of segregation and of what segregation looks like in the United States. We see that this is where we're heading."

Effects for Residents

A research review by Lina Aldén and Mats Hammarstedt at Linnaeus University (2016) discusses the impact of residential segregation. Newly arrived refugees are a particularly low-resource group in terms of financial assets, information, and access to the new country's social networks. From the beginning, they often end up in less attractive areas where housing is typically available, which gives them a weak start. Aldén and Hammarstedt (2016) write:

> The poor job market for foreign-born and the long time it takes for foreign-born to get into employment from the time of immigration means that foreign-born people, for resource reasons, have difficulties gaining access to the most attractive areas of the housing market in Sweden. This, in turn, leads to them not fully gaining access to the contacts and networks that are important in order to be able to establish themselves and improve their position in the job market.

One of the biggest problems with segregation is that low-resource children and young people end up with interacting mostly with others who have low levels of economic and social resources. Young people, whose character and human capital have not yet been shaped, are more easily influenced by their environment than adults. The risk of being impacted by negative social influences, attending a disorderly school, lacking positive role models, or of being drawn into drug abuse or a criminal subculture is greater.

At the same time, the effects of housing segregation should not be exaggerated. The most important reason for why those who live in segregated areas fare worse is not the effect of the residential area in itself, but rather that individuals with lower education and other problems often live in segregated areas. Again, it is key for social scientists to separate correlation from causality.

There is an extensive academic literature that, using different methods, tries to isolate the residential area's effects on social and economic outcomes from other explanations. Even if the negative effect from the residential area normally is not extremely strong, it is in many cases still a contributing explanation. This also applies to the residential area's most important effect: an individual's social networks. Aldén and Hammarstedt (2016) write:

> To live in areas with a high percentage of foreign-born may, due to lack of access to valuable contacts, thereby impair job market outcomes among foreign-born. Thus, much indicates that the opportunities of foreign-born people to succeed on the job market deteriorates from living in areas with a high percentage of foreign-born neighbors, since foreign-born in general have access to poorer networks and contacts than native-born Swedes. This reinforces the housing segregation and it thereby also becomes more difficult for foreign-born to gain access to better social networks.

COVID-19 Segregation

A very current consequence of segregation concerns how the COVID-19 crisis sharply impacted immigrants, both economically and in terms of health. A pattern that could also be observed in other Scandinavian countries as well as in other parts of the West is higher infection and mortality rates among the minority community—although as of writing, the causes are not well understood.

An analysis by the Public Health Agency of Sweden (2020) for the period of March 13 to May 7, 2020, demographically describes the incidence of infection and mortality rates, relative to each group's population share. Immigrants were on average more likely to have confirmed infections than native-born Swedes, in some cases dramatically higher. Immigrants born in Turkey, Somalia, Ethiopia, Chile, and Iraq had infection rates 3–4 times as high as native-born Swedes. Of the groups with a large enough sample size to be analyzed, only migrants from Poland had lower rates than the Swedish-born. Mortality in COVID-19 is highly age-dependent, but also here immigrants were disproportionately affected—with those born in Finland, Turkey, and Somalia being 2–4 times more likely to pass away than those born in Sweden. Again, only those born in Poland had lower mortality rates than the Swedish-born.

There are many potential explanations for this hitherto not well-understood pattern, including lack of language skills that made some immigrants less informed about public health information, poorer average health, a greater likelihood to work in service professions with personal interaction, less financial possibility to abstain from work, or cultural tendencies toward living with elderly generations. One potential explanation linked to the previous discussion may be residential segregation and the shortage of housing, where immigrants are more likely to live in crowded apartments in residentially segregated neighborhoods.

Many immigrants live with elderly relatives in small apartments and do not enjoy the possibilities of middle-class Swedes to, for instance, seek refuge from the pandemic in the densely populated cities in their summer cabins. The daily *Svenska Dagbladet* (2020) conducted interviews in the particularly hard-hit immigrant neighborhood of Järva, where locals pointed to the failure of the Swedish authorities to provide them with provisional housing for their elderly. Understanding the causes for the high burden of COVID-19 on low-income immigrant communities is an important topic for future empirical research.

White Flight

On a theoretical level, Schelling (1971) developed an influential model of segregation. When the segregation process is underway, social interaction leads even people with high tolerance of diversity to quickly move out, since they want to avoid becoming the "last remaining" person from their own group. A small influx may risk a chain reaction, where groups isolate themselves, which makes equilibria with mixed areas unstable.

In this and similar models, segregation does not occur gradually, but abruptly after the minority population in an area reaches a tipping point—after which the majority population moves out. The Schelling type of model has been used to study so-called white flight in the United States (Card et al. 2008). A study using the same method was performed in Sweden by Aldén et al. (2015). The study's conclusions were summarized in the popular science magazine *Forskning & Framsteg* (2015):

> "Yes, we found a so-called tipping point at 3–4 percent. When this proportion of non-European immigrants is reached in a residential area, the native Swedes start to move out of there," said Emma Neuman, economic researcher at Linnaeus University in Växjö. Highly educated and high-income earners are the first to leave, which leads to ethnic segregation occurring in parallel with economic segregation.

More recently, Böhlmark and Willén (2020) find a tipping point around 18% for the share of immigrants in a neighborhood in 1990, and that this tipping point is driven by non-Western immigrants. However, they find little support of negative effects on outcomes from living in a neighborhood with a high share of immigrants. Notably, the authors find that "the tipping behavior is driven exclusively by native aversion toward non-Western immigrants: the effects disappear when the model is re-estimated using Western immigrants."

There are also several studies, both in Sweden and internationally, which indicate discrimination in the rental market. Landlords and real estate agents are less likely to provide housing to people with an immigrant background, which is a contributing factor to housing discrimination. A convincing example is a so-called field experiment by Ahmed and Hammarstedt (2007). The authors submitted fictitious applications to rental offers on a classified ad website. Applications with Arabic-sounding names received far fewer positive responses and offers of viewings than in all other aspects similar applications with fictitious Swedish-sounding names, which points to the presence of discrimination.

A survey made by Swedish daily *Svenska Dagbladet* (2013) a few years ago showed that only just over 1% of Swedish members of parliament lived in any of the country's areas of social exclusion. It is common, not only among politicians, to speak warmly about diversity, but to quickly move away from actual diversity. An interesting interview study by Maja Lilja (2015), with 19 Swedish mothers, highlights a glaring discrepancy between expressed attitudes and actual behavior. In theory, the respondents embraced the benefits of multicultural residential areas, with quotes like "I'd love to live in a mixed area." The mothers praised ethnically mixed areas as not only beneficial for society but also beneficial for themselves and their children. The author explains:

> The women had slightly different arguments as to why it was important to allow the child to grow up in an environment where people had different backgrounds. Among other things, some of the women said that the child should grow up in an environment that reflected today's Sweden, which has become a multicultural society. However, the most common argument for their children to grow up in a culturally mixed environment was that their children could become "enriched" by meeting people of different backgrounds.

In their real-life choices, though, all interviewed women avoided mixed residential areas and schools. This was often coupled with references to the best interests of the child, who should grow up in a "calm and safe" environment. The Swedish mothers in this study unanimously stressed how important it is to grow up in a multicultural environment, but without exception made sure to prevent their own children from growing up in such an area. The interviews do not necessarily suggest that the interviewed women are aware of the paradox—which is managed through rationalization or doublethink.

This is a striking example of a more general tendency among Scandinavians: combing passionate public multicultural rhetoric with a vigilant avoidance of multicultural environments in their private lives.

Separate Societies in Ethnic Enclaves

Geographic segregation has contributed in strengthening cultural isolation, where there is such a strong concentration of immigrants with such a separate identity that they partially defect from the majority culture. The clash with Swedish society is strong when it comes to religion as well as clan structures. This often creates friction not only with Swedish society but also within the immigrant population—that is, between those who wish to integrate and those who want to hold on to their distinct customs and enforce their religious beliefs on the community.

Many aspects of the problems with segregation in parallel societies are traced out in a public report about one particular neighborhood (City of Borås 2019). This in-depth study is based on a large number of interviews and paints an unusually detailed picture of one such neighborhood in a medium-sized manufacturing town in western Sweden. Borås was once known as a center of the Swedish textile industry and has in recent years received attention due to the unusually large number of recruits to ISIS, who traveled to fight for the extremist Islamic Caliphate in Syria and Iraq. Norrby, with a population of roughly 4000 inhabitants, is one district in the city, and among the 22 areas designated by the police as particularly vulnerable.

The work to produce a status report for the district followed an initiative by The City Executive Office's department Center for Knowledge and Security in 2019. The main task was to draw up a status report for the area and attempt to identify underlying causes for the problems.

A particularly vulnerable area is defined as an area where it is difficult or almost impossible for police to carry out their duties; there are parallel social structures; residents are reluctant to partake in the judicial process; obstruction of justice is common, including systematic intimidation of witnesses and plaintiffs; people travel to participate in combat in conflict areas and fundamentalists restrict people's freedoms, such as the freedom of religion; and there is a high concentration of criminal residents.

Based on the interviews with the respondents, clan structures appear in Norrby and manifest themselves in several ways. This includes rivalry and stereotyping between the clans; hierarchical ranking of clans with tendencies to ascribe lower status to individuals within a group of friends based on clan affiliation. Persons from smaller clans are vulnerable as they are not allowed to take part in some contexts. Women are not present in public spaces, for instance the Somali association, and there are notions that one should or may not marry across certain clan lines. There exists a private, parallel legal system, and there are allegedly organizations in the area which are only open to certain clans, though the identity of this alleged type of organization could not be established by the report.

Professionals within the municipality's educational management report about the problems that arrive with parents with a very low education level. Many parents cannot help their children with homework due to insufficient knowledge of the Swedish language. The interviewed professionals also have the impression that some parents do not see the point in having their children go to school every day, and attendance at parent-teacher conferences is very low. School does not seem to occupy an important place in the lives of some students, and students often have difficulties achieving.

Police who work in the area have witnessed private justice systems, based on Somali customary law. This can occur in instances when a crime has been committed between individuals within the same clan or two different clans, and where the "conflict" has been resolved privately outside the bound of the Swedish legal system. According to residents in the area, some older men within a clan make sure that funds are raised for providing compensation to the damaged party. The clans can implement customary law between themselves, but can—in theory—turn to, e.g., a mosque to have the size of the damages appraised. Otherwise, clan elders meet and come to an agreement regarding the size of the damages. The Police Authority has also stated that a local mosque has been involved in the administration of private justice, though it has not been possible to establish how often this has occurred.

Ironically, some of the Somali customary law between clans used in conflict resolution bears some resemblance to the Germanic law documented in Viking Age Scandinavia, a less individualistic society where crimes could be settled by fines to the injured family (Dunbar et al. 1995)—a practice documented in the Icelandic tales. One difference with Viking Age Sweden or Iceland is that the Somali Clan elders collect fines using telephones, and conduct their private law not in an anarchy or a weak state but parallel to the formal legal system of an advanced welfare state.

Both police and professionals in the area have been informed that persons belonging to one ethnic group have demanded that other residents leave certain places, or created such an environment in the residential buildings in order to make people of other ethnicities move from the building. A majority of respondents said that they have experienced honor-related violence and oppression in Norrby in their work, and that it is even normalized in some environments. This includes the notion that girls are not allowed to leave the home, and that women who let their daughters move about unveiled are poor mothers. Arranged or forced marriage of women is believed to have taken place in the area, by sending daughters to the home country with the intent of marrying them off.

A number of branches within the municipal administration in the area claim that many of the children that they encounter are in Koranic schools, and that there is concern for what the children are taught there. Ranstorp et al. (2018) describe some of the believes of devout Salafists, who influence many Koranic schools:

> Boys and girls must be segregated according to gender and educated in their future roles. Boys are to be prepared in a patriarchal understanding of their duties as husbands, dads, and guardians of Islam, while girls are trained for their future roles as wives, motherhood, and their role as stay-at-home wives and how to dress properly as women. The importance of a separate religious education is something that is stressed by Salafist religious authorities in, for example, Saudi Arabia and Qatar.
>
> – – –
>
> Pressure is deemed to begin as early as at the age of seven, for instance, in the form of not speaking to children of the opposite sex, etc. Informants say that "youths disappear from school to the Koranic school." It has also occurred

> that youths after a day in school come to the mosque to "be washed" from what they have learned during their day in school. Informants also say that "the worst ones" (within extremist environments) offer activities for children aged 6–12 with juice, pastries, and computer games.

Residents as well as local professionals interviewed in the report often recount that they experienced or witnessed others experience encounters with what can be described as morality police. Examples include a relative, neighbor, or stranger who bother or harass women for walking unveiled, or for being "lightly dressed," and proclaim this to be morally wrong.

Many informants report that unveiled girls and women in the area and within communal institutions such as school, meeting spots, and playground are abused in various ways. It can take the form of questioning, reproach, degrading treatment, pressuring, exclusion, bullying, being called different names, as well as spitting and shouting at them if they are perceived as too lightly dressed. This allegedly happens especially in one particular local school. The people subjecting them to it are children as well as adults who may be known or unknown to the victim. The branches within the municipal administration are also aware that older people or relatives have on occasion either visited or contacted people who do not live according to the prevalent norm in order to compel them to comply. According to a number of informants in Norrby, LGBT persons are rarely visible in public spaces.

Within the education system, informants point to considerable problems with bullying of girls who do not live according to the norm and students who eat pork. Other children, for instance, stare at and reproach those who consume pork. According to school authorities, disputes involving children who are attacked for eating pork arise at a daily basis. Based on the collected material, many of the people in Norrby are hesitant toward certain parts and representatives of society, and have low trust in interpreters, social services, and the police authority.

Sweden often provides public interpreters to translate for those interacting with the public sector, such as medical care and public administration, which makes it an important profession to handle daily life. Lack of trust in interpreters is indicated by the fact that residents sometimes avoid using them if they hear that the person belongs to a different clan, since they believe that the interpreter will pass on what is said during the conversation. For that reason, some of the offices have to book interpreters who do not have any connection to the municipality.

Patriarchal Structures and the Morality Police

One of the sharpest areas where Swedish culture clashes with that of some immigrants is the issue of religion and gender norms. It should be emphasized that the majority of immigrants already share or readily adjust to modern Western norms about sexual liberation, personal freedom, and allowing boys and girls to interact. A minority of immigrants, however, hold on to the culture from their home countries. This socially reactionary group is mostly related to Muslim migrants, although similar norms exist among Christians, Yazidis, and other traditional clan cultures from the Middle East and Africa. Swedish studies and media outlets have reported on the extent of this problem.

Many immigrants today have secular values, and there are powerful movements for women's liberation and feminism also in Middle East. Indeed, for many immigrants the main reason for moving to the West was cultural and political freedoms rather than economic factors. Far from everyone from the Middle East or Africa holds religious values, and an intense culture war wages between modernism and traditionalism in these regions as well as within the immigrant populations in the West.

A study by Martin Ljunge (2017) examined attitudes among children of immigrants in Sweden and other European countries to the questions, "A woman should be prepared to cut down on her paid work for the sake of her family," and "When jobs are scarce, men should have more right to a job than women." Swedes have one of Europe's most gender equality-oriented cultures, though attitudes differ between immigrants compared to the native-born:

> There is a conflict between the indigenous Swedish values and migrant groups. Integration, from the Swedish perspective, seem to require the migrant groups to adopt more gender-equal attitudes.

Over time, an integration process occurs so that the attitudes of the foreign-born approach that of the majority population. This process is not automatic, though, and the convergence is sometimes only partial. There are strong conservative forces fighting cultural assimilation toward gender equality, especially in isolated immigrant suburbs.

Nevertheless, a significant minority of immigrants hold conservative views on women and through social control impart these values on their surroundings. Many women with an immigrant background live under substantial pressure from their families, and in the worst-case scenario they are at risk of shame culture and "honor" violence. For example, a survey by the National Board of Health and Welfare (2007) showed that 22% of women with a non-Nordic background did not feel free in their choice of partner, compared with less than 3% of women with a Nordic background.

A number of reports have portrayed honor culture and social pressure against women's freedom of movement. Swedish society has all too often legitimized these demands and retreated from the cultural conflict needed to resist them. Well-known examples include gender segregation in physical education classes in school, gender-segregated time slots in public baths, and the defense of the practice of refusing to greet women with a handshake. In doing so, mainstream society has accepted the reintroduction of conservative gender roles that had previously disappeared in Sweden. The Social Democrat Nalin Pekgul discussed this in an interview with journalist Ivar Arpi (*Neo* 2014):

> Together with her husband Cheko, Nalin Pekgul has written the book *But I'm Swedish*, which deals with conflicts that have emerged in Tensta and similar areas of social exclusion. The conflict is between Islamists—who are gaining in strength—and secular Muslims, says Nalin Pekgul. She has been questioned for not wearing a hijab. Even culturally, much has happened. Attitudes have changed. …
>
> "The Left and Right have traded places in these issues. Historically, it has been the Left who has defended the freedom of the individual. But suddenly there are those on the Left who themselves enjoy the right to independence and freedom, but at the same time show such an 'understanding' for other cultures that allow women and others to be oppressed. Even if they are against the conservative in their own culture, they defend other conservative cultures."

Similar warnings have been conveyed by the Swedish politician Amineh Kakabaveh who, like Nalin Pekgul, has a Kurdish background, and was cited by Swedish Public Television (2015) on male oppression in suburbs: "Women are no longer welcome at some cafes and in some places, young girls can't stay out after dinner time."

Patriarchal gender structures and the oppression of women are not merely cultural issues, but also constitute barriers to economic integration. Gender oppression can be observed in job market statistics, where the proportion of women outside the workforce is particularly high among migrants from the Middle East as well as Africa (Aldén and Hammarstedt 2015).

A research study on honor-based oppression among secondary school students, aged 13–15, in Uppsala showed some worrying results. A high proportion of immigrant girls and immigrant boys are not allowed to choose whom they will marry. The family or clan decides that they may only choose a partner of the same religion or ethnicity, or, in more extreme cases, they may only choose among partners that the family picks out and presents to them (*Upsala Nya Tidning* 2018):

> Two-thirds of foreign-born girls in Uppsala cannot decide entirely for themselves whom they will marry, according to a survey among all ninth-graders in Uppsala. … One question concerned respondents' own worry of being married off. One in four Swedish-born girls with foreign-born parents is worried of being married off, and among girls who are themselves foreign-born, 40 percent feel worried. … The survey further shows that 11 percent of girls and 5 percent of boys have in the past three years repeatedly been subjected to violence, violations, and threats by family or other relatives.

Associate Professor in Sociology, Astrid Schlytter, was interviewed on the harmful effects of the division of girls and boys on school busses, at physical education classes, and in swimming pools: "When you legitimize the values of the parents, integration is hampered," she said, claiming the problem has increased in recent years. "The main reason is that there are many more people in Sweden today with these values" (*Svenska Dagbladet* 2017).

Additionally, *Aftonbladet* (2017) reported on a seminar of Sweden United Muslims:

> Here, Sweden United Muslims, SFM, teach that women must not leave home, not wear perfume, not joke, and not show any skin.
>
> "She must not go out without the consent of her husband," says the lecturer, Sheikh Muhammad al-Shahrani. SFM received an economic grant from Gothenburg municipality as late as January. … If a woman has her husband's consent to leave the house, strict rules apply, al-Sharhani explains. She must be covered from head to foot and not show any skin. She must not wear any fragrance or colorful clothes.
>
> "She must go out without perfume," says al-Sharhani. In the next sentence, he however adds that perfume can be acceptable, if the woman is going to a party where only women are present. But then she must not put on the perfume before she gets to the party, and must not wear any fragrance when she leaves it.
>
> The woman may not smell of anything when she goes out, but she also must not smell bad, of onions, or of food.

The Caliphate in the North

The wars in Iraq and Syria contributed to a growth in Islamic sectarian extremism. Sweden is one of the European countries with the highest number of individuals who enlisted to fight for ISIS, sometimes referred to as "terror travelers." According to the Swedish Police Authority (2015), violence-promoting religious extremism is found in at least one-third of the areas vulnerable to crime. The concept is broad and includes everything from sympathizers with some kind of platform to ISIS combatants. In some areas, there are family connections between key players in criminal networks and religious extremism, and recruitment to crime and religious extremism often take place in the same circles. More generally, the increase in religious extremism has negatively affected religious freedom in a number of vulnerable areas, with residents avoiding to openly show religious affiliations.

The Director-General of the Swedish Security Service, Anders Thornberg, was interviewed on Sweden's status of Islamist extremists (*Expressen* 2017)—saying they estimate there are thousands of violence-promoting extremists in Sweden today. The increase in recent years has been explosive: "We've never seen anything like it to this extent before," says Thornberg, adding "We'd say that it has gone from hundreds to thousands at this point." He then concludes: "It is a new normal in the sense this is a historic challenge that extremist environments are growing."

The growth in religious extremism has also been accompanied by an emerging shame culture that is undermining the freedoms of girls and women living in these areas. The local newspaper *Mitt i* (2016) quotes the researcher Astrid Schlytter's views that shame culture norms have expanded and recently taken on new forms in regular Swedish residential areas: "The difference now is that it's no longer just the family or relatives who control girls. Nowadays, entire areas exert social control over girls. Parents who otherwise might not comply with shame culture now do so because they feel pressure from their surroundings." The article also highlights a report that was produced by the Stockholm district administration in Spånga-Tensta, which echoes similar problems:

> In it, it is described that the area has undergone a change with several isolated groups living under shame culture norms. There is control of girls' clothing and leisure activities, insults, and the spreading of rumors. About 100 girls from grade 6 to grade 9 in Hjulsta have been interviewed. 45 percent say they never go to the sports hall. 54 percent do not participate in activities in their free time. The older girls feel restricted by the spread of rumors and several avoid recreational centers: "If I go to the recreation center, I get a bad reputation," is a common comment in the report.

The emergence of these cultural difficulties was a gradual process, and one that some warned about. Sweden remains one of the world's most tolerant and liberal societies, but with pockets characterized by oppression and regressive values. Alas, the number of these pockets has grown over time.

References

Aftonbladet. 2017. "'Kvinnor får inte gå ut, ha parfym eller skoja'" ["Women Are Not Allowed to Go Out, Have Perfume, or Fun"]. By Olof Svensson, April 5, 2017. https://www.aftonbladet.se/nyheter/samhalle/a/ko7kA/kvinnor-far-inte-ga-ut-ha-parfym-eller-skoja.

Ahmed, Ali, and Mats Hammarstedt. 2007. "Diskriminering på bostadsmarknaden: Effekten av att heta Mohammed" [Discrimination in the Housing Market: The Effect of Being Named Mohammed]. *Ekonomisk Debatt* 35, no. 6: 34–41. https://www.nationalekonomi.se/filer/pdf/35-6-aamh.pdf.

Aldén, Lina, and Mats Hammarstedt. 2015. "Utrikes födda på 2000-talets arbetsmarknad – en översikt och förklaringar till situationen" [Foreign-Born in the Labor Market of the 21st Century—An Overview and Explanations of the Situation]. *Ekonomisk Debatt* 43, no. 3: 77–89. https://www.nationalekonomi.se/sites/default/files/NEFfiler/43-3-lamh.pdf.

———. 2016. "Boende med konsekvens – en ESO-rapport om etnisk bostadssegregation och arbetsmarknad" [Housing with Consequences—An ESO Report on Ethnic Housing Segregation and the Labor Market]. Rapport till Expertgruppen för studier i offentlig ekonomi (ESO) 2016:1, Wolters Kluwer, Stockholm. https://eso.expertgrupp.se/wp-content/uploads/2016/02/Hela-2016_1-till-webben.pdf.

Aldén, Lina, Mats Hammarstedt, and Emma Neuman. 2015. "Ethnic Segregation, Tipping Behavior, and Native Residential Mobility." *International Migration Review* 49, no. 1: 36–69. https://doi.org/10.1111/imre.12066.

Böhlmark, Anders, and Alexander Willén. 2020. "Tipping and the Effects of Segregation." *American Economic Journal: Applied Economics* 12, no. 1: 318–47. https://doi.org/10.1257/app.20170579.

Card, David, Alexandre Mas, and Jesse Rothstein. 2008. "Tipping and the Dynamics of Segregation." *The Quarterly Journal of Economics* 123, no. 1: 177–218. https://doi.org/10.1162/qjec.2008.123.1.177.

City of Borås. 2019. "Lägesbild Norrby: Perioden 2014–2019" [Snapshot Norrby: The Period 2014–2019]. Rapport, Dnr 2019-01055. Stadsledningskansliet, Centrum för kunskap och säkerhet. Borås: Borås stad. https://pdfhost.io/v/klZFDnON_Lgesbild_Norrby.pdf.

Dunbar, Robin I. M., Amanda Clark, and Nicola L. Hurst. 1995. "Conflict and Cooperation Among the Vikings: Contingent Behavioral Decisions." *Ethology and Sociobiology* 16, no. 3: 233–46. https://doi.org/10.1016/0162-3095(95)00022-D.

Expressen. 2017. "Skräcksiffran: Tusentals radikala islamister i Sverige" [The Horror Figure: Thousands of Radical Islamists in Sweden]. By TT/David Baas, June 16, 2017. https://www.expressen.se/nyheter/skracksiffran-tusentals-radikala-islamister-i-sverige.

Forskning & Framsteg. 2015. "Segregeringen ökar i Sverige" [Segregation Is Increasing in Sweden]. By Henrik Höjer, May 29, 2015. https://fof.se/tidning/2015/7/artikel/segregeringen-okar-i-sverige.

Gustafsson, Björn, Katarina Katz, and Torun Österberg. 2017. "Residential Segregation from Generation to Generation: Intergenerational Association in Socio-Spatial Context Among Visible Minorities and the Majority Population in Metropolitan Sweden." *Population, Space and Place* 23, no. 4: e2028. https://doi.org/10.1002/psp.2028.

Lilja, Maja. 2015. "'Det bästa för mitt barn': Nyblivna mödrar i den delade staden" ["The Best for My Child": New Mothers in the Split City]. Diss., Örebro Studies in Sociology 19, Örebro University, Örebro. https://www.diva-portal.org/smash/get/diva2:794168/FULLTEXT01.pdf.

Ljunge, Martin. 2017. "Cultural Determinants of Gender Roles: 'Pragmatism' as an Underpinning Attitude Toward Gender Equality Among Children of Immigrants." In *Social Economics: Current and Emerging Avenues*, edited by Joan Costa-Font and Mario Macis, 197–232. Cambridge: MIT Press. https://doi.org/10.7551/mitpress/9780262035651.003.0009.

Mitt i. 2016. "Larm: Ökat förtryck mot tjejer [Alarm: Increased Oppression of Girls]. By Johanna Edström, July 4, 2016, updated October 27, 2016. https://mitti.se/nyheter/larm-okatfortryck-mot-tjejer.

National Board of Health and Welfare. 2007. "Frihet och ansvar: En undersökning om gymnasieungdomars upplevda frihet att själva bestämma över sina liv" [Freedom and Responsibility: A Survey of High School Students' Perceived Freedom to Decide for Themselves]. Artikelnummer 2007-131-27, Socialstyrelsen, Stockholm. https://www.socialstyrelsen.se/globalassets/sharepoint-dokument/artikelkatalog/ovrigt/2007-131-27_200713127_rev.pdf.

Neo. 2014. "Intervju: Nalin Pekgul. 'Låt islamisterna bilda ett eget parti'" [Interview: Nalin Pekgul. "Let the Islamists form Their Own Party"]. By Ivar Arpi, no. 5, 2014. http://magasinetneo.se/artiklar/lat-islamisterna-bilda-ett-eget-parti/.

Public Health Agency of Sweden. 2020. "Covid-19: Demografisk beskrivning av bekräftade covid-19 fall i Sverige 13 mars–7 maj 2020" [Covid-19: Demographic Description of Confirmed Covid-19 Cases in Sweden, March 13–May 7, 2020]. Folkhälsomyndigheten, Solna. https://www.folkhalsomyndigheten.se/

contentassets/d6538f6c359e448ba39993a41e1116e7/covid-19-demografisk-beskrivning-bekraftade-covid-19-fall.pdf.

Ranstorp, Magnus, Filip Ahlin, Peder Hyllengren, and Magnus Normark. 2018. "Mellan salafism och salafistisk jihadism: Påverkan mot och utmaningar för det svenska samhället" [Between Salafism and Salafist Jihadism: The Impact of and Challenges for Swedish Society]. Centrum för asymmetriska hot- och terrorismstudier (CATS), Försvarshögskolan, Stockholm. http://fhs.diva-portal.org/smash/get/diva2:1231645/FULLTEXT02.pdf.

Schelling, Thomas C. 1971. "Dynamic Models of Segregation." *Journal of Mathematical Sociology* 1, no. 2: 143–86. https://doi.org/10.1080/0022250X.1971.9989794.

Svenska Dagbladet. 2013. "Fem av 349 riksdagsmän bor i utsatta områden" [Five of 349 MPs Live in Vulnerable Areas]. By Jenny Stiernstedt, Erik Paulsson Rönnbäck, and Lena Hennel, May 31, 2013, updated June 1, 2013. https://www.svd.se/fem-av-349-riksdagsman-bor-i-utsatta-omraden.

———. 2017. "Forskare: 'Svenska staten har varit oerhört feg'" [Researcher: "The Swedish State Has Been Extremely Cowardly"]. By TT, April 4, 2017. https://www.svd.se/forskare-svenska-staten-oerhort-feg.

———. 2020. "Stor virusrädsla i Järva: 'Situationen är akut'" [Great Virus Fear in Järva: "The Situation is Acute"]. By Negra Efendić, April 4, 2020. https://www.svd.se/stor-virusradsla-i-jarva-situationen-ar-akut.

Swedish Police Authority. 2015. "Utsatta områden – sociala risker, kollektiv förmåga och oönskade händelser" [Vulnerable Areas—Social Risks, Collective Ability, and Unwanted Events]. Dnr: HD 5800-61/2015. Underrättelsesektionen, Nationella operativa avdelningen (NOA), Polismyndigheten, Stockholm. https://polisen.se/siteassets/dokument/ovriga_rapporter/utsatta-omraden-sociala-risker-kollektiv-formaga-och-oonskade-handelser.pdf.

Swedish Public Television. 2015. "Männens förtryck växer i förorten" [Men's Oppression Is Growing in the Suburbs]. By Pererik Åberg, *SVT Nyheter*, June 24, 2015. https://www.svt.se/nyheter/lokalt/stockholm/vaxer-mannens-diktatur-i-fororten.

———. 2016a. "Ingen elev med svenska som förstaspråk – på 14 år" [No Student with Swedish as Their First Language—in 14 Years]. By Fredrik Skillemar and Ella Berger, *SVT Nyheter*, June 1, 2016. https://www.svt.se/nyheter/lokalt/skane/ingen-elev-med-svenska-som-forstasprak-pa-14-ar.

———. 2016b. "Ny studie om segregation: 'På väg att bli som i USA'" [New Study on Segregation: "About to Be Like the U.S."]. By Hedvig Eriksson and Niklas Forsberg, *SVT Nyheter*, August 27, 2016, updated August 28, 2016. https://www.svt.se/nyheter/inrikes/ny-studie-om-segregation-pa-vag-att-bli-som-i-usa.

Upsala Nya Tidning. 2018. "Utbrett hedersförtryck bland Uppsalas unga" [Widespread Repression of Uppsala's Youths]. June 26, 2018. https://www.unt.se/nyheter/uppsala/utbrett-hedersfortryck-bland-uppsalas-unga-5013910.aspx.

CHAPTER 9

Social Exclusion

> Human beings are members of a whole,
> In creation of one essence and soul.
> If one member is afflicted with pain,
> Other members uneasy will remain.
>
> —Saadi, *Gulistan*, 1258

The commonly used Swedish term *utanförskap* can be literally translated as "outsideness." *Nationalencyklopedin* (n.d.) defines it rather vaguely as "to stand outside a certain community in home, work, culture, or social life, between members of a country, people, etc." The term was coined in Sweden and has since been borrowed by its Nordic neighbors, but lacks an established English language equivalent. In sociology, the term is sometimes compared with "social exclusion," with roots in the France of the 1970s—and this is the translation used here.

That a vague concept quickly became so prevalent in the public debate is interesting in itself. This may indicate that the suggestive term *utanförskap* captures the zeitgeist and an intuitively recognizable phenomenon, still seeking a definition. Björkemarken (2014) writes that the concept "got its breakthrough due to the Liberal Party's reports on social exclusion." These reports, collectively known as *The Map of Social Exclusion*, were developed by Mauricio Rojas, Associate Professor of Economic History, who was for a time the Swedish Liberal Party's spokesperson on refugee and immigration issues.

Neo-Poverty

Historically, the word poverty would usually be used to describe social circumstances, similar perhaps to what today would be called social exclusion (Ravallion 2016). This is probably not a coincidence. Poverty primarily refers to the lack of material resources; it can either be about absolute destitution

T. Sanandaji, *Mass Challenge*,
https://doi.org/10.1007/978-3-030-46808-8_9

or relative poverty. Those who were socially excluded in the past were also poor. However, in today's society, what we fundamentally associate with social exclusion is neither material destitution nor relative poverty. Most people who today are considered, and consider themselves to be, socially excluded would be counted among high-income earners had they lived in the West a hundred years ago, or in many countries outside the Western world today. Sweden has, through a combination of high prosperity and low inequality, the perhaps lowest material poverty in Europe. That being said, relative poverty can still matter even in the absence of material poverty. The reason for this is that one's social position is influenced by how much one earns, compared to others in the same country.

Relative poverty is therefore closer to social exclusion, even though it is a narrower term defined only by material status. Consequently, it does not capture deprivations such as ethnic discrimination, physical segregation, psychological alienation, and involuntary exclusion. Moreover, while low income is an outcome, social exclusion also relates to the process that caused the outcomes, focusing on the exclusion of individuals or groups that are shut out from a core community. In this way, social exclusion—unlike poverty—also necessarily requires a theoretical explanation. Having—for various reasons—been excluded from communities such as the workplace, social networks, or attractive residential areas, leads to lower incomes and reduces the opportunity to fully participate in society.

In the first half of the twentieth century, economists with a material view of poverty, such as John Maynard Keynes, predicted that poverty would disappear as incomes increased. This, however, did not happen despite a sharp increase in material standards. An alternative perspective on poverty has been presented by Economics Nobel laureate Robert Fogel (1999), who believed poverty has a dimension beyond the material. "Spiritual" poverty can be seen as lacking human capital such as knowledge and skills, or a lack of social capital such as standards of behavior, character development, trust, and social networks. Lack of human and social capital leads to lower incomes, while increasing the risk of unfavorable behavior such as substance abuse, crime, chaotic living conditions, and broken families. This would explain why the social nature of poverty does not disappear despite rising incomes. Fogel emphasizes that "although material assistance is an important element in the struggle to overcome spiritual estrangement, such assistance will not be properly targeted if one assumes that improvement in material conditions naturally leads to spiritual improvement."

In Sweden, too, poverty has a material component. For example, there are many retirees with low incomes as well as households who live off social assistance and have a relatively low standard of living. Statistics Sweden reports disposable income for households of working age. In 1991, working households had about 25% higher income than non-working households—a difference that increased to almost 80% by 2013. At the same time, as income from work and capital has grown for those who are gainfully employed, many government-assistance programs have become significantly less generous.

Phenomena such as crime and substance abuse have a stronger connection to spiritual or social poverty than material poverty. One way to illustrate this is to look at students who live off student loans and grants. Students often have low incomes and live in cramped housing conditions, yet have a low incidence of crime, antisocial behavior, substance abuse, and other adverse behaviors common among the poor. The reason is that students have intangible assets in the form of high human and social capital, which is further strengthened by their studies. Those who have low incomes due to social or spiritual poverty are often also overrepresented in behaviors widely considered "unfavorable"—not because this behavior is caused by low incomes, but because social poverty causes low incomes as well as unfavorable behavior.

Outsiders

Originally, the concept of social exclusion seems mainly to have been used for marginal groups such as the homeless (Eriksson 1999). Over time, however, social exclusion has increasingly come to be associated with ethnic divides, as opposed to the past focus on class analysis.

Not having a job is probably the single most important measure of social exclusion. It is also a dimension where there is significant agreement among commentators and across political parties. Still, to date, a completely satisfactory theoretical definition of social exclusion has not been developed—part of the reason being that sociological and economic theory still is struggling to get to grips with the concept.

The study of residential areas has some clear advantages. One is that if we look at the individual level, if someone is not working, it does not necessarily reflect involuntary social exclusion. There are many reasons for why individuals are registered as not working, including parental leave, regular sick leave, or education. Hence, in every society, there is a certain percentage of the working-age population that is not employed, which has nothing to do with social exclusion.

One way to account for this, and to better measure involuntary social exclusion, is thereby to study residential areas, where the proportion of the population who are employed is below the national average. Another advantage of studying residential areas is that social exclusion is linked to residential segregation. Interestingly, the term social exclusion is often spatially defined—even in earlier studies about marginal Swedish groups.

The job market is a social institution, and unemployment may be seen as a form of social exclusion where some, for various reasons, are not let into a group. Using the labor market as a starting point, the Swedish center-right defined social exclusion to include those with weak connections to the job market as well as those who received financial assistance. This measurement was criticized, since it included groups that were voluntarily positioned outside the job market, but it was politically successful as it was simple and directed focus to the fact that many—in addition to the openly unemployed—lacked jobs. That the message got through, even to former Social Democrat voters, may in part reflect the Swedish Lutheran work ethic. The argument that many, due to the design of the system, lacked the opportunity or incentive to work collided with the ideal of social inclusion centered around work.

Social capital such as social status, trust, cultural awareness, values, and position in social networks are hard—if not impossible—to measure. An advantage of the measure of social exclusion developed by Rojas is that it also measures human capital by including the proportion of pupils in the area, who leave primary school without obtaining a complete set of passing grades.

A Map of Social Exclusion

Continuing along the path focused on integration that they embarked on in the run-up to their 2002 election success, the Liberal Party published the much talked about and innovative report entitled *The Map of Social Exclusion* in 2004. The report used Statistics Sweden's geographical measurement units to split the country into about five thousand residential areas, and examined how many of those were affected by deep social problems. The criteria for being defined as an area of social exclusion were the following: that 60% or fewer of the residents of working age are working; and that fewer than 70% complete primary school with complete grades, or that fewer than 70% voted in the most recent municipal election.

The Liberal Party's report showed that the number of areas of social exclusion had increased from three in 1990 to no less than 128 in 2002. It received a lot of media coverage, perhaps partly due its unusually high methodological ambitions. The Map of Social Exclusion was subsequently updated several times by the Liberal Party, and these maps were summarized several times by the Liberal Party. The last update came in 2008 and showed that the number of areas of social exclusion had increased further to 156 in 2006. After that, there was a reluctance from the Liberal Party to evaluate the developments during the period when the center-right Alliance was in power, with a Liberal Party Minister for Integration.

However, not everyone had forgotten about the Map of Social Exclusion. For example, *Svenska Dagbladet*'s (2013) editorial page called for an update under the headline "They Have Stopped Drawing the Map of Social Exclusion." In the following year, I updated the Map of Social Exclusion up until the year 2012 (Sanandaji 2014).

From existing geographical units, Sweden was divided into nearly five thousand residential areas. During the update of The Map of Social Exclusion for 2012, my report followed the Liberal Party's methodology as closely as possible (Sanandaji 2014). Mauricio Rojas wrote the introduction—commencing by citing the foreword of the first 2004 report:

> "A new social landscape has emerged in Sweden, a landscape characterized by exclusion from the job market, residential segregation, dependency on public assistance, powerlessness, and vulnerability.... There are areas where social exclusion has become the glue in a collective identity that is based on a strong sense of being shunned and not belong to the community in general."
>
> That a significant proportion of the population in these areas consisted of southern and in particular non-European refugees and immigrants made the situation even more charged. An ethnocultural dimension radically expanded the widening gap that separated the areas of social exclusion from the rest of the country. It should have served as a big, red flag, calling for action before it was too late. But nothing was done....
>
> Now we know exactly how it happened. Tino Sanandaji has documented the Liberal Party's and the center-right's failure to reverse the trend that condemns an increasing number of new and old Swedes to a life in social exclusion. The areas of social exclusion continued to grow between 2006 and 2012, when there were 186 areas of social exclusion scattered around Sweden. The same year, 566,000 people lived in these areas—an increase of 16 percent compared with the figure for 2006! Tino Sanandaji has used the same methodology I created for the development of the Map of Social Exclusion in 2004 and which was also used for the updated versions of the map in 2005, 2006, and 2008. It is also based on the same types of data. That's why his results are fully comparable with those of the earlier maps. When we presented the first Map of Social Exclusion, the Social Democrats tried to come up with one excuse after another in order to avoid having to acknowledge a historic failure that was about to become very costly for Sweden. We can only hope that the Liberal Party and the center-right will not repeat the same embarrassing spectacle now.

Table 9.1 summarizes the results from the 2014 update; in addition to the number of areas of social exclusion, it also shows the average outcomes for all these areas compared to the rest of the country.

Table 9.1 Comparison of social exclusion (2006–2012)

	2006	*2012*
Number of areas of social exclusion in Sweden	156	186
Number of people living in areas of social exclusion	488,000	566,000
Residents of areas of social exclusion as percentage of the Swedish population	5.4%	5.9%
Gainful employment rate in areas of social exclusion	50.7%	50.2%
Gainful employment rates in the rest of Sweden	78.3%	78.8%
Students without complete primary school grades in areas of social exclusion	49.9%	50.2%
Students without complete primary school grades in the rest of Sweden	22.4%	20.6%

Source Statistics Sweden

In 1990, using the same method, only three residential areas were areas of social exclusion, the most prominent of which was Rosengård in Malmö. The number of areas of social exclusion continued to increase between 2006 and 2012: in 2006, 156 residential areas were identified; in 2012, the number had increased to 186 residential areas. The number of residents in the areas of social exclusion was about 488,000 in 2006, and 566,000 people in 2012. Of the country's population, 5.4% lived in areas of social exclusion in 2006, and 5.9% in 2012.

A significant proportion of the residents in these areas are second-generation immigrants—in other words, the native-born children of foreign-born parents. Only 26% of the residents of the areas of social exclusion in 2006, and 25% of the residents in 2012, had Swedish background—defined as native-born with two native-born parents.

In 2012, 175 of 186 areas of social exclusion were more immigrant-heavy than the national average. However, there were some areas of social exclusion with a low or medium proportion of foreign-born, often in old mining towns and rural areas such as the district of Bojsenburg in Falun and Vasastaden in Arboga.

Development Over Time

While the overall problems in these neighborhoods have persisted, a positive trend is that the proportion of those gainfully employed has increased, particularly in the areas of social exclusion around Stockholm. By contrast, the average disposable income per resident has developed worse than in the rest of the country. Figure 9.1 shows that the disposable income per person only has increased slowly in these areas, so that the gap, compared to the national average, has grown sharply over time. As can be seen in Fig. 9.2, school results remain at a low level, with a high proportion of young people leaving primary school without access to secondary education.

Another report written by the Swedish Trade Union Confederation analyst Jan Edling (2015) provides an exhaustive analysis of Swedish integration policy. Swedish Public Television (2015) writes:

> Jan Edling's judgment of Swedish integration policy these past 20 years is harsh. "These suburbs are in serious trouble and you can't say that Sweden is an integrated country. We've used these suburbs as a repository for those who don't fit into ordinary society," says Edling.

Edling's report confirms that low employment rates are a severe drag on these areas. He also points out that many of the jobs that do exist in segregated areas are low-paying jobs. Swedish Public Television (2015) continues:

> Those who after all have jobs are according to the report employed in jobs with low wages and low social status. To a large extent, the women work as nurse's assistants or cleaners, while many men work as kitchen and restaurant helpers, cleaners, or personal assistants.

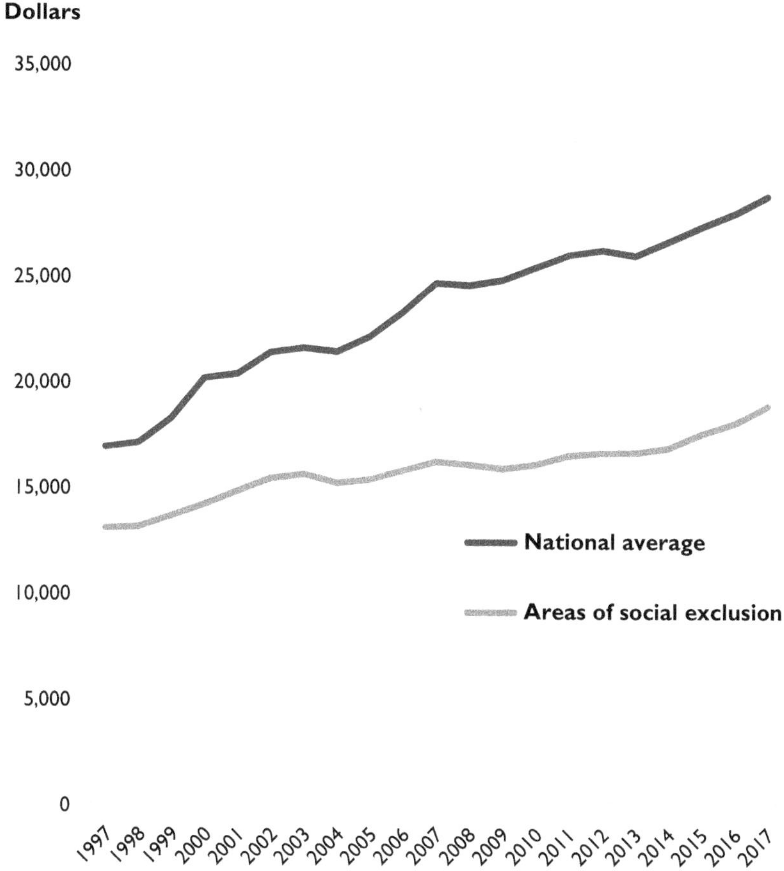

Fig. 9.1 Disposable income per person in areas of social exclusion vs. the national average (*Source* Statistics Sweden)

In summary, the large and growing number of areas of social exclusion in Sweden is a societal problem of historic proportions. This so-called challenge has been discussed since at least the 1990s, without a solution in sight. The main problem is not that the old areas of social exclusion—like Rinkeby, Rosengård, and Ronna—have become poorer relative to the rest of the nation since the 1990s, which they collectively have not. Instead, the problem is that an increasing number of previously normal residential areas have turned into areas of social exclusion. While the problems in Rinkeby have been discussed for a generation without a solution being found, new areas such as Araby in Växjö, Oxhagen in Örebro, and Krongården in Trollhättan have become worse than Rinkeby was when the discussion originally started.

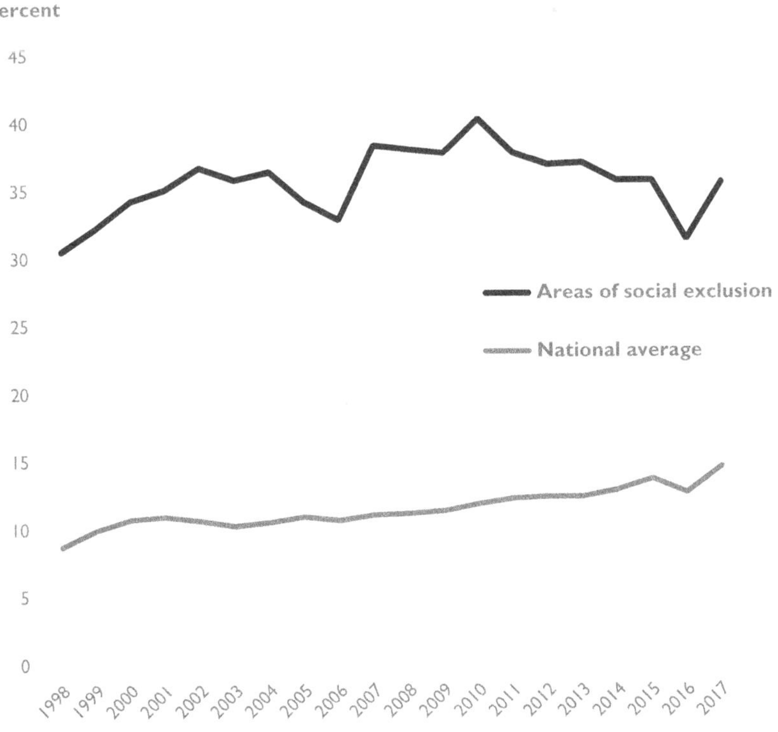

Fig. 9.2 Percentage of students without secondary school eligibility in areas of social exclusion vs. the rest of the country (*Source* Statistics Sweden)

References

Björkemarken, Mariann. 2014. "Begreppet 'utanförskap'" [The Term "Social Exclusion"]. LO-distriktet i Västsverige. Landsorganisationen i Sverige, Stockholm. https://vastsverige.lo.se/home/lo/res.nsf/vRes/lo_distriktet_i_vastsverige_1365671392950_2965_5_begreppet_utanforskap_webb_pdf/$File/2965-5_Begreppet%20utanförskap_webb.pdf.

Edling, Jan. 2015. "Förorterna som Moder Svea glömde: En dokumentation av en obefintlig integrationspolitik" [The Suburbs Mother Svea Forgot: A Documentation of a Non-Existent Integration Policy]. Flexicurity, Verdandi, Stockholm. http://www.verdandi.se/wp-content/uploads/2015/10/151014-Förorterna-som-Moder-Svea-glömde.pdf.

Eriksson, Catharina. 1999. "Det motsägelsefulla utanförskapet" [The Contradictory Social Exclusion]. *Socialvetenskaplig tidskrift* 6, no. 4: 293–312. https://journals.lub.lu.se/index.php/svt/article/view/15423.

Fogel, Robert W. 1999. "Catching Up with the Economy." *American Economic Review* 89, no. 1: 2–21. https://doi.org/10.1257/aer.89.1.1.

Liberal Party (Sweden). 2004. *Utanförskapets karta: En kartläggning över utanförskapet i Sverige* [The Map of Social Exclusion: A Survey of the Social Exclusion in Sweden]. Stockholm: Folkpartiet Liberalerna.

Nationalencyklopedin. n.d. "utanförskap." https://www.ne.se/uppslagsverk/ordbok/svensk/utanförskap.

Ravallion, Martin. 2016. *The Economics of Poverty History, Measurement, and Policy*. Oxford: Oxford University Press. https://doi.org/10.1093/acprof:oso/9780190212766.001.0001.

Sanandaji, Tino. 2014. "Utanförskapets karta – en uppföljning av Folkpartiets rapportserie" [The Map of Social Exclusion—A Follow-Up to the Liberal Party's Report Series]. Stiftelsen Den Nya Välfärden, Stockholm. http://www.dnv.se/wp-content/uploads/2014/05/Utanförskapets-karta-en-uppföljning-.pdf.

Svenska Dagbladet. 2013. "De har slutat rita Utanförskapets karta" [They Have Stopped Drawing the Map of Social Exclusion]. Editorial by Sanna Rayman, June 16, 2013. https://www.svd.se/de-har-slutat-rita-utanforskapets-karta.

Swedish Public Television. 2015. "Ny utredning: 'Förorterna har blivit en förvaringsplats'" [New Survey: "The Suburbs Have Become a Repository"]. By Andreas Liebermann and Elisabeth Marmorstein, *SVT Nyheter*, October 13, 2015. https://www.svt.se/nyheter/inrikes/ny-utredning-fororterna-har-blivit-en-forvaringsplats.

CHAPTER 10

Immigration and Causality

> Happy is the man who has been able to learn the causes of things.
>
> —Virgil, *Georgics*, 29 B.C.

Even after several decades with conspicuous socioeconomic problems among Sweden's immigrant population, it remains common to deny the role of immigration in issues such as inequality, unemployment, or crime. Even though the gang criminals overwhelmingly have immigration background, the Swedish Prime Minister Stefan Löfven famously stated that rising gang crime has nothing to do with immigration and could not have been foreseen (Swedish Public Television 2019). Even when the impact of immigration on various undesired outcomes is admitted, the analysis is often vague regarding effect sizes and causal relationships, with a tendency to minimize the role of immigration in favor of other explanations or pure obfuscation.

Overall, the Swedish public debate has had a hard time dealing with how immigration affects society. The strong moral desire for immigration to work well has made it painful to admit its role in socioeconomic problems. Moreover, after a long period with stable demographics and a homogenous population, few are accustomed to analyzing demographic effects—something that becomes necessary to incorporate following large-scale immigration. For decades, Sweden was a country with stable and predictable population trends, where demographic considerations were of secondary importance. The focus in the political debate, and related academic analysis, was instead placed on such issues as income distribution, social structures, tax levels, and macroeconomic topics like wage levels.

The type of standard theoretical models used in economics and other fields in the social sciences when discussing such topics is often implicitly based on closed societies, sometimes referred to as *autarky*. In some areas, demographics as an explanatory factor was neglected to the point where many simply were not anymore used to dealing with demographic changes such as

T. Sanandaji, *Mass Challenge*,
https://doi.org/10.1007/978-3-030-46808-8_10

immigration. An example of this is that economic growth often is reported as the change in total GDP, rather than GDP per capita. When population growth slowed down to a few fractions of a percent per year toward the end of the twentieth century, it was deemed unnecessary to spend the effort to adjust for GDP per capita—especially for short-term analysis.

This chapter discusses the issue of causality when accounting for the effects of immigration on the outcomes of the host country, and the extent to which observed changes can be said to be caused by immigration. Discussing causality can philosophically be viewed as a type of counterfactual analysis—that is, to ask how matters would have progressed in an alternative scenario without immigration, or with lower rates of immigration. This is different from the moral question of which group to "blame" for various problems, or to be grateful toward for various improved outcomes. If immigrants, for instance, are overrepresented in poverty and do not affect the poverty of natives, immigration can be said to increase the average incidence of poverty compared to a scenario with fewer migrants. It would, however, not follow from this that individual immigrants are to be collectively blamed for poverty. We will use the examples of unemployment and school performance to illustrate how one can think about immigration and causality.

Unemployment and School Performance

The share of immigrants among Sweden's unemployed has increased from 23% in 2006 to 58% in 2019. These are striking numbers given that the foreign-born make up about 19% of the population, and one quarter of those of working age. If we instead focus on the immigrants' share of the long-term unemployed, it is even higher: 66% of all those who have been unemployed for more than a year in Sweden are foreign-born. Consequently, in this period, unemployment among native-born has fallen significantly both in terms of absolute numbers and in percentages, whereas the nation's overall unemployment rate has hardly changed since it has been pushed up by more unemployed immigrants. Immigration is no longer a marginal phenomenon, but one of the main drivers behind unemployment trends in Sweden. Figure 10.1 shows the trend for foreign-born as the proportion of the working-age population—employed and unemployed, respectively.

Foreign-born still make up a minority of the population, but are so heavily overrepresented in negative socioeconomic outcomes that the group is a driving force in aggregated trends. This is true not only for unemployment but also for many other outcomes. According to the Swedish National Board of Health and Welfare statistics, immigrant households received about 65% of the disbursed social assistance payments in 2019, and accounted for two-thirds of the increase in disbursed social assistance since 1990. As is discussed below, children with immigrant background make up 77% of Sweden's

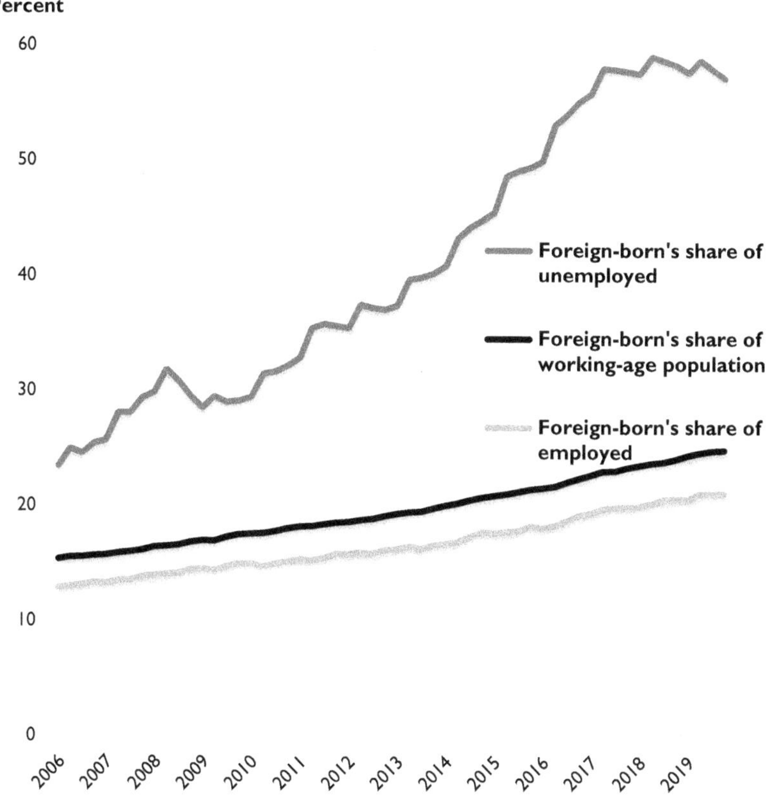

Fig. 10.1 Foreign-born's share of those unemployed (2006–2019) (*Source* Statistics Sweden; Swedish Public Employment Service)

children living in poverty. When interpreting these figures, it is important to understand that the increased impacts on socioeconomic outcomes that we observe for immigrants are not primarily driven by an increase in this group's problems, but rather by the group having become a larger proportion of the total population.

An important method when investigating the causal relationship of immigration is to break down the total numbers by different groups, which is also called decomposition. Immigration affects socioeconomic outcomes in society through two main mechanisms. One is that the immigration of new residents to a country makes their socioeconomic outcomes part of the country's aggregate outcome. The influx of unemployed immigrants increases unemployment. This is a direct effect that can easily be calculated with precision. Potentially, immigration could also affect the unemployment rate for those who are already in Sweden—a more indirect effect that is more difficult to calculate.

Many studies suggest that immigration may negatively affect wages and employment for the rest of the population, though effect sizes are often small (e.g., Borjas 1987; Card 1990; LaLonde and Topel 1991; Angrist and Krueger 1999; Borjas 1999, 2003; Coleman and Rowthorn 2004; Longhi et al. 2005, 2008; Bratsberg et al. 2014; D'Amuri et al. 2010; Engdahl 2016; Borjas 2017). There are also studies which conclude that immigration does not significantly affect the existing population's job market, as well as some that show positive effects (e.g., Dustmann et al. 2016). While there is an intense debate about these spillover or displacement effects in the job market, even estimates which find such effects suggest that they, in the long run, are considerably smaller than the direct impact of immigration. The main impact of immigration on Swedish unemployment figures arise from immigrants themselves having higher unemployment, so that the total unemployment increases when the group becomes a larger percentage of the population.

The increase of immigrants as a proportion of the population is most often gradual and may thus, in the short term, appear to be unimportant when compared to, for example, swings associated with macroeconomic cycles, but it has a powerful cumulative effect when the small changes from year to year are added on top of each other over time. In the long run, immigration's most important impact on society is, therefore, what is called a compositional effect. This refers to the mechanical effect that occurs when groups, which in various respects differ from each other, change their proportion of the population. All else equal, if society's composition is changed by groups with high unemployment, becoming a larger proportion of the population, unemployment increases. If immigration leads to many unemployed people moving into a country, the demographic composition is altered, which in turn leads to a rise in unemployment. The effect of immigration is not always so extensive that it dominates the development in the rest of society. Even when total unemployment drops, however, immigration may lead to it dropping less than it otherwise would have.

Another example is the share of those gainfully employed. Between 2000 and 2015, the gainful employment rate in Sweden increased by 4.3 percentage points for the foreign-born and by 4.4 percentage points for the native-born. However, the total rate only increased by 2.7 percentage points. It may seem paradoxical that the total rate increases less than the rate for each of the two subgroups, which make up the population. But the explanation can be found in the altered composition of the population.

In 2000, foreign-born made up 14.0% of the working-age population in Sweden. In 2015, the proportion of foreign-born had risen to 21.5%. Both in 2000 and 2015, the foreign-born's gainful employment rate was about 23 percentage points lower than of the native-born. When groups with lower gainful employment rates grow as a share of the population, the total average gainful employment rate is pushed down. In other words, between 2000 and 2015, the negative compositional effect of immigration caused a negative impact on the gainful employment rate by 1.7 percentage points. Although the gainful employment rate among both groups increased by 4.3 and 4.4 percentage points, respectively, the total increase was as a consequence only 2.7 percentage points. The growth in the immigrant share of the population ate up two-fifths of the increase in total gainful employment rate—even though the group's gainful employment rate relative to native-born did not change.

There were, thus, different forces in the job market, which pulled in different directions and partially canceled each other out. The growth of the proportion of immigrants in this case had a negative effect on the gainful employment rate for the population as a whole and pressed it down. The positive force in the form of a broad upswing, however, was greater during the period, so that the gainful employment rate increased on the aggregate—despite the fact that it was simultaneously pushed down by the compositional effect of immigration. However, the increase was lower than it would otherwise have been. In this case, the composition effect was not large enough to completely cancel out the positive trend in the economy, hence the total still showed a slight increase. In other cases, the negative composition effect boosts downward trends in general. Among other things, this is the case with school performance.

On average, first- and second-generation immigrants have poorer school performance than other students. Immigration has contributed to the drop in Swedish school performance—both through the composition effect, with those with immigrant background representing a higher proportion of students, and through the widening of the gap between those with native and immigrant backgrounds. These effects can be observed both in the results of the international knowledge test PISA, as well as in the proportion of students who leave primary school with incomplete grades. According to a Swedish National Agency for Education (2016) report, the proportion of students leaving primary school without being eligible for further studies increased from 8.7 to 14.3% between 1998 and 2015. The report calculates the effects of immigration: "All things equal, this means that if the share of students with foreign background increases, the national average performance level will be negatively impacted."

The increasing number of students who have arrived after the age when they would normally have started school in Sweden have had a decisive impact on the reduced eligibility rates to secondary school since the mid-2000s. Upwards of 85% of the increase of almost 4 percentage points in the proportion of ineligible in 2006–2015 can be explained by an increase in the proportion of students who immigrated after the age of six. The greatest impact comes from the fact that the share of this group of students is increasing, but its deteriorated eligibility rate has also had an impact. The eligibility rate of students who were born in Sweden with immigrant background has not deteriorated, but since their share has increased, they still contribute to the total decline in eligibility. If we look across the entire period 1998–2015, over half of the decline in eligibility can be explained by an increase in the proportion of students who have immigrated after starting school.

Immigration and the development among students with immigrant background have also affected Sweden's results in the PISA test. The effect is driven partly by widening knowledge gaps across groups, but even more by the composition effect of students with immigrant background having increased. There are different ways of counting; yet, students without a Swedish background drive around a third of Sweden's long-term decline in PISA up to 2015, and more than one half of the decline up to the 2019 round.

Explanations and Excuses

Traditionally, studies on inequality focused on topics such as macroeconomics, the factor distribution of income between capital, and workers and redistributive policy. Contemporary poverty in Sweden is, however, no longer exclusively driven by domestic economic development and the distribution of resources, but in part imported from abroad. The forces boosting poverty are not primarily related to the incomes of those who already live in Sweden, independently of background, but rather to the influx of new low-income people from abroad. These demographic effects are fundamentally simple, even if they are difficult to understand for those who are used to standard theories of distribution policy developed in societies with low immigration.

It is ideologically inconvenient for many to accept the connection between immigration of poor people and increased poverty—both among liberals, socialists, and conservatives. The prevailing societal analysis of problems such as poverty is adapted to societies which were assumed to be closed, or where immigration was not an important demographic factor. There is also a strong tendency to see the solution to all new social problems in light of already existing ideological tools. Among Social Democrats, increased poverty is assumed to be caused by cuts in the welfare state, which is solved by an expanded welfare state and higher taxes. Liberals usually prefer to see poverty as caused by too weak incentives to work, too much regulation, and high thresholds to enter the job market in the form of high salaries and collective bargaining agreements. In a similar fashion, conservatives explain the problem with standard theories, such as a lack of work ethic among the allegedly work-shy who lack employment, or with the decline of the nuclear family.

None of these explanations focusing on domestically fixated societal analysis are, however, adequate to explain the return of poverty, when it is in fact driven by an increased number of poor children and adults with foreign background. If increased poverty primarily was driven by any of the classic internal mechanisms—such as a weakened welfare state, the Employment Protection Act, collective bargaining agreements, and so on—then we would observe increased poverty also among the Swedish majority population, as well as among those immigrants who have already been living in Sweden for a while.

Instead, poverty, unemployment, child poverty, low school performance, and other problems in these groups have remained stable—or in some cases even declined—in recent years. What drives the development is instead that the population share of those groups suffering problems is growing through immigration. This is a strong indicator that the causal explanation is immigration itself—not domestic social changes.

Simpson's Paradox and Child Poverty

Child poverty is another interesting example of the importance of accounting for composition effects in the face of demographic change. A commonly used definition of child poverty is children living in households at or below the threshold for social assistance. Child poverty has come to be concentrated among children with foreign backgrounds. A recent report on child poverty by Save the Children (2015) states: "Nearly a third of children with a foreign background, 29.3 percent, live under conditions of financial hardship compared to 4.9 percent of children whose parents were born in Sweden."

As previously pointed out, foreign background includes both those who were born abroad, and second-generation immigrants born in Sweden. When it comes to children, the fact is that most of those with a foreign background were born in Sweden. It is mainly children in immigrant households and children with single parents who grow up in poverty in Sweden. Child poverty is the type of inequality that is most concentrated to those with foreign background. Save the Children (2015) writes: "Of all children in financially disadvantaged families in Sweden in 2013, 71.4 percent are children with foreign background."

In 1991, 39% of poor children were of immigrant origin. Over time, child poverty has dropped sharply among children of Swedish origin, while the number of poor children has been added to by children of immigrant origin. Total child poverty increased during the financial crisis in the 1990s, and then declined. On closer inspection, the trend in child poverty demonstrates the importance of discussing demographic effects as well as the importance of compositional change.

Between 1991 and 2013, child poverty among children of Swedish origin more than halved—from 11.3 to 4.9%. Total child poverty, however, only dropped slightly—from 14.5 to 12.0%. The reason is not that children of immigrant origin became more likely to be poor. On the contrary, the share was stable, and even fell marginally from 29.4 to 29.3%. However, child poverty was boosted by immigration, since immigrants' share of the population increased significantly during the period.

When the group with higher poverty becomes larger, total poverty in society is increased, even if the proportion of poor in that group remains unchanged. This compositional effect is often as important as the actual changes of the outcomes; in the long run, the compositional effect is often even more important.

For Sweden, the years between 2006 and 2013 show a fascinating statistical phenomenon related to child poverty. Note that the time period in itself is not of particular interest; rather, it is chosen for illustration. Between 2006 and 2013, child poverty dropped from 6.3 to 4.9% among those of Swedish origin. It also declined among children with immigrant background—from 30.2 to 29.1%. Given that child poverty declined for both of the two groups that make up the Swedish population, it is reasonable to assume that also the total dropped. Perhaps somewhat surprisingly, the answer is that total child poverty actually increased slightly—from 11.8 to 12.0%.

That two groups show a trend that is reversed when they are combined is an example of what in statistics is known as Simpson's paradox. In the above example, the reason for this is that the group with higher child poverty rate increased its share of the total population. Over time, the higher child poverty rate for immigrants weighs heavier and heavier on the total, which boosts child poverty. This compositional effect more than compensates for the drop in the averages of each of the two groups. For many alternative time periods, there is no pure Simpson's paradox. For example, if we instead had looked at the period 1991 to 2013, then we would have found that the changes within the groups were larger than the compositional effect, so that the total trend only was reduced—not reversed. Here too, however, the total average fell considerably less than in the two groups separately.

These examples illustrate that the biggest effect of immigration on the national economy and social outcomes in the long run are changes in group composition, rather than changes in outcomes for groups. Immigrants' problems have an increasingly large impact on society as the group gradually grows, even when differences in outcomes are constant.

In addition to immigrants' social exclusion pulling down Sweden's total outcome, today's trend leads to formerly broader social problems—such as crime, unemployment, and child poverty—being increasingly concentrated to those with immigrant background. After Sweden, with great effort, basically won the fight against the traditional class society, the country now heads in the direction of an ethnic class society. For those of Swedish origin, child poverty has never been lower. However, due to immigration, total child poverty has again become entrenched at relatively high levels.

References

Angrist, Joshua D., and Alan B. Krueger. 1999. "Empirical Strategies in Labor Economics." In *Handbook of Labor Economics*, vol. 3A, edited by Orley C. Ashenfelter and David Card, 1277–1366. Amsterdam: North Holland. https://doi.org/10.1016/S1573-4463(99)03004-7.

Borjas, George J. 1987. "Immigrants, Minorities, and Labor Market Competition." *Industrial and Labor Relations Review* 40, no. 3: 382–92. https://doi.org/10.1177/001979398704000305.

———. 1999. "The Economic Analysis of Immigration." In *Handbook of Labor Economics*, vol. 3A, edited by Orley C. Ashenfelter and David Card, 1697–1760. Amsterdam: North Holland. https://doi.org/10.1016/S1573-4463(99)03009-6.

———. 2003. "The Labor Demand Curve Is Downward Sloping: Reexamining the Impact of Immigration on the Labor Market." *The Quarterly Journal of Economics* 118, no. 4: 1335–74. https://doi.org/10.1162/003355303322552810.

———. 2017. "The Wage Impact of the *Marielitos*: A Reappraisal." *Industrial and Labor Relations Review* 70, no. 5: 1077–1110. https://doi.org/10.1177/0019793917692945.

Bratsberg, Bernt, Oddbjørn Raaum, Marianne Røed, and Pål Schøne. 2014. "Immigration Wage Effects by Origin." *The Scandinavian Journal of Economics* 116, no. 2: 356–93. https://doi.org/10.1111/sjoe.12053.

Card, David. 1990. "The Impact of the Mariel Boatlift on the Miami Labor Market." *Industrial and Labor Relations Review* 43, no. 2: 245–57. https://doi.org/10.1177/001979399004300205.

Coleman, David, and Robert Rowthorn. 2004. "The Economic Effects of Immigration into the United Kingdom." *Population and Development Review* 30, no. 4: 579–624. https://doi.org/10.1111/j.1728-4457.2004.00034.x.

D'Amuri, Francesco, Gianmarco I. P. Ottaviano, and Giovanni Peri. 2010. "The Labor Market Impact of Immigration in Western Germany in the 1990s." *European Economic Review* 54, no. 4: 550–70. https://doi.org/10.1016/j.euroecorev.2009.10.002.

Dustmann, Christian, Uta Schönberg, and Jan Stuhler. 2016. "The Impact of Immigration: Why Do Studies Reach Such Different Results?." *Journal of Economic Perspectives* 30, no. 4: 31–56. https://doi.org/10.1257/jep.30.4.31.

Engdahl, Mattias. 2016. "Invandringens arbetsmarknadseffekter" [The Labor Market Effects of Immigration]. Rapport 2016:11, Institutet för arbetsmarknads- och utbildningspolitisk utvärdering (IFAU), Uppsala. https://www.ifau.se/globalassets/pdf/se/2016/r-2016-11-invandringens-arbetsmarknadseffekter.pdf.

LaLonde, Robert J., and Robert H. Topel. 1991. "Labor Market Adjustments to Increased Immigration." In *Immigration, Trade, and the Labor Market*, edited by John M. Abowd and Richard B. Freeman, 167–200. Chicago: University of Chicago Press.

Longhi, Simonetta, Peter Nijkamp, and Jacques Poot. 2005. "A Meta-Analytic Assessment of the Effect of Immigration on Wages." *Journal of Economic Surveys* 19, no. 3: 451–77. https://doi.org/10.1111/j.0950-0804.2005.00255.x.

———. 2008. "Meta-Analysis of Empirical Evidence on the Labour Market Impacts of Immigration." IZA working paper no. 3418. https://ssrn.com/abstract=1136223.

Save the Children. 2015. "Barnfattigdom i Sverige: Årsrapport 2015" [Child Poverty in Sweden: Annual Report 2015]. Research and analysis by Tapio Salonen. Rädda Barnen, Sundbyberg. https://resourcecentre.savethechildren.net/node/9615/pdf/rb_barnfattigdom_2015_web_l.pdf.

Swedish National Agency for Education. 2016. "Invandringens betydelse för skolresultaten: En analys av utvecklingen av behörighet till gymnasiet och resultaten i internationella kunskapsmätningar" [The Importance of Immigration for School Results: An Analysis of the Development of Qualifications for High School and the Results of International Knowledge Surveys]. Skolverkets aktuella analyser 2016, Skolverket, Stockholm. https://www.skolverket.se/publikationsserier/aktuella-analyser/2016/invandringens-betydelse-for-skolresultaten.

Swedish Public Television. 2019. "Analys: 'Statsministerns svarta vecka'" [Analysis: "Prime Minister's Black Week"]. By Mats Knutson, *SVT Nyheter*, November 20, 2019. https://www.svt.se/nyheter/statsministerns-svarta-vecka.

CHAPTER 11

Law and Order

> For from within, out of the heart of man, come evil thoughts, sexual immorality, theft, murder, adultery, coveting, wickedness, deceit, sensuality, envy, slander, pride, foolishness.
>
> —Mark 7:21–22

One of the most important effects of social exclusion on society is crime—a sensitive and complex topic that will be discussed in detail in the following chapters. While crime has an economic dimension, it is also intimately linked to deeply rooted moral concepts such as guilt, justice, honor, and revenge. The fear of becoming the victim of crimes committed by the Other has often been used to collectively blame immigrants, outcasts, and minorities, as well as to incite hatred. History offers many examples of actual or imagined crimes that have provoked reprisals in the form of xenophobic violence—not seldom against innocent people. An atmosphere of threatening rhetoric and fear of violence facing the own group may risk stirring up primal instincts in the majority.

While crime and the rhetoric surrounding it may be emotionally charged, it is also an important issue that has been studied by social scientists using scientific methods, both quantitative and qualitative. The study of crime constitutes a separate field within the social sciences called criminology. Crime has also been extensively studied in related fields such as law, sociology, psychology, medicine, and—not the least—economics.

The fact that economists often study crime may come as a surprise to many laymen, who associate economics with various financial topics. But in fact, today, a significant proportion of the research on crime is performed by economists, either directly or in relation to economic issues. A practical reason for this is that the modern statistical and econometric methods developed within economics are well suited for criminology. Studies performed by economists in the field of criminology have been very influential. A concrete example of

T. Sanandaji, *Mass Challenge*,
https://doi.org/10.1007/978-3-030-46808-8_11

this is that a majority of the most downloaded studies in the field of criminology in the online research archive Social Science Research Network are actually written by economists.

There are also links between crime and economic issues that justify economic analysis of crime. Property crimes and organized crime are largely about making money. Poverty and the pursuit of the same material standard as the rest of society can be an important driving force behind crime. Crime can be affected by economic factors, and—as discussed in Chapter 16—crime can have significant socioeconomic impact.

Measuring Crime

There are many forms of crime, and several ways in which crime can be measured. The results sometimes differ depending on which crime category is studied, and what methods of measurement are used. For Sweden, it is clear that most forms of crime are more common today than in, say, 1950—but it is harder to address the question whether crime has dropped, increased, or remained stable in recent years. The answer depends on the crime category and social group studied, and in addition there are important methodological problems with measuring crime that make it difficult to draw clear conclusions.

The number of reported crimes has in general increased sharply since 1950, both in the aggregate and adjusted for population. Total reported crimes per inhabitant set a record in 2015 and have since remained high, slightly below this record by 2019. It is a controversial issue to what extent this is driven by a greater inclination in society to report crime, or whether it is the result of an actual increase in crime. All types of reported crimes do not move in the same direction. Certain forms of crime, such as burglaries and bicycle theft, have dropped in recent decades, and car thefts have declined so sharply that they are now approaching lower levels of the 1950s. The perhaps most important and noticeable crime category is violent crime. The number of reported violent crimes per inhabitant increased steadily from 1950 to a peak in 2010. It then fell several years in a row, but has again begun to increase, and was in 2019 only slightly below its historical peak.

When interpreting these trends, it should be noted that the number of reported crimes may be affected by changes both to laws as well as to current norms, and is not an exact measurement of actual crimes. For example, in the past, brawls among young school-age boys were typically not reported to police. Even today, far from all these brawls are reported, but as society's tolerance for violence has dropped, it has become more common to report this type of crime to police—which in part explains the increase that we observe.

Based on an EU survey, Statistics Sweden (2019) notes that crime is increasing, and that Sweden nowadays is one of the most crime-affected countries in the EU, to the extent that "About 13% of the population in Sweden are exposed to crime, violence, or vandalism in their own neighborhoods," which corresponds to "one of the highest rates in Europe." A more detailed regional comparison is then presented:

> In 2017, 13 percent reported that they are exposed to crime, violence, or vandalism in their neighborhood. The other Nordic countries are among the countries with the lowest proportion of the population exposed to these problems in their own neighborhood. In Norway, about 4 percent are exposed to violence, crime, and vandalism. The corresponding rate for Denmark and Finland are 8 and 6 percent, respectively.

The survey also showed that exposure to crime is more common among low-income earners.

Self-Reported Surveys of Crime

Another measurement of crime is given by the so-called Swedish Crime Survey, which is an annual survey conducted by the Swedish National Council for Crime Prevention (SNCCP), where a large sample of individuals aged 16 to 84 are asked to self-report their exposure to crime. The survey has been carried out since 2006 and asks about the exposure to crime in the previous year, so that the 2019 measurements refer to events that occurred during 2018.

For comparability reasons, the SNCCP reports trends between 2006 and 2018, and while they adjust the results, it should be noted that survey methods have changed during this period—and that the data reported here are based on the latest revised estimates using the new method. The proportion of respondents who stated that they had been exposed to crimes against their person generally increased between 2006 and 2018, although the trend differs between different types of crime. The incident of assault increased from 3.0 to 3.5%, the share who were robbed increased from 0.8 to 1.4%, whereas victims of sex crimes increased from 1.5 to 6.0%.

The number of crimes increased even more than the share of the population exposed to crime, since many victims of crime are exposed to more than one crime per year. Most violent crimes are committed by a small group of criminals, while the overwhelming majority of the population never commit violent crime. A recent high-profile study tracking all individuals born in Sweden 1958–1980 up to adulthood found that 1% of the population account for almost two-thirds of all violent crime (Falk et al. 2014). It is sometimes forgotten that there is also a high concentration among victims, where an estimated half of all crimes reflect repeated exposure among a relatively small proportion of the population (SNCCP 2016a).

Returning to the Swedish Crime Survey, a potentially important problem to keep in mind when interpreting its results is a high and, over time, increasing non-response rate. That is to say, many who are asked to participate do not respond to the survey, and thus their experiences are not captured in the statistics. The proportion who do not respond is particularly high among people born outside the Nordic countries, which may bias the results. The SNCCP (2016a) writes that "It is also likely that the most marginalized groups in the population, such as homeless, addicts, and career criminals, are not represented in the material, which is particularly unfortunate as they tend to be more victimized by crime than others."

If more people from groups exposed to crime are overrepresented among those who have stopped responding to the survey, a distortion is created so that it underestimates the trend in crime. The type of bias created by this statistical problem cannot be solved by weighting the results if those who do not respond systematically differ from others in ways that are not observable. The very low response rate in these surveys from the immigrant population makes the results obtained from areas of social exclusion unreliably low—in particular when compared to more readily observable measures of crime such as homicides and shootings.

Sex Crime

One crime category that, according to several metrics, has increased in recent years is sex crimes, which includes unwanted touching, indecent exposure, and rape. It is more difficult to measure sex crimes than many other types of crime, in particular since there is likely to be many hidden crimes when it comes to rape, where many violations are not reported—especially when it comes to rape perpetrated in relationships or by someone close to the victim. To the extent that social change leads to more people having the courage to report rape, the number of reported crimes may increase without the actual number of rapes increasing as much. The vast majority of the victims are women who are exposed to sex crimes perpetrated by men, but not all.

Sex crimes are measured both by examining police reports and through self-reported surveys, where hidden crimes are less of an issue. According to self-reported data in the Swedish Crime Survey, exposure to sex crimes has increased sharply among women. The proportion of women who report that they have been the victims of sex crimes increased from 2.5% in 2006 to 9.9% in 2018—a remarkable and widely debated increase.

Reported rapes have increased significantly in Sweden and are among the highest in Europe. Rapes reported in relation to the population quadrupled between 1975 and 2005, and have since continued to increase—almost doubling once again by 2018. While the increasing trend is dramatic and stands out compared to many other countries, it is difficult to tell how much of the increase is due to an increase in the actual number of rapes, and how much is due to changes in the propensity to report rapes and to legislation. Crucially, the legal definition of rape was expanded in April 2005 to also include some situations previously categorized as sexual abuse, where the victims are deemed to have been in a helpless state due to, for instance, severe intoxication, unconsciousness, or sleep. Moreover, social change and movements such as Metoo are likely to have increased the likelihood that victims report rape.

It is well-known that many rapes are not reported to the police. In fact, this is more likely to be true for most countries than for Sweden, as rape is still considered shameful for the victim in many cultures. Therefore, Sweden's high number of reported rapes compared to other countries to a large extent reflects more modern sexual norms and greater intolerance of sexual violence. For the same reason, it is difficult to estimate what the trend over time looks like for Sweden; more modern sexual norms are likely to lead to more reported rapes without an actual increase.

Even so, it is also possible that both reporting and the actual number of rapes increase. One indication that this may indeed be the case is the increase in rapes preceded by assault, which are less likely to go unreported. These are defined as rapes that start with a sudden attack and where the perpetrator is unknown to the victim. Most assault rapes are committed outdoors and tend to be concentrated to the summer period. While the number of assault rapes increased from the mid-1990s to the mid-2000s (SNCCP 2008), between 2005 and 2017, however, the number of rapes classified as assault rapes did not increase further—although there was a general increase in rapes overall (SNCCP 2019a). In addition to assault rapes, there has also been an increase in the number of gang rapes, defined as rape with several offenders, which increased both in the comparison of the mid-1990s to the mid-2000s as well as between 2005 and 2017 (SNCCP 2008, 2019a).

Hence, we do not know by how much actual rapes have increased, and how much of the trend reflects a higher reporting rate; yet, the increase in sex crimes in self-reported surveys along with more assault rapes being reported indicates that there has indeed been an actual increase. Furthermore, the SNCCP (2008) argue that since the increase in reported "nightlife-related rapes"—that is, those which are preceded by the victim and the perpetrator meeting in a nightlife venue such as a restaurant or a nightclub—coincides with both an increased range of nightlife activities (and later the rise of online dating), it probably also in part reflects an increase in actual rapes. The analyses by SNCCP (2019a) emphasized uncertainty, but similarly concluded that the increase in reported rapes may well reflect both rising reporting and a real increase.

There are major differences between groups when it comes to the likelihood of becoming the victim of a sex crime. The group of women who are most vulnerable to sex crimes is—interestingly enough—not those with Swedish background, but second-generation immigrants. One possible explanation for this is that second-generation immigrant women more often live in areas with high crime, and thereby find themselves living in a higher risk zone for sexual abuse. For both groups, the risk of victimization is higher among young women. The proportion exposed to sex crimes over time according to the Swedish Crime Survey 2019 is presented in Fig. 11.1 (SNCCP 2019b).

Among the general public, the risk of sexual abuse seems to be an important part of the fear of crime. From 2005, The Public Health Agency of Sweden has, through the National Public Health Survey, studied the share of the population who stated that they are afraid to go out alone. The

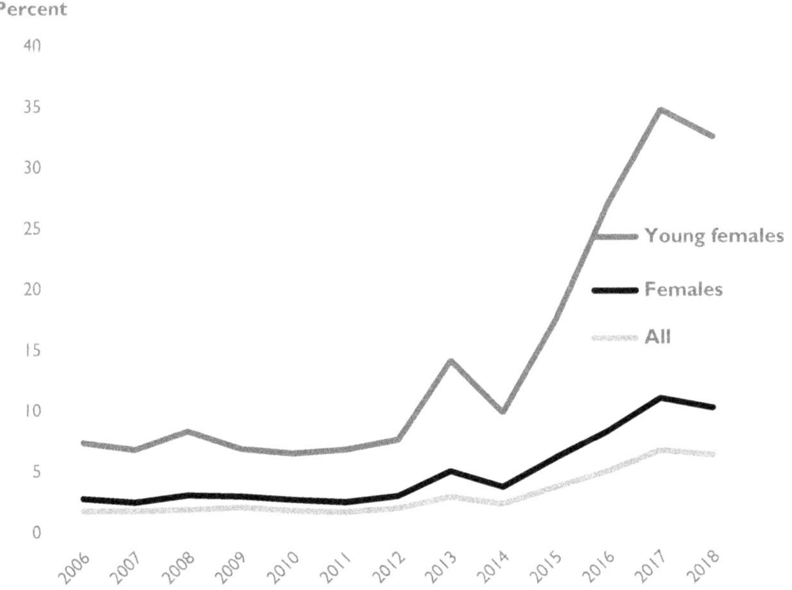

Fig. 11.1 Percentage of victims of sex crimes (2006–2018) (*Source* SNCCP)

proportion has increased in recent years, especially among women. In 2018, 12% of men and 44% of women in Sweden indicated they were afraid to go out alone. Unsafety has increased particularly among young women, of whom 58% in 2018 stated that they were afraid to go out alone. The pattern is similar to that for victims of sex crimes reported in the Swedish Crime Survey, in the sense that exposure is particularly high among young women. Figure 11.2 presents the proportion who are afraid to go out alone according to the National Public Health Survey.

The Swedish Crime Survey also shows an increase of unsafe sentiments and crime-avoidance behavior accompanying the rise of victimization. Of the respondents in the 2018 round, 43% report that they at some point during the year have chosen a different route or other means of transport as a result of being worried about crime—whereas 29% sometimes or often have abstained activities such as dining out, meeting others, or taking walks, in order to avoid crime. The rate of crime-avoidance behavior is higher among women than men and has increased over time. Likewise, 41% stated that their quality of life has been adversely impacted as a result of feeling unsafe.

The impact of the lack of safety on quality of life in the Swedish Crime Survey 2019 remained at the highest level recorded since the survey was launched. It is worth pointing out that the negative effect of safety on the quality of life was a bigger problem among respondents with a foreign origin. The concern for crime is not only a question of individual safety, as many report they do not expect to be victims of crime themselves, but rather fear for the safety of their family members or other members of society.

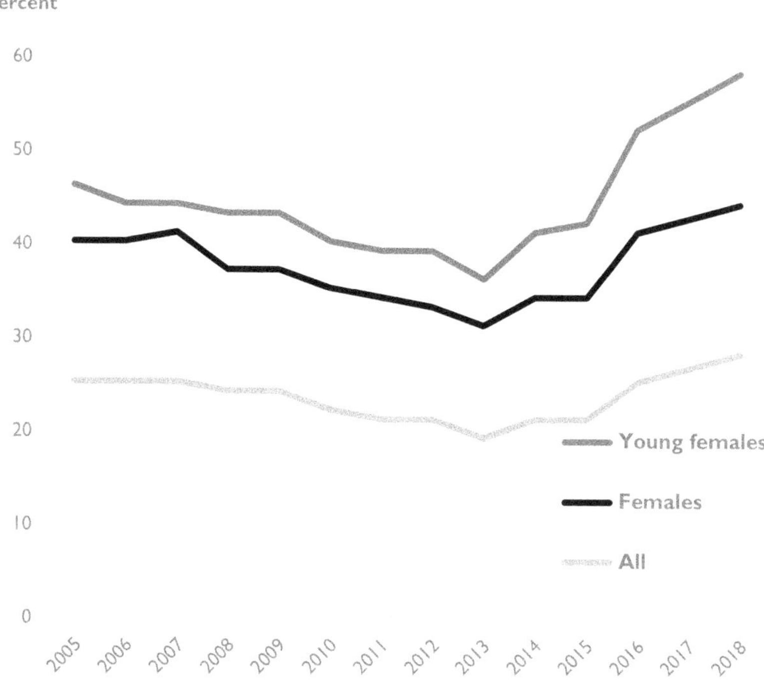

Fig. 11.2 Percentage afraid to go out alone (2005–2018) (*Source* Public Health Agency of Sweden)

Property Crime

While some types of crimes such as theft have fallen, others have risen. One of the areas where crime has risen rapidly in recent years is child robbery, where gangs of adolescents usually threaten or beat up other children and rob them of jackets, mobile phones, and other valuables. Often, the robbery is accompanied by acts of humiliation. One problem is that children do not dare to report the crime, for fear of being harassed further. Swedish Public Radio (2019) reports on the difficulties of victim protection, which are so severe that authorities themselves sometimes suggest to the victims not to report the crime, out of concerns for their well-being.

> Some officials, such as police and support persons employed by municipalities, discourage victims of crime from reporting to the police….
>
> "We have interviewed government officials and people who support victims and witnesses. Especially when it comes to relationship abuse and in socially vulnerable areas, some of them feel that it is difficult to recommend crime victims to go to the police. Because they doubt that the legal system has the ability to solve the crimes," says Johanna Skinnari, investigator at the authority. According to the SNCCP, this involves police and support persons, both employed by the municipalities and those who work in the nonprofit sector.

"They have somehow become hardened, they've experiences that it hasn't led to anything, and it can be very traumatic for individuals to participate in judicial processes. That is why they feel that it is very difficult to recommend it," says Johanna Skinnari.

Vimmerby is the hometown of the beloved Swedish children's author Astrid Lindgren, depicted in the books about Emil, and a symbolically interesting example of rising brutality of behavior among adolescents. The local daily *Dagens Vimmerby* (2018) describes violent sexual harassment against young girls:

> Two boys tormented two teenage girls for an hour. They groped them, threatened them with a knife, hit and kicked them—and threatened to kill them.
>
> "They pushed the girls up against a board fence and jabbed a knife right next to them," says the mother of one of the victims. The girls had just been at Body Gym & Relax for a workout and were on their way home. Behind ICA Supermarket, they were attacked by two boys.
>
> "Two guys started calling at them in a threatening manner. My daughter and her friend turned around and ran and hid in some bushes, but were of course found.... They took out a knife and pushed the girls up against a board fence and jabbed the knife around their heads.... They said that they would lie floating in blood and 'if you tell anything, we will kill you'."
>
> "They repeatedly jabbed at my daughter's stomach and they were really close, just some four inches away. My daughter was really afraid, and they also bit her neck."

Another brutal category of crime that have experienced an increase is home-invasions and crimes against the elderly—sometimes combined. In some instances, several elderly inhabitants have been targeted for violent home invasion, so that the police went out with warning to those living in isolated homes to be cautious (*Sydsvenskan* 2020).

Historical Homicide

Reported crimes is a measure that includes all types of crimes—from shoplifting to violent crime to homicide. Taking someone's life is the most severe type of crime, making homicide particularly important to study. In addition, homicide is a type of crime that rarely goes unreported, and, consequently, it can be used for reliable comparisons over time as well as between countries. Figure 11.3 shows the homicide rate in relation to the population of Sweden from 1754 to 2015. The data are based on a compilation by criminologist Hanns von Hofer (2011), with a moving average, and have here been updated until 2015 with data from the SNCCP (2016b).

Before continuing, it may be worth noting that Sweden and Finland have one of the world's most thorough historical data series on homicide. The statistics on homicide and manslaughter date back to 1754, when Sweden

Fig. 11.3 Homicide rate in Sweden per 100,00 inhabitants from 1754 (*Source* von Hofer 2011; SNCCP)

and Finland were parts of the same country. Sweden was the first country in the world with modern population statistics and is unique in having such a long and unbroken series of population statistics (Statistics Sweden 2000). In 1686, church law made it mandatory to keep church records of baptisms and funerals as well as of the residents in the congregation. In 1749, the predecessor to Statistics Sweden was established, with the task of compiling the church records for the entire country. From 1754, cause-of-death statistics are included, which can be used to estimate the number of homicides.

Looking at Fig. 11.3, we can observe that the trend in the homicide rate has gone up and down in different periods. These changes coincide with various technological and societal changes related to healthcare, drinking habits, reform of the justice system, and the proliferation of firearms. Homicide was at its lowest in the 1920s and 1940s. It gradually increased from the 1950s to about 1990. From the early 1990s to the early 2010s, the homicide rate in Sweden dropped, but this trend was broken in 2012. Between 2012 and 2018, the number of homicides increased from 68 to 108. In relation to the population, however, homicide is still lower than for Sweden's modern peak years of 1989–1991.

It is important to emphasize that these movements are part of powerful international trends in homicide rate, and thus should not be analyzed out of context. In most of the Western world, homicide rates increased from roughly 1960 to a peak in the late 1980s or early 1990s, after which they declined sharply. This general tendency is true for the United States, Canada, Australia, Japan, as well as virtually all European countries. Oberwittler (2019) outlines homicide trends in Europe and North America: "The rates first increased and then declined between ca. 1960 and today in most developed nations in a synchronized manner, hinting at common influences."

The causes for the historic variation in homicide rates are complex and not fully understood, both regarding the broad increase in the postwar era and the broad decline from the late 1980s. Some explanations are given in Steven Pinker's seminal book *The Better Angels of Our Nature: Why Violence Has Declined* (2011), including a civilizing process toward greater self-control and taboo against violence. A plethora of additional explanations have been put forward for the shifts—including age distribution, drug and alcohol consumption, policing, cultural change, and improvements in technology saving more victims of violence from death (e.g., Harris et al. 2002; Eisner 2003; Farrell et al. 2014; Eisner 2014; Lappi-Seppälä and Lehti 2014).

However, Oberwittler (2019) points out, "to the extent that improvements in the medical treatment of victims resulting in higher survival rates have an impact on this long-term trend, the decline in homicide rates would not necessary represent a decline in serious interpersonal violence." While the causes are debated, the trends for homicide victimization are clear, which means that the Swedish homicide victimization rates must be viewed in this context.

Compared to the other Nordic countries, the homicide rate per inhabitant in Sweden is below that of Finland but above those in Denmark, Norway, and Iceland. Historically, Finland has been notable for having a high number of homicides per inhabitant, although the country has converged to levels closer to that of Sweden. In 2018, based on criminal statistics, 108 cases of homicide were registered in Sweden, compared to 58 in Finland, 51 in Denmark, and 25 in Norway. The figures based on healthcare cause-of-death registers are similar, if not identical—for instance, 102 in Sweden, 68 in Finland, 29 in Denmark, and 23 in Norway for the same year. In both cases, preliminary homicide figures are subject to some revaluations, for instance, if later cases of murder are discovered.

Per 100,000 inhabitants, the figures based on criminal statistics correspond to 1.1 in Sweden, 1.1 in Finland, 0.9 in Denmark, and 0.5 in Norway. The average of the past three or five years is nearly identical. The Swedish figures have now been evaluated for several years in a row, which suggests that the increase is not merely an outcome of random chance and yearly fluctuation, which may influence homicide figures in small countries.

Comparing the latest five-year period to the first half of the 1990s, we can see that the Swedish homicide rate has fallen, by roughly 15% adjusted for the population. But during the same period, the homicide rate per inhabitant fell by almost 30% in Denmark, 50% in Norway, and 60% in Finland. For the average of Western Europe, based on WHO's figures, the homicide rate fell by more than 50%. Similarly, the American homicide rate fell by 45% during this period—from 9.1 per 100,000 inhabitants in the first five years of the 1990s to 5.1 in the average for the last five years, up to and including 2018.

Again, estimating the homicide rate can be complicated by definitional differences, misclassification, and other measurement problems. A study by Thomsen et al. (2019) carefully examined the data in Denmark between 1992 and 2016, finding a decline of the population-adjusted homicide rate close to 40% in this particular period. Based on these figures, in the early 1990s, the rate of homicide in Denmark was somewhat above that of Sweden, but is today slightly below the Swedish.

Figure 11.4 shows the development of homicide rate per 100,000 inhabitants since 1970 in Sweden, the EU, and the EU-15—that is, the 15 Western European Union countries (SNCCP 2016b; WHO Mortality Data Base). The rate of homicide has decreased both in Sweden and in the EU since the late 1980s and early 1990s, but—as explicated above—fell less in Sweden than in the rest of the EU.

The homicide rate has thus fallen across virtually all Western countries during the past decades, but where Sweden stands out is that killings have long-term fallen less than in most other countries, once trends reversed—to a large extent driven by gang shootings. It is common for biased accounts to portray the debate on rising Swedish violence as a myth, by only pointing out the long-term decrease in Sweden. Once we put this minor decrease into a broader framework of a sharp and systematic decline in homicides rate in all other Western countries, it becomes clear why the Swedish situation raises concerns. It is deceptive to celebrate a 15% decline in the homicide rate without pointing out that the homicide rate fell by 40 to 60% in comparable countries during the same period, in part due to common social and technological trends. Likely, what has happened is that Sweden benefited from the same fundamental causes that led to fewer homicides in the rest of the West, but at the same time experiences other countervailing forces in the opposite direction.

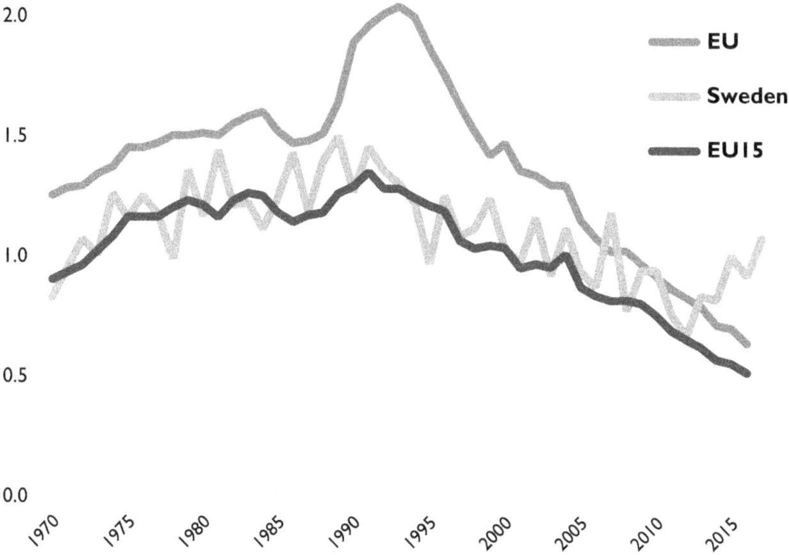

Fig. 11.4 Homicide rate per 100,000 inhabitants since 1970 (*Source* WHO)

SNCCP (2015a) analyzes all of the cases of homicide reported by the police, along with those for manslaughter and assault with lethal outcome, in the period 1990–2014, using data both from the judiciary and the National Board of Health and Welfare's healthcare records. Fatalities legally classified as self-defense or as a result of the legal carrying out of official duties are not defined as homicide. The conclusion was that the rate of homicide has decreased in Sweden since the 1990s. An important explanation is related to a change in alcohol consumption, lower tolerance toward violence, and changed habits among the young. Other potential explanations include a more advanced security industry and improvements in technology that saves more lives. At the same time, the rate of homicide related to gang crime has increased, particularly in areas of social exclusion in urban cities.

There is a striking concentration of homicide to the areas of social exclusion. The SNCCP report divides fatal violence between areas of social exclusion and the rest of the country for the period 2011–2013. According to this division, 270,000 of the just over five million residents of the metropolitan areas lived in one of these areas of social exclusion, which corresponds to approximately 5% of the population of the metropolitan areas. In spite of this, 40% of lethal firearms violence in metropolitan areas occurred in these areas of social exclusion. While firearms violence has increased, there have also—as previously mentioned—been changes in the types of firearm used. Fewer homicides are perpetrated with legal weapons, such as hunting rifles, while homicides committed with illegal smuggled weapons have increased (SNCCP 2015a).

Shootings

Another report from the SNCCP (2015b) studies shootings more generally, between 2006 and 2014. It should be noted that Sweden does not keep any systematic statistics on shootings, and that the analysis of the SNCCP is based on estimates derived from police data:

> According to the report, a total of 365 confirmed or probable shootings occurred in 2014. This corresponds to 3.7 shootings per 100,000 inhabitants. The corresponding number for 2006 is 306 shootings, which corresponds to 3.4 shootings per 100,000 inhabitants.

Medical records also indicate that the number of shootings has increased, albeit more strongly so. The Swedish medical records are valuable for estimating gun-wounds, since most victims who are treated by the emergency healthcare system are included. However, this data source is not useful for measuring the general level of violence, including less serious cases, since the health records only include parts of the medical system but excludes, for instance, primary care. The number of people receiving treatment for gunshot wounds has increased dramatically. Figure 11.5 shows the number of people

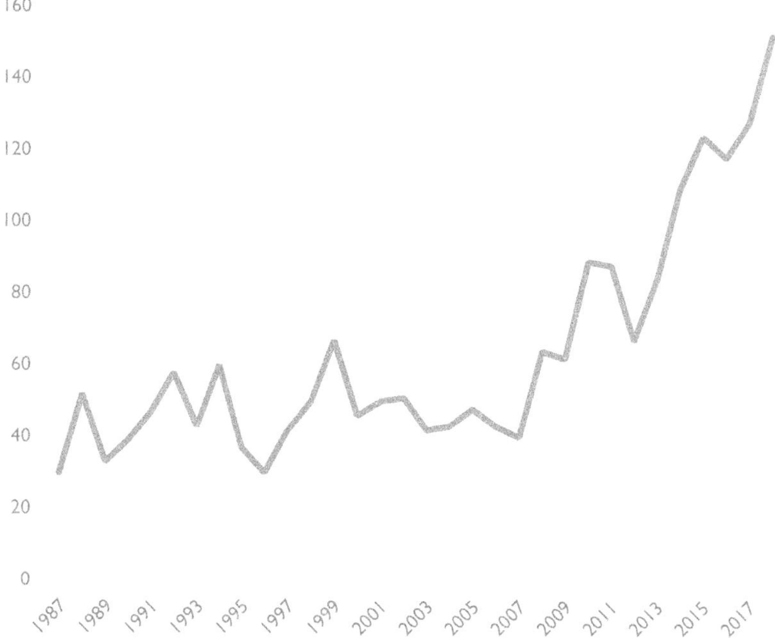

Fig. 11.5 People treated in hospital for gunshot wounds (1987–2018) (*Source* Swedish National Board of Health and Welfare)

admitted to hospital for gunshot wounds since 1987. In addition to those hospitalized, there are annually a number of people with less serious gunshot wounds, who are treated directly by paramedics or in a primary care setting.

The report splits shootings between areas of social exclusion and the rest of Sweden. Areas of social exclusion are defined in the same way as in the report on homicide mentioned above. However, an important difference between these two reports is that the comparison for shootings looks at the whole country and not just the metropolitan areas. Another difference is, of course, that it also includes shootings where no one died, while the previous analysis concerns violence resulting in fatalities. SNCCP shows that in 2005, it was about five times as common with shootings in areas of social exclusion as in the rest of the country. As shown in Table 11.1, the entire increase in shootings in Sweden between 2006 and 2014 can be attributed to areas of social exclusion—despite the fact that people living in these areas only represent 4% of the population (SNCCP 2015b). In total, the number of shootings per inhabitant in Sweden increased by 12%. A striking result from the report is that the number of shootings increased by 163% in the areas of social exclusion, but fell by 3% in the rest of the country.

Swedish police has compiled data on lethal shootings in criminal contexts, reported by the media outlets (e.g., Sydsvenskan 2016; Swedish Public

Table 11.1 Number of shootings in areas of social exclusion and the rest of the country (2006 and 2014)

	2006		*2014*	
	No.	*Per 100,00*	*No.*	*Per 100,00*
Shootings in areas of social exclusion	19	6.0	56	15.8
Shootings in the rest of the country	286	3.3	296	3.2
Crime scene coordinates unavailable	1		13	
Total shootings nationwide	306	3.4	365	3.7

Source SNCCP

Television 2018). Between 1990 and 1994, the average number of these shootings was 4 per year—already an increase compares to past figures. This figure gradually increased to 7 per year in 1995–1999, 8 per year in 2000–2004, 9 per year in 2005–2009, and 14 per year in 2010–2014. Similar numbers for 1990–2013 have also been reported by Granath and Sturup (2018). The number of lethal shooting tied to criminal conflicts further escalated to 28 in 2015–2016, and to 37 in 2017. In 2018, 45 individuals were killed in shootings, although this figure includes a handful of shootings not tied to criminal contexts. Since the early 1990s, the number of lethal criminal shootings in Sweden increased by an order of magnitude, a stunning trend that demands an explanation. The increase in total gun homicides, including those outside of gang environment, was somewhat less.

In 2019, SNCCP created an updated version of the geographic distribution for the period 2014–2017, using a slightly different definition of vulnerable areas based on the police classification. Also using this definition, the disparity in crime rates is readily observed, as the homicide rate is over three times higher in these areas than in the rest of the country—3.1 per 100,000 inhabitants compared to 0.9 for the rest of the country. The report states that the share of homicides in these areas increased from 9% of the national total in the period 2005–2008 to 17% during 2014–2017 (SNCCP 2019c).

A recent review by Khosnood (2018) on the scientific literature on firearm-related violence in Sweden confirmed the above impression: "firearm-related violence is significantly increasing in the country and foremost when discussing gang-related crimes." Comparisons with other Western European countries also show that Sweden stands out. A study by Sturup et al. (2018) found that:

> In a comparative perspective the rate of gun homicide victimization among males 15 to 29 years was higher in Sweden compared to other Western European countries, while the risk for males over age 30 was at an average level. Based on the results of this study we conclude that gun violence among young males in Sweden has been on the rise and is at a high level compared to other Western European countries. The development of gun violence in Sweden can be characterized as endemic, prevalent in both population and socially vulnerable areas.

And one of the authors of the study, Joakim Sturup, was quoted in Swedish Public Radio (2017):

> In relation to population size, there are between four and five times as many deadly shootings in Sweden as in Norway and Germany …
>
> "When we speak to police or researcher colleagues abroad, it is hard to find counterparts in other countries," he says.

What stands out with Swedish crime is not only the number of incidents, but the intensity and heavy armament used. While statistics only started to be compiled from 2018, in 2019 there were 257 reported attacks using explosives, both including hand grenades and bombings of buildings by criminals. *Dagens Nyheter* (2019) cites researchers who estimate that Sweden has the highest number of explosions in Western Europe.

> "Attacks with explosives are unparalleled in Europe, perhaps in the world," according to criminologist Amir Rostami. The wave of explosions makes Sweden unique among prosperous peacetime countries in Europe, perhaps in the world. It is not possible to make any certain comparisons with other Western European countries, because outside Sweden, explosions are so rare that the statistics are rarely compiled.
>
> "I have been in contact with countless police agencies in both Europe and North America, and no one has seen anything like what we are experiencing in Sweden.… Sadly, we have to look to war zones, or countries with a long history of terrorism, to find an equivalent."

The particular way in which violence has developed among criminal gangs in Sweden has in fact aroused great interest abroad. Police and researchers visit to see if they can learn something. They want to prevent anything similar from happening in their countries. Rick Fuentes, former superintendent of the New Jersey State Police, currently at Rutgers University, cooperates with the Stockholm police to reduce the number of shootings. In *Svenska Dagbladet* (2019), he provides the following remarks: "I was baffled by the use of grenades in Sweden. I'll be honest with you. I've worked in the police for 40 years and I have never heard or seen anything like it."

Criminal Behavior

Interestingly, two well-cited studies of crime and causality in recent years were performed in Sweden by researchers at the Karolinska Institute. Sariaslan et al. (2013) study the connection between crime and residential area, whereas Sariaslan et al. (2014) examine the link between crime and family income. A striking finding is that the relationship between socioeconomic factors and crime does not involve direct causation, where poverty leads to higher crime, but deeper family-related factors. Other studies have reached similar conclusions, even if the two Swedish studies are exceptionally well-made.

Sariaslan et al. (2014), for example, is the world's most comprehensive individual-based study on the relationship between income and crime, in terms of the size of the surveyed population. The study included the total population born in Sweden from 1989 to 1993—over half a million individuals. Sariaslan et al.'s study (2013) is similarly extensive and includes about 300,000 children born in Sweden, who were followed during several years. Both studies take advantage of Sweden's unusually detailed social and demographic data, which is considered to belong to the best in the world for research purposes.

Sariaslan et al. (2014) examine the relationship between income and socioeconomic status and crime—one of the most important and controversial issues when it comes to crime. Low-income earners have significantly higher crime risk than high-income earners. In the public debate, this is often interpreted as crime being caused by low income or by other socioeconomic problems. Establishing a causal relationship is, however, far from obvious in research. The causal link between violence and socioeconomics in modern studies that take causality into account is far weaker than what many imagine. The complexity of the problem is not only evident in modern individual-based studies, but also in the trend over time. For example, the rate of homicide in Sweden was at its lowest during the period 1920–1950, when Sweden was much poorer than today.

It is clear that there is a strong correlation between the crime risk of individuals and socioeconomic problems, but not what the relationship depends on. In discussing such an important and controversial topic, it is important to make the distinction between correlation and causality. The fact that violent crime and low income are highly correlated does not prove that low income leads to more violent crimes. It may, for instance, at least in part, be the other way around that it is criminal behavior which leads to problems in the job market. If this is the case, we talk about reverse causality. An even more important underlying explanation is likely to be that individual and familial characteristics, which increase the likelihood of crime, at the same time tend to increase the risk of worse performance outcomes in education and in the job market. The absence of support at home, poor upbringing, drug problems, and poor education are all examples of factors that increase the risk of criminal behavior and of socioeconomic problems simultaneously.

Sariaslan et al. (2014) is a study that convincingly demonstrates that the link between crime and socioeconomic issues are due to factors that run deeper than low income simply leading to crime. While it was found that the difference in how likely it was that children from the families with the lowest and the highest incomes were convicted of violent crimes was seven times, these differences largely disappeared after controlling for family effects. This was done by comparing relatives of different degrees of relatedness, who grew up under different economic circumstances, and it turned out that close relatives had similar risks regardless of them being poor or not. The authors conclude that: "There were no associations between childhood family income and subsequent violent criminality and substance misuse once we had adjusted for unobserved familial risk factors." They also point out that many other studies and research reviews have arrived at similar conclusions, namely that the correlation between socioeconomic problems and violent crime is complex and not necessarily causal (Sariaslan et al. 2014): "Our finding that the associations between childhood family income and adolescent violent criminality and substance misuse are unlikely to be causal has been suggested in prior systematic reviews on SES and criminality."

A study by Cambridge researchers Wikström and Treiber (2016) discusses the difficulty of untangling the causal link between crime and socioeconomic background. The authors write:

> It is difficult to imagine any criminological topic that is more debated but less scientifically understood than the extent and nature of the relationship between social disadvantage and crime (e.g., Katz, 1988; Sampson, 2000, 2012; Tittle & Meier, 1990). While research findings generally suggest that social disadvantage (typically in reference to families and neighborhoods) is somehow implicated in crime causation, there is far from a simple one-to-one relationship, and researchers avidly disagree about the strength and nature of this relationship, with some even questioning whether there is a relationship at all.

A paradox discussed in the study is that most offenders have low socioeconomic background, while the vast majority of those with low socioeconomic background do not commit crimes. The correlation between socioeconomic background and crime is relatively low at the individual level. The majority of the most criminally active individuals had low socioeconomic status, while 93% of those with low socioeconomic status were not charged with crimes.

That the relationship at the individual level is weak is in itself not a paradox. Regardless of social background, most people do not commit crimes. At the individual level, most of the variation is driven by immeasurable individual factors, chance, annual variation, and what is technically referred to as classical measurement error. When societal groups are aggregated to enable comparison of groups instead of individuals, these immeasurable individual factors are evened out, so that the link between crime and social background become much stronger at the group level. For crime, as well as many other outcomes, weak explanatory value at the individual level does not stand in opposition to strong structural explanations at the societal level.

Wikström and Treiber's explanatory model is called *situational action theory*, where individual risk factors are combined with environmental risk factors. Simplified, the theory is that crime is a deliberate choice to break society's rules. This is more likely when the checks from the social environment are weak and where there is motivation for crime. Crime is committed when two factors coincide. The first one is "crime propensity"—personal criminal inclination in terms of morality and self-control. The second is the degree of "criminogenic exposure" from the surrounding community—that is to say, whether the surroundings encourage crime or prevent crime by exerting social control. Wikström and Treiber suggest that lower socioeconomic status does not lead to crime in itself, but that it increases the likelihood of developing criminally inclined personal characteristics and ending up in a crime-promoting environment:

> Specifically, we propose social and self-selection processes lead to young people from disadvantaged backgrounds being more profoundly exposed to (a) settings and circumstances which lead them to develop and sustain a high crime propensity (weak personal morality and a lack of ability to exercise self-control) and (b) moral contexts that are conducive to engagement in acts of crime (i.e., those in which rules of law are loosely applied and/or weakly enforced).

Personality traits that increase the risk for crime include reduced self-control, lower future-orientation, and whether a person easily loses their temper. Among other things, the effects of the surroundings are measured by examining the criminality of friends and parental control. The conclusion is that criminally inclined personal characteristics and crime-promoting environments are much more strongly linked to criminality than socioeconomic background. The authors conclude: "Our overall conclusion is that social disadvantage is only moderately related to factors related to crime involvement (crime propensity and criminogenic exposure)."

In wealthy nations, even low-income people are not so poor that they must commit crimes to survive. Low-income earners in Sweden are significantly wealthier than the middle class was in the 1950s, when crime rates were much lower. In addition to that, for many crimes—such as rape or vandalism—there is no economic motive whatsoever.

It is clear that crime and poverty are linked to each other, but it is far from obvious that it is low income that causes crime. It is more likely that the same individual underlying factors that lead to problems in the job market simultaneously increase the risk of crime. Examples of these individual factors are low education, lower degree of future-orientation, poor self-control, impulsivity, insufficient social control exerted by the surroundings, weaker work ethic, a lack of standards regarding good character, macho culture, drug and alcohol abuse, antisocial values, and a criminal subculture in which violent criminals have status. These factors are all components of low human and social capital, both of which tend to be transmitted within families and social groups. Individuals and groups with lower human and social capital tend to be both poorer and more likely to commit crimes. In this case, socioeconomic problems and crime are both outcome variables caused by more profound latent factors—not an explanation of crime in itself.

An example of an important individual factor is future-orientation; the psychological tendency to value the future instead of the present. Impulsive people with weaker self-control, who discount the future more compared to the present, are more likely to commit crimes. At the same time, short-term time preferences adversely affect education, work, savings, and other economic outcomes. Åkerlund et al. (2016) show that psychological time preferences among youth at the age of 13 in Sweden are an important explanatory factor for crimes later in life. Short-term time preferences are influenced by upbringing, social environment, norms and culture, and is one reason why crime correlates with other negative life outcomes.

There is a strong correlation between unemployment and crime—not because the unemployed in Sweden are forced to steal bread to feed their children, but because the same qualities and behavior that increase the risk of unemployment also increase the risk of crime. This may explain paradoxes such as why the link between residential areas with high unemployment and crime is strong, while crime is only slightly impacted when unemployment drops during economic booms. However, it is possible that socioeconomic problems amplify the likelihood of crime by creating resentment against society, and that financial problems thereby enhance antisocial values. Rostami (2013) writes about the link between low incomes and gang formation, and concludes that the link is not that strong, but that "It is, in my opinion, rather a consequence of the implications of social exclusion. It is not only about economic exclusion, but also about cultural, ethnic and normative exclusion."

Similar to Sariaslan and co-authors, Eriksson et al. (2016) examine explanations for criminal behavior in Sweden by comparing siblings. There are similarities in the crime risk of siblings, which suggest that common family factors partly explain criminality. By comparing siblings, one can more causally examine which factors are most important for family effects. Conditions that the child receives through family, and that reappear at the family level, include parents' income and education, residential area, culture, religion and values, whether the child has a single mother, and whether the parents themselves are criminally active.

The comparison shows that factors such as residential area and parental income explain a relatively small proportion of the systematic variation in crime. On the other hand, children of parents with criminal records had higher crime risk themselves. Family structure while growing up also turns out to be important, so that children with single parents or teenage mothers tend to have higher risk for crime and other social problems. Parents' criminal background and family structure explain more of the systematic similarities of crime than household income and education level: "These results suggest that both parental criminality and family structure are relatively more important in explaining sibling correlations in crime than parental education and income" (Eriksson et al. 2016).

These results strengthen the idea that income is not an important direct explanation for crime, as well as that there are deeper and more complex connections between crime and socioeconomic status—which will be demonstrated more clearly in the following chapters.

References

Åkerlund, David, Bart H. H. Golsteyn, Hans Grönqvist, and Lena Lindahl. 2016. "Time Discounting and Criminal Behavior." *Proceedings of the National Academy of Sciences* 113, no. 22: 6160–65. https://doi.org/10.1073/pnas.1522445113.

Dagens Nyheter. 2019. "Kriminolog: Sprängdåden i Sverige unika för Europa" [Criminologist: The Explosions in Sweden Unique to Europe]. November 3, 2019. https://www.dn.se/nyheter/sverige/kriminolog-sprangdaden-i-sverige-unika-for-europa.

Dagens Vimmerby. 2018. "Drama i en timme – hotade att döda tonårstjejerna" [Drama for an Hour—Threatened to Kill the Teenage Girls]. By Jakob Karlsson, May 17, 2018. https://www.dagensvimmerby.se/nyheter/e/21708/drama-i-en-timme-hotade-att-doda-tonarstjejerna.

Eisner, Manuel. 2003. "Long-Term Historical Trends in Violent Crime." *Crime and Justice* 30: 83–142. https://doi.org/10.1086/652229.

———. 2014. "From Swords to Words: Does Macro-Level Change in Self-Control Predict Long-Term Variation in Levels of Homicide?" *Crime and Justice* 43, no. 1: 65–134. https://doi.org/10.1086/677662.

Eriksson, Karin Hederos, Randi Hjalmarsson, Matthew J. Lindquist, and Anna Sandberg. 2016. "The Importance of Family Background and Neighborhood Effects as Determinants of Crime." *Journal of Population Economics* 29, no. 1: 219–62. https://doi.org/10.1007/s00148-015-0566-8.

Falk, Örjan, Märta Wallinius, Sebastian Lundström, Thomas Frisell, Henrik Anckarsäter, and Nóra Kerekes. 2014. "The 1% of the Population Accountable for 63% of All Violent Crime Convictions." *Social Psychiatry and Psychiatric Epidemiology* 49, no. 4: 559–71. https://doi.org/10.1007/s00127-013-0783-y.

Farrell, Graham, Nick Tilley, and Andromachi Tseloni. 2014. "Why the Crime Drop?" *Crime and Justice* 43, no. 1: 421–90. https://doi.org/10.1086/678081.

Granath, Sven, and Joakim Sturup. 2018. "Homicide Clearance in Sweden 1990–2013 with Special Reference to Firearm-Perpetrated Homicides." *Journal of Scandinavian Studies in Criminology and Crime Prevention* 19, no. 1: 98–112. https://doi.org/10.1080/14043858.2018.1449412.

Harris, Anthony R., Stephen H. Thomas, Gene A. Fisher, and David J. Hirsch. 2002. "Murder and Medicine: The Lethality of Criminal Assault 1960–1999." *Homicide Studies* 6, no. 2: 128–66. https://doi.org/10.1177/108876790200600203.

Khosnood, Ardavan. 2018. "Firearm-Related Violence in Sweden—A Systematic Review." *Aggression and Violent Behavior* 42: 43–51. https://doi.org/10.1016/j.avb.2018.07.008.

Lappi-Seppälä, Tapio, and Martti Lehti. 2014. "Cross-Comparative Perspectives on Global Homicide Trends." *Crime and Justice* 43, no. 1: 135–230. https://doi.org/10.1086/677979.

Oberwittler, Dietrich. 2019. "Lethal Violence: A Global View on Homicide." In *Oxford Research Encyclopedia of Criminology and Criminal Justice*. https://doi.org/10.1093/acrefore/9780190264079.013.402.

Pinker, Steven. 2011. *The Better Angels of Our Nature: Why Violence Has Declined*. New York: Viking.

Rostami, Amir. 2013. "Tusen fiender – en studie om de svenska gatugängen och dess ledare" [A Thousand Enemies—A Study of the Swedish Street Gang and Its Leaders]. Edited by Rolf Granér and Elisabet Hellgren. Linnæus University studies in policing, nr. 001, 2013, Polisutbildningen, Linnéuniversitetet, Växjö. http://lnu.diva-portal.org/smash/get/diva2:712083/FULLTEXT01.pdf.

Sariaslan, Amir, Niklas Långström, Brian D'Onofrio, Johan Hallqvist, Johan Franck, and Paul Lichtenstein. 2013. "The Impact of Neighbourhood Deprivation on Adolescent Violent Criminality and Substance Misuse: A Longitudinal, Quasi-Experimental Study of the total Swedish Population." *International Journal of Epidemiology* 42, no. 4: 1057–66. https://doi.org/10.1093/ije/dyt066.

Sariaslan, Amir, Henrik Larsson, Brian D'Onofrio, Niklas Långström, and Paul Lichtenstein. 2014. "Childhood Family Income, Adolescent Violent Criminality and Substance Misuse: Quasi-Experimental Total Population Study." *The British Journal of Psychiatry* 205, no. 4: 286–90. https://doi.org/10.1192/bjp.bp.113.136200.

SNCCP. 2008. "Våldtäkt mot personer 15 år och äldre: Utvecklingen under åren 1995–2006" [Rape Against Persons 15 Years and Older: Developments in the Years 1995–2006]. By Klara Hradilova Selin, Swedish National Council for Crime Prevention. Rapport 2008:13, Brottsförebyggande rådet (Brå), Stockholm. https://www.bra.se/download/18.cba82f7130f475a2f180008010/1371914724593/2008_13_valdtakt_mot_personer_over_15_ar.pdf.

———. 2015a. "Det dödliga våldet i Sverige 1990–2014: En beskrivning av utvecklingen med särskilt fokus på skjutvapenvåldet" [Homicide in Sweden 1990–2014: A Description of the Development with a Special Focus on Firearm Violence]. By Sven Granath, Swedish National Council for Crime Prevention. Rapport 2015:24, Brottsförebyggande rådet (Brå), Stockholm. https://www.bra.se/download/18.31d7fffa1504bbffea086b7a/1449670735846/2015_24_Det%20dödliga%20våldet.pdf.

———. 2015b. "Skjutningar 2006 och 2014 – omfattning, spridning och skador" [Shootings 2006 and 2014—Extent, Spread, and Damage]. By Jonas Öberg, Swedish National Council for Crime Prevention. Kortanalys 7/2015, Brottsförebyggande rådet (Brå), Stockholm. https://www.bra.se/download/18.31d7fffa1504bbffea044822/1447769941578/2015_Skjutningar%202006%20och%202014.pdf.

———. 2016a. "Nationella trygghetsundersökningen 2015: Om utsatthet, otrygghet och förtroende" [The Swedish Crime Survey 2015: On Vulnerability, Insecurity, and Trust]. By Thomas Hvitfeldt, Sara Westerberg, Åsa Irlander Strid, Anna Frenzel, and Sahar Ashir, Swedish National Council for Crime Prevention. Rapport 2016:1, Brottsförebyggande rådet (Brå), Stockholm. https://www.bra.se/download/18.47fa372d1520dfb2fc51c5e2/1452520810398/2016_1_NTU_2015.pdf.

———. 2016b. "Konstaterade fall av dödligt våld – en genomgång av anmält dödligt våld 2015" [Confirmed Cases of Homicide—A Review of Reported Homicide in 2015]. By Nina Forselius, Swedish National Council for Crime Prevention. URN:NBN:SE:BRA-659, Brottsförebyggande rådet (Brå), Stockholm. https://www.bra.se/download/18.358de3051533ffea5ea7eaf8/1462804743722/2016_Dödligtvåld_2015.pdf.

———. 2019a. "Indikatorer på sexualbrottsutvecklingen 2005–2017" [Indicators of the Development of Sex Crimes 2005–2017]. By Swedish National Council for Crime Prevention. Rapport 2019:5, Brottsförebyggande rådet (Brå), Stockholm. https://www.bra.se/download/18.62c6cfa2166eca5d70e1919f/1565079287510/2019_5_Indikatorer_%20pa_sexualbrottsutvecklingen_2005_2017.pdf.

———. 2019b. "Nationella trygghetsundersökningen 2019: Om utsatthet, otrygghet och förtroende" [The Swedish Crime Survey 2019: On Vulnerability, Insecurity, and Trust]. By Maria Molin, Sofie Lifvin, and Åsa Irlander Strid, Swedish National Council for Crime Prevention. Rapport 2019:11, Brottsförebyggande rådet (Brå), Stockholm. https://www.bra.se/download/18.62c6cfa2166eca5d70ec536d/1570520930995/2019_11_Nationella_trygghetsundersokningen_2019.pdf.

———. 2019c. "Dödligt våld i Sverige 1990–2017: Omfattning, utveckling och karaktär" [Deadly Violence in Sweden 1990–2017: Extent, Development, and Character]. By Jonas Öberg and Klara Hradilova Selin, Swedish National Council for Crime Prevention. Rapport 2019:6, Brottsförebyggande rådet (Brå), Stockholm. https://www.bra.se/download/18.62c6cfa2166eca5d70e1dc50/1560341522859/2019_6_Dodligt_vald_i_Sverige_1990_2017.pdf.

Statistics Sweden. 2000. "Befolkningsstatistik 1999. Del 3: Folkmängen efter kön, ålder och medborgarskap m m" [Population Statistics 1999. Part 3: Distribution by Sex, Age, and Citizenship, etc.]. Programmet för Befolkningsstatistik, Statistiska centralbyrån (SCB), Örebro. http://share.scb.se/ov9993/data/historisk%20statistik//SOS%201911-/Befolkningsstatistik/Befolkningsstatistik%20Del%203%20Folkmängden%20efter%20kön%20ålder%20medborgarskap%20(SOS)%201991-2001/Befolkningsstatistik-1999-3-Folkmangden-kon-alder-medborgarskap.pdf.

———. 2019. "Fler upplever brottslighet och vandalisering i sitt bostadsområde" [More People Experience Crime and Vandalism in Their Neighborhood]. By Philip Andö, Short analysis, April 25, 2019. Statistiska centralbyrån (SCB), Stockholm. https://www.scb.se/hitta-statistik/artiklar/2019/fler-upplever-brottslighet-och-vandalisering-i-sitt-bostadsomrade.

Sturup, Joakim, Amir Rostami, Hernan Mondani, Manne Gerell, Jerzy Sarnecki, and Christofer Edling. 2018. "Increased Gun Violence Among Young Males in Sweden: A Descriptive National Survey and International Comparison." *European Journal of Criminal Policy and Research* 25: 365–78. https://doi.org/10.1007/s10610-018-9387-0.

Svenska Dagbladet. 2019. "USA-polis om granaterna: 'Aldrig sett nåt liknande'" [U.S. Police on the Grenades: "Never Seen Anything Like It"]. By Adrian Sadikovic, September 17, 2019. https://www.svd.se/usa-polis-om-vapenvaldet-aldrig-sett-nat-liknande.

Swedish Public Radio. 2017. "Fler skjutningar i Sverige än i många andra länder" [More shootings in Sweden Than in Many Other Countries]. By Daniel Persson, *P4 Stockholm*, September 5, 2017. https://sverigesradio.se/sida/artikel.aspx?programid=103&artikel=6770056.

———. 2019. "Brå: Myndighetspersoner avråder brottsoffer att anmäla" [SNCCP: Officials at Government Agencies Discourage Victims of Crime from Reporting]. By Simon Andrén, *Ekot*, October 2, 2019. https://sverigesradio.se/sida/artikel.aspx?programid=83&artikel=7313223.

Swedish Public Television. 2018. "Siffrorna visar: Kraftig ökning av dödsskjutningar" [The Figures Show: Strong Increase in Fatal Shootings]. By Marit Sundberg, *SVT Nyheter*, January 20, 2018. https://www.svt.se/nyheter/inrikes/siffrorna-visar-kraftig-okning-av-dodsskjutningar.

Sydsvenskan. 2016. "Dödliga uppgörelser eskalerar" [Deadly Settlements Escalate]. By TT, November 12, 2016. https://www.sydsvenskan.se/2016-11-12/dodliga-uppgorelser-eskalerar.

———. 2020. "Man misshandlad och rånad – polisen varnar boende på avsides belägna gårdar" [Man Beaten and Robbed—The Police Warns Residents of Remote Farms]. By My Östh Gustafsson, January 22, 2020. https://www.sydsvenskan.se/2020-01-22/man-misshandlad-och-ranad-polisen-varnar-boende-pa-avsides.

Thomsen, Asser H., Hans Petter Hougen, Palle Villesen, Ole Brink, and Peter M. Leth. 2019. "Homicide in Denmark 1992–2016." *Journal of Forensic Sciences*, November 20, 2019. https://doi.org/10.1111/1556-4029.14244.

von Hofer, Hanns. 2011. "Brott och straff i Sverige: Historisk kriminalstatistik 1750–2010. Diagram, tabeller och kommentarer" [Crime and Punishment in Sweden: Historical Crime Statistics 1750–2010. Charts, Tables, and Comments]. 4th rev. ed. Edited by Felipe Estrada. Rapport 2011:3, Kriminologiska institutionens rapportserie, Stockholms universitet, Stockholm. http://www.criminology.su.se/polopoly_fs/1.88252.1337171877!/menu/standard/file/2011_Brott-o-Straff.pdf.

Wikström, Per-Olof H., and Kyle Treiber. 2016. "Social Disadvantage and Crime: A Criminological Puzzle." *American Behavioral Scientist* 60, no. 10: 1232–59. https://doi.org/10.1177/0002764216643134.

CHAPTER 12

Immigration and Crime

> Crime is common. Logic is rare. Therefore it is upon the logic rather than upon the crime that you should dwell.
>
> —Arthur Conan Doyle, *The Adventures of Sherlock Holmes*, 1892

In recent years, immigrant crime in Sweden has been a hotly debated issue, even reaching the level of international news. The phenomenon invokes strong opinions and emotions, and many contradictory statements have confidently been made—even about basic facts such as the levels of crime or whether immigrants are overrepresented or not. This has caused the issue to appear intricate and shrouded in secrets, something that is both unnecessary and unfortunate as there actually is extensive research on immigrants' overrepresentation in crime. However, since historically immigration to Sweden was small and the source material is limited, there are not many relevant studies older than a couple of decades, and thus the scope for historical comparisons is limited. A few studies have, given the data that exist, reviewed immigrants' historical share in specific types of crime such as homicide in Stockholm (Sveri 1973, 1980; Wikström 1992; Kaspersson 2000).

The Swedish National Council for Crime Prevention (SNCCP) has published two high-profile reports on immigrant crime in Sweden: *Criminality of Immigrants and Immigrants' Children—A Statistical Analysis* (1996); and *Violence among Individuals Born in Sweden and Abroad* (2005). These reports compare registered crime across groups, based on country of birth and the parents' background, for the years 1985–1989 and 1997–2001, and find that foreigners have higher rates of registered crime than people with Swedish backgrounds.

Note that the figures use a broad definition of foreign background, including those with one foreign-born parent, and that they focus on age groups (such as 15–44), who commit most crime, rather than the entire population. The figure for crime registration is mostly based on suspects,

T. Sanandaji, *Mass Challenge*,
https://doi.org/10.1007/978-3-030-46808-8_12

but comparisons show that the relative numbers at the group level are near-identical for those convicted for crime. Therefore, SNCCP's cumbersome term "registration as suspects for crime" will be used interchangeably with crime in the discussion below, although it should be kept in mind that the figures are estimates based on observed crime, rather than all actual crime. Of course, a great deal of crime is never reported or remains unsolved, and it is possible for innocent individuals to be registered for crimes they did not commit. As will be discussed below, there is little reason to believe that actual immigrant crime is overestimated by these figures due to bias, and even some reason to suspect that it may be underrepresented.

Recently, I assisted in a study by Sociology Associate Professor Göran Adamson (2020) that updated these figures until 2017, using data provided by the SNCCP. The findings are summarized in Table 12.1.

Breaking down these numbers for 1997–2001 and adjusting for population, the SNCCP found that the foreign-born are two-and-a-half times more likely to be registered as suspects of crimes compared to Swedish-born individuals with two Swedish-born parents. Second-generation immigrants born in Sweden to two foreign-born parents were twice as likely to be suspects of crimes. Adjusting for differences in age, sex, and income across the groups reduces the overrepresentation somewhat, but the basic pattern remains the same.

The updated figures for the 2013–2017 period suggest that over time, the overrepresentation of first-generation immigrants declined, whereas the overrepresentation of second-generation immigrants increased. This development has made Sweden more similar to the pattern observed in several other countries that second-generation migrants are more likely to engage in crime than their first-generation parents. In the United States as well as in many other countries, it is primarily second-generation immigrants who are overrepresented in crime—not first-generation immigrants (Killias 2011; Bersani 2014).

In these figures, foreigners registered for crime who are not registered as residents in Sweden are reported separately. Studying the table, it is interesting to first note that people who were not even registered as residents in Sweden at the time of committing the crime were estimated to account for

Table 12.1 Different groups' share of crimes reported to police

	Registered crime 1985–1989 (%)	*Registered crime 1997–2001 (%)*	*Registered crime 2013–2017 (%)*
Not registered in the country	3	7	13
Foreign-born	14	19	24
At least one parent born abroad	15	19	21
Both parents born in Sweden	69	55	42

Source SNCCP; Adamson (2020)

3% of all crimes in 1985–1989, 7% of all crimes in 1997–2001, and 13% in 2013–2017. This group consists, among others, of individuals waiting for a decision on a residence permit, individuals temporarily staying in Sweden during the five-year period as tourists or students, and individuals who have deliberately come to Sweden for criminal purposes. Consequently, this group effectively includes temporary visitors, international burglary gangs, asylum seekers not yet registered as residents, and various categories of unlawful immigrants.

This overall category used to be marginal, but their share of crime has increased dramatically over time—a tendency that has also been documented in Norway (Mohn and Ellingsen 2016). Calculating the overrepresentation of this groups requires assumptions, since it is unknown how many unregistered individuals actually reside in Sweden. Adding the category of unregistered foreign-born to the registered foreign-born diminishes the decline in their overrepresentation and makes the overall numbers more stable.

Adamson (2020) provides estimates of the elevated risk of being registered for crime among individuals with foreign background compared to the Swedish-born with two Swedish parents. The figure was 2.1 in 1985–1989, increased to 2.5 in 1997–2001, and remained fairly stable at 2.6 in 2013–2017. Most of the increase in the share of crime registered among those with foreign background thus reflects a growing population share—not higher relative or absolute tendencies to engage in crime. Between 1985–1989 and 2013–2017, the foreign-origin population's share of total registration for crime as suspects increased from 31 to 58%, and from 42 to 72% for homicide.

The population share registered as suspects of crimes also vary between different countries of origin, where the SNCCP (2005) notes that "Those from North Africa and the Middle East have the highest recorded crime rates." Foreign-born have, as previously mentioned, a particularly elevated risk when it comes to more serious violent crime. The relative risk in the surveyed period was 3.0 for assault, 4.1 for robbery, and 5.0 for rape. However, risk of crime is lower among immigrants from Southeast Asia and in later periods immigrants from Western Europe. For several categories of crime, immigrants from East and Southeast Asia have lower rates of crime than for those with Swedish origin (Adamson 2020).

Similar results are found in the older report of the Swedish Prison and Probation Service's (2010), which instead of crime suspects focuses on inmates serving long prison sentences—defined as four years or more for men, and two years or more for women. The report notes that "A majority (52.9%) of those serving long-term sentences originated from other countries than Sweden." This number includes foreign-born with Swedish citizenship, asylum seekers, those with residence permits, and temporary visitors. It is not clear from the report what proportion of the remaining 47% that were second-generation immigrants, but since other data suggest this is a significant proportion, the total share of inmates with foreign origin was likely even higher than 53%. The most common crimes for both native- and foreign-born long-term inmates were felony narcotics offenses or drug smuggling. Many of the foreign-born were from Eastern Europe and the Middle East: "The most common nationality of origin after Sweden was Poland, closely followed by Iran and Finland." These figures underestimate the proportion of crimes committed by those from abroad, as they exclude criminals who have been transferred to their home country in order to serve their sentence.

In lieu of reports by government agencies, Swedish journalists have in recent years taken initiatives to compile crime statistics available in public records. The program *Uppdrag Granskning* of Swedish Public Television (2018) surveyed every single individual registered for rape or attempted rape during 2012–2017. The result was that 58% of the perpetrators were foreign-born. Although the exact proportion was not presented, there were additional individuals with migrant background among the remaining 42% native-born Swedes. Reported separately, though, were those registered for attempted and completed sexual assault, where victim and criminal were strangers; more than 80% of these perpetrators were foreign-born.

Another compilation conducted about the same time was commissioned by the tabloid *Aftonbladet* (2018), focusing on 112 individuals registered for group rape—defined as having at least two offenders—since 2012. Out of this population, 73% were foreign-born. When adding those born in Sweden with two migrant parents, the figure increased to 88%. Similarly, the tabloid *Expressen* (2018) compiled all those sentenced for gang rape in the years 2016 and 2017. The examination showed that among the fairly small total sample of 43 such men, one was born in Sweden to two Swedish-born parents, 10 born in Sweden to one or two foreign-born parents, whereas 32 were foreign-born.

Additionally, using police files, *Expressen* (2017) surveyed 192 individuals in Stockholm, who were either members of criminal gangs or had links to criminal networks—categorized on the basis of court sentences or preliminary investigations. 82% were migrants, either born abroad or with two foreign-born parents; adding those with one foreign-born parent, the figure rose to 95%.

Yet another compilation was assembled by *Dagens Nyheter* (2017), consisting of 100 registered or suspected criminals in investigations on gunfire in public places during 2013–2017. Out of these, 90% had one or two foreign-born parents. Among this group, roughly half were born in Sweden in migrant households, whereas the rest were first-generation immigrants. Interestingly, the data confirmed that men with foreign background were also strongly overrepresented among the victims of the shootings.

There are also some compilations from neighboring countries by media outlets. A Norwegian TV channel investigates who was convicted of serious violent criminal offenses in Oslo and concludes that 7 out of 10 had a foreign background (*TV 2* 2019):

> TV 2's investigation shows that out of the 140 perpetrators, 70 percent had an immigrant background. In other words, more than two out of three serious violent offenses in Oslo were committed by immigrants. This in spite of the fact that immigrants, according to Statistics Norway, make up 33 percent of Oslo's population.... Even though the number seems high, violence researcher Ragnhild Bjørnebekk is not surprised. She argues that one of the reasons is that many of them come from cultures where violence is more widespread.
>
> "They are more vulnerable, they have experienced more trauma. Some come from violent cultures, and they bring that with them."

Research on Immigrant Overrepresentation

Kardell (2011) compares overrepresentation in crimes between first- and second-generation immigrants in Sweden, Norway, and Denmark, measured as adjudicated crimes—that is, crimes where someone has been found guilty. Interestingly, the picture is about the same among both first- and second-generation immigrants in all three countries, with an elevated risk of between 1.9 and 2.7. The elevated risk compared to the native population is highest in Denmark, the second highest in Sweden, and lowest in Norway.

Rostami et al. (2012) studied street gang structures in Sweden using police records. 239 gang members in the seven gangs categorized by the police as the most prominent were examined in the study. All gang members are men, and 76% of the street gang members are first- or second-generation immigrants.

A study by Skardhamar et al. (2014), consisting of both Norwegian and Finnish criminologists, compares immigrants' crimes in Norway and Finland. The research summary discusses overrepresentation in crime among immigrants in Sweden, Denmark, Norway, and Finland—a pattern that has been found in a range of studies (e.g., von Hofer et al. 1997; Gundersen et al. 2000; Andersen and Tranæs 2013; Hällsten et al. 2013; Lehti et al. 2014). The overrepresentation of immigrants in crime is higher in Finland than in Norway. An interesting conclusion is that it is generally the same immigrant countries which have high elevated risk in Norway and Finland. Immigrants from the Middle East and Africa account for a relatively higher proportion of crime, while immigrants from Southeast Asia and Western Europe account for a lower proportion of crime in both Finland and Norway.

The SNCCP (2019) summarizes studies about immigration and crime in the Scandinavian countries. One general finding for Sweden is that the overrepresentation of different immigrant groups varies significantly. Overall, participation in crime is higher for immigrants from countries that have lower levels of economic development, lower levels of education attainment, and that are geographically more distant from Sweden. One notable exception here is East Asian countries, including low-income East Asian countries, whose immigrants despite this have low crime rates. An interesting result from Norwegian studies is differences within immigration categories:

Immigrants who came as refugees have higher rates of crime than those who came as family migrants, while labor migrants have even lower rates of crime.

Agersnap et al. (2019) utilize a Danish policy reform that cuts welfare benefits for immigrants to evaluate the theory that generous benefits act as a welfare magnet and attract immigrants. The study finds sizeable effects from benefit reduction on the net flow of immigrants.

Dagnelie et al. (2019) report the employment rate of refugees without former ties to the United States, who arrived in the country between 2005 and 2010. Three months after arrival, 30% of refugees had a job, which is a striking figure compared to Sweden. The employment rate after this period was the lowest among Afghani refugees, although even within this group 20%. In contrast, it takes nine years in Sweden for immigrants from Asia and Africa to reach an employment rate of 30%, excluding labor market programs and jobs with extremely low pay (Bornhäll et al. 2019).

The comparison with Sweden is not identical since the American figures do not exclude those with extremely low wages and those in labor market programs. Nevertheless, even including a broad definition, an employment rate of 30% for refugees in Sweden is generally not reached before three years after being publicly registered in a Swedish municipality, which is, in turn, typically one–two years after arriving in Sweden. Regardless of how we count, it is clear from these figures that refugees settled in the United States integrate in the labor market far more rapidly than in Sweden. In fairness, some of this difference reflects the linguistic disadvantage of Sweden compared to the United States, as many refugees have English language skills.

Another pertinent study was conducted by Pfeiffer et al. (2018), who investigated the effect of refugees on crime in the German state of Niedersachsen using crime participation over time. They noted both that refugees were overrepresented in crime and that crimes where refugees were registered increased over time. *BBC News* (2018) reports:

> Migrants may be responsible for most of a recent rise in violent crime in Germany, research commissioned by the government suggests.... The report used statistics from Lower Saxony—regarded as an average state—where police saw an increase of 10.4% in reported violent crimes in 2015 and 2016. Based on figures from the state's interior ministry, which keeps a separate record of alleged crimes by migrants, the report suggested that 92.1% of this increase was attributable to migrants.

The German study includes fascinating data on cross-cultural differences that may be relevant for crime. Among young people with German origin, roughly 3% subscribe to the masculinity norm that men who are unwilling to react violently to insults are weak. In contrast, among German youth with origin in the former Yugoslavia and Turkey, the corresponding share is 13–15%.

There is also research on the importance of which residential areas immigrants end up in, and how this can affect the risk of crime. Between 1985 and 1994, Sweden applied the so-called All-of-Sweden strategy, where the Swedish Migration Board—the responsible government organization—placed refugees all across the country. The purpose was to avoid a concentration to the metropolitan areas in response to the segregation and social problems that were already visible at this time. Due to the housing shortage that often prevailed in Sweden, refugees who were granted asylum and left free to find housing in many cases ended up in municipalities where there was vacant housing due to a weak job market, and where there were already many immigrants. In order to combat this tendency, attempts were made to steer the location decision.

The responsibility for the introduction of refugees into Swedish society was transferred to the municipalities. It was determined that individuals did not have the right to choose where to live. The policy had some flexibility, and migrants who managed to find a home on their own were entitled to move where they wanted, which some migrants did immediately and many migrants did over time. Nevertheless, many stayed where they were assigned, and this policy led refugees to become scattered across Sweden—more likely to end up in rural areas and the northern parts of Sweden. An interesting consequence of this policy is that it allows researchers to study the effects of residential environment with it being in part exogenous, even if the quasi-experiment as such was not entirely streamlined. Often, a problem in the identification of causal effects of residential area is that it is not chance that determines where individuals live; yet here we have an instrument which in theory allows scholars to isolate the effect of the residential area itself rather than other factors.

The placement of refugees has been used to examine a range of socioeconomic outcomes. Åslund et al. (2010) study the effect of placement in different areas based on job opportunities. Those immigrants who from 1990 to 1991 were placed in residential areas with better access to jobs were more likely to be working some years later. However, the effect was limited and concerned the fact that immigrants who ended up in areas with a strong job market had a few percentage points higher gainful employment rate.

Grönqvist et al. (2015) compare those who were placed in different types of areas. Young people with immigrant backgrounds, who were placed in segregated residential areas with a higher proportion of other refugees, were more likely to commit crimes in the future—especially young people with low-skilled parents. However, the study found no statistically significant effect of segregated areas on violent crime. The effects were most apparent for drug-related crimes.

Damm and Dustmann (2014) use a similar Danish refugee placement program to study the impact of residential area on crime. Boys who during childhood ended up in residential areas with a higher proportion of criminals had a slightly higher risk of ending up in crime as adults. The effect was not driven by reported crimes in the residential area, but by whether or not a high proportion of the neighbors were convicted criminals. The probability of the young people being negatively affected was higher if the criminal neighbors belonged to the same ethnic group. This suggests that the effect is driven by social interaction and learning of crime. Environmental influ ences on the probability of falling into crime were strongest between 10 and 14 years of age—an age when young boys tend to be easily influenced.

Discrimination

There are several studies that show that for immigrants, there are differences in the probability of becoming a suspect or being convicted of a crime at different levels of the legal system. However, the effects do not unequivocally indicate discrimination. For example, it is immigrants from Western countries that prove to be more likely to be sentenced to prison, not non-Western immigrants (Kardell 2006). If the higher risk of conviction is a matter of discrimination, one could expect that it would primarily affect non-European immigrants.

One problem is that these studies do not isolate the effect of immigrant background per se, and, therefore, they can reflect that the type of crime differs in a way that is not captured by background factors. Groups who commit many crimes also tend to commit more serious crimes, which leads to more severe punishment. Studies in other countries have shown that disparities, which at the outset appears to be discrimination by the police and the legal system, sometimes instead reflect other factors such as police contacts (Knowles and Todd 2001; Anwar and Fang 2006; Fryer 2019; Johnson et al. 2019; Streeter 2019; Tregle et al. 2019). There are, however, other studies from various regions which show that racial bias in policing and sentencing due to either explicit or implicit prejudice can be documented, as well as many anecdotal examples of immigrants who experience negative differential treatment by the Swedish legal system itself (e.g., SNCCP 2008; Anwar et al. 2012, Alesina and La Ferrara 2014; Arnold et al. 2018; Knox et al. 2019; Shjarback and Nix 2020).

Another problem that is often highlighted is stereotypical views among the police and the judiciary, where some immigrant groups are believed to be more inclined to crime. However, the fact that the legal system discriminates against immigrants does not have to lead to an overestimation of immigrants' crime. One possible reason is that discrimination and inferior treatment may also apply to immigrants as victims. Crime often occurs within the same geographical areas and social groups; immigrants are more likely to be subjected to crimes by other immigrants.

If the legal system discriminates against immigrants who are victims of crime, it may lead to perpetrators going free, so that crime problems among immigrants are instead underestimated. This is not necessarily based on conscious discrimination, but may also be due to the fact that the Swedish legal system has more difficulties in dealing with crimes involving immigrants—for example, due to linguistic and cultural reasons. Immigrants may also be less likely to testify. If discrimination or difficulties in investigating crimes lead to fewer crimes where both victim and perpetrator are immigrants being registered, immigrants' crimes and exposure to crime will rather be underestimated.

An investigation of all cases of homicide between 2007 and 2009 found that about 21% of cases with foreign-born victims remained unsolved, compared to only 10% of homicides with native-born victims (Sturup et al. 2015). For cases with known offenders, we know that homicides with foreign-born victims are considerably more likely to have foreign-born perpetrators. This probably means that perpetrators with foreign backgrounds are more likely to avoid identification, which makes the overrepresentation of the foreign-born in crime appear lower than it actually is.

Cultural Factors

Kivivuori and Lehti (2011) discuss homicides in Sweden and Finland from a historical perspective. Although these two countries are similar in many respects, Finland has a significantly higher rate of homicide, and has been far above Sweden since the 1750s when systematic data are first available. The rate of homicide in Finland in relation to the population was for a long time 2.5 to 3 times above the Swedish level, although the two countries have converged in recent years, as homicide rates declined less in Sweden than in Finland.

Interestingly, the large Finnish immigrant group in Sweden has also had a high number of homicides and cases of manslaughter in relation to the population—that is to say, an elevated risk of approximately 4 times that of the Swedish-born. These are severe and far-reaching differences that are difficult to explain with poverty or socioeconomic factors. Finland and Sweden have similar welfare states and income distribution, where Finland, if anything, has less income inequality. Kivivuori och Lehti (2011) write:

> Finnish and Swedish societies are fairly similar when we look at their general welfare state indices. Finland's significantly higher homicide rate cannot be explained by differences in its economy or welfare state expenditures.

There is thus reason to believe that the explanation is in part cultural, for example, related to alcohol or macho culture. The authors emphasize the importance of alcohol abuse—both for the increase of the rate of homicide in Sweden during the postwar period and for the lasting differences with Finland. They further state:

> The main explanations for the increase in homicide rates in Sweden since the 1960s have been increasing alcohol consumption (Lenke 1990), large-scale immigration, and an increase in the population of habitual criminals and substance abusers (Lenke 1990; Wikström 1992; von Hofer 2008, p. 49). There is evidence for all. Alcohol consumption has quadrupled since the 1960s, and a very large percentage of homicide perpetrators are today immigrants. The annual average rate of homicides perpetrated by native Swedes has not increased significantly since the interwar years (von Hofer 2008, p. 49). Wikström (1992), however, has shown that a significant percentage of the increase in the number of homicides in Stockholm is linked to the activity of the subcultures of habitual criminals and substance abusers.

Alcohol plays a key role in homicides in both countries. This applies not the least to homicides committed by Swedish-born perpetrators outside gang environments. Such violence is often the consequence of drunk friends, or acquaintances ending up in a fight. A historical analysis of homicide in Sweden and Finland shows that this was common and even typical also in the past. Even today, almost two-thirds of offenders in Finland are known addicts, mostly alcoholics, and an even higher proportion of perpetrators were drunk when the homicide or manslaughter was committed: eight out of ten in Finland (2003–2007), and six out of ten in Sweden (1990–1998). According to Kivivuori and Lehti (2011), alcohol to a large extent explains Finland's higher rate of homicide: "Alcohol-related crimes are more common and make up a larger proportion of homicidal crime in Finland than in Sweden."

There are also speculations that macho culture is a partial explanation for the high level of violence in Finland (Spierenburg 1998). Although this is contested in the particular case of Finland, a macho culture and the will to uphold one's honor are important explanations for the degree of violence in a society (Nisbett and Cohen 1996; Pinker 2011; Mosquera 2013). Violence tends to be more common in societies with macho ideals and norms relating to male honor. In these societies, it is considered important to avenge perceived insults. Letting insults pass unpunished, or backing away from conflict, is considered disgraceful and damaging to one's reputation, which increases the likelihood of violence.

Controlling for Socioeconomic Factors

Despite immigrants' overrepresentation in crime, many have denied that immigration causes an increase in crime. An often both cited and criticized claim was made by Criminology Professor Jerzy Sarnecki (2016), who argued that "If it were the case that the extent of crime in Sweden really was influenced by the number of immigrants in the country, then crime should increase as the proportion of immigrants increases. In Sweden, however, most crime types have not increased since the early 1990s despite the sharp increase in immigrants."

This argument is methodologically flawed, both regarding socioeconomic factors and the comparison over time. Even if crime had dropped over the same period as the proportion of immigrants increased, it does not prove that immigration does not have an effect on crime. Crime can increase among immigrants, while simultaneously decreasing among those with Swedish background. Another possibility is that crime falls in both groups, while the immigrant proportion of the population increases and boosts crime. In such case, crime would have dropped even more without immigration. The reasoning is a logical misconstruction—*post hoc ergo propter hoc*.

Moreover, it is doubtful whether crime overall really has decreased since the early 1990s. The number of reported crimes and the total number of crimes in the self-reported Swedish Crime Survey have increased. Attempted murder and shootings have also increased. Other forms of crime have fallen, and the rate of homicide is still lower than the record years around 1990. Here, too, it is possible that the explanation is not a reduction in violence but that improved emergency care, widespread access to cell phones, and quicker rescue efforts save the lives of more victims of violence than in the past. The question of whether total crime has increased or decreased since 1990 is difficult to answer accurately, and the most likely case is that the answer varies depending on the type of crime and social group studied. Violent crimes, juvenile offenses, and alcohol-related crimes seem to have fallen among the Swedish working and middle classes, as well as among well-integrated immigrants, while gang violence has increased in vulnerable areas. In any case, whether crime has fallen or increased overall is not key to answering the question of how immigrant crime has affected crime over time.

The argument about socioeconomic factors made by Sarnecki is also incorrect. Since it is commonly used in the Swedish debate, it is worth scrutinizing in detail. Even if socioeconomic factors had completely explained immigrants' overrepresentation in crime statistics, it would not change the relationship between immigration and crime. In that case, major socioeconomic problems would simply be the mechanism through which immigration boosts crime. Controlling for poverty and other socioeconomic problems is interesting in order to form a better understanding of what causes crime, as well as a moral counter-argument against those who blame immigrants collectively. Nevertheless, in a discussion of how immigration has impacted crime, it is an irrelevant objection. If poverty causes crime and the number of poor increases through immigration, immigration will increase crime. It is not logical to say that immigrants do commit more crimes, but that immigration does not increase crime because criminal immigrants are poor.

Controlling for socioeconomic factors contributes to an increased understanding of crime but does not magically erase the overrepresentation in crime. Attempting to control for socioeconomic factors in an analysis of immigration's impact on crime is a textbook example of the statistical mistake commonly referred to as overcontrol. The conclusions regarding immigration's impact on crime are not affected by the degree to which crime is explained by socioeconomic factors. This only changes the analysis from immigration increasing crime to immigration increasing the number of people with socioeconomic problems—which, in turn, increases crime.

The argument about socioeconomic factors would have been more meaningful if Sweden had the tools with which it could easily solve those "socioeconomic problems." However, this is not the case. With effort, it is possible to reduce socioeconomic problems, but until the day someone actually fixes them, they are a part of reality and not something that can be excluded from the analysis. Neither are they temporary, transient phenomena that will resolve themselves on their own. Both immigrants' overrepresentation in crime and immigrants' overrepresentation in socioeconomic problems have been constant—or even increased somewhat—in recent decades.

It is worth noting that the claim of socioeconomic factors being a key driver of crime is also empirically questionable and may be driven by faulty statistical interpretations. One problem here is that the correlation between socioeconomic factors and crime may not reflect a causal link, but instead be driven by omitted variables, where unobserved cultural or individual-level factors simultaneously lead to greater socioeconomic problems and higher overrepresentation in crime—thereby creating a spurious correlation. Often, low socioeconomic outcomes can be described as symptoms of deeper factors that additionally cause elevated crime risk. In this case, relying on simple correlations will lead to misidentification, where symptoms are spuriously misinterpreted as underlying causes. This is a well-known statistical problem; any claim that socioeconomic factors "cause" or "explain" crime, which only relies on correlations without a method to identify causal links, should be dismissed as unscientific.

It is possible that individual-level factors, such as mental health issues and substance abuse, cause people to become more likely to commit crime as well as more likely to display socioeconomic problems. If so, these deeper underlying causes will create a positive correlation between crime and socioeconomic problems, beyond any causal link between the latter two variables. Examples of cultural factors that affect both socioeconomic outcomes and crime risk include levels of trust, macho culture, patriarchal norms, or alcohol habits. In such cases, controlling for socioeconomic factors will also indirectly lead to one controlling for unobserved cultural factors. Thus, socioeconomic family variables influenced by cultural factors are not necessarily independent explanatory mechanisms, but proxy variables, or mechanisms through which deeper factors influence the risk of crime.

Assume for argument's sake that a patriarchal culture increases both the risk of violence against women and the likelihood that women do not work. Controlling for upbringing in a family where the mother does not work would then reduce overrepresentation in crime, as family relationships are an indirect measurement of cultural differences. In other words, it is methodologically incorrect by Hällsten et al. (2013) to conclude that culture can only explain the overrepresentation that remains when socioeconomic factors have been controlled for. Part of the explanatory power of cultural factors has already been included in the analysis, simply by controlling for socioeconomic factors, as these are influenced by culture.

Another example where controlling for socioeconomic factors constitutes overcontrol is the relationship between immigration and falling school performance. As with crime, it is common to deny the impact of immigration on school performance, with the argument that the effect decreases after controlling for socioeconomic factors. Socioeconomic problems such as low education can in themselves be caused by deeper underlying factors such as cultural differences, individual-level factors, or social capital, and cannot, in that case, be interpreted as an independent explanatory variable. Either way, no matter how they have arisen, socioeconomic problems cannot be eliminated from the analysis as long as they actually exist in reality.

Despite intensive efforts, Sweden has not eliminated socioeconomic problems, and as long they exist, socioeconomic problems must inevitably be considered. The socioeconomic problems of immigrants cannot be magically separated from analyses of the effects of immigration. In general, there is a widespread misconception that one—by referring to controlling for background factors—can conjure away unwanted effects of immigration. This type of reasoning is, however, based on a fundamental misunderstanding of basic statistical methods, as well as of what "controlling" means.

After all, controlling for fat and carbohydrates such as sugar, cookies contain as many calories as celery sticks. That hardly means that you can change your snack of choice from celery sticks to cookies without gaining weight. A higher content of fat and sugar are properties which cause cookies to contain more calories. Statistical controls cannot eliminate the relatively higher number of calories in cookies. Similarly, a statistical analysis that breaks down immigrants' overrepresentation in crime into various constituent parts, through controlling for background factors, cannot be used to deny the causal effect of immigration on crime.

This does not mean that the overrepresentation is permanent or that it cannot be resolved. Immigrants' crime risk varies between different societies, over time, and across different immigrant groups. However, the significant overrepresentation observed in Sweden today cannot be ignored. The elevated risk is especially great for serious crimes and in socially vulnerable areas, where many of the victims also have immigrant backgrounds. At the same time as the public debate for a long time rejected the problem of higher crime in immigrant areas, the concentration of aggravated violence in these areas has started to approach American levels—a presence of gang crime, shootings, and murders far beyond what Sweden previously was used to. In these violence-stricken areas, immigrant overrepresentation in crime is not just an interesting statistical issue, but a matter of personal safety and security—and even about life and death.

References

Adamson, Göran. 2020. "Migrants and Crime in Sweden in the Twenty-First Century." *Society* 57: 9–21. https://doi.org/10.1007/s12115-019-00436-8.

Aftonbladet. 2018. "Unik granskning: 112 pojkar och män dömda för gruppvåldtäkt" [Unique Review: 112 Boys and Men Convicted of Group Rape]. By Joachim Kerpner, Kerstin Weigl, and Alice Staaf, May 7, 2018, updated October 21, 2019. https://www.aftonbladet.se/nyheter/a/rLKwKR/unik-granskning-112-pojkar-och-man-domda-for-gruppvaldtakt.

Agersnap, Ole, Amalie Sofie Jensen, and Henrik Kleven. 2019. "The Welfare Magnet Hypothesis: Evidence from an Immigrant Welfare Scheme in Denmark." NBER working paper no. 26454, National Bureau of Economic Research. https://doi.org/10.3386/w26454.

Alesina, Alberto, and Eliana La Ferrara. 2014. "A Test of Racial Bias in Capital Sentencing." *American Economic Review* 104, no. 11: 3397–3433. https://doi.org/10.1257/aer.104.11.3397.

Andersen, Lars Højsgaard, and Torben Tranæs. 2013. "Etniske minoriteters overrepræsentation i strafferetlige domme" [The Overrepresentation of Ethnic Minorities in Criminal Sentences]. Rockwool Fondens Forskningsenhed, Arbejdspapir 23, Syddansk Universitetsforlag, Odense. https://www.rockwoolfonden.dk/app/uploads/2015/12/Arbejdspapir-23-Etniske-minoriteters-overrepræsentation-i-strafferetlige-domme-rev..pdf.

Anwar, Shamena, and Hanming Fang. 2006. "An Alternative Test of Racial Prejudice in Motor Vehicle Searches: Theory and Evidence." *American Economic Review* 96, no. 1: 127–51. https://doi.org/10.1257/000282806776157579.

Anwar, Shamena, Patrick Bayer, and Randi Hjalmarsson. 2012. "The Impact of Jury Race in Criminal Trials." *The Quarterly Journal of Economics* 127, no. 2: 1017–1055. https://doi.org/10.1093/qje/qjs014.

Arnold, David, Will Dobbie, and Crystal S. Yang. 2018. "Racial Bias in Bail Decisions." *The Quarterly Journal of Economics* 133, no. 4: 1885–1932. https://doi.org/10.1093/qje/qjy012.

Åslund, Olof, John Östh, and Yves Zenou. 2010. "How Important Is Access to Jobs? Old Question—Improved Answer." *Journal of Economic Geography* 10, no. 3: 389–422. https://doi.org/10.1093/jeg/lbp040.

BBC News. 2018. "Germany: Migrants 'May Have Fuelled Violent Crime Rise'." January 2, 2018. https://www.bbc.com/news/world-europe-42557828.

Bersani, Bianca E. 2014. "An Examination of First and Second Generation Immigrant Offending Trajectories." *Justice Quarterly* 31, no. 2: 315–43. https://doi.org/10.1080/07418825.2012.659200.

Bornhäll, Anders, Sven-Olov Daunfeldt, and Hans Seerar Westerberg. 2019. "Less than 30 Percent of Non-Western Immigrants Earn a Monthly Wage That Exceeds 2,000 Euro After Nine Years in Sweden." HFI Notes no. 1, Institute of Retail Economics. https://handelnsforskningsinstitut.se/wp-content/uploads/2019/12/hfinote01rev1-1.pdf.

Dagens Nyheter. 2017. "Unga, oorganiserade och bor kvar hemma – de ligger bakom den nya mordvågen" [Young, Disorganized, and Living at Home—They Are Behind the New Murder Wave]. May 15, 2017, updated May 16, 2017. https://www.dn.se/nyheter/sverige/unga-oorganiserade-och-bor-kvar-hemma-de-ligger-bakom-den-nya-mordvagen.

Dagnelie, Olivier, Anna Maria Mayda, and Jean-François Maystadt. 2019. "The Labor Market Integration of Refugees in the United States: Do Entrepreneurs in the Network Help?" *European Economic Review* 111: 257–72. https://doi.org/10.1016/j.euroecorev.2018.10.001.

Damm, Anna Piil, and Christian Dustmann. 2014. "Does Growing Up in a High Crime Neighborhood Affect Youth Criminal Behavior?" *American Economic Review* 104, no. 6: 1806–32. https://doi.org/10.1257/aer.104.6.1806.

Expressen. 2017. "Gängen inifrån: 192 gängmedlemmar" [Inside the Gangs: 192 Gang Members]. By Claes Petersson and Tomas Carlsson, June 30, 2017. https://www.expressen.se/nyheter/qs/gangen-inifran/konfliktzon-stockholm/192.

———. 2018. "Gruppvåldtäkterna: De är män som våldtar kvinnor tillsammans" [Gang Rape: They Are Men Who Rape Women Together]. By Mattias Wikström and Kim Malmgren, March 20, 2018. https://www.expressen.se/nyheter/brottscentralen/qs/de-ar-mannen-som-valdtar-tillsammans.

Fryer Jr., Roland G. 2019. "An Empirical Analysis of Racial Differences in Police Use of Force." *Journal of Political Economy* 127, no. 3: 1210–61. https://doi.org/10.1086/701423.

Grönqvist, Hans, Susan Niknami, and Per-Olof Robling. 2015. "Childhood Exposure to Segregation and Long-Run Criminal Involvement: Evidence from the 'Whole of Sweden' Strategy." Working paper 1/2015, Institutet för social forskning, Stockholms universitet. http://www.diva-portal.org/smash/get/diva2:794902/FULLTEXT01.pdf.

Gundersen, Frants, Ulla Haslund, Arnt Even Hustad, and Reid Jone Stene. 2000. "Innvandrere og nordmenn som offer og gjerningsmenn" [Immigrants and Norwegians as Victims and Perpetrators]. Rapporter 2000/18, Statistisk sentralbyrå. Statistics Norway, Oslo–Kongsvinger. https://www.ssb.no/a/publikasjoner/pdf/rapp_200018/rapp_200018.pdf.

Hällsten, Martin, Ryszard Szulkin, and Jerzy Sarnecki. 2013. "Crime as a Price of Inequality?: The Gap in Registered Crime Between Childhood Immigrants, Children of Immigrants and Children of Native Swedes." *The British Journal of Criminology* 53, no. 3: 456–81. https://doi.org/10.1093/bjc/azt005.

Johnson, David J., Trevor Tress, Nicole Burkel, Carley Taylor, and Joseph Cesario. 2019. "Officer Characteristics and Racial Disparities in Fatal Officer-Involved Shootings." *Proceedings of the National Academy of Sciences* 116, no. 32: 15877–15882. https://doi.org/10.1073/pnas.1903856116.

Kardell, Johan. 2006. "Diskriminering av personer med utländsk bakgrund i rättsväsendet – en kvantitativ analys" [Discrimination Against Persons with a Foreign Background in the Judicial System—A Quantitative Analysis]. In *Är rättvisan rättvis? Tio perspektiv på diskriminering av etniska och religiösa minoriteter inom rättssystemet*, SOU 2006:30, edited by Jerzy Sarnecki, 67–110. Rapport av Utredningen om makt, integration och strukturell diskriminering, Statens offentliga utredningar (SOU), Fritzes, Stockholm. https://www.regeringen.se/contentassets/106cc584ae1a489db46fde9bbbc090ab/ar-rattvisan-rattvis-tio-perspektiv-pa-diskriminering-av-etniska-och-religiosa-minoriteter-inom-rattssystemet-sou-200630.

———. 2011. "Utländsk bakgrund och registrerad brottslighet – överrepresentationen i den svenska kriminalstatistiken" [Foreign Background and Registered Crime—The Overrepresentation in Swedish Crime Statistics]. Rapport 2011:1, Kriminologiska institutionen, Stockholms universitet, Stockholm. http://su.diva-portal.org/smash/get/diva2:418645/FULLTEXT01.pdf.

Kaspersson, Maria. 2000. "Dödligt våld i Stockholm på 1500-, 1700- och 1900-talet" [Homicide in Stockholm in the 16th, 18th, and 20th Centuries]. Diss., Avhandlingsserie 4, Kriminologiska institutionen, Stockholms universitet, Stockholm.

Killias, Martin. 2011. "Immigration and Crime: The European Experience." Improving EU and US Immigration Systems' Capacity for Responding to Global

Challenges: Learning from Experiences. EU-US Immigration Systems, 2011/19, Robert Schuman Centre for Advanced Studies, European University Institute, San Domenico di Fiesole. http://hdl.handle.net/1814/18960.

Kivivuori, Janne, and Martti Lehti. 2011. "Homicide in Finland and Sweden." *Crime and Justice* 40, no. 1: 109–98. https://doi.org/10.1086/658889.

Knowles, John, Nicola Persico, and Petra Todd. 2001. "Racial Bias in Motor Vehicle Searches: Theory and Evidence." *Journal of Political Economy* 109, no. 1: 203–29. https://doi.org/10.1086/318603.

Knox, Dean, Will Lowe, and Jonathan Mummolo. 2019. "Administrative Records Mask Racially Biased Policing." *American Political Science Review: forthcoming*. https://doi.org/10.1017/S0003055420000039.

Lehti, Martti, Mikko Aaltonen, Ville Hinkkanen, and Hannu Niemi. 2014. "Maahanmuuttajat rikosten uhreina ja tekijöinä rekisterilähteiden valossa" [Immigrants as Crime Victims and Offenders in Finland, Register-Based Analysis]. Oikeuspoliittisen Tutkimuslaitoksen Tutkimuksia 265. National Research Institute of Legal Policy, Helsinki. https://helda.helsinki.fi/bitstream/handle/10138/152441/265_Lehti_ym_2014.pdf.

Mohn, Sigmund Book, and Dag Ellingsen. 2016. "Unregistered Residents and Registered Crime: An Estimate for Asylum Seekers and Irregular Migrants in Norway." *Journal of Scandinavian Studies in Criminology and Crime Prevention* 17, no. 2: 166–76. https://doi.org/10.1080/14043858.2016.1260329.

Mosquera, Patricia M. Rodriguez. 2013. "In the Name of Honor: On Virtue, Reputation and Violence". *Group Processes & Intergroup Relations* 16, no. 3: 271–78. https://doi.org/10.1177/1368430212472590.

Nisbett, Richard E., and Dov Cohen. 1996. *Culture of Honor: The Psychology of Violence in the South*. Boulder, CO: Westview Press.

Pfeiffer, Christian, Dirk Baier, and Sören Kliem. 2018. "Zur Entwicklung der Gewalt in Deutschland. Schwerpunkte: Jugendliche und Flüchtlinge als Täter und Opfer" [On the Development of Violence in Germany. Focus: Young People and Refugees as Perpetrators and Victims]. Departement Soziale Arbeit, Institut für Delinquenz und Kriminalprävention, Zürcher Hochschule für Angewandte Wissenschaften (ZHAW). https://doi.org/10.13140/RG.2.2.29322.98245.

Pinker, Steven. 2011. *The Better Angels of Our Nature: Why Violence Has Declined*. New York: Viking.

Rostami, Amir, Fredrik Leinfelt, and Stefan Holgersson. 2012. "An Exploratory Analysis of Swedish Street Gangs Applying the Maxson and Klein Typology to a Swedish Gang Dataset." *Journal of Contemporary Criminal Justice* 28, no. 4: 426–45. https://doi.org/10.1177/1043986212458195.

Sarnecki, Jerzy. 2016. "Ökad invandring leder inte till ökat antal brott" [Increased Immigration Does Not Lead to an Increased Number of Crimes]. *Dagens Nyheter*, op-ed, August 26, 2016. https://www.dn.se/debatt/okad-invandring-leder-inte-till-okat-antal-brott.

Shjarback, John A., and Justin Nix. 2020. "Considering Violence Against Police by Citizen Race/Ethnicity to Contextualize Representation in Officer-Involved Shootings." *Journal of Criminal Justice* 66: 101653. https://doi.org/10.1016/j.jcrimjus.2019.101653.

Skardhamar, Torbjørn, Mikko Aaltonen, and Martti Lehti. 2014. "Immigrant Crime in Norway and Finland." *Journal of Scandinavian Studies in Criminology and Crime Prevention* 15, no. 2: 107–27. https://doi.org/10.1080/14043858.2014.926062.

SNCCP. 1996. "Invandrare och invandrares barns brottslighet – en statistisk analys" [Criminality of Immigrants and Immigrants' Children—A Statistical Analysis]. By Jan Ahlberg, Swedish National Council for Crime Prevention. Rapport 1996:2. Stockholm: Brottsförebyggande rådet och Fritzes.

———. 2005. "Brottslighet bland personer födda i Sverige och i utlandet" [Violence Among Individuals Born in Sweden and Abroad]. By Peter Martens and Stina Holmberg, Swedish National Council for Crime Prevention. Rapport 2005:17, Brottsförebyggande rådet (Brå), Stockholm. https://www.bra.se/download/18.cba82f7130f475a2f1800012697/2005_17_brottslighet_bland_personer_fodda_sverige_och_utlandet.pdf.

———. 2008. "Diskriminering i rättsprocessen: Om missgynnande av personer med utländsk bakgrund" [Discrimination in the Judicial Process: On the Disadvantage of Persons with a Foreign Background]. By Peter Martens, David Shannon, and Nina Törnqvist, Swedish National Council for Crime Prevention. Rapport 2008:4, Brottsförebyggande rådet (Brå), Stockholm. https://www.bra.se/download/18.cba82f7130f475a2f180007887/1371914724514/2008_4_diskriminering_i_rattsprocessen.pdf.

———. 2019. "Nordiska studier om brottslighet bland personer med utländsk och inhemsk bakgrund: En kartläggande litteraturöversikt av publicerad forskning och statistik 2005–2019" [Nordic Studies on Crime Among Persons of Foreign and Domestic Background: A Surveying Literature Review of Published Research and Statistics 2005–2019]. By Mona Backhans and Petra Sundlöf, Swedish National Council for Crime Prevention. PM, Brottsförebyggande rådet (Brå), Stockholm. Stockholm. https://www.bra.se/download/18.62c6cfa2166eca5d70eed454/1571297186393/2019_Nordiska_studier_om_brottslighet_bland_personer_med_utlandsk_och_inhemsk_bakgrund.pdf.

Spierenburg, Pieter. 1998. "Masculinity, Violence, and Honor: An Introduction". In *Men and Violence: Gender, Honor, and Rituals in Modern Europe and America*, edited by Pieter Spierenburg, 1–36. Columbus, OH: Ohio State University Press.

Streeter, Shea. 2019. "Lethal Force in Black and White: Assessing Racial Disparities in the Circumstances of Police Killings." *The Journal of Politics* 81, no. 3: 1124–1132. https://doi.org/10.1086/703541.

Sturup, Joakim, Daniel Karlberg, and Marianne Kristiansson. 2015. "Unsolved Homicides in Sweden: A Population-Based Study of 264 Homicides." *Forensic Science International* 257: 106–113. https://doi.org/10.1016/j.forsciint.2015.07.050.

Sveri, Britt. 1973. "Utlänningars brottslighet: En kriminalstatistisk jämförelse mellan svenska och utländska medborgare" [Criminality of Foreigners: A Crime Statistics Comparison Between Swedish and Foreign Citizens]. *Svensk Juristtidning* 69, no. 4: 279–310. https://svjt.se/svjt/1973/279.

———. 1980. *Utlänningars brottslighet: En jämförelse mellan om grövre brott övertygade personer 1967 och 1977* [Criminality of Foreigners: A Comparison of Major Crimes Convicted Persons in 1967 and 1977]. Kriminalvetenskapliga institutet vid Stockholms universitet. Stockholm: Stockholms universitet.

Swedish Prison and Probation Service. 2010. "Långtidsdömda män och kvinnor i Sverige: Kriminalvårdens riksmottagningar 1997–2009" [Men and Women in Sweden Sentenced to Long Prison Terms: National Reception Centers of the Prison and Probation Service 1997–2009]. By David Johansson, Mats Dernevik, and Peter Johansson, Kriminalvårdens Utvecklingsenhet, Kriminalvården, Norrköping. https://www.kriminalvarden.se/globalassets/publikationer/forskningsrapporter/langtidsdomda-man-och-kvinnor-i-sverigepdf.

Swedish Public Television. 2018. "Ny kartläggning av våldtäktsdomar: 58 procent av de dömda födda utomlands" [New Survey of Rape Convictions: 58 Percent of Convicted Born Abroad]. By Petter Ljunggren, Johan Frisk, and Kalle Thorslund, *SVT Nyheter*, August 22, 2018. https://www.svt.se/nyheter/granskning/ug/ny-kartlaggning-av-valdtaktsdomar-58-procent-av-de-domda-fodda-utomlands.

Tregle, Brandon, Justin Nix, and Geoffrey P. Alpert. 2019. "Disparity Does Not Mean Bias: Making Sense of Observed Racial Disparities in Fatal Officer-Involved Shootings with Multiple Benchmarks." *Journal of Crime and Justice* 42, no. 1: 18–31. https://doi.org/10.1080/0735648X.2018.1547269.

TV 2 (Norway). 2019. "Stor gjennomgang av voldsdommer avslører: Innvandrere står bak nesten tre av fire grove voldshendelser" [Large Review of Violence Convicts Reveals: Immigrants Are Behind Almost Three in Four Serious Incidents of Violence]. By Kadafi Zaman, Mathias Ogre, and Anne Sofie Mengaaen, February 25, 2019. https://www.tv2.no/a/10432505.

von Hofer, Hanns, Jerzy Sarnecki, and Henrik Tham. 1997. "Minorities, Crime, and Criminal Justice in Sweden." In *Minorities, Migrants, and Crime: Diversity and Similarity Across Europe and the United States*, edited by Ineke Haen Marshall, 62–85. Thousand Oaks, CA: Sage.

Wikström, Per-Olof H. 1992. "Context-Specific Trends in Criminal Homicide in Stockholm 1951–1987." *Studies on Crime and Crime Prevention* 1, no. 1: 88–105. https://psycnet.apa.org/record/1994-17952-001.

CHAPTER 13

Gang Crime

Fear follows crime and is its punishment.

—Voltaire, *Sémiramis*, 1749

One of the trials facing Sweden is the rise in organized crime, where armed gangs can control neighborhoods and engage in crime—ranging from extortion and systematic threats against witnesses to shootings and bombings. The Swedish police designates 60 districts in the country as vulnerable areas, areas where criminals have an impact on the local community and where gangs have often gained a firm foothold. The areas are to varying degrees characterized by a culture of silence, high concentration of criminals, religious extremism, and parallel social structures. In the worst inflicted 22 areas, the grip of crime is so strong that that law enforcement is unable to fully carry out its mission due to the risk of interference. A police report interestingly points out that this anomalous situation has over time often normalized, so that neither inhabitants nor the police themselves any longer even reflect on it (Swedish Police Authority 2019).

In recent years, several in-depth studies on gang crime have been carried out. The studies of organized crime conducted by the Swedish National Council for Crime Prevention (SNCCP 2012, 2015, 2016) cited here are largely based on interviews with police employees, and shed some light on the question of how this development has come about in an advanced and wealthy welfare state. Although many studies in Sweden on the topic discussed here are carried out by state anti-crime agencies, the results are in line with that of recent academic studies (e.g., Rostami 2016; Skinnari et al. 2016; Valasik and Tita 2018; Ahrne and Rostami 2019).

T. Sanandaji, *Mass Challenge*,
https://doi.org/10.1007/978-3-030-46808-8_13

Organized Crime

According to the SNCCP (2016), most individuals in organized crime environments are best described as belonging to networks of friends, rather than being formal gang members. Gangs often have a solid core consisting of professional criminals. Around the core there is a loosely assembled network of young people without substantial criminal records, who can join the group when something is about to go down. The network is usually mobilized for rock-throwing and similar activities using cell phones as a means of organization. The solid core may also change if the leadership is challenged or other organizational divisions occur. These criminal networks are often dependent on strong leaders, and when these disappear, the gangs may break up. This tends to happen, for example, when the leader is serving a prison sentence.

Early on, these gangs were dominated by individuals with roots in the Balkans, whereas today the Middle Eastern and African influence is growing. That said, the gangs are not typically ethnically homogeneous, even if many include kinship-based networks at their core. Instead, the gangs are often based on geographic proximity with members growing up together. While gangs often stick to the same type of crime, they are opportunist and adaptable with regard to new possibilities. Their loose network structure makes them flexible both in terms of the crimes they commit and their constellation of members. A representative gang can, for instance, consist of a core from a certain family such as brothers or cousins, as well as members from other families or ethnic groups, who are friends with each other and often come from the same neighborhoods. In other cases, the gangs are more homogeneously ethnic—for instance, the gangs from neighborhoods where one ethnicity predominates, or those that consist entirely from one clan. While the members overwhelmingly have first- or second-generation immigrant background, immigrant gangs sometimes include associates with Swedish ancestry, and even more often members who have part Swedish and part foreign descent.

The gangs are thus not political constellations and are hardly engaged in a "war" against the white ethnic population, as sometimes claimed by far-right sources. While criminal gangs in Sweden stand out for their use of military-grade weaponry such as automatic weapons, hand grenades, and bombs, the focus of this violence is crime—not politics or religious terrorism. Since gang violence in Sweden has been exploited for far-right propaganda abroad, it is important to emphasize that the direct motivations for the violence in Sweden are not ideological or anything resembling an ethnic conflict. Indeed, the victims of the gang violence overwhelmingly have immigrant background themselves. Of course, ethnic identity and ideology can still play more subtle roles—for instance, if feelings of alienation increase the likelihood of individuals becoming criminals, and by increasing the resentment against the police and other uniformed state employees.

An article in *Forskning & Framsteg* (2015) describes how the suburban gangs initially were inspired by the biker gangs of the 1990s—for example, when it came to organization, behavior, and dress codes. However, there are also clear differences. The suburban formations are less structured and more impulsive when it comes to the use of violence (SNCCP 2012). Biker gangs are hierarchical and internationally organized and therefore tend to abide to the orders handed down by the organization when turning to violence. The street gangs are local networks with the autonomy to act impulsively and are consequently more event-driven.

Both street gangs and biker gangs are involved in advanced heavy crime like shootings. While the street gangs overwhelmingly have members with immigrant background, it should be noted that those with immigrant background in one recent estimate constitute close to half the members also of biker gangs in Sweden (Swedish Public Television 2020). It should also be noted that this figure is a rough estimate, based on estimates of membership rather than convicts for violent crime.

The street gangs have been described as project-driven network constellations, with a solid core that collaborate on an ad hoc basis. Individuals with different loyalties interact in criminal transactions with each other or by carrying out projects. It is individuals who act, not groups collectively. When criminal projects are implemented, available actors band together in an ad hoc formation, sometimes with different functions.

An important aspect of gang crime is social capital. Being part of a gang protects from attacks and provides "fear capital" that can be used to make money. Violence and fear capital and gang membership may, for the individual gang member, serve as a safety net. As one respondent expressed it (SNCCP 2012): "It's a question of survival to constantly maintain your position in the criminal environment. It's sort of the law of the jungle, you have to defend your position every day."

Two types of criminal activities that are particularly dependent on violence capital are extortion and racketeering. To be profitable, they both require a violence capital that is intimidating and not easily parried, so that the threat of violence is credible enough to make victims pay up. To back up the threat, the gang needs to have several members who instill fear. Gang tattoos and other attributes are often used to signal a gang's violence capital. However, the structure of these networks and the low level of organization and cohesion mean that they often remain local.

In areas where many in the community are involved in criminal gangs, the risk increases for someone who decides not to participate in gang activities. For those living in an environment where nobody is a member of a criminal gang, the likelihood of ending up in conflict with someone else are limited. However, where gangs have taken root, those who stand alone risk ending up at a disadvantage should they end up in a dispute with someone who is part of a gang. This leads to a downward spiral where violence and gang formation become self-reinforcing, so that even those who would otherwise have remained outside of gangs are forced to join a gang out of fear. The criminal environment is also fraught with conflict and, perhaps surprisingly, conflicts are in general personal rather than commercial. The causes of these conflicts are often trivial, at least outside of a context where the ability to cope with perceived insults and threats are key components for establishing a reputation for being tough among other criminals.

There are thus inherent and expanding dynamics to gang conflicts. In recent years, this has led to violence becoming more brutal and more ruthless, as well as being backed by heavier weaponry. Enhanced access to weapons in an environment already filled with conflicts and violence-prone individuals contributed to this rise in brutality. However, contrary to popular beliefs, shootings are often not directly motivated by commercial considerations. Rather, they are about other conflicts or about signaling territorial control (SNCCP 2012).

Disorganized Crime

The parallel between Swedish suburban gangs and well-organized international crime syndicates such as the Cosa Nostra, the Camorra, or the Mexican cartels should not be exaggerated. Within Swedish suburban gangs, formations are often loose and organizational capital is weak. The gangs are often dependent on a core of relatives or close friends, while many other members are more loosely connected. With strong and charismatic leaders, the gangs can flourish, but they often dissolve without these key members. The phrase *organized crime* conjures up an image of structured syndicates, but reality is more amorphous. The majority of criminally charged persons linked to organized crime do not belong to any named gangs. In fact, rather than organized crime, this may be described as *disorganized crime*.

The police distinguish between, on the one hand, younger criminals and, on the other hand, older, more experienced criminals. The younger criminals often have less respect for authority, are more impulsive, and more prone to violence against real or perceived insults. This impulsivity often ignites conflict with little consideration of consequences. Once a challenge has been made, it is difficult to back down without losing credibility—which contributes to an excess of violent clashes.

Violent gang crime tends to be primitive, small-scale, and not particularly profitable. Law enforcement and competitors also make it difficult to grow and attain economies of scale. One indication of the lack of profitability is that many criminals supplement their income with social benefits, relying on the welfare state to make up for the often limited and uneven income from their criminal enterprise.

Yet another example of the inefficiency of core operations is the importance of entry fees as an income source for gangs. At the top, there is a small group of leaders, to which remaining individuals have to pay a certain percentage of their criminal earnings. This also implies a significant cost for the individual to terminate their membership. The system has been described as the criminal gangs' version of the classical pyramid scheme, where those who enter the scheme are expected to pay. A police respondent explains what happens to the person who succeeds in gaining membership (SNCCP 2012): "You receive a bulletproof vest and a t-shirt with the name of the gang, and then you're the king for a while. Then, of course, the gang requires that you perform criminal acts." The report adds that should the gang member wish to exit, it costs some $2500.

The glamorous image of the criminal lifestyle is often a fantasy, while reality is much bleaker: "The individuals in the brotherhood groups are, according to the police intelligence service, living far from 'a life of luxury.' Most lack the discipline and skill to manage their criminal earnings." Nonetheless, the glamour and status of criminals and their lifestyles make them role models for some youths in areas of social exclusion. Younger kids, who perhaps performed poorly in school and do not see a bright future for themselves in conventional society, view older criminals in the same neighborhood as role models, and emulate them in attempting to obtain status and respect by committing crimes (SNCCP 2012).

Many young people slide into crime simply because they live in the area and know criminally active individuals. Being associated with criminals provides status. The SNCCP (2012) explains that some young people think it is "super cool" to do favors for criminal networks. Committing crimes gives prestige, both directly by creating an image of toughness and indirectly through the potential of earning fast money later. A police respondent makes the following observation confirming the pursuit of social status: "Most of our young robbers all have nice clothes; they have Fred Perry, Boss, Marco Polo, Canada Goose."

More productive criminals enjoy a lifestyle with luxury cars and other attributes that signal success. The most prominent criminals achieve a kind of local celebrity status, and often manifest their position to the surroundings by, for example, skipping the line to popular nightclubs. Popular culture amplifies the romanticized aura of crime, to which young men in particular are attracted.

Social Impact

As pointed out above, criminal activities such as robbery and theft often have low returns. In recent years, there has been a gradual movement of criminals from traditional crimes toward modern white-collar crime. The SNCCP (2012) writes about white-collar crime: "A trend within organized crime is the growing interest in business and entrepreneurship." Traditional criminals with violence capital in many cases cooperate with modern specialists in financial crime for the purpose of exploiting business. Examples include credit card skimming, fake invoices, tax evasion, and taking over companies with the intention of either looting them or ordering large amounts of goods without paying.

There is also an increased shift to public benefits fraud targeting the welfare system (Swedish Public Radio 2016). Defrauding government agencies, such as the Public Employment Service and the Social Insurance Agency, is replacing bank and armored car robberies: "If you look at crimes against the welfare system and fraud, they have increased. Organized crime targets fraud and the welfare system because we have shortcomings in control measures," says one police chief. The new organized crime trend is discussed in an editorial in the tabloid *Expressen* (2016), which stated that seven out of every hundred businesses started in Sweden are believed to have been created for the purpose of committing crimes. Individuals are allowed to engage in this type of activity even when they have several bankruptcies behind them or are targets in ongoing white-collar crime investigations. It can even be permissible to register new companies when one is in jail. Free market reforms and deregulations aimed at increasing entrepreneurship have had the unintended consequence of making it easier to commit crime.

When criminals advance their positions, local civil society is impacted. Here too, there is a downward spiral in that the more the criminals take, the more the local community tends to retreat. In some parts of the country—particularly around Stockholm, Gothenburg, and Malmö—it is no longer uncommon for the police and other representatives of the government to be threatened or attacked. Stone-throwing occurs in conjunction with riots, cars have been torched, and police stations have even been the target of shootings (SNCCP 2012). Incidents like these send a strong message and "according to interviewed police officers, this leads people in the area to perceive that criminals are in control, while the authorities have retreated and do not exercise their power."

The SNCCP (2012) further discusses crimes against local businesspeople, and concludes that "extortion has developed into a business idea.... Threats and violence are not necessary, and the victim is often convinced that there is power behind the words. Extortion is thus significantly less risky than robbery."

There is also a strong territorial dimension to gang crime. Different gangs take over areas, often public spaces, considered to belong to them and which others are not allowed to use freely. Attitudes toward uniformed representatives of the state appear to have hardened over time, so that nowadays "control is not limited to criminal markets but may also include a provocative warning in the form of threats and violence against residents in the area, police officers, social workers, paramedics, firefighters, school staff, security guards, and so on" (SNCCP 2016).

Criminals have fairly easy access to firearms in all three Swedish metropolitan areas. The origin of the firearms has changed over time—from registered hunting weapons and stolen military hardware to illegal weapons smuggled into Sweden. These are primarily military weapons from former Yugoslavia, but there is still some demand for more exclusive high-status weapons produced in the West. Nowadays, hunting rifles are rarely used by gang criminals, whereas it is considered high status to own some unusual weapons such as Glock and Smith & Wesson (SNCCP 2012).

More generally, being armed provides status and weapons also command an economic value. Weapons that have already been used in previous crimes are "hot," as they can tie the former user to the crime committed. It still happens, however, that resource-weak criminals, out of thrift, reuse weapons in new crimes. The SNCCP (2012) explains that "especially younger people do not consider themselves able to afford to throw away a used weapon"—which may be worth around $1000. It is not uncommon for poorer criminals to reuse weapons already used in past crimes despite the higher risk of being caught, due to stinginess and the relatively high cost of replacing weapons.

Dynamic Effects

Over time, criminal structures have emerged in Swedish cities. While the street gangs have moved toward smaller and more loose organizations, they have grown in competence, armament, and violent sophistication. Neighboring Denmark in 2019 enacted border controls as a response to the gang criminals crossing from Malmö to Copenhagen, carrying out bombings, shootings, and other violent crime. Indeed, Sweden is now an exporter of criminals across Europe—as far south as Spain. An article in *Expressen* (2018) reports on this development:

> The Swedes have been described as the most violent group ever seen in the tourist paradise. The suspicion: Double contract killings, murder through torture, and a bombing targeting a family with children. Now, Spanish police declare victory against "Los suecos," since some ten people have been taken into custody in different investigations.... This year, a wave of violence has swept the Costa del Sol, and now a criminal gang from Malmö is suspected to be behind at least two contract killings and two bombings. In Spanish media, they have been dubbed "Los suecos"—the Swedes....
>
> "One of the Malmö residents who is suspected of murder in Spain was wearing a watch worth 250,000 euro. It has been confiscated by the Spanish police. It is no ordinary Malmö resident who walks around with such a watch," says Petra Stenkula, head of the police investigation unit.... Spanish police describes the Swedes as "the worst group of torpedos ever seen in Costa del Sol."

While there are many similarities across metropolitan areas, there are also differences in crime between Stockholm, Gothenburg, and Malmö. Some of these differences are driven by geography. For example, areas of social exclusion in Malmö are close to the city center, while those in Stockholm and Gothenburg are literal suburbs. When it comes to areas of social exclusion, it is impossible to say where crime is the highest. The most violence-affected areas in the three cities vary from year to year, and statistics are impacted by where gang conflicts flare-up.

In the media's reporting, Malmö often appears as the most crime ridden. There is some truth to this perception, which is primarily based on the fact that areas of social exclusion make up a relatively larger part of Malmö than of Stockholm and Gothenburg. Overall, the criminal dynamics of the metropolitan areas of social exclusion are similar. Violence has become part of everyday life here. The SNCCP (2012) quotes a respondent at the police department in the province of Scania: "It used to be a big deal if there was a shooting in Malmö. You almost started calling each other up. 'Did you hear that there was a shooting?' Now it happens once a week."

One significant contributing factor is that Malmö is small in relation to Stockholm and Gothenburg: "It's possible to get anywhere on a bike in 20 minutes," as one police officer put it. What are considered isolated suburban problems in Stockholm and Gothenburg are city problems in Malmö. The Rosengård district is fairly close to Malmö's medieval city center, thus making its inescapable mark on the city in a manner that the geographically isolated Tensta and Alby do not. Rosengård, like Fosie and Hyllie, has witnessed the emergence of territorial gang formations where criminals try to control geographic areas. The SNCCP (2012) writes:

> In some of these residential areas, district-bound criminal networks try control geographical territories. In the areas that criminal networks claim, it happens that police officers, firefighters, and other representatives of public functions are exposed to threats, harassment, and violence in the form of, for example, rock- and egg-pelting, the firing off of targeted fireworks, and vandalism. The neighborhood with its people can serve as a buffer between the criminals and external threats in the form of both law enforcement agencies and rival criminal individuals. However, this buffer is only achieved if the locals understand and follow the criminals' system of values and standards. Hence, some of the district-bound networks aim to influence the structures of the local community and undermine the legitimacy of other systems, for example, through different forms of provocative acts against public functions. In this way, the network demonstrates its power to the residents of the area. When people feel that the authorities no longer have control, many do not dare to report crime or otherwise collaborate with police and prosecutors. Self-censorship is spreading.

Another distinctive feature of Malmö is the deep penetration of white-collar crime and the creation of an extensive gray sector. The criminal economy has in many cases integrated with the local business community. There is widespread use of black-market labor, tax evasion, smuggling, and public benefits fraud. Organized crime has taken over all or part of the business in certain sectors—not least those which are cash-intensive. In addition to serious crime, there is a widespread culture of dodging taxes and regulations.

There are no accurate estimates of the extent of this problem. A calculation, based on rough estimates, by the local newspaper *Sydsvenskan* (2012) estimated that in Malmö $570 million are annually lost in unpaid tax revenues. Additionally, the problem appears to be growing. A news story by Swedish Public Radio (2015) quotes the Swedish Tax Agency's national coordinator for the fight against serious financial crime: "We notice that there's a large black sector in Malmö, and that there's a strong connection to organized crime." The SNCCP (2012) discusses the black sector in Malmö in detail:

> In Malmö's shops, contraband cigarettes are plentiful, and it is organized crime that supplies retailers and restaurants with these goods. Besides tobacco, contraband alcohol also ends up in restaurants. Stolen goods also take that route and are sold on or used in the business. Illegal taxicabs are common as well. Illegal labor is a way of keeping costs down in legal businesses. Illegal immigrants have a weak position in the job market and are forced to accept low wages. The consequence is that a parallel economy arises.

The dynamic economic effects of multicultural society in Sweden were not, like so many predicted, an innovative Silicon Valley, but rather the formation of a parallel society with widespread tax fraud and off-the-books labor. The dynamic impact on the economy is rather that honest companies are corrupted or driven out of business by extensive illegal activities. The SNCCP (2012) concludes: "If a business dumps prices because it does not pay taxes or because it uses black money, then those businesses that try to be legitimate must keep up in order to compete."

In addition to tax evasion, the Swedish job market model has been eroded by irregular work for wages far below agreed rates. This is often done in combination with tax evasion and sometimes also public benefits fraud. The SNCCP (2012) explains: "They end up in a bad work environment and with the lowest wages. There are gases and smoke, risks of falling, and risks of crush injuries." For instance, a car may be washed for as little as $5.

Financial crime affects tax revenues and honest businesses—but at the same time, it enables low prices for Malmö's consumers. One factor that keeps the black economy in check is that the rest of society has standards against cheating and is prepared to pay for the maintenance of law and order. If this is eroded, a culture that has a high tolerance for corruption, tax evasion, and illegal work can be created—similar to those in countries like Greece and Mexico. In these cultures, even people with a political preference for the welfare state and trade union rights may, in their personal behavior, opt out of more expensive but legally produced services. Here, personal interest collides with the collective social interest, which increases the temptation to base actions on self-interest rather than on the effect on society at large.

References

Ahrne, Göran, and Amir Rostami. 2019. "How Is 'Organized Crime' Organized?" In *Organization Outside Organizations: The Abundance of Partial Organization in Social Life*, edited by Göran Ahrne and Nils Brunsson, 253–70. Cambridge: Cambridge University Press. https://doi.org/10.1017/9781108604994.012.

Expressen. 2016. "Annie Lööf saknar all trovärdighet mot buset" [Annie Lööf Lacks All Credibility with the Thugs]. Editorial by Anna Dahlberg, August 27, 2016. https://www.expressen.se/ledare/anna-dahlberg/annie-loof-saknar-all-trovardighet-mot-buset.

———. 2018. "'Los suecos' – svenskarna sprider skräck på solkusten" ["Los suecos"—The Swedes Are Spreading Fear on the Sun Coast]. By Kim Malmgren, Kvällsposten, December 30, 2018. https://www.expressen.se/kvallsposten/los-suecos-svenskarna-sprider-skrack-pa-solkusten.

Forskning & Framsteg. 2015. "Därför ökar de kriminella gängens makt" [That Is Why the Power of the Criminal Gang Increases]. By Henrik Höjer, May 11, 2015. https://fof.se/tidning/2015/5/artikel/darfor-okar-de-kriminella-gangens-makt.

Rostami, Amir. 2016. "Criminal Organizing. Studies in the Sociology of Organized Crime." Diss., Faculty of Social Sciences, Department of Sociology, Stockholm University, Stockholm. http://su.diva-portal.org/smash/get/diva2:921818/FULLTEXT01.pdf.

Skinnari, Johanna, Lars Korsell, and Helena Rönnblom. 2016. "Welfare Fraud and Criminal Infiltration in Sweden." In *Organised Crime in European Businesses*, edited by Ernesto U. Savona, Michele Riccardi, and Guiliana Berlusconi, 87–101. Abingdon: Routledge. https://doi.org/10.4324/9781315640617.

SNCCP. 2012. "Brottslighet och trygghet i Malmö, Stockholm och Göteborg: En kartläggning" [Crime and Security in Malmö, Stockholm, and Gothenburg: A Survey]. By Emma Ekström, Annika Eriksson, Lars Korsell, and Daniel Vesterhav, Swedish National Council for Crime Prevention. Brottsförebyggande rådet (Brå), Stockholm. https://www.bra.se/download/18.1ff479c3135e8540b29800013583/1371914737955/2012_Brottslighet_och_trygghet.pdf.

———. 2015. "Det dödliga våldet i Sverige 1990–2014: En beskrivning av utvecklingen med särskilt fokus på skjutvapenvåldet" [The Deadly Violence in Sweden 1990–2014: A Description of the Development with a Special Focus on Firearm Violence]. By Sven Granath, Swedish National Council for Crime Prevention. Rapport 2015:24, Brottsförebyggande rådet (Brå), Stockholm. https://www.bra.se/download/18.31d7fffa1504bbffea086b7a/1449670735846/2015_24_Det%20dödliga%20våldet.pdf.

———. 2016. "Kriminella nätverk och grupperingar: Polisers bild av maktstrukturer och marknader" [Criminal Networks and Groupings: Police Officers' Picture of Power Structures and Markets]. By Daniel Vesterhav and Lars Korsell, Swedish National Council for Crime Prevention. Rapport 2016:12, Brottsförebyggande rådet (Brå), Stockholm. https://www.bra.se/download/18.3c6dfe1e15691e1603e1b5ca/1471871016717/2016_12_Kriminella_natverk_och_grupperingar.pdf.

Swedish Police Authority. 2019. "Kriminell påverkan i lokalsamhället – en lägesbild för utvecklingen i utsatta områden" [Criminal Impact in the Local Community—A Snapshot of the Development in Vulnerable Areas]. Diarienummer A309.000/2018, Polisen, Nationella operativa avdelningen (NOA), Underrättelseenheten. https://polisen.se/siteassets/dokument/ovriga_rapporter/kriminell-paverkan-i-lokalsamhallet.pdf.

Swedish Public Radio. 2015. "Samband mellan svarta pengar och våldsdåd" [Relationship Between Black Money and Violent Acts]. *P4 Malmöhus*, July 27, 2015. https://sverigesradio.se/sida/artikel.aspx?programid=96&artikel=6220090.

———. 2016. "Organiserad brottslighet slår till mot välfärden" [Organized Crime Strikes Against Welfare]. By Evalisa Wallin, August 21, 2016. https://sverigesradio.se/sida/artikel.aspx?programid=83&artikel=6499436.

Swedish Public Television. 2020. "Det dolda hotet från mc-gängen – den största kriminella gruppen i Sverige: 'Väljer att inte synas'" [The Hidden Threat from the MC Gangs—The Largest Criminal Group in Sweden: "Chooses Not to Be Seen"]. By Dante Thomsen, *SVT Nyheter*, January 28, 2020, updated January 29, 2020. https://www.svt.se/nyheter/inrikes/mc-gangen-storsta-gruppen-kriminella-enligt-rapport.

Sydsvenskan. 2012. "Vita och svarta Malmö" [White and Black Malmö]. By Jens Mikkelsen, February 5, 2012. https://www.sydsvenskan.se/2012-02-04/vita-och-svarta-malmo.

Valasik, Matthew, and George Tita. 2018. "Gangs and Space." In *The Oxford Handbook of Environmental Criminology*, edited by Gerben J. N. Bruinsma and Shane D. Johnson, 839–67. Oxford: Oxford University Press. https://doi.org/10.1093/oxfordhb/9780190279707.013.25.

CHAPTER 14

No-Go Zones

Laws build the land.

—Swedish medieval law, 14th century

The expression "no-go zones" is at times used to denote places that are heavily impacted by crime. The term is suggestive, although not very well defined. A no-go zone is an informal concept without a precise definition. The origin is military slang for rebel-controlled areas, and it is believed to have come into use during the 1964–1979 war in present-day Zimbabwe. Over time, the term has made it into civilian use and is as such used to describe areas exposed to crime, where government authorities have—to a varying degree—lost control.

As for the lexical definitions of the English expression *no-go area*, the *Oxford Dictionary* (n.d.) denotes it as "an area, especially in a city, which is dangerous for people to enter, or that the police or army do not enter, often because it is controlled by a violent group." The dictionary by Merriam-Webster gives the similar definition of "an area that is dangerous or where people are not allowed to go."

A common misconception is that no-go zones is a categorical term for areas that are completely closed off, though it rather applies to areas that are to some extent dangerous. When classifying areas as no-go zones, one sometimes refers to difficulties encountered by the police and other first responders in entering them, and sometimes to difficulties encountered by visitors in general. Thus, the term does not only refer to areas taken over by insurgents and where danger is guaranteed, but also to crime-stricken areas that should be avoided where there is a heightened risk compared to normal areas. This conceptual confusion has often been used to deny that no-go zones exist in Sweden—for example, by defining the concept as areas taken over and closed off by, e.g., Islamists. Naturally, using such a definition, there are no no-go zones in Sweden. However, this is a (sometimes deliberate) misunderstanding

T. Sanandaji, *Mass Challenge*,
https://doi.org/10.1007/978-3-030-46808-8_14

of how the concept is commonly defined that serves to create confusion. The point of using an exaggerated definition is to create a straw man in order to easier deny the existence of no-go zones, even where the term would be applicable using a reasonable definition.

Media reports and official documents until recently used to define no-go areas as being exposed to crime, not as war zones or completely closed-off areas that are impossible to enter. A report by the Swedish Association of Local Authorities and Regions (2007) discussed the term in connection with an analysis of the fear of crime: "Fear can cause some places in a neighborhood to turn into no-go areas. This entails that people avoid certain places because it causes discomfort." In the Swedish parliament, Liberal Party MP Roger Haddad (2015) summarized the concept as follows: "A rough definition of a no-go area is an area where the major criminal impact on the local community has led to difficulties for the police to work in these areas and to investigate crimes committed there."

Criminally Exposed Areas

In December 2015, the national operative unit of the Swedish Police Authority (2015) published a nationwide report on criminally exposed areas, based on the National Criminal Investigation Division's pilot study (NCID 2014). According to their definition, there are 53 criminally exposed areas in Sweden, of which 15 are considered to be particularly exposed. By 2019, these figures had changed to 60 and 22, respectively. These areas are defined as areas where "local criminal networks are considered to have a negative impact on the local community." Crimes that regularly occur and have become normalized in these areas include violence, riots, rock-throwing, drug trafficking, and so on.

According to the Swedish Police Authority (2015), the criminally exposed areas are characterized along four criteria for social risks, namely reluctance to participate in the legal process, inability by the police to fulfill its mission, parallel social structures, and religious extremism. It is rare for entire neighborhoods to be characterized by serious crime. Instead, it is usually about "specific places, courtyards, or streets where the problems are most concentrated, and these places then affect outsiders' or the media's description of the entire residential area" (Swedish Police Authority 2015). These particularly exposed locations are referred to as hotspots.

With only a few exceptions, most criminally exposed areas are so-called Million Program areas, and none are found in Northern parts of the country. The seriousness of the situation is evidenced by the NCID's (2014) discussion:

> All expressions publicly manifest criminal power and become a reminder of what the criminal operators are capable of. It is believed to be the basis for the unsafety that prevails in the areas and the reluctance of residents to participate

> in legal proceedings. For the police, this has led to difficulties in solving crime in the areas, which probably has reduced the confidence in the police as a guarantor of public order and safety. This may eventually lead to people being even less likely to cooperate with the police and turn to the police for help. In cases where the public has perceived that the police has failed to stop and investigate these crimes, it may have contributed to the perception that criminals "rule" in the area. The fact that the police has adapted its operating procedures by, for example, increased security measures in cases of enforcement, sends a signal to the public that the police assesses the area as dangerous, which may have stigmatizing effects. Overall, the situation may create a downward spiral that feeds fear and unsafety without the need to make concrete threats. In this way, an informal power structure is established in the local community, which in the long run favors the criminal operators. In several areas, police officers experience that such a process has occurred, and that the public's fear of reprisals entails that the ordinary legal system to some extent has been eliminated. This is expected to risk undermining the confidence in the state's monopoly on violence.

The Swedish Police Authority (2015) discusses the historical background to the problem, which dates back to the so-called Million Program, and the mass construction of public housing in the 1960s and 1970s. The primary goal of the Million Program was to mitigate the postwar problem of poor housing standards and housing shortage by building one million new units—a form of urban planning characterized by progressive social engineering (Goldfield 1982; Schulz et al. 2007). The program was successful in expanding the supply of housing, and by the early 1970s shortage had turned in to a housing surplus with empty apartments in many areas. An unintended consequence of this program was that many areas with newly built housing experienced a social downward spiral, with poorer people moving in and those better off moving out.

Many of those who moved in or remained were immigrants living in social exclusion. As the demographic makeup of the areas changed, more and more Swedes left, whereas future waves of immigration disproportionally ended up in the areas built as part of the Million Program. Because of these historical circumstances, today most criminally exposed areas are Million Program areas built between 1965 and 1975. These areas are not geographically deprived, and to the contrary often have access to public transportation, schools, hospitals, parks and green areas, close proximities to urban areas, and a range of government-provided services. Foreign observers are often surprised at the high quality of housing and infrastructure in Sweden's deprived areas, where the problem is social rather than material. At the same time, the progressive architectural ideals of the period when they were built also present additional challenges to policing beyond those related to social exclusion.

The police has indicated there are several problematic design features of such Million Program areas: They are generally separated from the rest of the city in a green area, and consist of high and efficiently built housing units, surrounding an inner common area where inhabitants were expected to meet each other, with relatively few roads linking it to the outside. The Swedish Police Authority (2015) writes:

> From a police point of view, the Million Program areas are often difficult to work in since there are no retreat routes. Moreover, the location of roads makes it easy to stop vehicles from leaving the area. The areas are also difficult when it comes to surveillance, since the buildings are positioned so that the residents overlook courtyards. The police's feeling of being watched is palpable.

Unintentionally, the attempts by city planners to socially engineer communities and integrate the area with nature have made it resemble a Teutonic fortress closed off to the outside world.

The effects of these features would only become clear in the decades to come. Although its roots can be traced back historically, it was only towards the end of the 1990s that the police began to see the emergence of a new phenomenon in some suburbs. Criminals started to join forces, thereby increasing the threat of violence and their power. This created an atmosphere of fear and unsafety, further increasing the power of these criminal organizations, and by "the turn of the millennium, local criminal networks tied to geographic areas ha[d] become a growing problem in Sweden" (NCID 2014).

The members of these organizations and their extended communities are not keen on cooperating with authorities and often meet police investigations with silence. The share of violent crimes that are solved is far lower than normal. Whereas Swedish police used to solve up to 80 or 90% of non-gang-related murders or those without firearms, the share of gang-related murders that are solved in recent years is as low as 20–30% (Swedish Public Television 2018a). According to police criminologist Mikael Rying, one explanation is that individuals in criminal environment know facts needed by the law enforcement to solve the crime, but do not want to cooperate: "They are afraid or loyal" (Swedish Public Radio 2017).

The widespread code of silence among broader communities is a new phenomenon in Sweden, which in part has cultural roots. While criminals come from diverse backgrounds, there are family-based groups that can loosely be termed as clans. An article in *Forskning & Framsteg* (2015) further explains:

> Such constellations are "often pervaded by traditional norms, which means that perceived injustices and violations must be responded to in order for the group to maintain its honor and respect." The consequence is that quite trivial events can trigger spirals of serious violence.

The Nature of Crime

As mentioned in the previous chapter, the police divides criminals into a younger and an older group for analytical purposes. The younger group is made up of criminals younger than 23, and their crimes are typically less complex and committed locally. The organization of these criminals are described by the police (NCID 2014):

> Criminal cooperation among the younger is then often described by a number of influential people with "hangarounds." During the talks with the police authorities, it has emerged that on average, the number of influential criminals in the areas concerned are three to ten individuals.

These younger criminals often use drugs and can rarely support themselves on their criminal activities, which usually are small-time and in addition to the sale of drugs include thefts and burglaries.

It is interesting to note the low degree of sophistication regarding the types of crimes that are committed as well as the fact that crime does not seem to generate major financial returns. That most criminally active individuals earn surprisingly little from their activities has also been shown in US studies on drug-selling gangs (e.g., Levitt and Venkatesh 2000). The profits from drug sales are often used to finance personal drug consumption. Another common way to finance substance abuse use is theft. The absence of sophistication can be illustrated by the fact that theft often occurs spontaneously in local stores and primarily involves tobacco, consumer goods, and petty cash.

The older group—i.e., individuals aged 23 and older—is more problematic due to a higher degree of sophistication. They focus on various types of theft, carry out extortion and racketeering, and perform so-called smash-and-grab robberies, where display windows are shattered by tools or by driving a motor vehicle into the store. Older criminals are also more likely to work outside of their own areas and are overall more disciplined: "Cooperation between the older criminals is more characterized by ethnicity, family ties, or friendship bonds than the importance of the geographical location" (NCID 2014).

There is definitely an air of business sense and entrepreneurial spirit about some of the more seasoned criminals, who are more likely to be able to support themselves through crime. This group opportunistically adjusts its activities to changes in the surrounding economic environment. The Swedish National Council for Crime Prevention (SNCCP 2012) explains: "According to the police intelligence service, some operators are specialized, but it is common for persons involved in organized crime to engage in various crimes. The police call the latter multi-criminals."

Drug trafficking is perhaps the most important component of criminal activity, and often it takes place more or less in the open. The most common substance is cannabis, although the trade also involves heavier drugs, such as cocaine and methamphetamine. The NCID (2014) finds that "Younger criminals in these types of areas finance their addiction mainly in two ways: by selling, or by committing larceny. In this way, drug use is a natural gateway to crime."

In order to protect the commercial criminal enterprise, various methods and tools are employed—including the monitoring of passing vehicles in the areas, shakedowns, joint weapons caches, and mopeds. A shakedown is a form of extortion or robbery, where a debt is somehow engineered and a sum is meant to be paid as compensation for a perceived or imaginary offense. Weapons are hidden from the police by giving individuals in the younger group the task of storing and transporting them to more senior members. Mopeds are important tools in the business in order to move both weapons and drugs, but also to engage in surveillance and to observe the vehicles that pass by the territory.

As a direct consequence of drug trafficking, there are substantial problems with public displays of violence, in particularly in the centers of criminally exposed areas. In addition, this trend has been accompanied by threats and violence against eyewitnesses and plaintiffs. Many residents have adapted to this unsafe environment by avoiding public squares and other places at night. The Swedish Police Authority (2015) writes: "The public violence is also seen in the school environment. It has happened that school staff have been threatened or abused by students who have felt offended, and in many cases schools have been robbed in the daytime."

Journalists have also been subjected to threats. One of several examples is a Norwegian Public Broadcasting (NRK) interview with me. Swedish Public Television (2016a, b) writes:

> It was last week when Norwegian journalist Anders Magnus and the photographer Mohammed Alayoubi were going to interview the economist and commentator Tino Sanandaji in a restaurant in Husby, when they were confronted by some masked youths. In a film clip from NRK that Swedish Public Television News Stockholm has seen, you can hear Tino Sanandaji during an interview saying, "Sweden has failed in integration," after which you hear a chair being pulled out at an opposite table, and Sanandaji then telling the people that "I'm not denigrating your area, I'm not talking about Husby."
>
> Later in the clip, the TV team chooses to leave the restaurant while the men follow and yell "bang, bang, bang" after them and tell the TV team not to film in Husby. In connection with the feature, the TV team followed the police in the area and then a bunch of masked youngsters started throwing rocks at the police. It was after the police had arrested a person on suspicion of selling drugs, NRK writes.
>
> – – –
>
> Alayoubi has worked for NRK in several dangerous areas. But he says that the experience in Sweden was one of the most unpleasant days he ever had at work.
>
> "It was scary to be in Sweden on this job. They're so many, and they move around in gangs. We hear the police talking about hand grenades being thrown, shootings, and rock-pelting. It's like a war zone," he says. Like Mohammed Alayoubi, Anders Magnus has several times found himself in many dangerous locations due to his work. But he says that what happened now is not common.

This is only one of many similar incidents against journalists, albeit one in which I partook myself. Another example was reported in the tabloid *Expressen* (2018) as its team was chased away from the central square:

> They shout, wave, threaten us with assault, and rock-throwing if we don't leave. We mustn't film anything from the square, not even if they are not in it.
>
> "Don't you get what we're saying? Go away," shouts a man who has pulled up his sweater over his mouth. We move 20 meters to the bus stop. But the guys are agitated and come over to us.
>
> "Do you know who rules Botkyrka? Do you want us to show you?" We are no longer allowed to be on their square—and we can't ever come back. 20 people at the bus stop witness the event. No one says anything, no one does anything.

A World Apart

In some cases, the impact of crime on the local community is so profound that it leads to the emergence of so-called parallel societies. These types of societies have components such as a separate justice system, where conflicts are resolved outside of the regular legal system. Over time, what was once exceptional has become normalized in Sweden, including car-burning, explosions, shooting, and criminal control of entire areas. The willingness to report crime and assist with investigations is low in these neighborhoods, and the police is often hindered when carrying out their duties. This is true even for more serious crimes, so that shooting with multiple witness can go unreported. Fear of reprisals and a lack of trust and confidence in the Swedish justice system have undermined law enforcement in exposed areas (NCID 2014).

In some areas, there is direct pressure on the residents not to cooperate with the police. *Expressen* (2016) reports on instances of parallel justice involving "blood money," where murderers offer their victims' families blood money in exchange for their silence. The combination of threats and blood money convinces many witnesses not to participate in the legal process. In mob environments, to combine threats against those who cooperate with law enforcement with rewards for silence is a proven way of silencing relatives. For example, Mexican cartels are known to offer silver or lead—"Plata o Plomo." The threat makes it psychologically easier to accept the bribe, while the blood money takes the edge off the humiliation of being silenced by threats. In the same article, a police chief comments on the danger for the Swedish justice system: "We're heading towards a gangster society, where people shut themselves in and solve things themselves. We're talking about a parallel society."

The Swedish Police Authority (2015) report contains an interesting discussion about the more in-depth sociological mechanisms, which may explain the emergence of parallel societies in these areas. A key factor is low trust:

> The lower level of confidence entails that the local community has a harder time coping with emerging problems. Fewer cooperate with authorities, sometimes because of fear, perhaps most clearly illustrated by the will to testify or report crimes. Many feel abandoned by society, and when society is perceived as insufficient, the residents adapt to the situation.

Parallel societies result in the emergence of new norms and institutions. Examples include "criminal networks that allocate money to a so-called security fund, from which relatives of sentenced criminals may turn to receive financial support during the time the sentence is served." Through institutions like this security fund, criminal activity is likely to increase even further, since the criminal career becomes like any profession—with its own social insurance system.

Policing the Police

An unmistakable sign of the emergence of a parallel society is when it has become difficult for the state to enforce laws. The residents become less likely to testify or choose to withdraw their testimonies—sometimes due to local attitudes and sometimes as the direct result of threats. The Swedish Police Authority (2015) describes the force's difficulty in fulfilling its mission in these areas:

> The areas are generally considered to be very difficult in terms of, for example, surveillance since undercovers and unmarked units are rapidly identified by young people in the area. When the police approaches the area, criminals warn each other. At times of major police presence in the vulnerable areas, this may result in public displays of dissatisfaction. For instance, a vehicle check can give rise to a large crowd gathering around, with both attempts to free the suspect and actual success in doing so as a consequence. It also happens that instigators call on the crowds to attack the units. In the particularly vulnerable areas, a police intervention can lead to violent riots, with car fires and rock-throwing as a consequence. Therefore, the police are sometimes forced to hold off with intervening.

Against this background, the police has been forced to develop specific methods and measures for criminally exposed areas. For example, they always work in double units. The task of the extra unit is to ensure that the police vehicle is not vandalized while the regular unit carries out its mission. The vehicles also have reinforced windows to protect against rocks and other objects thrown at them. For the same purpose, the individual police officers routinely wear body armor, helmets, and shields. Protective goggles are also an increasingly important tool used to protect against the green lasers, with which police are increasingly being attacked.

Järvafältet is a large area extending through northwest parts of Stockholm and its suburbs. It was a park area until the 1970s when

Rinkeby, Tensta, Husby, Hjulsta, Kista, and Akalla were built as part of the Million Program. Today, the concentration of social exclusion in Järvafältet is very high. The Swedish Police Union magazine (*Polistidningen* 2016) discusses the difficulties that police officers face commuting to work in Rinkeby:

> "I don't look over my shoulder, but sure, if you've participated in a tough operation, you may not want to hang out in downtown Rinkeby after work," says Martin. None of them see public transportation as an option.
>
> – – –
>
> All people are not positive about the police presence. For example, those who hide their drugs around the subway entrance. Sometimes even inside the goods in the convenience store, says one of the police officers.
>
> "Sometimes, they also leave us notes. What did it say again? 'Fuck your mom, greetings from the guys'."

One of the solutions that have been developed in response to the situation is special so-called secure parking lots for the private vehicles of police officers. Another solution adopted is a kind of coordinated joint transportation to and from work for the individual police officers.

The pressure against the police by criminals is becoming increasingly fierce and has taken its toll. A police inspector at the operational unit in Stockholm warns about the situation (*Aftonbladet* 2018):

> Threats and serious violence against police officers are becoming increasingly common. Hundreds of policemen testify of serious violence and threats on the job in the past years; often in connection with having to go on missions alone. The Police Union is now putting pressure on the police management to try to prevent police from being sent alone into hazardous environments. Martin Melin, 51, is a police inspector at the operational unit in Stockholm.
>
> "Generally speaking, it would be good if the employer decided that we can't work alone, that would be the best solution. No police officer wants to work alone." … Aftonbladet has previously reported on how violence and threats against police have changed character in the past ten years: police cars that explode, hand grenades, attacks against police stations, and criminals attacking individual police officers.

The same article recounts a telling example of what has now become part of everyday Swedish police work: "On Wednesday night, a plain-clothes police officer was assaulted at a bus station in Skövde. He suffered a concussion and lost a number of teeth. The next squad that arrived at the scene was also attacked by the group. The fighting was stopped only when additional police squads arrived."

Further on the subject, the report *Threats and Violence against Police Officers* by the Swedish Police Union (2017) paints the following gloomy picture:

> Seven out of ten police officers report that exposure to threats, violence, and harassment has increased in the past two years, according to a recent survey on behalf of the Police Union. … As the Police Union now for the first time has asked questions about rock- and bottle-throwing and shootings with fireworks, 30 and 26 percent, respectively, of those who have been subjected to threats or violence reply that this is something that they have experienced. When the Police Union conducted similar surveys in 2008 and 2010, they were not even included as possible answers. Because of the developments in recent years, this has become a given question to ask.

Some additional numbers are reported by Swedish Public Television (2017a), commenting on police cars that have been torched, had their windows shattered, or their tires slashed: "An increasing number of police cars are vandalized in Stockholm County, and in only one year repair costs have doubled. During 2016, 87 police cars were reported for damage."

Not surprisingly, security professionals other than the police have also been exposed. The member magazine of the Swedish Transport Workers' Association reports that security guards are now prohibited from working at a public square in Gothenburg, following an aggravated assault on a security guard (*Transportarbetaren* 2017):

> "There's a small group that fully controls the square," says Ulf Jarnefjord, regional safety officer at the Swedish Transport Workers' Union in Gothenburg. The security guard who was assaulted could have been killed. Last Sunday, two security guards were attacked by about ten people in the same spot. One of them was beaten with his own baton. He was taken to hospital with multiple wounds to the head and a number of crushed fingers.

One strategy followed by the police to hold down crime is building massive, fortified police stations in troubled areas. An ironic example of this is the difficulties encountered in the project to build a police station in the neighborhood of Rinkeby. Swedish Public Television (2017b) reported that the high crime rate made it difficult to find contractors willing to accept the project:

> No one wants to build the new police station in Rinkeby. The construction of the new police station in Rinkeby has dragged on. According to sources to Swedish Public Television, there have not been any tenders from applicants, since many big construction companies do not want the job for security reasons.
>
> "It is much too dangerous to build a police station in the area," say several police officers, who want to remain anonymous. …
>
> "It has to be guarded around the clock. It is both a matter of risk of theft, but also of threats against the staff who are going to work at the construction site."

The new police station was scheduled to open in the summer of 2018, then in the fall of 2019. As of writing this book, it is still not finished.

Sabotaging Public Services

When a parallel society is established, it is not only difficult for the police to work in the area. Workers at the Social Insurance Agency and Social Services as well as parking enforcement officers increasingly find themselves under pressure. Dealing with applications for economic assistance and having the ability to impose fines becomes associated with frictions, pressure, and threats. Sometimes there is direct unlawful influence, but often it is rather the fear of being subjected to a crime or a threatening reaction that forces civil servants to preemptively modify their behavior (NCID 2014).

An undeniable example of areas being formal no-go zones for some professionals is the metro system in Stockholm, where some stops can temporarily become designated with Code Red—that is to say, too dangerous for tickets control officers to visit alone. *Svenska Dagbladet*'s (2018) article "Four Stations in the Metro 'No Go' for Security Guards" explains:

> Four subway stations have been marked red for ticket inspectors and security guards. Only with support from police are they allowed to perform their duties at the stops Rinkeby, Tensta, Rissne, and Hjulsta. In red areas, ticket inspectors and security guards are deemed unable to carry out their duties without police presence, out of concern for their own safety.
>
> "We are often numerically inferior, and are targets of threats and rock-throwing," says one security guard.

The Swedish postal service has also on several occasions designated some areas as too dangerous for their drivers to enter. One example is from a neighborhood in Malmö, Seved, where *force majeure* has been declared (*Sydsvenskan* 2017):

> Deliveries to Seved have been suspended for years. The measure is called "force majeure," and can be applied in the case of war, natural disasters, or other serious events that prevent deliveries. Many Seved residents are unaware of this and pay for home delivery of goods—but then receive a notice that the goods could not be delivered. Now they are tired. …
>
> "There are a number of streets where our drivers have been subjected to threats and violence. As a consequence, I've taken the decision to suspend distribution there. I must be able to guarantee the safety of drivers when they're working."

Similar halts have been decided on subsequently, and sometimes lifted only to be reinstated later. Swedish Public Television (2018b) reported on another postal stop in a nearby neighborhood: "When an announced delivery from the postal service never arrived the other day, Sylvia Ziegler went to its terminal in Toftanäs, and was then informed that her address was blocked. Sylvia's address at Augustenborg, next to Seved, is not safe to drive to."

No No-Go Zones?

There has been a reluctance to shed light on crime in vulnerable areas. For example, in 2015, Left Party MP Ali Esbati on Twitter accused the daily *Svenska Dagbladet*'s (2015) editorial page of spreading suggestive rumors when they wrote about "so-called no-go zones—places where rescue services, healthcare, and police cannot go without risk being attacked." Others show a greater concern for the criminal development in these areas, such as the former Norwegian Minister of Justice, Anders Anundsen: "We must ensure that we don't get the kind of conditions that the Swedes have. We will not have no-go zones for Norwegian police. We will have a much safer society than that" (Norwegian Public Broadcasting 2016).

In fact, this reluctance has often morphed into an outright denial of the violence in the suburbs by, for instance, intentionally misunderstanding what is meant by no-go zones. Other popular rhetorical tricks include relativization, using anecdotal examples such as personally feeling safe in criminally exposed areas, or pointing out that the majority in these areas do not commit crimes.

An illustrative example of the desire to downplay the severity of problems in the suburbs is the journalist Johanna Langhorst's 2013 book about Tensta, entitled *Hatred of the Suburb*. In the tabloid *Aftonbladet* (2013), she explained that the purpose of the book was to give the district a vindication and criticize the media's allegedly biased reporting: "It's common to just spread prejudice without thinking through it and making a further analysis, says Johanna, aiming a well-directed punch at investigative journalist Janne Josefsson." However, later in the article it becomes clear that during 17 years of living in Tensta, her son was robbed several times on the way home from school, to the effect he started taking detours and even refused to go to school. Eventually, the family moved to a safer area south of Stockholm, although in the words of Johanna herself: "I felt like a traitor, who gave in to all the haters who claim that Tensta is rife with crime. Statistically speaking, it's not more dangerous than in Southern Stockholm."

In sharp contrast to Johanna Langhort's assertions, *Dagens Nyheter* (2012) reported on a survey by the Safer Sweden Foundation on residents' assessment of safety in a number of affected areas in the following fashion: "Tensta is the most unsafe area in Sweden, according to the residents themselves." More extensive surveys focusing on Tensta have been conducted by the Stockholm municipally-owned housing company Svenska Bostäder. Their 2009 survey showed that a high proportion of the inhabitants were affected by crime, but that about half of them did not report it to the police. The survey also showed exceptionally high levels of perceived unsafety: "A total of 92 percent of the residents see crime in Tensta/Hjulsta as a problem. 62 percent consider it a major problem. Only 8 percent feel that crime in Tensta/Hjulsta is not a problem" (Svenska Bostäder 2009).

References

Aftonbladet. 2013. "Bok hänger ut Josefsson som rasist" [Book Hangs Out Josefsson as a Racist]. By Jenny Agö, April 18, 2013. https://www.aftonbladet.se/nyheter/a/qnmadE/bok-hanger-ut-josefsson-som-rasist.

———. 2018. "Polisen och tv-profilen Martin Melin: 'Ingen polis vill jobba ensam'" [Police and TV Profile Martin Melin: "No Police Officer Wants to Work Alone"]. By Helena Trus, October 7, 2018. https://www.aftonbladet.se/nyheter/a/xRkL8X/martin-melin-ingen-polis-vill-jobba-ensam.

Dagens Nyheter. 2012. "Tensta är den mest otrygga förorten" [Tensta Is the Most Unsafe Suburb]. By Stefan Lisinski, July 4, 2012. https://www.dn.se/sthlm/tensta-ar-den-mest-otrygga-fororten.

Expressen. 2016. "Mördarna köper sin frihet för blodspengar" [The Killers Buy Their Freedom for Blood Money]. By Micke Ölander, Kvällsposten, September 17, 2016. https://www.expressen.se/kvallsposten/mordarna-koper-sin-frihet-for-blodspengar.

———. 2018. "Här betalar kvinnorna för knarket med sex" [Here the Women Pay for the Drugs with Sex]. By Frida Sundkvist and Claes Petersson, July 1, 2018. https://www.expressen.se/nyheter/brottscentralen/qs/gangen/gang-2-fittja-kvinnor-betalar-med-oralsex--for-knarket.

Forskning & Framsteg. 2015. "Därför ökar de kriminella gängens makt" [That Is Why the Power of Criminal Gang Increases]. By Henrik Höjer, May 11, 2015. https://fof.se/tidning/2015/5/artikel/darfor-okar-de-kriminella-gangens-makt.

Goldfield, David R. 1982. "National Urban Policy in Sweden." *Journal of the American Planning Association* 48, no 1: 24–38. https://doi.org/10.1080/01944368208976164.

Haddad, Roger. 2015. "Skriftlig fråga till statsråd 2015/16:884: Extra resurser till no-go-områden" [Written Question to Minister: Extra Resources for No-Go Areas]. Sveriges riksdag, Stockholm. https://data.riksdagen.se/fil/6C7351BF-4D17-4A50-9FC9-0418E751A5AE.

Levitt, Steven D., and Sudhir Alladi Venkatesh. 2000. "An Economic Analysis of a Drug-Selling Gang's Finances." *The Quarterly Journal of Economics* 115, no. 3: 755–89. https://doi.org/10.1162/003355300554908.

NCID. 2014. "En nationell översikt av kriminella nätverk med stor påverkan i lokalsamhället: Sekretessprövad version" [A National Overview of Criminal Networks with Major Impact in the Local Community: Confidentiality-Approved Version]. National Criminal Investigation Division, Dnr: A452.732/2014. Underrättelsesektionen, Rikskriminalpolisen, Stockholm. https://snpf.org/wp-content/uploads/2015/09/En-nationell-översikt-Kriminella-nätverk-med-stor-påverkan-på-lokalsamhället.pdf.

Norwegian Public Broadcasting. 2016. "Sverige er ille. Men vi ser de samme krisetegnene i norsk politi" [Sweden Is Bad. But We See the Same Crisis Signs in Norwegian Police]. By Anders Magnus, *NRK*, September 18, 2016. https://www.nrk.no/urix/_-sverige-er-ille.-men-vi-ser-de-samme-krisetegnene-i-norsk-politi-1.13139913.

Oxford Advanced Learner's Dictionary. n.d. "no-go area." https://www.oxfordlearnersdictionaries.com/definition/english/no-go-area.

Polistidningen. 2016. "Edvard, polis i Rinkeby/Tensta: 'Vi har svikit de här områdena'" [Edvard, Police in Rinkeby/Tensta: "We Have Failed These Areas"]. By Emma Eneström, *Swedish Police Union magazine*, April 6, 2016. https://polistidningen.se/2016/04/vi-har-svikit-de-har-omradena.

Schulz, Solveig, Bengt J. O. Johansson, and Sonja Vidén. 2007. "State of the Art: Sweden." In *COST C16 Improving the Quality of Existing Urban Building Envelopes: State of the Art*, edited by Maria Therèse Andeweg, Silvia Brunoro, and Leo G. W. Verhoef, 31–44. Amsterdam: IOS Press. http://ebooks.iospress.nl/volumearticle/23234.

SNCCP. 2012. "Brottslighet och trygghet i Malmö, Stockholm och Göteborg: En kartläggning" [Crime and Security in Malmö, Stockholm, and Gothenburg: A Survey]. By Emma Ekström, Annika Eriksson, Lars Korsell, and Daniel Vesterhav, Swedish National Council for Crime Prevention. Brottsförebyggande rådet (Brå), Stockholm. https://www.bra.se/download/18.1ff479c3135e8540b29800013583/1371914737955/2012_Brottslighet_och_trygghet.pdf.

Svenska Bostäder. 2009. "Trygghet och socialt liv i Tensta/Hjulsta 2009 – en uppföljning" [Safety and Social Life in Tensta/Hjulsta 2009—A Follow-Up]. By Ulf Malm/ Malm Kommunikation AB, Svenska Bostäder, Stockholm. http://webbplatsarkivet.stockholm.se/_sites/www.svenskabostader.se/2016/04_09/Global/Pdfer/Om/TrygghetJarva/Trygghet_Tensta_Hjulsta_2009.pdf.

Svenska Dagbladet. 2015. "Det politiska ansvaret efter Ikeamorden" [The Political Responsibility After the IKEA Murders]. Editorial by Tove Lifvendahl, August 11, 2015. https://www.svd.se/det-politiska-ansvaret-efter-ikeamorden.

———. 2018. "Fyra stationer i t-banan 'no go' för ordningsvakter" [Four Stations in the Metro "No Go" for Security Guards]. By Jan Majlard, June 3, 2018. https://www.svd.se/fyra-stationer-i-t-banan-no-go-for-ordningsvakter.

Swedish Association of Local Authorities and Regions. 2007. "Trygghet, säkerhet, oro eller risk? Begreppsdefinitioner och mått" [Security, Safety, Concern, or Risk? Concept Definitions and Measures]. By Marie Torstensson Levander. Sveriges Kommuner och Regioner (SKR), Stockholm. https://webbutik.skl.se/bilder/artiklar/pdf/7164-309-4.pdf.

Swedish Police Authority. 2015. "Utsatta områden – sociala risker, kollektiv förmåga och oönskade händelser" [Vulnerable Areas—Social Risks, Collective Ability, and Unwanted Events]. Dnr: HD 5800-61/2015. Underrättelsesektionen, Nationella operativa avdelningen (NOA), Polismyndigheten, Stockholm. https://polisen.se/siteassets/dokument/ovriga_rapporter/utsatta-omraden-sociala-risker-kollektiv-formaga-och-oonskade-handelser.pdf.

Swedish Police Union. 2017. "Polisförbundets rapport: Hot och våld mot poliser" [Police Union Report: Threats and Violence Against Police Officers]. June 2017, Polisförbundet, Stockholm. https://www.polisforbundet.se/globalassets/publika-dokument/rapporter/hot-och-vald-mot-poliser-polisforbundets-rapport-2017.pdf.

Swedish Public Radio. 2017. "Färre mord klaras upp" [Fewer Murders Are Cleared Up]. By Evalisa Wallin, *I lagens namn*, July 2, 2017. https://sverigesradio.se/sida/artikel.aspx?programid=83&artikel=6725371.

Swedish Public Television. 2016a. "Norskt tv-team utsatta för stenkastning i Husby" [Norwegian TV Team Exposed to Rock-Pelting in Husby]. By Olof Thorell, *SVT Nyheter*, May 6, 2016, updated May 12, 2016. https://www.svt.se/nyheter/lokalt/stockholm/norskt-tv-team-utsatta-for-stenkastning-i-husby.

———. 2016b. "Hot och stenkastning mot norska journalister" [Threats and Rock-Pelting Against Norwegian Journalists]. By Johanna Eklundh, *SVT Nyheter*, May 6, 2016. https://www.svt.se/nyheter/inrikes/hot-och-stenkastning-mot-norska-journalister-1.

———. 2017a. "Allt fler polisbilar vandaliseras – stort problem för polisens arbete" [Increasingly More Police Cars Are Being Vandalized—A Major Problem for the Police's Work]. By Cecilia Ingvarsson, *SVT Nyheter*, April 27, 2017. https://www.svt.se/nyheter/lokalt/stockholm/allt-fler-polisbilar-vandaliseras-stort-problem-for-polisens-arbete.

———. 2017b. "Källor till SVT: Ingen vill bygga ny polisstation i Rinkeby" [Sources to Swedish Public Television: Nobody Wants to Build a New Police Station in Rinkeby]. By Andreas Björklund, *SVT Nyheter*, March 10, 2017, updated October 16, 2017. https://www.svt.se/nyheter/lokalt/stockholm/inga-anbud-pa-ny-polisstation-i-rinkeby.

———. 2018a. "Allt färre mord med skjutvapen klaras upp" [Increasingly Fewer Murders with Firearms Are Being Solved]. By Rebecca Randhawa Bergmark, *SVT Nyheter*, May 17, 2018. https://www.svt.se/nyheter/val2018/ny-studie-allt-farre-mord-med-skjutvapen-klaras-upp.

———. 2018b. "Malmöbon Sylvias adress är för farlig att leverera paket till" [Malmö Resident Sylvia's Address Is Too Dangerous for Delivery of Packages]. By Fanny Palm, *SVT Nyheter*, July 7, 2018, updated July 8, 2018. https://www.svt.se/nyheter/lokalt/skane/malmobon-sylvias-adress-ar-for-farlig-att-leverera-paket-till.

Sydsvenskan. 2017. "Inga paket levereras till Seved – nu har de boende tröttnat" [No Packages Are Delivered to Seved—Now the Residents Have Grown Tired]. By My Östh Gustafsson, June 6, 2017. https://www.sydsvenskan.se/2017-06-06/leveransstopp-i-seved-omradet-for-farligt-enligt-postnord.

Transportarbetaren. 2017. "Väktare förbjuds jobba på torg i Göteborg" [Security Guards Are Prohibited from Working at a Public Square in Gothenburg]. By Lena Blomquist, October 6, 2017, the member magazine of the Swedish Transport Workers' Association. http://www.transportarbetaren.se/vaktare-forbjuds-jobba-pa-torg-i-goteborg.

CHAPTER 15

Antisocial Behavior

Some say the world will end in fire,
Some say in ice.
From what I've tasted of desire
I hold with those who favor fire.
But if it had to perish twice,
I think I know enough of hate
To say that for destruction ice
Is also great
And would suffice.

—Robert Frost, *Fire and Ice*, 1920

One of the most conspicuous challenges facing Sweden is the rise of antisocial behavior, ranging from minor transgressions such as littering in libraries, all the way up to grenade attacks that have taken the lives of innocent children. Antisocial behavior includes violations of the formal and informal norms that govern social interaction, and which have elements of aggression or hostility. Therefore, behaviors that unintentionally violate rules or disrupt the surroundings should not be defined as antisocial; this could, for instance, include misuse of the laundry room due to lack of experience or language skills.

Antisocial behavior such as throwing rocks and verbal epithets, however, constitutes conscious acts that express antagonism. Another category of antisocial behavior, such as littering or speaking loudly in public environments, can occur both as a demonstration of dominance, or simply as a consequence of putting personal comfort above the well-being of others. Not showing consideration for one's surroundings, by deliberately breaking the rules of order that others follow, may also be regarded as a milder form of antisocial behavior.

Antisocial behavior is typically local in nature and thus mainly affects neighbors, classmates, and those living in the same area. It occurs to varying

T. Sanandaji, *Mass Challenge*,
https://doi.org/10.1007/978-3-030-46808-8_15

degrees among both native- and foreign-born. To the extent it is more common in areas of social exclusion, much of this antisocial behavior affects victims with a foreign background.

Public Disorder

Many antisocial problems are most common in places where young people gather such as schools, entertainment venues, and shopping centers. Disorder, however, also spill over into places frequented by a broader public—including hospitals and public baths. Libraries are public spaces that often are conveniently located, indoors, and with comfortable chairs and sofas. This makes them popular with youths and a hotbed for antisocial behavior.

The daily *Svenska Dagbladet* (2015a) reviewed two-and-a-half years' worth of incident reports from libraries in the Stockholm area during 2013–2015, and found that there were nearly 500 cases of violence, thefts, and brawls—concluding that "the sheer amount of incidents testifies to serious problems." In the article, library staff describe youth gangs that disrupt by yelling, arguing, harassing staff and visitors, watching Internet porn, and using libraries as substitutes for recreation centers:

> "Security guards are called; they are unable to bring order to the premises and thus call for backup. The youth gang ignores both staff and guards, and eventually they start an incident with one of our patrons. They physically attack the patron."
>
> – – –
>
> "The four form a menacing ring around the part-time librarian, and the boys say offensive and inappropriate things, including 'I'm gonna kill you,' 'I'm gonna show you my cock,' and so on."

Similarly, there are many reported cases of antisocial behavior in public baths, for example, Karlslundsbadet in Landskrona. The local newspaper *Helsingborgs Dagblad* (2016) writes:

> On Thursday evening, a large youth gang suddenly started throwing tables, chairs, and other things into the pool and mess with the staff. It was early in the evening when about 15 young people around 12 years old and up, some of whom were adults, suddenly began to behave badly.
>
> "They were rude and aggressive and threw tables around," said one of the staff who was present at the time.

But even more disruptive and disconcerting than the incidents in public libraries and pools is the fact that first responders—police, firefighters, and paramedics—are unusually severely impacted by antisocial behavior; even to the extent that they in several areas have encountered difficulties in carrying out their work. According to an article in the tabloid *Aftonbladet* (2016a) about the southwest Stockholm neighborhoods of Hallunda and Norsborg, attitude towards the police is so spiteful that they enter with at least two units in order to provide each other support. Public utilities such as elderly care providers, the post service, as well as the neighborhoods commercial landlords, have had to adapt and introduce new routines. Strikingly, we can read that "janitors have on occasion been forced to wear helmets, since residents throw things from the balconies."

Henrik Johansson, a representative for a trade union organizing ambulance staff, was interviewed in the liberal journal *Neo* (2015) and in *Svenska Dagbladet* (2015b)—saying that he has indeed been requesting specially trained "tactical units" with gas masks, riot helmets, and bulletproof vests for areas that are particularly troublesome and dangerous for first responders. He also relates that an acceptance has developed, where ambulance staff consider violence as part of everyday life. One consequence of the risk of assault is that patients living in areas of social exclusion do not receive emergency care as quickly they should, since ambulances must wait for a police escort before they dare to enter the area.

The same sentiments are echoed in an interview with firefighter Kaj Engelke in *TV4-Nyheterna* (2016), where he cites a survey revealing that three out of ten firefighters in and around Malmö and Stockholm received threats of violence during the previous year, and nearly half stated that there had been delayed responses due to threats of violence. Speaking of his own experiences, he said:

> "I've had paving stones thrown at me. I've had canned foods thrown at me. I've had cops with drawn weapons behind me when I've broken down doors, because there are known criminals behind the door that may attack you when you get the door open."

Henrik and Kaj are far from alone; many others also confirm the impression that the problems of attacks and harassment against rescue personnel have increased over time, and that they are not just isolated incidents. A study by Petzäll et al. (2011) found that threats and violence in ambulance care were on the rise already in the early 2000s. More recently, a crisis support coordinator for ambulance operations at the company Falck commented on the situation in a news segment in Swedish Public Television (2016a): "When I started in ambulance operations in the late '80s, the situation didn't look like today. It was a nicer climate." We are also told that as late as 2011, Falck only had five reported incidents were staff somehow ended up in distress. In 2015, the number had increased to 23, and in the first eight months of 2016 alone there were 28. A quote from an ambulance service officer illustrates how respect for healthcare services has disappeared: "You used to be able to leave the ambulance with the back door open, and nobody would touch the vehicle. Now people even walk into hospitals and steal things from the ambulances."

There are numerous examples of how assault on rescue services make their work difficult and cause harm for the general public. *Aftonbladet* (2019) reports:

> When they arrived at the burning preschool, the fire fighters were shot at with pyrotechnics. A number of rockets were fired at the firetruck as it approached the preschool.
>
> "When I drive into the area, I'm shot at with fireworks. I continue anyway, but then they've put up a hurdle. We cannot get through," Mats Olsson, the responsible officer at the Landskrona rescue services, tells Aftonbladet's photographer on the scene.
>
> "So we turn around and go back to another, safe, location and await the police. ... It can injure us and it can injure third parties who are prevented from receiving aid. It's dreadful," says Mats Olsson at the rescue services.

Upsala Nya Tidning (2017) reports on the traumatic effects of unrest on local residents.

> Fourteen cars were torched in total, an apartment was attacked with fireworks, and there were attempts to set fire to the school Gottsundaskolan. Police confirm that they knowingly delayed sending in squads ... Only when a sufficient number of squads had been assembled to escort emergency services, they entered Gottsunda to put out the fires.
>
> "It is, of course, regrettable for residents in the area. But we have to prioritize the safety of our staff." UNT interviews local residents who feel abandoned: "They have left us to our fate." Zahra Sameti says that she thinks that Gottsunda and Valsätra have changed; that safety in the area has deteriorated over the past years, and that she is now afraid to go out after dark.
>
> "It is 100 percent unsafe. I don't know what will happen when I walk here when it's dark. Anytime, anyone can appear and take my bag. Many people in the area that UNT speaks to are outraged about the fact that it took so long before police and emergency services arrived."

Violent antisocial behavior is not always planned, but can easily escalate from a lower-level hostility. The local newspaper *Mitt i* (2016) reports on how a "Snowball-fight ended with threat at gunpoint":

> A group of youths attacked security guards and construction workers at the city's "dialogue pavilion" in Bagarmossen. Both construction workers and security guards were at the scene, when some 15 youths appeared and started throwing snowballs both at the stand and at the security guard car. According to police statements, when staff told the youths to stop, they instead began kicking the guard's car until the alarm was set off. The security guard then felt obliged to alert their command center. At the same time, the row took a completely different turn. "Two masked men appear and point a gun at one of the construction workers."

Threats and unprovoked assaults also occur in different areas of healthcare. Local newspaper *Sydsvenskan* (2016a) writes in an article on intimidations against healthcare professionals in Malmö that there were hundreds of incidents reported in less than three years. Some of these only involve verbal abuse, while others are more serious such as the threat to stab a nurse. Yet another story from *Sydsvenskan* (2016b) describes the turbulent working environment for security guards in emergency care:

> The environment in the emergency room at Scania University Hospital in Malmö is sometimes filled with threats and violence, and it has become worse over the years. Last year, several serious incidents occurred and the security guards sounded the alarm. The Swedish Work Environment Authority made an inspection and concluded that the work situation for the security guards was very tough—to the extent that they made it mandatory to work in pairs. At the same time, the security guards started using bulletproof vests.

Healthcare operations have been impacted by large and unruly crowds of friends and relatives of victims, who do not necessarily mean to cause problems for healthcare workers, but act chaotically due to emotional stress of their injured loved ones. *Aftonbladet* (2017) reports:

> There is unrest outside the emergency room at Karolinska Hospital after the murder in Östberga. A witness told Aftonbladet that some 40 people have been in a row with the police. … Suddenly, the group ran for the entrance and banged on the windowpanes. People who sat in the waiting room have been moved to another room, according to the witness. The group has been in a fight with the police, and smashed trash cans in the waiting room.

Swedish Public Television (2018) cited a doctors' union survey among medical professionals about the extent of the problem, revealing that threats and violence increased by 50% between 2010 and 2015, whereas one-fourth of all members reported having been subjected to threats or violence in 2016 and 2017: "With the present trend, I can't rule out that we will need armed security guards in the emergency rooms within five or ten years if nothing is done," said union chairman Andreas Fischer.

In addition to medical care, schools have also been exposed to these problems. *Göteborgs-Posten* (2017) reports on the potential violence facing teachers in dealing with criminal youths: "Students threaten teachers with their families. A teacher at a school in Västerås has been subjected to stalking by a student's relatives, and is forced to have a personal assault alarm and security guards outside the home." Even more widespread is cases of threats and lower-level violence against teachers. *Sydsvenskan* (2018) reports the results from a survey in Malmö:

> Teachers who are afraid, break into tears, and cancel classes. Teachers who are humiliated, receive death threats, and are physically abused by students. Sydsvenskan examines testimonies from ten schools in Malmö. A few weeks before Malmö's primary school students and teachers went on summer holiday in 2017, The National Union of Teachers in Sweden sounded the alarm: The work environment at the city's schools was desperate—something had to be done. Almost 700 teachers had by then responded to the union's work environment survey. More than half of the teachers responded that they had sleep problems, suffered from stress and from the loud sound volume in the schools. 38 percent claimed that they had been subjected to pressure in connection to grading. More than ten percent had received threats or suffered physical abuse from students. ... [An example:] Student is told off after cutting the lunch line. The student then head-butts the teacher in the chest and says repeatedly that they will bring a knife to school to stab the teacher. During recess, the student tells their friends that they will stab the children and the teacher. A little later, the student again head-butts, hits, and kicks the teacher.

As the problem spreads, exposed occupations also include park workers who are weeding leaves. Swedish Public Radio (2016a) reports about recurrent incidents in the city of Västerås, requiring the police to be summoned to the aid of park workers:

> "It's been threatening situations with rock-throwing, and they've been jumping on cars. The atmosphere hasn't really been pleasant, simple as that."
>
> *What reactions have you received from the staff?*
>
> "They're super-worried and feel unsafe. Once surrounded, they've heard things like 'We're gonna kill you,' or 'Fucking whore'."

Swedish Public Radio (2017) reported that "Early this morning, staff who were cleaning the streets at Järntorget, among others, were subjected to a gang that threw rocks and glass bottles at them." The work climate for cleaners and street cleaners in Gothenburg has deteriorated so much that it triggered new security directives.

Attacks on Rescue Services

Sweden does not keep national statistics on rock-throwing incidents against first responders. Despite occurring regularly, this phenomenon is so new that the police has not yet introduced a crime code for rock-throwing that allows for the compiling of statistics. However, there are sporadic reports in the media about how widespread this phenomenon has become.

The Swedish Rescue Services Agency's magazine *Sirenen* (2005) contains one of the earliest articles discussing systematic problems with attacks on first responders, against the back-drop of two incidents of rocks being thrown against fire trucks. Three years later, the Swedish Police Union magazine (*Polistidningen* 2008) wrote about the fire department's need for police escort in Rosengård—something that had already then become standard in Malmö, but was still a rarity in the rest of the country:

> When there's a fire in Rosengård, the fire trucks are idling, waiting for the police before the firefighting can begin. Rock-pelting and death threats from children and adolescents have led the fire department to refuse to enter the area without police protection. … Often, children and young people are waiting by the fire, and sometimes threatening situations arise where firefighters are attacked with stones and eggs during their extinguishing efforts. In mid-June, a firefighter was subjected to a death threat, and during the same extinguishing effort, both police and firefighters became targets for egg-pelting. When they responded to a call the following day, a fire truck was attacked with rocks. Since then, the rescue service requires police escort to enter and put out the fires in the district.

The reporting above is similar to what we now see on a regular basis. The difference between now and then is that what a good decade ago was a phenomenon more or less unique to Malmö has now spread to other parts of the country, along with the expansion of the number of areas of social exclusion. Attacks against first responders have thus gone from being something unusual and startling to a normalized part of the everyday working environment for these occupational groups. An article from 2015 summarizes the developments during the preceding decade (Swedish Public Television 2015a):

> "The rock-pelting against police officers started in about 2006–2007. Then, these were exceptional events. Today, it's part of everyday life in some areas," says Swedish Police Union president Lena Nitz. A uniformed police officer in the Stockholm area describes the attacks to the reporter:
>
> "We're not talking about gravel. These are fist-sized rocks that will crack your head open."

Another article (*Dagens Nyheter* 2016) found that there were 30 incidents of rock-peltings of police during the first four months of 2016 in—Rinkeby alone. Police constable Biljana Flyberg tells of everyday police work after nightfall:

> "Now, all the 'ordinary' people go home and shut the doors behind them. The risk of getting stoned upon just entering the area now is unfortunately great. For me as a commanding officer, it feels extremely frustrating, I can no longer guarantee the safety of my colleagues." …
>
> "We want to work in this area. The majority of the population are incredible grateful that we're here, and we know we could do a great deal of good. But now it's about to go too far. We're too few and we're too often met with insults and violence." She's one of all the police officers who have been exposed to rock-pelting in the area—several times. In 2011, she was struck by a rock on the bridge of her nose, since then she hasn't been hit, but it's been a close call several times. Now she crouches automatically when she crosses under bridges—even when she's off-duty.

The strain on first responders from working under these conditions is a serious work environment issue that may also have repercussions on their spare time and private life. The stress that it creates is, arguably, a contributing factor to high levels of attrition among police.

In areas of social exclusion, there are frequent fights between young people and police, and it is not rare for the criminals to emerge victorious. For instance, the Swedish Public Radio (2016b) reported on attacks against police and rescue services from the area Kronogården in Trollhättan. Some 30 to 40 youths had gathered, stopped cars, and threw rocks and firecrackers at the police as well as others. Despite this, no one was arrested. The response from the police is telling and follows a pattern that is commonly repeated in these types of skirmishes: "The police chose not to confront the young people, because the attitude was so upset." Or as expressed by the deputy police chief: "If we had approached them, there would probably had been some form of riots. We chose instead to wait them out."

The tabloid *Expressen* (2016a) also reported on the unrest in Trollhättan. In addition to burning of tires, the riot included throwing rocks at the police, security guards, and tow trucks:

> "40 to 60 young people have mobilized. They have thrown at least four small paving stones and a big firecracker against police cars," said Karl-Johan Främling, desk sergeant at the Trollhättan police.

Another uniformed occupational group that has also been affected is parking enforcement officers. Norwegian Public Broadcasting (2016) was among the first to report that—for reasons of personal safety—parking companies do not send parking enforcement officers to Rinkeby and Tensta in the afternoons and evenings. In a similar vein, the local daily *Upsala Nya Tidning* (2016) reported that parking enforcement officers had been surrounded by hostile individuals and threatened also in Uppsala's suburbs. Some of these threats were extremely aggravated; an example was given in a report to the Work Environment Authority: "During usual monitoring of the no-parking zone at Bandstolsvägen, I was threatened by about nine people not to report two vehicles. Then they would fuck me, break me, and make chaos with me." Yet again, retreat seem to have been the instinctive response: "Now, the company is considering just going to the areas in the mornings when those making threats are presumed to be asleep."

An increasingly common phenomenon is that youth gangs set up an ambush, lure the police to a chosen location, and then attack them. In connection with unrest, an unusually ruthless attack also took place against an assisted living facility:

> The glazier company arrives at the building that had its windows smashed. It's a municipal assisted living facility for the mentally ill, and when the paving stones began to pour down at the entrance during Friday evening, many became scared. The reaction triggered the youth gang.

> "When they realized that there were actually people in there, they became excited and started throwing more stones. It was probably pure luck that more people weren't injured," says Johan Sjöholm.

In Cold Blood

There is a ruthless and destructive streak in the emerging suburban violence that has led to innocent people being victimized. A tragic example of this is that of a hand grenade thrown into an apartment in Biskopsgården in Gothenburg. The grenade killed eight-year-old Yuusuf Warsame, who was visiting his Swedish relatives. The tabloid *Aftonbladet* (2016b) visited Biskopsgården in the aftermath of the event. The news story describes the escalation of social unrest, to the extent that police cars could not drive into the area without the risk of being smashed: "The police was patrolling in teams of no less than four officers on foot, much like occupation forces in the West Bank or in Baghdad."

Aftonbladet's reporter also reproduced an interesting conversation with the locals on whether the lack of material resources explains the violence. In the story, it is noted that society has already made huge investments in Biskopsgården. This is illustrated by recording the variety of professional titles encountered in meetings with public officials. In addition to those associated with schools, the police, and social services, there were also more unusual and exotic titles like "Safety ambassador, culture coordinator, student assistant, auxiliary resource, comfort manager, equal treatment manager, job ambassador, and association consultant."

The hand grenade in Biskopsgården is an example of a particularly brutal form of antisocial behavior involving highly destructive weapons. But unfortunately, it is not unique in involving hand grenades. The extraordinary nature of this development is highlighted in a recent study by Sturup et al. (2019), which documented 77 recorded incidents between 2011 and 2016. The study writes that "In a European perspective, the increasing use of hand grenades seems to be unique to Sweden," noting that the only other country where hand grenades were used as much by criminals was Mexico, a country plagued by cartel violence. Given the dramatically higher rate overall of crime in Mexico, the mere hint of resemblance in the use of explosive weaponry between these two countries is astonishing.

The daily *Svenska Dagbladet* (2016) writes: "The influx of hand grenades into Sweden has increased over the last two years and does not seem to be slowing down. Sweden is one of the countries in Europe where the use of hand grenades has increased the most." In 2015, Swedish Public Television (2015b) reported the mind-blowing story that a hand grenade in Malmö can be cheaper than ice cream or falafel:

> "There's a greater supply of hand grenades today, and the risk is that use will spread to other cities because of the spiral of violence we're now seeing. Once you have used a grenade, you cross a mental barrier and it becomes easier to continue using them," said detective chief inspector Gunnar Appelgren.

The so-called Drug Roundabout in central Malmö became notorious in the fall of 2016, when a preschool chose to move its activities to the central public park, so that the children would not be threatened by the drug dealers. In a follow-up article, some parents of young children were interviewed (*Expressen* 2016b). A father relates how he left his sons for a moment on a football field near the roundabout, where his eldest son was playing football with some boys in their late teens. The game went a bit rough and when things soured, the eldest son was threatened with a gun held to his head. The article also reports:

> The three parents of small children constantly refer to major shootings and explosions when they're talking about the time of events. It was "the week after the Docentgatan shootout," and "just after the Babel explosion." At the same time, most events, small and large, have not been investigated.

The level of brutality in violent crime has risen so suddenly that the Swedish system has not been able to catch up. Law enforcement and legislation are in many cases not equipped to meet these new forms of antisocial violence. One example is that Swedish legislation for a long time did not classify hand grenades as weapons.

In societies that are used to antisocial behavior, the police and other authorities have greater capabilities to stop the violence. When the trend has lasted long enough, Sweden will no doubt also build up these capabilities. At the same time, the price for this is a tougher social climate. There is already rhetoric from the Moderate Party and other center-right parties about water cannons, curfews, and generally tougher measures. Among the general public, there is a strikingly strong sympathy for vigilante committees, the police using rubber bullets, extended powers for the state to engage in surveillance and monitoring of citizens, and a general loosening of civil rights. Attempts to counteract crimes and antisocial behavior through external control are costly and only a matter of treating the symptoms. Instead, the ideal way of solving the problem is to try to change the incentives and internal psychological driving forces that motivate this behavior.

The Social Impact of Antisocial Behavior

Much of the burden of crime and antisocial behavior have been on local residents, who in many cases have immigrant background themselves. Indeed, interviews with locals suggest that there is widespread law-and-order mentality among immigrants in these areas fed with crime, perhaps even more so than among the Swedish majority population. The hostile reaction of the youth against the majority society does not appear to have broad local support, which clearly separates the phenomenon from the type of ethnic unrest we have observed in, for instance, Northern Ireland or Basque regions of Spain.

In reason is the massive cost of this type of crime on immigrants who work hard in local small businesses, and that have seen their efforts sabotaged by destructive behavior. An extensive report by *fPlus* (2019) is worth citing on how economically devastating the combination of high crime and widespread disorder has been in a neighborhood of Malmö's Rosengård area—causing blighted economic activity and reducing the quality of life for the residents.

> Rosengård's police station looks robust and impenetrable, almost like a concrete bunker. When it was built in 2014, security was important—it was equipped with perimeter protection, defense against shootings, and a secure parking lot to thwart vandalism of police vehicles.
>
> "The perimeter protection is necessary. Last year, a hand grenade detonated in the courtyard, leaving a large crater here," says the photographer as we park the car. At the reception, there is something that looks like a big cat litter box with sand. The receptionist tells us that this is where you are supposed to put weapons and explosives if you want to hand them into the police. ... We continue past a row of closed business premises with empty windows. Former furniture stores, Glen informs us. But, clearly, you can't run such things here anymore, he says. There's neither the purchasing power here, nor the personal security. ...
>
> "Here, a store clerk had their throat cut as recently as last autumn ... The criminals are the ones who run society in there. We call it 'parallel social structures.' Crime isn't reported. The groupings have their own tribunals. They have their own trials and issue their own fines or other, worse, punishments. No one dares to tell us," he says. ... Inside the actual Seved center is one of the few remaining shops in Seved. But there are empty, former shops here and there. Police very rarely enter here to work, and almost never by foot patrol ...
>
> "They've driven through here with cars and shot people to death from the car window with a Kalashnikov. But since we put up these concrete slabs, this type of fatal shootings has stopped. They can't drive through and it's more difficult for them to escape the crime scene." ... Cameras are placed high up on the walls of the buildings and can withstand external impact. The area is also strongly lit at night. Maybe that is why curtains are shut in almost every apartment.

An editorial in *Göteborgs-Posten* (2018) depicts the situation for local business owners in so-called particularly vulnerable areas:

> Two-thirds of business owners have been victims of crime in the past year. Almost one-third has experienced threats or violence, according to a survey by Swedish Public Television among 101 business owners in the 23 areas that are classified as particularly vulnerable. The selection has focused on businesses in connection to or close to public squares. Of business owners who have responded that they have been victims of crime, more than one-third have chosen not to report this to the police. That is regarded as pointless. One business owner explains:

> "I don't have time to report everything when 100 percent of the cases are dropped. I was robbed some years ago—six hours later the robber came to my store. It was a threat, to show that he was out again." ... Another example of how a particularly vulnerable area differs from the rest of society comes from the business owner Ali Jomaa at Lindängen in Malmö. Of the eight languages that he speaks, Swedish is the one that he has least use for, though he lives and works in Sweden. Yet, Jomaa doesn't feel that the neighborhood where he lives is part of Sweden:
>
> "Lindängen isn't ruled by Swedish laws, but by the traditions from the home countries. What matters is the size of ones extended family."

While the degree differs from neighborhood to neighborhood, crime and antisocial behavior have had a negative impact throughout Sweden and have made many local victims dissatisfied—both with the criminals and the ineffectual Swedish authorities. Swedish Public Television (2016b) reports on attempts to organize protests:

> Salam Kurda has worked in the [Husby] area for 30 years. He is also the chairman of the local association of small business owners, and he says that they have now had enough of crime.
>
> "There are constant burglaries and we have sounded the alarm on the matter for a long time, but the response we get from the police is that they lack resources and that this is not a highly prioritized area. We feel abandoned. We simply cannot continue to run our businesses in the area.... All business owners have been subjected to crime in the form of daily threats, vandalism, burglary, shoplifting, and robbery."

Crime and high levels of disorder are sometimes described as a symbolic issue, but of course have wide-reaching implications for the surroundings. The next chapter goes beyond the anecdotes cited above and discusses the empirical support for the link between local crime and depressed economic activity.

References

Aftonbladet. 2016a. "Polisens hemliga rapport: Här är Stockholms läns farligaste områden" [Secret Police Report: Here Are Stockholm County's Most Dangerous Areas]. By Anders Johansson and Linda Hjertén, February 4, 2016, updated February 10, 2016. https://www.aftonbladet.se/nyheter/krim/a/J1LP38/polisens-hemliga-rapport-har-ar-stockholms-lans-farligaste-omraden.

———. 2016b. "Hans åttaåring blev offer för gängvåldet i Göteborgsförorten" [His Eight-Year-Old Became a Victim of Gang Violence in the Gothenburg Suburb]. By Peter Kadhammar, September 23, 2016. https://gangvaldet.story.aftonbladet.se.

———. 2017. "Oroligt vid akuten efter mordet – polis på plats" [Unrest at the Emergency After the Murder—Police on Location]. By Adam Westin, Jamshid Jamshidi, and Linn Dahlgren, August 15, 2017. https://www.aftonbladet.se/nyheter/a/1L17K/oroligt-vid-akuten-efter-mordet–polis-pa-plats.

———. 2019. “Brandmän beskjutna med raketer vid utryckning” [Firefighters Attacked by Rockets at Emergency Call]. By Joakim Magnå, December 30, 2019, updated December 31, 2019. https://www.aftonbladet.se/nyheter/a/Op20JA/brandman-beskjutna-med-raketer-vid-utryckning.

Dagens Nyheter. 2016. “Stenkastning allt vanligare mot poliser i Rinkeby” [Stone-Throwing Is Increasingly Common Against the Police in Rinkeby]. By Ulrika By, May 11, 2016. https://www.dn.se/sthlm/stenkastning-allt-vanligare-mot-poliser-i-rinkeby.

Expressen. 2016a. “Maskerade ungdomar kastade sten på polis” [Masked Youth Threw Stones at the Police]. By Sanna Wikström, August 31, 2016. https://www.expressen.se/gt/maskerade-ungdomar-kastade-sten-pa-polis.

———. 2016b. “Langare och dagisbarn möts i knarkrondellen” [Pushers and Kindergarten Children Meet in the Drug Roundabout]. By Johanna Karlsson, November 17, 2016. https://www.expressen.se/nyheter/langare-och-dagisbarn-mots-i-knarkrondellen.

fPlus. 2019. “Våldet tog död på företagandet – ‘nu skjuter man direkt i huvudet’” [Violence Killed Business Enterprise—“Now They Shoot Directly in the Head”]. By Henrik Sjögren, March 12, 2019, updated March 13, 2019. https://www.fplus.se/valdet-tog-dod-pa-foretagandet-nu-skjuter-man-direkt-i-huvudet/a/3jWVd0.

Göteborgs-Posten. 2017. “Skolvåldet: Elever hotar lärare med familjen” [School Violence: Pupils Threaten Teachers with Family]. By Katri Artta Svarfvar, TT, October 7, 2017. https://www.gp.se/nyheter/sverige/skolvåldet-elever-hotar-lärare-med-familjen-1.4710160.

———. 2018. “Svenska områden som inte är en del av Sverige” [Swedish Areas That Are Not Part of Sweden]. Editorial by Alexandra Boscanin. May 16, 2018. https://www.gp.se/ledare/svenska-områden-som-inte-är-en-del-av-sverige-1.6033452.

Helsingborgs Dagblad. 2016. “Ungdomsgäng härjade på Karlslundsbadet – polisen kom inte” [Youth Gang Raged at Karlslundsbadet—Police Did Not Come]. By Mikael Brandt, September 2, 2016. https://www.hd.se/2016-09-02/ungdomsgang-harjade-pa-karlslundsbadet---polisen-kom-inte.

Mitt i. 2016. “Snöbollskrig slutade med pistolhot” [Snowball-Fight Ended with Threat at Gunpoint]. By Anna Alexandersson, November 29, 2016. https://mitti.se/nyheter/snobollskrig-slutade-pistolhot.

Neo. 2015. “Det är definitivt ett nytt fenomen att vi är så utsatta” [It Is Definitely a New Phenomenon That We Are So Exposed]. By Paulina Neuding, February 6, 2015. http://magasinetneo.se/artiklar/det-ar-definitivt-ett-nytt-fenomen-att-vi-ar-sa-utsatta/.

Norwegian Public Broadcasting. 2016. “Kvinner i flere svenske bydeler tør ikke å gå ute om kvelden” [Women in Several Swedish Neighborhoods Dare Not Go Out at Night]. By Anders Magnus, *NRK*, May 8, 2016. https://www.nrk.no/urix/_-kvinner-i-flere-svenske-bydeler-tor-ikke-a-ga-ute-om-kvelden-1.12929688.

Petzäll, Kerstin, John Tällberg, Tom Lundin, and Björn-Ove Suserud. 2011. “Threats and Violence in the Swedish Pre-Hospital Emergency Care.” *International Emergency Nursing* 19, no. 1: 5–11. https://doi.org/10.1016/j.ienj.2010.01.004.

Polistidningen. 2008. “Brandkåren kräver poliseskort i Rosengård” [The Fire Brigade Requires Police Escort in Rosengård]. By Ulf Eliasson, *Swedish Police Union Magazine*, August 26, 2008. https://polistidningen.se/2008/08/brandkaren-kraver-poliseskort-i-rosengard.

Sirenen. 2005. “Stenkastning mot brandbilar” [Stone Throwing at Fire Trucks]. *The Swedish Rescue Services Agency’s Magazine*, no. 3, 2005. https://www.tjugofyra7.se/globalassets/sirenen/sirenen_2005_nr_03.pdf.

Sturup, Joakim, Manne Gerell, and Amir Rostami. 2019. “Explosive Violence: A Near-Repeat Study of Hand Grenade Detonations and Shootings in Urban Sweden.” *European Journal of Criminology*. https://doi.org/10.1177/1477370818820656.

Svenska Dagbladet. 2015a. “Stöket på biblioteken: Låt inte detta normaliseras” [The Mess in the Libraries: Do Not Allow This to Become Normalized]. Editorial by Paulina Neuding, June 6, 2015, updated June 7, 2015. https://www.svd.se/lat-inte-detta-normaliseras.

———. 2015b. “Våld ett allt större problem” [“Violence Is a Growing Problem”]. Editorial by Paulina Neuding, July 26, 2015. https://www.svd.se/vald-ett-allt-storre-problem.

———. 2016. “‘Unik’ ökning av handgranater – Sverige sticker ut i Europa” [Unique Increase in Hand Grenades—Sweden Stands Out in Europe]. By Frida Svensson, August 25, 2016. https://www.svd.se/unik-okning-av-handgranater--sverige-sticker-ut-i-europa.

Swedish Public Radio. 2016a. “Parkarbetare hotas och utsätts för stenkastning” [Park Workers Are Threatened and Subjected to Stone-Throwing]. *P4 Västmanland*, August 24, 2016. https://sverigesradio.se/sida/artikel.aspx?programid=112&artikel=6502560.

———. 2016b. “Polisen flydde Kronogården efter stenkastning i natt” [Police Fled Kronogården After Stone-Throwing Last Night]. *P4 Väst*, August 31, 2106. https://sverigesradio.se/sida/artikel.aspx?programid=125&artikel=6507667.

———. 2017. “Kvinnor allt mer otrygga i samhället” [Women Are Becoming Increasingly Insecure in Society]. By TT, January 10, 2017. https://sverigesradio.se/sida/artikel.aspx?programid=83&artikel=6604950.

Swedish Public Television. 2015a. “Vanligt med attacker mot polisen” [Usual with Attacks Against the Police]. By TT, August 31, 2015. https://www.svt.se/nyheter/vanligt-med-attacker-mot-polisen.

———. 2015b. “Billigare att köpa handgranat än en glass” [Cheaper to Buy Hand Grenades Than an Ice Cream]. By Diana Olofsson, *SVT Nyheter*, July 31, 2015. https://www.svt.se/nyheter/lokalt/skane/billigare-att-kopa-handgranat-an-en-falafel.

———. 2016a. “Allt vanligare med attacker mot ambulanser” [Increasingly Common with Attacks Against Ambulances]. By Thomas Jonasson, *SVT Nyheter*, August 24, 2016. https://www.svt.se/nyheter/inrikes/allt-vanligare-med-attacker-mot-ambulanser.

———. 2016b. “Butiksägare i Husby: ‘Vi känner oss övergivna’” [Shop Owners in Husby: “We Feel Abandoned”]. By Amela Mahovic, *SVT Nyheter*, December 26, 2016, updated December 30, 2016. https://www.svt.se/nyheter/lokalt/stockholm/smash-and-grab-i-husby.

———. 2018. "'Kan behövas beväpnade skyddsvakter på akuten inom fem till tio år'" ["Armed Security Guards May Be Required in the Emergency Within Five to Ten Years"]. By Tommy Bergman, *SVT Nyheter*, July 1, 2018, updated July 2, 2018. https://www.svt.se/nyheter/lokalt/stockholm/lakarforbundet-kan-behovas-bevapnade-skyddsvakter-inom-fem-ar.

Sydsvenskan. 2016a. "Akutsjuksköterskan blev attackerad på jobbet: 'Han bara fortsatte slå'" [The Emergency Nurse Was Attacked at Work: "He Just Kept Beating"]. By Oskar Ahlqvist, August 28, 2016. https://www.sydsvenskan.se/2016-08-26/han-bara-fortsatte-sla.

———. 2016b. "Sjukhuset vill öka säkerheten – kan ta bort ordningsvakterna på akuten" [The Hospital Wants to Increase Safety—Might Remove the Emergency Guards at the Emergency]. By Oskar Ahlqvist, August 29, 2016. https://www.sydsvenskan.se/2016-08-29/sjukhuset-vill-oka-sakerheten-kan-ta-bort-ordningsvakterna-pa-akuten.

———. 2018. "Malmölärare börjar gråta, blir slagna och ställer in lektioner" [Malmö Teachers Begin to Cry, Get Beaten, and Cancel Classes]. By Andreas Persson and Olof Westerberg, January 10, 2018. https://www.sydsvenskan.se/2018-01-10/malmolarare-borjar-grata-blir-slagna-och-staller-in-lektioner.

TV4-Nyheterna. 2016. "Var tredje brandman utsätts för hot – 'jag är rädd'" [Every Third Firefighter Is Threatened—"I'm Scared"]. October 1, 2016. https://www.tv4.se/nyheterna/klipp/var-tredje-brandman-utsätts-för-hot-jag-är-rädd-3549012.

Upsala Nya Tidning. 2016. "P-vakter hotas på tre platser i Uppsala" [Parking Guards Are Threatened at Three Locations in Uppsala]. By Håkan Frisell, July 28, 2016. https://www.unt.se/nyheter/uppsala/p-vakter-hotas-pa-tre-platser-i-uppsala-4314391.aspx.

———. 2017. "Brandattentat mot bostad i Gottsunda" [Fire Attack Against Housing in Gottsunda]. By Jon Velander, November 24, 2107. https://www.unt.se/nyheter/uppsala/brandattentat-mot-bostad-i-gottsunda-4827350.aspx.

CHAPTER 16

The Socioeconomic Cost of Crime

Miserable it is to be to others cause of misery.

—John Milton, *Paradise Lost*, 1667

The analysis of the socioeconomic effects of immigration is usually separated from the analysis of crime and antisocial behavior, such as gang-related crime in problem neighborhoods. But crime and antisocial behavior are very much socioeconomic issues. Crime is impacted by economic factors such as poverty, while crime prevention measures such as burglar alarms and security guards are significant industries. An even more important but indirect link is that crime has socioeconomic costs. Crime is per definition undesirable. By harming others and reducing their well-being, crime leads to high costs for society. This applies both to more serious crimes like assault and murder, as well as less serious but more common crimes like harassment and vandalism.

Crimes such as vandalism, robbery, and arson cause damage to property and often directly harm economic activities. Convenience stores are robbed, shops face problems with shoplifting, and merchants get their premises scrawled with graffiti. These types of costs are fairly straightforward to quantify. The largest cost item for crime is, however, likely to be human costs—which are significantly more difficult to measure. Violent crime and sexual offenses cause suffering both for those affected and for their families. A philosophical discussion exists about whether it is appropriate to put economic price tags on psychological pain and human lives. Calculations that estimate the costs of injuries and deaths should not be seen as cynical exercises, when they are aimed at preventing crime or accidents. For example, by assigning each traffic accident an economic cost, it has become easier for authorities to justify investments in road safety, as well as to guide the allocation of resources to the measures that are the most effective in preventing injuries and deaths.

The socioeconomic burden of crime is difficult to estimate, although it is known to be substantial (Cohen and Bowles 2010; Chalfin 2015; DeLisi

T. Sanandaji, *Mass Challenge*,
https://doi.org/10.1007/978-3-030-46808-8_16

2016). For instance, when including the psychological costs caused by crime, the total cost of crime in the United States has been estimated to one trillion dollars per year, at the time equivalent to 12% of GDP (Anderson 1999). Estimates in countries with low crime have similarly shown significant social costs associated with crime—for example, 6.5% of GDP in England and Wales (Brand and Price 2000). Beyond these costs, long-term costs affecting productivity and investment may also arise if organized crime impacts business, creates corruption, and reduces foreign investment (Detotto and Otranto 2010).

To the extent that crime is impacted by immigration, the cost of crime is part of the socioeconomic effects of immigration. Crime and disorder are not minor details or symbolic issues but primary factors in the debate on immigration. For example, in a research review, Bell and Machin (2013) write that "the economic and social costs of crime are usually estimated to be large, so any link between immigration and crime should be of significant concern to researchers and to policymakers alike."

The effect of immigration on crime differs between different types of immigration, and from country to country. In countries where immigration has reduced crime, this effect becomes a social gain from immigration. In countries such as Sweden, where immigration has pushed crime up beyond the level where it would have been without immigration, it is instead an added cost. There are, however, no estimates of these costs for Sweden comparing them to the direct economic costs on, for instance, public finances. Since crime causes significant adverse effects, it is not impossible that the increase in crime and antisocial behavior is the greatest socioeconomic cost item of immigration for Sweden.

Card et al. (2012) suggest that the effects of immigration on quality of life can be a more important explanatory factor for resistance to immigration than its direct economic costs. Immigration impacts not only the economy but also cultural life, social cohesion, school performance, crime, and other aspects which affect quality of life. Except directly negative effects, it may also simply be the case that the majority population prefer to live surrounded by their own culture, cuisine, language, and religion. The authors write:

> A distinctive feature of immigration is that it changes the composition of the receiving country's population, imposing potential externalities on the existing population. Several previous studies have focused on the fiscal spillovers created by redistributive taxes and benefits (e.g., MaCurdy, Nechyba, and Bhattacharya, 1998; Borjas, 1999, Hanson, Scheve and Slaughter, 2007). A broader class of externalities arises through the fact that people value the "compositional amenities" associated with the characteristics of their neighbors and co-workers.
>
> – – –
>
> But standard economic studies generally ignore the value that people place on having neighbors and co-workers who share their language, ethnicity, culture, and religion. A large body of research has shown that concerns over

> "compositional amenities" affect decisions about what neighborhood to live in, what schools to attend, and which employees to hire. In this paper we argue that similar concerns play an important part in mediating views about immigration policy.

According to the study, these effects can cause immigration to be perceived as something that reduces quality of life—even when the direct economic impact is only marginally negative or even positive.

Estimates of Socioeconomic Costs of Crime

The costs of social externalities, such as crime and disorder, are more difficult to capture using traditional methods than the direct effects of immigration on, for example, public finances. An interesting way to estimate the size of these indirect effects is to study home prices. When immigration leads to positive social externalities, such as a richer cultural life and other ambient advantages, homebuyers will be willing to pay more to live in an area with a higher density of immigrants. On the contrary, if immigration leads to negative externalities such as crime and disorder, these areas are less attractive—which, in turn, is reflected in home prices. There are several studies examining the effect of crime on home prices, and also a few studies examining the effect of immigration on home prices through both crime and other channels. Although they are more difficult to calculate, methods to indirectly calculate the cost of crime and other externalities have been developed in empirical research.

One method is to use surveys to assess the public's valuation of conveniences and other factors that are valued but not priced in markets. For example, in environmental research, the public's evaluation of different aspects of a better environment, such as cleaner lakes, is estimated. The goal is to establish an approximate monetary valuation in order to justify expenditures intended to preserve the environment. The value of clean lakes comes mainly in the form of psychological well-being, and this benefit is something important that the public is willing to pay money for. A technique developed for this purpose uses survey methods to ask the public about their long-term willingness to pay to avoid pollution.

Cohen et al. (2004) used the same technique to calculate the public's willingness to pay to avoid crime in the United States. The study shows that the public has a high collective valuation of low crime. It confirms the impression that the material costs of crime are secondary, compared to the immaterial costs, and that safety is highly valued in monetary terms. The negative effect of crime on life and health is, thus, considerably more significant than the purely material damage. In today's money, the collective willingness to pay amounted to over \$80,000 for each reduction of aggravated assault, and over \$10 million for each reduction in homicide. Similar calculations by DeLisi et al. (2010) estimated the cost of a murder to more than \$15 million.

The cost of crime includes concerns about future crimes as well as suffering from crime that affects others—both close relatives and other members of the community. This is not irrational but a natural consequence of human psychology. Most of us have empathy and care about others, not just ourselves. Research in economic psychology also shows that most people have an aversion to risk, uncertainty, and loss. This explains why many are willing to pay a premium for insurance, or prefer a secure income over the chance to gain an expectedly higher but more uncertain income. The same psychological mechanisms explain why people experience a psychological cost from the risk of future crime, which is greater than the psychological cost of crimes that have already occurred in their society (Anderson 2012).

Home Prices as a Measure of Social Externalities

Another extensive research literature uses hedonic price theory to examine how society values the different things that normally are not priced in a market, such as clean air and school quality (Harrison and Rubinfeld 1978; Saiz and Wachter 2011). The underlying assumption of hedonic price theory, as applied to housing, is that a home can be viewed as a collection of factors that jointly determine the property price. These are partly related to the property itself (number of square meters, year built, etc.), and partly the location of the property—i.e., the area in which it is located, the distance to various facilities, and how vulnerable the home is to various disturbances and risk factors such as crime and noise.

Hedonic price theory is, then, used to estimate what consumers value by dividing the complex pricing model into its components (Rosen 1974). The valuation of, for example, a car, a computer, or a home depends on its properties. Car buyers are interested in factors like horsepower, safety, environment, and comfort. But the car is purchased as a single package, which means that these properties cannot be measured directly, but instead must be estimated indirectly through a model. Similarly, homes are valued based on their characteristics such as size, views, balconies (or lack thereof), equipment, and location (Sheppard 1999; Boyle and Kiel 2001; Wilhelmsson 2002; Fransson et al. 2002; Lind and Bergenstråhle 2004; Werner 2008; Bayer et al. 2016). One of the characteristics that residents value the most is safety and the absence of crime and disorder, which is evident both from surveys and from comparisons of home prices. Consequently, an indirect way to estimate the negative socioeconomic costs of crime is to estimate how much crime lowers home prices.

Simplified, immigration can be said to have two effects on the real estate market. One is that the increase in population—no matter the success rate of integration—tends to increase real estate prices by increasing the demand for housing and drive up prices in the areas where housing is limited. In the long run, a larger population usually leads to more construction of housing where free space is available, which abates the effect of immigration on the real estate market. Increased housing prices are not a straightforward profit for the recipient nation, but is rather a redistribution between different population groups. It favors property owners, but hurts those who rent, or young people who have not yet had time to buy their first home.

The second, more complex, and probably more important effect of immigration on home prices occurs through social externalities. The attractiveness of a residential area largely depends on the residents' behavior and social situation. Most people prefer to live in areas with "well-behaved" neighbors. Part of the value of living in nice areas is a question of prestige and status, which from a socioeconomic perspective is dubious to analyze because it probably involves a zero-sum game—which is not affected by immigration on the aggregate level. Some areas, like Stockholm's posh Östermalm district, would have been considered more exclusive than others regardless of the size of immigration. But status is not the only reason why some neighborhoods are more attractive than others. Other factors relate to non-zero-sum benefits for residents, such as safety, and are thus part of the socioeconomic calculation when determining the impact of immigration.

Attractive areas have schools and preschools with better outcomes, more positive peer effects from other students, and fewer social disturbances. Higher purchasing power leads to the establishment of more shops, cafes, restaurants, and other services. These areas tend to be more physically attractive, both when it comes to private residences and commercial premises as well as public infrastructure. Well-being and job satisfaction are not small details in economic analysis; they are the very point of economics. Contrary to what many believe, economics is not about the narrow concern for money and purely material factors; it is rather fundamentally about what people value in terms of life satisfaction—that is, what economists call utility. The economy is, of course, measured in terms of money, but money is not considered to have any intrinsic value. It only has value insofar as people require material consumption for their life satisfaction. The bulk of the value and utility in society is probably created outside of markets—for instance, in the family and through leisure activities.

As usual when it comes to immigration, it is not a uniform phenomenon, which makes it impossible to talk about a generally positive or negative effect on home prices. The effect may, for instance, vary between different immigrant groups (Zhu et al. 2016). The influx of high-skilled immigrants with low crime rates tends to increase home prices, while the immigration of low-skilled individuals—resulting in increased poverty and antisocial behavior—tends to lower the attractiveness of areas and home prices.

There are a number of studies on the relationship between crime and home prices that are worth considering. The first modern study using the hedonic method was performed in 1978 by the Chicago economist and 2017 Nobel laureate Richard Thaler. Crime was shown to reduce home prices with an elasticity of 0.07. Elasticity is a measure of how much a 1% change in a variable impacts another variable. Gibbons (2004) examined the relationship between crime and home prices in London in a similar study, which also further developed the method. There was a clear negative effect of crime with a standard deviation's increase in crime, reducing home prices by 10%. Another study that gained attention for its methodology is Linden and Rockoff (2008), who with high precision estimated the effect of a particular type of crime on home prices. The study showed that when a registered sex offender moves in, their neighbor's home drops in value by an average of 12%.

Ihlanfeldt and Mayock (2010) studied the relationship between crime and home prices in Florida, using a model that takes into account that crime and low property prices are endogenous—i.e., that crime both affects and is affected by low home prices. Their conclusion is that each percent increase in crime in a residential neighborhood leads to 0.1–0.3% lower home prices. In other words, residents are willing to pay a premium to live in areas with fewer violent crimes, such as assault and robbery. Tita et al. (2006) also found significant negative effects of crime on home prices in the United States, with the greatest impact coming from violent crime. Pope and Pope (2012) investigated how the reduction of crime in the United States in the 1990s affected property prices, and concluded that each percent of crime reduction led to 0.15–0.35% higher property prices at the national level.

There are also studies in Sweden which show that crime reduces home prices. Two studies on Stockholm by Ceccato and Wilhelmsson (2011, 2018) found a negative impact of crime on home prices. A similar paper on Jönköping by the same authors confirmed that the link between a lack of safety and home prices also exists in smaller cities (Ceccato and Wilhelmsson 2014).

The above studies examine the effects of crime on home prices. Immigration is, of course, not the only factor affecting crime, and immigration does not only impact home prices through effects on crime but also through, for example, effects on the local schools. Additionally, there is a literature that directly estimates the effects of immigration on home prices. The effects have differed between different countries and forms of immigration. Saiz (2003, 2007) found a correlation between immigration and higher rents in the United States. Likewise, Gonzalez and Ortega (2013) identified a positive effect between immigration and home prices in Spain.

Saiz and Wachter (2011) found a negative correlation between the proportion of people with immigrant background and the development of home prices in the United States, which is driven by the exodus of wealthier white households—in other words, so-called *white flight*. There are, as mentioned earlier, major differences between various immigrant groups, where the negative effects tend to be linked to a larger proportion of immigrants with lower education levels. For example, immigrants from the Indian subcontinent and Europe have no negative effect on home prices, while immigration from Latin America does have negative effects.

Sá (2015) similarly finds a strong negative effect on home prices driven by the relocation of the native population in the UK. The estimate is that immigration equivalent to 1% of the initial population reduces average home prices by 1.7%. Lastrapes and Lebesmuehlbacher (2019) also study the impact of refugee immigration on English home prices and find negative effects.

Bakens et al. (2013) examine the relationship between the proportion of those with immigrant background and home prices in the Netherlands. The conclusion is that there are both negative and positive effects of diversity, but that the negative effects (e.g., crime) are greater than the positive ones (e.g., a greater range of services and restaurants). Accetturo et al. (2014) examine immigration's effect on home prices in Italy. The study separates the effect of population growth and changes in perceived quality of life, and states:

> The impact is also quantitatively significant: a 10% increase in immigrant population decreases local prices by nearly 2 percentage points with respect to the city average. According to the theoretical model, this effect is entirely determined by the impact of immigration on the level of the natives' satisfaction with local amenities. This implies that the areas hit by immigration are likely to experience a deterioration of local amenities.

The weakening of public utility is not only influenced by the proportion of immigrants in itself, but also by the fact that the degree of so-called ethnic fragmentation reduces the strength of the social ties that bind the local community together.

Algan et al. (2016) use housing allocation to study the effects of different degrees of diversity on social cohesion in France. Ethnic fragmentation led to "anomie"—a sociological term that can be translated into apathetic norm dissolution—and weakened social ties. Residential areas with larger number of ethnicities had lower ability to maintain public utility and to combat vandalism and graffiti, but not more violent crimes.

The Impact of Crime on Business

Beyond negative effects on households, crime also entails costs for businesses. One indication of this is that almost all large and medium-sized companies in Sweden, as well as three-quarters of small businesses, pay for private security solutions. Problems tend to be greatest in areas that have been affected by social exclusion for some time. These areas are already characterized by low purchasing power, which in itself makes companies less interested in establishing themselves there. Another negative effect on local business is that crime tends to drive away people from cities and their centers (Cullen and Levitt 1999).

Crime affects businesses in several ways. First and foremost, there is a direct cost of theft, robbery, extortion, shoplifting, vandalism, and harassment. Business owners must, therefore, dedicate time and resources to prevent and deal with crime, which thereby takes time and resources away from core operations. In addition to these direct costs, there is also the indirect effect of a decrease in entrepreneurship and business expansion. Another negative effect is that market functions deteriorate due to the transaction costs and the inefficiency caused by crime.

Criminal activity can create a negative spiral. The risk of individuals ending up in a criminal career is the highest in socially disadvantaged areas that have fewer economic opportunities. At the same time, crime primarily impacts local business, which limits their ability to offer new jobs. Therefore, crime is not just a result but also a cause of higher unemployment.

Lens and Meltzer (2016) examine the impact of crime on the value of commercial property, such as stores and other business activities in New York. Crime has a strong negative impact on local business, an effect that is even stronger in already poor minority areas. The authors conclude that law enforcement is an important mechanism to relaunch the economy in affected areas: "crime control, especially in poorer communities of color, can revitalize economic activity by reducing the cost of doing business."

In Sweden, there are now several areas where local business owners are subjected to pressure, racketeering, and extortion. Typically, the victims are restaurant and convenience store owners, and some have even been coerced into selling their businesses at a loss. In these areas, it is not uncommon that criminals take over public spaces and try to enforce their own rules—while taking things from shops and eating in restaurants without paying.

The popular science magazine *Forskning & Framsteg* (2015) quotes a police officer regarding the adverse effect of crime on various businesses in Rinkeby and Tensta: "The last bank moved when someone sent in fireworks, so that it suffered fire damage. The pharmacy was robbed over and over again, and they finally got tired of it. The Social Insurance Agency has moved away."

Social unrest with gross vandalism, stone throwing, and car burnings often occur in the center of these areas, where commercial activities tend to be located. Naturally, this impacts business. Another example is the phone operator Tele2's shop in Rinkeby, which only lasted for a few months. After one robbery, a burglary attempt, and several other unpleasant incidents in a short period of time, the shop was closed permanently citing personnel safety (*Mitt i* 2016). The most spectacular of these incidents was a smash-and-grab attempt, when a wheel loader was crashed into the entrance of the shop.

It is not only Swedish media that have taken notice of this development. The World Bank also comments on corporations' crime-related costs in a report on Swedish business climate (World Bank Group 2015):

> Somewhat surprisingly, 40 percent of the firms in Sweden suffer losses due to theft and other crime, and 85 percent spend on security. Losses due to crime and expenses on security as a proportion of firm's annual sales in Sweden are comparable to those found in developing countries in such regions as Latin America.

Business owners in social exclusion areas are well aware of the fact that crime is an obstacle to entrepreneurship. As mentioned in the previous chapter, on December 30, 2016, all business owners in Husby center closed their shops as a protest against crime. Covering the protest, the Swedish Public Television (2016) reported that "They argue that it's not possible to operate businesses in the area before the problems are fixed, and now demand that the police and the politicians in the city of Stockholm take action."

Disorder and Unsafety

James Wilson and George Kelling's classic "Broken Windows" from 1982 is one of the most influential articles in the social sciences. Their theory is that the visible signs of decay, such as broken windows that are not being repaired, signal that an area is not characterized by care and social control, which invites more crime. The theory has also been confirmed empirically, among others by Keizer et al. (2008). Wilson and Kelling (1982) write:

> Many citizens, of course, are primarily frightened by crime, especially crime involving a sudden, violent attack by a stranger. This risk is very real, in Newark as in many large cities. But we tend to overlook another source of fear—the fear of being bothered by disorderly people. Not violent people, nor, necessarily, criminals, but disreputable or obstreperous or unpredictable people.
>
> ---
>
> Second, at the community level, disorder and crime are usually inextricably linked, in a kind of developmental sequence. Social psychologists and police officers tend to agree that if a window in a building is broken and is left unrepaired, all the rest of the windows will soon be broken.
>
> ---
>
> But vandalism can occur anywhere once communal barriers—the sense of mutual regard and the obligations of civility—are lowered by actions that seem to signal that "no one cares."

Even if the issue of visible vandalism like shattered windows has received the most attention, there are many other important insights in the article. Wilson and Kelling present a wider range of disturbances than traditional crime, noting that the public "apparently assign a high value to public order."

Antisocial behavior can be viewed as a continuum with various degrees of severity—from serious but rare crimes, such as murder and rape at the one end, to less serious but common occurrences, such as vandalism and disorder at the other (Ross and Mirowsky 1999; Sampson and Raudenbush 1999). The aggregated negative effects of disturbances should not be underestimated; although the cost per incident is small relative to violent crime, the number of incidents is much greater.

The public's strongly negative reaction to crime is also clear from surveys, and it is precisely a lack of safety that is the most common problem voiced by those who have left immigrant areas. In 2004, the city of Malmö sent a questionnaire to all households who moved from Malmö to other areas in Scania County. The headline from the study of the reasons given for abandoning Malmö was "Unsafety most important cause." There are, of course, many who move for everyday reasons such as work, studies, or larger living space for the children. But the dissatisfaction with Malmö, despite its otherwise favorable location, is rooted in a fear of crime and antisocial behavior. The city of Malmö (2005) report states: "The most important cause for moving is lack of safety. Safety includes a safe environment, few external disturbances, and a good environment for children to grow up in. Three-quarters believe that a safe environment is a cause that justified moving away."

Similar patterns are found in surveys of people's reasons for moving from areas of social exclusion, such as Rågsved in Stockholm (City of Stockholm Dept. of Statistics and Analysis 2011). A large proportion of respondents provided lack of safety, vandalism, and crime in general as reasons for moving.

Being forced to live in an area that is unsafe due to crime and disorder has a negative effect on human well-being. Feelings of lack of safety have a continuous impact on everyday life and restrict freedom of action. Many are forced to change their lifestyle, for example, in the way that parents can no longer let their children play outside or walk home from school by themselves. Even when crime prevention activities keep crime in check, many prefer a more open lifestyle to safety provided by surveillance cameras, a neighborhood watch, gated communities, or the constant mistrust of strangers that often characterize unsafe areas. This explains why many have a very high willingness to pay to avoid the risk of exposure to crime.

Crime Prevention Measures

An important dimension that is rarely discussed in Sweden is preventive measures in order to avoid crime. Everyone takes, to varying degree, measures to avoid crime—even those who are never victims of crime. Obvious examples are to lock the door, not go out alone late at night, or to avoid areas with high risk of crime. In his groundbreaking paper on crime, Gary Becker (1968) writes:

> A variety of private as well as public actions also attempt to reduce the number and incidence of crimes: guards, doormen, and accountants are employed, locks and alarms installed, insurance coverage extended, parks and neighborhoods avoided, taxis used in place of walking or subways, and so on.

The social cost of crime includes all measures to lower the number of crimes committed. In addition, preventive measures absorb a part of any increase in the underlying latent criminal risk. This means that the number of crimes actually committed may underestimate an increase in unsafety and crime risk. A somewhat extreme example can illustrate this: Imagine an unusually dangerous street where the probability of being robbed is 100%. If everyone in the city knows this and acts based on this information, no robberies will be observed on the street, since everybody avoids it and instead takes other routes. Therefore, if we look at the number of robberies on the street, we will underestimate the latent crime risk. The example is extreme, but the logical point is important to consider.

We noted in Chapter 11 that the number of women who become victims of sexual crimes and young women's fear of going out by themselves have increased. Young women often adapt their behavior to the risk of violations—for example, by not going out alone, being vigilant, carrying panic alarms, taking taxis, and by avoiding certain locations. Even the risk of violation thus leads to the restriction of women's freedom of movement. A clear example of this was reported by the Swedish Public Television (2017) in the article "Women Opted out of New Year's Celebration at Larmtorget":

> Last New Year's Eve, 33 women filed police reports that they had been victims of sexual harassment at Larmtorget Square in Kalmar. This year, not a single case was reported. At midnight, women were nowhere to be found at Larmtorget ...
>
> "Women and young girls have opted out of the square," says municipal police officer Lotta Petersson.

In the subsequent year—in immediate response to the previous year's mass violations—women avoided central Kalmar at the New Year's celebrations, which led to the number of crimes committed plummeting to zero. That no molestation occurred cannot be interpreted as a sign of low risk of violation. Despite no crime being committed, the community was forced to adapt by restricting women's freedom of movement.

In recent years, technology for preventing car theft has sharply reduced property crime, without the underlying crime risk necessarily having declined to the same extent. Another trend is that more people have installed locks, alarms, and gates in their homes. All these costly measures have led to fewer crimes, but are nonetheless reactions to an increase in crime risk. Some behavioral changes that reduce crime, such as lower cash use, only partly depend on crime and would have occurred anyways. Other measures are taken automatically without further reflection, such as locking your car door and switching on your alarm. But if the crime risk had been zero, few would have installed car alarms and advanced locks. Likewise, since residents adjust their behavior, an increased crime risk rarely leads to a proportionate increase in the number of observed crimes.

A study in Argentina tried to empirically estimate the importance of crime prevention measures (Tella et al. 2010). In the 1990s, the capital Buenos Aires was struck by a crime wave. The study observes that wealthy residents responded with a sharp increase in security measures taken, such as alarms and private guards, in order to protect their homes. But the rich had no greater possibility of reducing the risk of being the victim of robbery on the street than the poor. The study finds that the number of street robberies rose as much for wealthy people as for others, while robbery in the home increased less among the rich. The authors write:

> An important finding is that robberies in the street, where the rich cannot do better than mimic the behavior of the poor, show similar increases in victimization for both income groups. For home robberies, where the rich can protect themselves with expensive protection devices, we find larger increases in victimization rates among the poor.

Similarly, Levitt (1999) explains that different risks of being a victim of a crime for the rich and the poor may partly be because the rich are more able to take security measures, and that the costs of the crimes that actually occur are not the only price that we pay for crime:

> The natural tendency is to calculate the extra burden borne by the poor as a result of higher crime victimization. Such a calculation, however, would ignore the fact that individuals distort their behavior in costly ways (for example, by moving to the suburbs, investing in security systems, or not going out after dark). Any measure of the burden of crime should incorporate not only the costs of those victimized, but also the investment made to avoid victimization.

Crime prevention measures in Sweden have increased in recent years. Statistics Sweden (2004) examined crime prevention measures among Swedish households over time. Between the early 1990s and early 2000s, there was a sharp increase in the incidence of burglar alarms as well as security grilles and gates. The increase was primarily found in metropolitan areas. Regarding the number of homes that had installed security gates, the report states that "As the case with burglar alarms, there has been almost a doubling in the 1990s."

According to more current figures from Statistics Sweden, the turnover for security and guard services was close to $2 billion in 2015. During the period 2000–2015, it increased three times faster than the turnover of other businesses. The private security industry now has, according to some estimates, more employees than there are police officers. *Göteborgs-Posten* (2016) writes: "Today, the security industry has overtaken the police in terms of both financial and human resources. Around 31,000 people work in private security companies, while the number of police officers is 20,000." Other figures confirm the picture of a greater focus on crime prevention measures. According to the international study ICVS, the proportion of households in Sweden with burglar alarms increased from 5% in 1992 to about 16% in 2004, and about 25% in 2010 (Dijk 2010).

When one takes these crime prevention measures into account, it is easier to understand why there is concern about crime in groups who are not victims of crime to a very high degree. It is common for women and older people to be more worried about crime than young men, who are more exposed to crime. Many have interpreted this—sometimes in contemptuous terms—to mean that women and older people are irrational. This, however, indicates an unsophisticated analysis of the effects of crime. Those who are more vulnerable to crime tend to adjust their behavior and act more cautiously, while young men do not let the risk of crime limit their mobility to an equal degree. Hence, there is no automatic paradox or irrationality in that women and older people are more worried about crime, although they rarely suffer from violent crime. Bushway and Router (2008) explain this in their review of how economic analysis has contributed to studies on crime:

> Women are particularly vulnerable to threats of force and present attractive targets to potential robbers, who are primarily male. And women are more frightened of robbery than are men. But, men were 2.7 times more likely to be victims of robbery than women in 2005 (US Department of Justice 2006). From criminal opportunity theory perspective, this is not because men are inherently more attractive targets than women, but because women, on average, take steps to prevent robbery that men do not take, and as a result of these steps, men are more attractive targets on average. From this perspective, researchers must always remember that one observes the result of actions taken by both potential criminals and potential victims.

Similar reasoning can also be found in Wilson and Kelling's (1982) above-mentioned "Broken Windows" article:

> Surveys of citizens suggest that the elderly are much less likely to be the victims of crime than younger persons, and some have inferred from this that the well-known fear of crime voiced by the elderly is an exaggeration: perhaps we ought not to design special programs to protect older persons; perhaps we should even try to talk them out of their mistaken fears. This argument misses the point. The prospect of a confrontation with an obstreperous teenager or a drunken panhandler can be as fear-inducing for defenseless persons as the prospect of meeting an actual robber; indeed, to a defenseless person, the two kinds of confrontation are often indistinguishable. Moreover, the lower rate at which the elderly are victimized is a measure of the steps they have already taken—chiefly, staying behind locked doors—to minimize the risks they face. Young men are more frequently attacked than older women, not because they are easier or more lucrative targets but because they are on the streets more.

In countries with high crime, so-called gated communities are common—i.e., neighborhoods that are separated from their surroundings with gates, fences, or other forms of access control for external parties entering the building. Gated communities have been criticized for increasing segregation and reducing social capital, and many perceive it as an unpleasant development that wealthier people shut themselves off from the rest of society by excluding others. Some areas in Sweden have already been called gated communities. For example, *Aftonbladet* (2015) writes: "Gated communities have arrived in Sweden. In Kungsbacka, a construction project consisting of several buildings behind walls and gates is being planned."

A paper by cultural geographer Mikaela Herbert (2014) studied the phenomenon and its development in Malmö since the early 2000s, when a housing co-op in the central parts of the town applied for planning permission to install walls, fences, and gates. Initially, creating such enclosed areas was controversial and sparked debate, but the author nonetheless concludes that "During the last decade, enclosed apartment buildings have become a more common sight in Malmö." About three-quarters of enclosed apartment buildings in Malmö are located in areas with a high concentration of foreign-born residents. Many residents in less socioeconomically deprived areas also experience problems from surrounding areas.

Herbert's interviews with residents showed that from a societal perspective, they are often negative toward the development of enclosed areas and reduced openness, which they compare to United States, but at the same time they feel compelled to put up barriers to protect themselves. In the words of a deputy chairman of a housing co-op in western Malmö, cited in the article, "People want peace and quiet where they live."

One of the most interesting measurements of reduced safety and lower openness in Sweden is found in the Swedish Transport Administration's studies on the freedom of movement of children. As part of traffic-related research, studies of children's way to school and other destinations were conducted in the years 1981 and 1983. Since 2000, these questions and new ones are asked by the Transport Administration every three years. Fewer and fewer parents allow children to walk to school, recreation centers, sports fields, public swimming pools, libraries, and shops on their own (Public Health Agency of Sweden 2008; Björklid 2012; Transport Administration 2012; Swedish Association of Local Authorities and Regions 2013).

The reduction in children's freedom of movement in Sweden has been significant. The proportion of children aged seven to nine, who are allowed to walk to school without being accompanied by an adult, fell from 94% in 1981 to 47% in 2009—while the percentage that may go to shops unaccompanied by an adult fell from 82 to 24% during the same period (Björklid 2012). The trend is, however, not unique to Sweden, and the proportion of children who get to school on their own has also decreased in the United States (Pinker 2011).

A report by the Swedish Association of Local Authorities and Regions (2013) discusses the reasons for this change, including increased traffic risk, changed norms, and higher risk aversion among parents. Interviews with parents also suggest that concerns about crime is an important factor. The report includes an interview with a father:

> He described the children's way to school and possible events based on the risk of assault. He wondered "what people can you trust?" …
>
> "There have been muggings, juvenile robberies. I don't want him to go there. I don't trust those surroundings. Girls had been raped."

A Transport Administration (2012) report also indicates that declining perception of the safety of free-roaming children is not only about traffic. Perceived safety of the route to school declined between 2003 and 2012—although perceived traffic safety increased slightly. Similarly, the perceived safety of traffic environment for routes to recreation centers, playgrounds, sports fields, green areas, and playmates was stable, with a slight tendency toward improvement. At the same time, the proportion of children with permission to go unaccompanied to all these destinations fell.

It is difficult to determine the extent to which children's reduced mobility reflects lower risk tolerance among parents, and if the parents' concern is well-founded. At the same time, the sharp reduction in the freedom of movement of children in Sweden since 1981 is consistent with the overall story of a wider reduction in the sense of safety.

References

Accetturo, Antonio, Francesco Manaresi, Sauro Mocetti, and Elisabetta Olivieri. 2014. "Don't Stand so Close to Me: The Urban Impact of Immigration." *Regional Science and Urban Economics* 45: 45–56. https://doi.org/10.1016/j.regsciurbeco.2014.01.001.

Aftonbladet. 2015. "Här kan du bo bakom murar och spärrar" [Here You Can Reside Behind Walls and Barriers]. By Josefin Westin, April 13, 2015, updated April 14, 2015. https://www.aftonbladet.se/nyheter/a/L0a0z1/har-kan-du-bo-bakom-murar-och-sparrar.

Algan, Yann, Camille Hémet, and David D. Laitin. 2016. "The Social Effects of Ethnic Diversity at the Local Level: A Natural Experiment with Exogenous Residential Allocation." *Journal of Political Economy* 124, no. 3: 696–733. https://doi.org/10.1086/686010.

Anderson, David A. 1999. "The Aggregate Burden of Crime." *The Journal of Law and Economics* 42, no. 2: 611–42. https://doi.org/10.1086/467436.

———. 2012. "The Cost of Crime." *Foundations and Trends® in Microeconomics* 7, no. 3: 209–265. https://doi.org/10.1561/0700000047.

Bakens, Jessie, Peter Mulder, and Peter Nijkamp. 2013. "Economic Impacts of Cultural Diversity in the Netherlands: Productivity, Utility, and Sorting." *Journal of Regional Science* 53, no. 1: 8–36. https://doi.org/10.1111/jors.12012.

Bayer, Patrick, Robert McMillan, Alvin Murphy, and Christopher Timmins. 2016. "A Dynamic Model of Demand for Houses and Neighborhoods." *Econometrica* 84, no. 3: 893–942. https://doi.org/10.3982/ECTA10170.

Becker, Gary S. 1968. "Crime and Punishment: An Economic Approach." *Journal of Political Economy* 76, no. 2: 169–217. https://doi.org/10.1007/978-1-349-62853-7_2.

Bell, Brian, and Stephen Machin. 2013. "Immigration and Crime." In *International Handbook on the Economics of Migration*, edited by Amelie F. Constant & Klaus F. Zimmermann, 353–72. Cheltenham: Edward Elgar.

Björklid, Pia. 2012. "'Hur kom du till skolan idag?' Vad har hänt sedan 80-talet?" ["How Did You Get to School Today?" What Has Happened Since the 1980s?]. Institutionen för pedagogik och didaktik, Stockholms universitet, Stockholm. http://m.ansvarforframtiden.se/client/files//content/projekt_vi_driver/Tylosandseminariet/Presentationer_2012/O_1130_Pia_Bjorklid.pdf.

Boyle, Melissa, and Katherine Kiel. 2001. "A Survey of House Price Hedonic Studies of the Impact of Environmental Externalities." *Journal of Real Estate Literature* 9, no. 2: 117–44. https://www.aresjournals.org/doi/abs/10.5555/reli.9.2.23u082061q53qpm3.

Brand, Sam, and Richard Price. 2000. "The Economic and Social Costs of Crime." Home Office Research Study 217, Home Office, London. https://mpra.ub.uni-muenchen.de/74968.

Bushway, Shawn, and Peter Reuter. 2008. "Economists' Contribution to the Study of Crime and the Criminal Justice System." *Crime and Justice* 37, no. 1: 389–451. https://doi.org/10.1086/524283.

Card, David, Christian Dustmann, and Ian Preston. 2012. "Immigration, Wages, and Compositional Amenities." *Journal of the European Economic Association* 10, no. 1: 78–119. https://doi.org/10.1111/j.1542-4774.2011.01051.x.

Ceccato, Vania, and Mats Wilhelmsson. 2011. "The Impact of Crime on Apartment Prices: Evidence from Stockholm, Sweden." *Geografiska Annaler: Series B, Human Geography* 93, no. 1: 81–103. https://doi.org/10.1111/j.1468-0467.2011.00362.x.

———. 2014. "The Impact of Safety on a Small Town's Housing Market." CEFIN—School of Architecture and the Built Environment, Royal Institute of Technology (KTH), Stockholm. https://www.researchgate.net/publication/265414862_The_impact_of_safety_on_a_small_town's_housing_market.

———. 2018. "Gangs and Space." In *The Oxford Handbook of Environmental Criminology*, edited by Gerben J. N. Bruinsma and Shane D. Johnson, 518–44. Oxford: Oxford University Press. https://doi.org/10.1093/oxfordhb/9780190279707.013.30.

Chalfin, Aaron. 2015. "Economic Costs of Crime." In *The Encyclopedia of Crime & Punishment*, edited by Wesley G. Jennings. Chichester: Wiley. https://doi.org/10.1002/9781118519639.wbecpx193.

City of Malmö. 2005. *Flyttlassen kommer och går: Fakta och attityder kring hushåll som flyttat till eller från Malmö under år 2004* [The Loads of Furniture Come and Go: Facts and Attitudes about Households that Moved To or From Malmö in 2004]. Malmö: Stadskontoret, Kommunikation & Utveckling.

City of Stockholm Dept. of Statistics and Analysis. 2011. "Vilka flyttar från Rågsved och varför?" [Who Moves from Rågsved and Why?]. By Jennie Westman and Jan-Ivar Ivarsson. Stockholms Stads Utrednings- och Statistikkontor, Stockholm. https://insynsverige.se/documentHandler.ashx?did=102221.

Cohen, Mark A., and Roger Bowles. 2010. "Estimating Costs of Crime." In *Handbook of Quantitative Criminology*, edited by Alex R. Piquero and David Weisburd, 143–62. New York: Springer.

Cohen, Mark A., Roland T. Rust, Sara Steen, and Simon T. Tidd. 2004. "Willingness-To-Pay for Crime Control Programs." *Criminology* 42, no. 1: 89–110. https://doi.org/10.1111/j.1745-9125.2004.tb00514.x.

Cullen, Julie Berry & Steven D. Levitt. 1999. "Crime, Urban Flight, and the Consequences for Cities." *Review of Economics and Statistics* 81, no. 2: 159–69. https://doi.org/10.1162/003465399558030.

DeLisi, Matt. 2016. "Measuring the Cost of Crime." In *The Handbook of Measurement Issues in Criminology and Criminal Justice*, edited by Beth M. Huebner & Timothy S. Bynum, 416–33. Chichester: Wiley. https://doi.org/10.1002/9781118868799.ch18.

DeLisi, Matt, Anna Kosloski, Molly Sween, Emily Hachmeister, Matt Moore, and Alan Drury. 2010. "Murder by Numbers: Monetary Costs Imposed by a Sample of Homicide Offenders." *The Journal of Forensic Psychiatry & Psychology* 21, no. 4: 501–13. https://doi.org/10.1080/14789940903564388.

Detotto, Claudio, and Edoardo Otranto. 2010. "Does Crime Affect Economic Growth?" *Kyklos* 63, no. 3: 330–45. https://doi.org/10.1111/j.1467-6435.2010.00477.x.

Dijk, Jan van, Pat Mayhew, John van Kesteren, Marcelo Aebi, and Antonia Linde. 2010. "Final Report on the Study on Crime Victimisation." INTERVICT, Tilburg University, Tillburg. https://serval.unil.ch/resource/serval:BIB_0F-77D65C5D99.P001/REF.pdf.

Forskning & Framsteg. 2015. "Därför ökar de kriminella gängens makt" [That Is Why the Power of the Criminal Gang Increases]. By Henrik Höjer, May 11, 2015. https://fof.se/tidning/2015/5/artikel/darfor-okar-de-kriminella-gangens-makt.

Fransson, Urban, Gunnar Rosenqvist, and Bengt Turner. 2002. "Hushållens värdering av egenskaper i bostäder och bostadsområden (Household Preferences for Housing Attributes)." Institute for Housing and Urban Research, Uppsala University, Gävle.

Gibbons, Steve. 2004. "The Costs of Urban Property Crime." *The Economic Journal* 114, no. 499: F441–F463. https://doi.org/10.1111/j.1468-0297.2004.00254.x.

Gonzalez, Libertad, and Francesc Ortega. 2013. "Immigration and Housing Booms: Evidence from Spain." *Journal of Regional Science* 53, no. 1: 37–59. https://doi.org/10.1111/jors.12010.

Göteborgs-Posten. 2016. "Fler väktare och ordningsvakter än poliser" [More Watchmen and Security Guards Than Police]. By Sanna Arbman Hansing, July 13, 2016. https://www.gp.se/nyheter/västsverige/fler-väktare-och-ordningsvakter-än-poliser-1.3477377.

Harrison, David, and Daniel L. Rubinfeld. 1978. "Hedonic Housing Prices and the Demand for Clean Air." *Journal of Environmental Economics and Management* 5, no. 1: 81–102. http://dx.doi.org/10.1016/0095-0696(78)90006-2.

Herbert, Mikaela. 2014. "Låsta grindar i den polariserade staden" [Locked Gates in the Polarized City]. In Att laga revor i samhällsväven – om social utsatthet och sociala risker i den postindustriella staden, by Richard Ek et al., 90–100. Malmö University Publications in Urban Studies 18, Malmö University, Malmö. http://muep.mau.se/handle/2043/18123.

Ihlanfeldt, Keith, and Tom Mayock. 2010. "Panel Data Estimates of the Effects of Different Types of Crime on Housing Prices." *Regional Science and Urban Economics* 40, no. 2: 161–72. https://doi.org/10.1016/j.regsciurbeco.2010.02.005.

Keizer, Kees, Siegwart Lindenberg, and Linda Steg. 2008. "The Spreading of Disorder." *Science* 322, no. 5908: 1681–85. https://doi.org/10.1126/science.1161405.

Lastrapes, William D., and Thomas Lebesmuehlbacher. 2019. "Asylum Seekers and House Prices: Evidence from the United Kingdom." Working paper. https://doi.org/10.2139/ssrn.2868420.

Lens, Michael C., and Rachel Meltzer. 2016. "Is Crime Bad for Business?: Crime and Commercial Property Values in New York City." *Journal of Regional Science* 56, no. 3: 442–470. https://doi.org/10.1111/jors.12254.

Levitt, Steven D. 1999. "The Changing Relationship Between Income and Crime Victimization." *Economic Policy Review* 5, no. 3: 87–98. https://papers.ssrn.com/sol3/papers.cfm?abstract_id=1014080.

Lind, Jan-Erik, and Sven Bergenstråhle. 2004. *Boendets betydelser och boendes värderingar* [The Meanings of the Accommodation and the Values of the Residents]. Göteborg: Göteborgs universitet, Sociologiska institutionen.

Linden, Leigh, and Jonah E. Rockoff. 2008. "Estimates of the Impact of Crime Risk on Property Values from Megan's Laws." *The American Economic Review* 98, no. 3: 1103–27. https://doi.org/10.1257/aer.98.3.1103.

Mitt i. 2016. "Tele2 lämnar Rinkeby" [Tele2 leaves Rinkeby]. By Johanna Edström, May 4, 2016. https://mitti.se/nyheter/tele2-lamnar-rinkeby.

Pinker, Steven. 2011. *The Better Angels of Our Nature: Why Violence Has Declined.* New York: Viking.

Pope, Devin G., and Jaren C. Pope. 2012. "Crime and Property Values: Evidence from the 1990s Crime Drop." *Regional Science and Urban Economics* 42, no. 1–2: 177–88. https://doi.org/10.1016/j.regsciurbeco.2011.08.008.

Public Health Agency of Sweden. 2008. "Aktiv transport – på väg mot bättre förutsättningar för gång- och cykeltrafik" [Active Transport—On the Way to Better Conditions for Pedestrian and Bicycle Traffic]. By Johan Faskunger, R 2008:31. Statens folkhälsoinstitut, Östersund. https://www.folkhalsomyndigheten.se/contentassets/9621865e6bbc4d2c94ea689596bc73e3/r200831_aktiv_transport_08111.pdf.

Rosen, Sherwin. 1974. "Hedonic Prices and Implicit Markets: Product Differentiation in Pure Competition." *Journal of Political Economy* 82, no. 1: 34–55. https://doi.org/10.1086/260169.

Ross, Catherine E., and John Mirowsky. 1999. "Disorder and Decay the Concept and Measurement of Perceived Neighborhood Disorder." *Urban Affairs Review* 34, no. 3: 412–32. https://doi.org/10.1177/107808749903400304.

Sá, Filipa. 2015. "Immigration and House Prices in the UK." *The Economic Journal* 125, no. 587: 1393–1424. https://doi.org/10.1111/ecoj.12158.

Saiz, Albert. 2003. "Room in the Kitchen for the Melting Pot: Immigration and Rental Prices." *Review of Economics and Statistics* 85, no. 3: 502–21. https://doi.org/10.1162/003465303322369687.

———. 2007. "Immigration and Housing Rents in American Cities." *Journal of Urban Economics* 61, no. 2: 345–71. https://doi.org/10.1016/j.jue.2006.07.004.

Saiz, Albert, and Susan Wachter. 2011. "Immigration and the Neighborhood." *American Economic Journal: Economic Policy* 3, no. 2: 169–88. https://doi.org/10.1257/pol.3.2.169.

Sampson, Robert J., and Stephen W. Raudenbush. 1999. "Systematic Social Observation of Public Spaces: A New Look at Disorder in Urban Neighborhoods." *American Journal of Sociology* 105, no. 3: 603–51. https://doi.org/10.1086/210356.

Sheppard, Stephen. 1999. "Hedonic Analysis of Housing Markets." In *Handbook of Regional and Urban Economics*, vol. 3, edited by Paul Cheshire and Edwin S. Mills, 1595–1635. Amsterdam: North-Holland. https://doi.org/10.1016/S1574-0080(99)80010-8.

Statistics Sweden. 2004. "Offer för våld och egendomsbrott 1978–2002" [Victims of Violence and of Property Crimes 1978–2002]. By Lars Häll, Rapport 104, Enheten för Social Välfärdsstatistik. Stockholm: Statistiska centralbyrån (SCB).

Swedish Association of Local Authorities and Regions. 2013. "Varför skjutsar föräldrarna barnen till skolan?" [Why Are Parents Driving the Kids to School?]. Avdelningen för tillväxt och samhällsbyggnad, Sveriges Kommuner och Landsting, Stockholm. https://webbutik.skr.se/bilder/artiklar/pdf/7164-956-0.pdf.

Swedish Public Television. 2016. "Butikerna i Husby stänger i protest" [The Shops in Husby Close in Protest]. By Richard Ekman and Aymen Mussa, *SVT Nyheter*, December 30, 2016. https://www.svt.se/nyheter/lokalt/stockholm/butikerna-proteststanger-i-husby.

———. 2017. "Kvinnorna valde bort nyårsfirande på Larmtorget" [The Women Opted Out of New Year's Celebrations at Larmtorget]. By Ricardo Garcia Canchaya, *SVT Nyheter*, January 3, 2017, Updated November 30, 2017. https://www.svt.se/nyheter/lokalt/smaland/kvinnorna-valde-bort-nyarsfirande-pa-larmtorget.

Swedish Transport Administration. 2012. "Barns skolvägar 2012" [Children's School Roads 2012]. Publication No. 2013:006, TRV 2010/21715. Trafikverket, Borlänge. https://trafikverket.ineko.se/Files/sv-SE/11519/RelatedFiles/2013_006_Barns_skolvagar_2012.pdf.

Tella, Rafael Di, Sebastian Galiani, and Ernesto Schargrodsky. 2010. "Crime Distribution and Victim Behavior During a Crime Wave." In *The Economics of Crime: Lessons for and from Latin America*, edited by Rafael Di Tella, Sebastian Galiani, and Ernesto Schargrodsky, 175–204. Chicago: University of Chicago Press.

Tita, George E., Tricia L. Petras, and Robert T. Greenbaum. 2006. "Crime and Residential Choice: A Neighborhood Level Analysis of the Impact of Crime on Housing Prices." *Journal of Quantitative Criminology* 22, no. 4: 299–317. https://doi.org/10.1007/s10940-006-9013-z.

Werner, Inga Britt. 2008. "Bostadskvalitet idag – en utvärdering av nybyggda bostäder, ur kundens synvinkel" [Housing Quality Today—An Evaluation of Newly Built Housing, from the Customer's Point of View]. Urbana och regionala studier, Skolan för arkitektur och samhällsbyggnad, KTH. https://vpp.sbuf.se/Public/Documents/ProjectDocuments/3f577f5b-8aca-4e20-acca-78bdce75a6c1/FinalReport/SBUF%2011660%20Slutrapport%20Utvärdering%20av%20nybyggda%20bostäder%20rev%2027sept.pdf.

Wilhelmsson, Mats. 2002. "Household Expenditure Patterns for Housing Attributes: A Linear Expenditure System with Hedonic Prices." *Journal of Housing Economics* 11, no. 1: 75–93. https://doi.org/10.1006/jhec.2002.0308.

Wilson, James Q., and George L. Kelling. 1982. "Broken Windows." *The Atlantic Monthly* 249, no. 3: 29–38. https://www.theatlantic.com/magazine/archive/1982/03/broken-windows/304465.

World Bank Group. 2015. "Sweden's Business Climate: A Microeconomic Assessment." International Bank for Reconstruction and Development, The World Bank, Washington, DC. https://www.enterprisesurveys.org/content/dam/enterprisesurveys/documents/reports/sweden/Sweden-Business-Climate-2015.pdf.

Zhu, Jiazhe, Sarah Brown, and Gwilym Pryce. 2016. "Local House Price Effects of Immigration in England and Wales: The Role of Regional Employment Accessibility and Ethnic Heterogeneity." Working Paper, The Applied Quantitative Methods Network (AQMeN). https://www.research.aqmen.ac.uk/wp-content/uploads/sites/27/2017/07/Working-paper-immigration_house_prices_zhu.pdf.

CHAPTER 17

Failed Integration

Man is the child of customs, not the child of his ancestors.

—Ibn Khaldun, *Muqaddimah*, 1377

Sweden has a knowledge-intensive economy. Swedish export companies such as ABB, Electrolux, Volvo, Scania, Sandvik, and Atlas Copco do not compete with low wages but with advanced technology, skilled labor, high quality, and innovation.

The level of prosperity in a society is predominantly determined by productivity, that is, by how much each person produces. Since the industrial revolution, the standard of living has gradually risen due to increased labor productivity—not because the number of hours worked per person has increased. On the contrary, the number of hours worked per person has fallen as we have become wealthier. The fundamental explanation for increased productivity is the dissemination of knowledge and technology. Productivity growth is thus crucial for a sustained increase in living standards. It also determines companies' labor demand and the wages they are willing to offer.

Hence, productivity plays a major role in social exclusion. One of the most important policies to combat social exclusion is to raise the level of knowledge and, thus, the productivity of those who find it hard to get jobs. In this way, those who are currently un- or underemployed become more attractive to hire at good wage levels. Tackling the problem by lowering wages without raising the productivity of unemployed people is not an attractive solution for high-tech countries.

Increasing demand for skills raises the bar for new arrivals. In the case of Sweden, nearly one-third of refugee immigrants do not have a nine-year elementary education, and many are functionally illiterate. Among native-born Swedes, the share who lack primary education is less than 1%. Illiterate adults naturally have difficulties learning Western languages at the level required for carrying out the jobs offered in today's labor market.

T. Sanandaji, *Mass Challenge*,
https://doi.org/10.1007/978-3-030-46808-8_17

It is often argued that the solution is more simple jobs. At first glance, this seems to make sense, but it overlooks the fact that in today's modern economy, there are few truly simple jobs that are in demand. In practice, less qualified jobs—like working in a grocery store—are not simple but require knowledge of cash handling, computers, customer service, language skills in Swedish and preferably some English, and so on.

The International Labour Organization has created the category "elementary occupations," which captures the least human capital-intensive professions. This means jobs such as street vendors, berry pickers, farmhands, and shoe shiners—jobs that today mostly are found in developing economies. There is demand for some of these jobs—such as movers and window and house cleaners—even in modern economies. However, there is no demand for street-based chewing gum vendors or hand washing of cars at stoplights. These types of simple jobs, which still exist in the Third World, gradually disappear with technological advances and have long since been rationalized away in advanced economies.

While many acknowledge the low employment rates among many immigrant groups in European welfare states, the problem formulation and consequently the proposed solutions are often based on wishful thinking about the underlying causes. The fundamental explanation for the low employment rate is low skill levels, coupled with the increasing demands of today's knowledge-intensive job market. Instead of soberly admitting that this is the case, both the left and the right have preferred to re-frame the issue according to their respective ideological pet ideas.

Public Opinion and the Migration Debate

A brief discussion of the political debate on immigration in Sweden may be useful to understand integration policy and its ideological forces. In the post-Soviet era, Sweden's political division can be described as a two-block party system dominated on the left by Social Democrats, Greens, and Socialists, while on the right by liberal or libertarian leaning center-right parties. Whereas views on domestic economic policy differed, the political leadership in both blocks had reached a consensus on generous refugee policy; the general public, though, was far cooler to the idea.

One example of this is the regularly recurring SOM survey conducted by Gothenburg University. The survey asked if it is a good idea for Sweden to take fewer refuges. Between 1990 and 2018, a plurality in every single survey supported reducing refugee immigration. Respondents also have the choice of not taking a stand on the issue. Excluding these non-committal replies, on average 66% of respondents with an opinion on the issue stated that it was a good suggestion to take fewer refugees. On average for this period, 50% stated that reducing the number of refugees was a good suggestion, 25% stated that it was a bad suggestion, while 25% picked neither option.

The same question was asked of Sweden's members of parliament in some years, with strikingly different results. Between 1994 and 2010, for instance, less than 10% of Swedish members of parliament agreed that taking fewer refugees was a good suggestion (Esaiasson 2016). This can be compared to almost 50% among the general public, corresponding to over 70% of those that opted to state their opinion. The gap in opinion between the Swedish political elite and the general public on refugee policy was among the largest in any political issue in the survey (Karlsson 2018).

One reason that this division did not create more of a tension is that refugee policy for a long time was a fairly unimportant issue for voters. Once the salience of the issue increased in the 2010s, the opinion gap sharpened, which contributed to the growth of the anti-immigrant Sweden Democrats as well as pushing the positions of the political parties to more closely align with voters.

The Education Mirage

In the buildup to the 2015 refugee crisis, Prime Minister Stefan Löfven reassured the public in a TV interview (Swedish Public Television 2015) that "Up to 30 percent of people now coming from Syria, for example, have a college education. Doctors, engineers, and other well-educated groups that we need are coming to Sweden." This claim was however inaccurate, as the Prime Minster misinterpreted basic education statistics. In fact, only a little more than one in ten of the people coming from Syria had degrees equivalent to a college education, whereas four in ten lacked even high school degrees (Statistics Sweden 2017). Overall, 15% of Syrians in Sweden have college degrees, including those who came prior to the 2015 migrant wave as well as those who obtained their college degrees in Sweden.

To be fair to the Prime Minister, the tendency to grossly inflate the share of highly educated asylum seekers is not unique to Sweden and occurs in most countries based on the same misunderstanding. A widely reported UNHCR (2015) estimate concluded that "86 per cent say they have secondary school or university education. Half of that group had studied at university." These figures were far from accurate and were exaggerated due to a combination of misleading classifications and biased sampling.

The definition of post-secondary education in international statistics is education after high school, not academic education at college level. Hence, post-secondary education also includes short vocational programs and is not synonymous with an academic education or a college degree. Many of those who are chefs, welders, hairdressers, or indeed dancers have post-secondary education, but are not academics. Someone with a few years of mechanical training in the Syrian military is not considered highly educated according to the Western definition, but may be defined as possessing tertiary education in statistics and put in the same broad category as a civil engineer. This misclassification is quite common and easily gives rise to false impressions.

When measuring education across different countries, broad categories are used by statistical organizations. This way, a high school degree or a master's degree can be roughly matched between, say, the United States, France, and Japan. These types of degrees may have different names in different systems but are roughly equivalent in terms of academic content. This standardization, however, can become misleading when applied to countries far behind in terms of economic development. When interpreting education statistics from developing countries, it is often forgotten that graduates from Koran schools in the Afghan countryside are put in the same category as mathematics graduates from Oxford. Consequently, these classifications can be highly deceptive, both when it comes to length, quality, and content of education, if they are not used with care.

When doing so, it is clear that based on official Swedish education statistics, the proportion of highly educated new arrivals is low by Swedish standards. According to Statistics Sweden (2014), approximately 10% of those newly arrived of working age are highly educated, compared to approximately 25% of the total Swedish population.

It is not only Statistics Sweden that has estimated the percentage of highly educated Syrians. Their Norwegian counterpart Statistics Norway defines college education as at least four years. Their estimate is that 6% of newly arrived Syrians have a college education of at least four years. As there is no data available for just over a third, this means that 9% of those who Statistics Norway has information on are highly educated. These numbers have been reported by Norwegian Public Broadcasting (2015), who concluded, among other things, that "Refugees from Syria to Norway have lower education than many had believed." Similarly, Danish Public Television estimated the proportion of highly educated among new arrivals to 13%, a number that includes both Syrians and other nationals (*TV 2* 2015).

In a German study (Ceritoglu et al. 2017), the education level among Syrians in Turkey was investigated. Barely 9% of the Syrian respondents had an academic education. Finally, the World Bank has estimated the proportion of Syrians with an academic education before the start of the war to 4%. Naturally, those who are more well-educated tend to be more mobile than those with lower education, but one must still be realistic about how much of an effect this overrepresentation can have when a large proportion of the country's population is fleeing a war.

Misinterpreting educational statistics like the Swedish Prime Minister did is of course in the short run both more convenient and gives more cause for optimism than the truth. If a large share of immigrants is well-educated, then it becomes easier to defend the theory that the immigration policy of recent years is economically beneficial in the long run. It also suggests an opportunity for simple policy interventions. For instance, the difficulties that new arrivals encounter in the job market could be caused by their foreign degrees in engineering, teaching, nursing, and medicine not being given proper formal recognition. This, in turn, implies that minor adjustments to Swedish bureaucracy could fix the problem.

Among university graduates with a foreign degree, many work in professions that do not correspond to their actual education, for example as taxi drivers or cleaners. To the extent that formal education does not correspond to the job that an individual has, overqualification is sometimes an issue, which may in part reflect discrimination. Interestingly, as it turns out, this is only an issue for those with foreign degrees. The fact that immigrants with Swedish degrees are doing much better in the job market than those with foreign degrees indicates that discrimination is not a primary explanation for the problems that immigrants face on the job market, but rather that employers in Sweden prefer Swedish degrees. In 2009, Statistics Sweden examined how well-established foreign-born university graduates were in the job market. The survey concerned those who had arrived in Sweden at the age of 15 or older. There were clear differences between immigrants who had a foreign degree and those with a Swedish degree, where the latter group fared significantly better. Statistics Sweden (2010) writes: "Of those educated in Sweden, 78 percent were working, while the proportion among those with foreign university education was 69 percent."

A more recent study by Eklund and Larsson (2020) investigated the share of immigrants with earnings high enough to be classified as self-sufficient. For the native-born and immigrants from other Nordic countries in 2016, the share among the population aged 20–64 with self-sufficient labor market income was 73%. The corresponding figure was only 38% for immigrants born in Africa, and 36% for those born in the Middle East. The education rate played an important role, as immigrants with college degrees were around 10% points more likely to be self-sufficient than those with high school degrees—who, in turn, were around 10% points more likely to be self-sufficient than those without high school degrees. Importantly, the authors point out that the degree of self-sufficiency is considerably lower than the official employment rate.

Blaming Big Government

The establishment right and those with libertarian or neoliberal inclinations often blame the welfare state, high wages, unions, and labor market regulations for low employment rates among immigrants. A common argument is that the thresholds to the job market must be lowered. By lowering taxes, minimum wages, removing labor legislation, and making public benefits less generous, more people—and immigrants in particular—can start working. There is some merit to this argument, and it is supported by simple economic models. It is, therefore, commonly cited by influential voices such as the Economist, the Wall Street Journal, the World Economic Forum, and the

OECD. There is, however, a strong case to be made that these factors have been exaggerated, and that even highly free market economic policy would not lead to full employment.

This school of thought is a fairly attractive view for those who consider immigration as analogous to free trade, and who explicitly or implicitly analyze these issues based on the first welfare theorem of Adam Smith's invisible hand. The idea is that given the existence of the rule of law and functioning markets, laissez-faire and minimum state intervention will guarantee optimal outcomes. Since problems are viewed as the result of economic distortions, it is natural for someone who applies this conceptual framework to come up with the conclusion that the unemployment rate of immigrants in welfare states is caused by social policy. This market liberal view based on classical economics should not be dismissed outright and, indeed, describes many situations fairly well, such as free enterprise and free trade. Nonetheless, immigration is not comparable to free trade since immigrants are not merely economic goods (such as Chinese textiles) but are also citizens. In Western European welfare states, public spending constitutes close to 50% of the economy, which makes conclusions based on models of free markets misleading.

The conclusion of the first welfare theorem assumes that government plays no significant part in economic redistribution, a conclusion that can be drastically altered if we are in fact operating in a world where there are substantial redistributive government policies already in existence. In a theoretical world with no government, it may be economically beneficial to allow low-skilled migration with very low productivity in order to produce cheap services. However, if we for ethical reasons have government policy that guarantees subsidized healthcare, the analysis becomes complicated since it is possible that the cost of providing healthcare is higher than the benefits generated by cheaper service provision.

This illustrates how existing government policies can invalidate laissez-faire presumptions underpinning open immigration policies. Moreover, sophisticated economics has shown that labor markets cannot be assumed to be characterized by the perfect conditions required for the first welfare theorem due to various distortions, externalities, and market failures—including transaction costs and imperfect information. Market imperfections mean that we cannot simply assume that all observed problems are caused by the government and that they can, hence, be solved by cutting down on government intervention. In practice, attempts to liberalize the labor market, cut taxes, and to deregulate have not solved the integration problem as was once expected. Sweden is not only a suitable case study for large-scale refugee migration, but also for the limits of lower-wage and lower-tax policies.

The Swedish welfare state has been cut back and the labor market deregulated in various waves since the early 1990s, both by social democratic and center-right governments. The magnitude of these reforms has been substantial—for instance, the government's share of the economy has been reduced from about 60% of GDP in the late 1980s to just below 50% today. At the same time, the Swedish labor market has gone from being one of the most regulated in the OECD, characterized by strong employment protection, to being fairly average. Wage dispersion has increased during the same period, so that de facto minimum wages set by unions are more flexible and far lower compared to the median. These reforms have likely had some effect on the employment of immigrants, but it is difficult to detect any major shift in aggregate data.

The failure of such policies to solve the problem strongly undermines any analysis based on the simple textbook model, which emphasizes high thresholds that keep out immigrants from the job market. It is understandable that the conclusion that social democratic policies were causing the problem appeared convincing. We have in this book observed that the countries with the biggest gaps between non-immigrant and immigrant employment tend to be precisely the most generous welfare states. The high correlation between immigrant integration and small-size government has led many to conclude that government must be causing the problem.

There is, however, a subtle reason why this superficial impression is an illusion. The key explanation for low employment is not the size of the welfare state, but rather the skill level of immigrants relative to natives. Immigrants who have high skill levels compared to the rest of the population tend to have high employment rates in all OECD countries—both those that have large welfare states and those that do not. Conversely, immigrants with low skill levels relative to the native average have lower employment rates, even in free market countries with smaller welfare states. The reason that we observe large employment gaps in welfare states is not a direct effect of their generous social and labor market policies, but rather that these countries are more likely to pursue generous refugee policies and take in large numbers of unskilled immigrants (Calmfors and Sánchez Gassen 2019; Lazear 2019; Brell et al. 2020; Henrekson et al. 2020).

The more market liberal OECD economies such as the United States, Australia, Canada, Switzerland, and New Zealand have far better labor market integration of immigrants, but tend to pursue policies where they mainly take in labor migrants. To the extent that these countries do take in refugees in sizeable numbers, as Switzerland and Canada have done during some periods, the integration outcomes are less impressive. Studies that compare refugees from the same country of origin with the same education do not find that, for instance, Canada outperforms Sweden by much. The type of high-skilled labor migrants Canada prioritized has favorable integration levels in Sweden as well. The vast differences in aggregate outcomes between Canada and Sweden are chiefly driven by the fact that they take different types of immigrants, so that the composition of the overall migrant population drives most of the outcome.

This does not just apply to Canada and Sweden but constitutes a general tendency, where large welfare states are more likely to pursue humanitarian immigration policies and take in low-skilled migrants, which causes the spurious correlation between welfare state policy and a lack of integration. It should be noted that the United States in this kind of analysis stands out as a country with impressive labor market integration of immigrants, even for the low-skilled. This is not to say that skill does not matter for employment in the United States, which it does, but that it simply outperforms other countries controlling for skill.

From 2006 onwards, the strategy forcefully pursued by Swedish governments to get migrants into work emphasized lowering the cost of labor through cutting payroll taxes and providing firms with generous subsidies. However, employers' price sensitivity turned out to be weaker than expected. Job market programs where the state subsidizes wage costs have similarly limited effects. Employers have simply demonstrated little interest in hiring low-skilled people, even after substantial discounts.

If the wage cost had been decisive, subsidies of 50–80% for companies that want to hire new arrivals would already have solved the problem. In fact, few additional jobs were created. Similarly, the experiment with reduced employer payroll taxes for young people indicates a low demand elasticity of only about 0.2–0.3 (Egebark and Kaunitz 2014; Skedinger 2014). This means that each percent of the reduction in wage costs only increased employment by 0.2–0.3%. In order to put that into perspective, such a weak effect size entails, if extrapolated, that a halving of the wage would only increase employment by about one-tenth. These experiences are devastating to theories that presuppose that the social exclusion of immigrants can be solved if only wage costs decreased sufficiently.

Blaming Small Government

For their part, the left often emphasizes that integration problems are due to a lack of social investment. The fact that Sweden already invests large amounts in a broad spectrum of social programs is in this context rarely mentioned. If the solution was to be found in social programs, Sweden would be the world champion of integration—not like today, performing worse than many other developed countries. It is also commonplace to argue that immigrants are in fact a well-educated group, and that the core problem is job market discrimination.

In response, the Scandinavian countries have introduced a myriad of social and job market programs to ensure integration. While there are programs that somewhat alleviate the problem, many are quite futile. Overall, it is clear that even massive spending on job market programs and subsidies have not closed the gap, although it could be argued that the situation would be ever worse without these interventions. Today, a sizable number of immigrants in Sweden live in an artificial "job market" that revolves around various state programs—sometimes jumping from program to program, without ever having regular employment in a real job.

One example of such a job market program is the Job Garage in the Stockholm suburb of Tensta, a project aimed at reducing youth unemployment in an immigrant-heavy suburb. The daily *Svenska Dagbladet* (2014, 2015) wrote about the project, as well as how young men in this neighborhood spent their time, in a couple of articles—one with the title "Being 30 and Never Having Had a Job Is Not Uncommon Here":

> "I've never had a job. None of my friends have jobs, and I have quite a large circle of friends. It's totally messed up," says a 29-year-old Tensta resident. He says he could imagine working with anything. He's soon starting an education program and maybe it will lead to a first job.
>
> ---
>
> Mustafa Zatara isn't enrolled in the Job Garage. He's there to make routines and everyday life work. Now he's angry and says that everything is shutting down in Tensta, everything moves away. Some claim that the area's young people are used as guinea pigs for different projects that lead nowhere.
>
> "You have no idea how hard it is to go to the Employment Service. The officers only want you to email, write resumes, and a lot of other things. But we're talking about people who don't even have email accounts. Where do you start then?" He and others there say that it's shameful in some circles to go to the Employment Service, or to seek help from the government. You lose your street cred, and for some people, that's all they have.
>
> "To ask for help is a failure out there." He points to the gray street and stresses that he knows what he's talking about. He knows many who hang out in the center all day long.
>
> "You see, if you want to hang with the boys, you don't go to the Employment Service. In the short term, hanging out in the street gives you more than going there."
>
> ---
>
> They've been rapping for former Prime Minister Fredrik Reinfeldt—and former Director-General of the Public Employment Service, Angeles Bermudez-Svankvist, invited them to her 50th birthday party. Now, many of the young people who worked in the project feel used and deceived.

Another more exotic example of a failed integration program is subsidies to a Somali cultural association to create a camel farm on the outskirts of Gothenburg. An article in *Göteborgs-Posten* (2017) provides the background to the venture of establishing a Scandinavian camel industry:

> Over $100,000 in tax money and grants have been awarded, but there is still no trace of the promised camel center in Angered. Despite the lack of building permits, money has been spent on fences, souvenirs, and camel milk imports.
>
> "It is said that the milk helps against autism … There is research showing that camel milk is particularly healthy. Among other things, they have taken blood tests on children with autism and seen that they benefit from drinking

> camel milk", says Malin Larsson (Green Party), and later clarifies that the existing studies have been on a smaller scale.
>
> ---
>
> However, this has not stopped the camel center from operating. Among other things, the land has been enclosed for $12,500, they have gone on study trips to Germany and Kazakhstan, and bought souvenirs in the form of alpaca wool, stuffed animals, and t-shirts. 1,500 liters of camel milk has also been imported from the Netherlands, which has been sold to private individuals.

One reason tax-subsidized hip-hop programs, camel farms, and countless other less flamboyant interventions have not solved the employment problem is that they do not get at the core of the issue. The fundamental explanation for the difficulties migrants experience in European labor markets is neither the lack of social programs, as the European left argues, or too many social programs, as the European right proclaims. The core problem is a lack of skills in an increasingly skill-intensive economy. The simple manufacturing jobs that used to be the gateway to integration for many immigrants no longer exist, and even the service sector can no longer absorb everyone as it is becoming more advanced.

Blaming Borders

In the Swedish immigration debate, libertarians and the progressive left were often allies—both arguing for a vision of open borders and contending that borders and regulated immigration are immoral, since it blocks the global poor from accessing the higher standard of living in the West. The support for open borders was particularly strong among the youth organizations of the political parties, both on the left and on the right. By the time in 2006 when the so-called Alliance of four right-of-center parties came to power, many of the leaders belonged to a generation fostered in youth organizations that supported a vision of open borders, often passionately so. The center-right combined pro-market views with socially liberal attitudes, including a belief in multiculturalism and a vision of a world without borders.

These views were often fused with preexisting political visions. The cultural left viewed immigrants as oppressed, and naturally resisted racism and Nazism that were associated with immigration restrictionism. Libertarians, in turn, were already against the welfare state, and could add to their list of criticism that the Swedish welfare state and unions, which upheld high wages, were immoral since they prevented the policy of alleviating global poverty through open borders. The influence of libertarian pro-immigration philosophy in Sweden should not be underestimated, since it becomes a dominant ideology of the Alliance government in 2006–2014, and afterward has remained influential among several political parties as well as Sweden's well-organized business lobby.

The libertarian proponent of open borders, Fredrik Segerfeldt, is worth citing here since he is among those who championed this view in explicit terms, while taking his ideology to its logical conclusion. For instance, Segerfeldt (2012) stated, "Our walls, our barbed wire, and our armed patrols hold millions of people in misery," and as a consequence, our "Closed borders are the rich countries' real debt to the poor of the world." He argues that living standards in many countries are so low that even opening immigration while establishing shanty towns in Sweden would bring relief. Indeed, Segerfeldt (2015) argues, "Shanty towns in Sweden may indeed be a solution to acute poverty in other countries." Consequently, it is selfish of Sweden to control immigration from countries like Somalia.

These reform proposals gained some political influence, but they have also been subject to criticism. In response, Fredrik Segerfeldt developed a controversial argument for the libertarian think tank Migro—a branch of the Swedish business lobby. He argued that it is possible to live on $45 a month in Sweden just like in Somalia, and that incomes higher than this imply a welfare improvement—even if they are significantly below the current Swedish levels (Norberg and Segerfeldt 2012):

> Let's see how you would do it in Sweden with $45. The cheapest way to get carbohydrates would be to eat rice. One kilogram of rice contains about 3,500 calories. To get 2,500 calories, you would have to eat 0.7 kilograms of rice. Hence, you need 21 kilograms of rice a month. A quick Google search indicates that the lowest price of rice in Swedish grocery stores is $1.5 per kilogram. The total monthly cost of carbohydrates will thus be $31.5. Hence, it is possible to survive on $45 in Sweden, just as it is possible to survive on the corresponding income in Somalia. In fact, it is not only possible to survive, but it is everyday life for billions of people. According to the World Bank, there are 1.4 billion people who live on a maximum of $1.25 a day adjusted for purchasing power. And another billion live on the double, that is, barely $2 a day with Swedish prices. If the rich world would give these people the opportunity to live and work here for, e.g., $10 ($300 per month), their situation would improve five-fold. The increase in human welfare is enormous.

One objection to this line of reasoning is that the comparison of purchasing power between Sweden and Somalia is dubious, since the baskets of goods available in these countries differ too much, which makes simplistic purchasing power adjustments invalid. Given the prices for housing, energy, clothing, medicine, etc., $45 would not cover a reasonable living standard in Sweden—since, for instance, cheap Somali-level housing is simply not available, and no shelter from the cold can be purchased with a few tens of bucks per month.

Also, in the example with rice diet, the budget leaves no room for the costs of preparing the rice or for the consumption of protein or vegetables. Even more worryingly, a strict rice diet can in the long run lead to deficiency disorders. In addition, exceptionally low economic, social, and health standards for migrants—even if an improvement compared to their country of origin—cannot exist in isolation. Rather, they tend to spill over to the rest of society.

The Importance of Human Capital

In order to understand the integration challenge, more important than regulation is the fact that Scandinavian job markets are characterized by high thresholds in the form of demanding knowledge requirements. The human capital gap compares the knowledge level of native- and foreign-born individuals. Overall, countries where there is a greater gap in knowledge between native- and foreign-born also have a greater gap in employment. Figure 17.1 shows the correlation between the knowledge and employment gap among native- and foreign-born in the OECD, as measured in the PIAAC knowledge test.

As noted earlier, there is no significant difference in the likelihood of being employed between the native- and foreign-born, after taking the actual measured knowledge of adults into account; nor is there any difference in the proportion who have highly qualified professions when actual skills are measured. Of foreign-born who have good or high skills in reading or math, approximately 54% of foreign-born and 49% of native-born work in professions that require a college education. The Long-Term Survey (SOU 2015:104) states:

Fig. 17.1 Relationship between knowledge and employment gap among native- and foreign-born (*Source* OECD)

> These results from the PIAAC surveys can be interpreted as it is essentially differences in language and general proficiency which explain that a higher proportion of native-born than foreign-born are working.

The gaps in job market outcomes between native- and foreign-born, which have sometimes been interpreted as structural discrimination, thus mostly reflect average differences in human capital and productivity. The lack of clear effects of job market discrimination on the aggregate level after taking human capital into account does not prove that discrimination never occurs. It is probable that positive special treatment of certain immigrants exists in certain contexts, as well as negative discrimination in other contexts, which, in turn, partly cancel each other out.

Direct discrimination, where high-productivity immigrants are rejected for racist reasons, is probably uncommon. This form of discrimination driven by aversion against certain groups is called preferential discrimination. However, discrimination can also be more subtle. For example, immigrants may have poorer opportunities in school and when it comes to getting their first job, thereby making it more difficult for them to build human capital. There are also clear signs of so-called statistical discrimination, where employers weed out immigrants when they have many job seekers (Carlsson and Rooth 2007).

Statistical discrimination works like this: If an employer knows that an immigrant group on average is more poorly educated or speaks worse Swedish, this employer can take a shortcut by excluding all applications from the group, including those who are highly educated and speak perfect Swedish. The employer's picture is statistically correct, but the effect may lead to unfair discrimination of the individual immigrant. This type of discrimination is most common when many are applying for the same job and for more standardized jobs. Economists like Gary Becker have pointed out that xenophobic discrimination affects the employers themselves, who lose out on skills since they reject productive workers. Hence, there are incentives also for employers to avoid preferential discrimination.

Important to note is that ethnic discrimination tends to differ between various immigrant groups, where Roma or those from African countries are more likely to experience prejudice than immigrants from neighboring European countries or from East Asia. This is one reason why discrimination may not show up clearly in aggregate labor market statistics, even though it does exist for some groups. The reality is even more complex and context-dependent; the degree of discrimination differs in industries, regions, and among social groups and may perhaps be higher among immigrant groups that between Swedes and immigrants. An African-American tourist with a New York accent might experience positive and welcoming attitudes when visiting Stockholm, whereas a Swedish-born person whose parents are from Somalia might be treated as an outsider and not let into clubs in their home city.

The self-perception of Swedes as tolerant may also make dealing with subtle racism more difficult. Many Swedes readily condemn racist comments by Donald Trump and criticize his mishandling of race relations in the United States, but still paid little attention to Black Lives Matter protests in Sweden focusing on the difficulties experienced by the Swedish Black population. One not uncommon attitude is that since they or their parents came as migrants and are granted access to the welfare state, they cannot have anything to complain about.

Negative Productivity

One major question is why the focus on cheaper labor did not work, contrary to what was expected based on simple textbook models. One hypothesis worth mentioning is that many of those who lack employment are so-called negative productivity workers—that is, workers who create greater costs than value for employers. Tyler Cowen and Jayme Lemke (2011) explain why not even the US job market can create full employment any longer:

> In essence, we have seen the rise of a large class of "zero marginal product workers," to coin a term. Their productivity may not be literally zero, but it is lower than the cost of training, employing, and insuring them. That is why labor is hurting but capital is doing fine; dumping these employees is tough for the workers themselves—and arguably bad for society at large—but it simply doesn't damage profits much. It's a cold, hard reality, and one that we will have to deal with, one way or another.

This may sound cynical, but the observation is based on empathy with the unemployed. In order to fix unemployment and the social exclusion it entails, we must have a better understanding of these phenomena. It would be more inhumane to accuse unemployed people that nobody wants to hire of being lazy, and sharply cut their unemployment benefits to make them work. One example of negative productivity workers might be illiterate immigrants, who do not speak the language in their new country. It may not matter how much employer payroll taxes are reduced in order to make these workers attractive to Volvo, Siemens, or even to McDonald's.

Someone who is not productive in one task can, of course, be productive in another, or become productive after training and with experience. The problem is that truly simple tasks that employers are willing to pay for are becoming fewer and fewer in number. Technology is gradually replacing the tasks that used to be performed by low-skilled workers, which means that these workers are not as sought after anymore. It has become less profitable for employers to spend resources on expensive supervision of low-productivity workers conducted by highly qualified managers. In skill-intensive companies, great value is created by experienced and qualified teams, but only if operations run smoothly. Thus, even a single unproductive person who disrupts production can cause significant losses. Unproductive workers can cause losses by lowering product quality, increasing production costs, creating conflict, contributing to a bad social atmosphere, giving poor customer service, or simply by being incompetent. In modern economies, the weakest link in the chain increasingly determines the productivity of the entire team.

The model based on these observations is sometimes called the "O-ring theory," after a small mechanical component in a space shuttle that failed and caused the Challenger disaster (Kremer 1993). Unemployment due to high public benefits and taxes is relatively straightforward to solve; but if Cowen and Lemke are right about unemployment increasingly being about negative productivity workers, the issue must be rethought.

Both the right and the left cling on to ideologically orthodox solutions that were tailored for a bygone era. While the economy has changed, their policy manuals have not been updated. Decades-old reform proposals do not provide answers to how the knowledge-intensive job market can absorb large groups lacking the skills required in today's economy—that is to say, both those with foreign and native backgrounds who are being left behind.

Increased Refugee Aid

In the Swedish original version of this book, 25 policy proposals are put forward to help solve the integration problem—mainly focusing on raising human capital and increasing productivity through public investments. In this book, that discussion is not included since it is of peripheral interest for foreign readers. One component, however, is even more important to include in a book aimed at an international audience.

Although it may sound far-fetched, the most important integration policy measure that can be taken is solving the global refugee crisis. This can in fact be done if the resources currently spent on expensive refugee reception in the West are instead used for humanitarian aid and large-scale refugee programs in peaceful developing countries.

Sweden and the other Scandinavian countries are sparsely populated, wealthy, and have high costs for receiving refugees. Sweden, Denmark, Finland, and Norway have a combined population of just over 25 million, and a combined GDP of $1.5 trillion. It would be nearly impossible for these small countries to solve the refugee problem for some 80 million displaced people in the world by inviting them in—particularly since the number of potential refugees willing to move once given the possibility is far larger. On the other hand, it would be quite realistic for these countries to double the UNHCR budget. Scandinavian countries can afford to give all refugees protection, but not through immigration.

The primary disadvantage of reduced immigration is that it prevents Sweden from helping refugees who are in distress because of war or for other reasons. My proposal for Sweden is to restrict refugee inflow while donating two dollars to international refugee aid for each dollar saved on reduced immigration. This can be combined with commitments regarding quota refugees and temporary residence permits for those with protection needs. If other Western countries followed suit, support for the approximately 80 million refugees in the world would be multiplied.

An irrational refugee policy that, with great strain on the own society, helps a fraction of those on the run is not the only option available. If the will existed, it would not be impossible to act as a true Moral Superpower and make a real difference to the global refugee problem.

References

Brell, Courtney, Christian Dustmann, and Ian Preston. 2020. "The Labor Market Integration of Refugee Migrants in High-Income Countries." *Journal of Economic Perspectives* 34, no. 1: 94–121. https://doi.org/10.1257/jep.34.1.94.

Calmfors, Lars, and Nora Sánchez Gassen, eds. 2019. *Integrating Immigrants into the Nordic Labour Markets*. Copenhagen: Nordic Council of Ministers. https://doi.org/10.6027/Nord2019-024.

Carlsson, Magnus, and Dan-Olof Rooth. 2007. "Evidence of Ethnic Discrimination in the Swedish Labor Market Using Experimental Data." *Labour Economics* 14, no. 4: 716–29. https://doi.org/10.1016/j.labeco.2007.05.001.

Ceritoglu, Evren, H. Burcu Gurcihan Yunculer, Huzeyfe Torun, and Semih Tumen. 2017. "The Impact of Syrian Refugees on Natives' Labor Market Outcomes in Turkey: Evidence from a Quasi-Experimental Design." *IZA Journal of Labor Policy* 6, no. 1: 5. https://link.springer.com/article/10.1186/s40173-017-0082-4.

Cowen, Tyler, and Jayme Lemke. 2011. "10 Percent Unemployment Forever?" *Foreign Policy*, January 6, 2011. https://foreignpolicy.com/2011/01/06/10-percent-unemployment-forever.

Egebark, Johan, and Niklas Kaunitz. 2014. "Do Payroll Tax Cuts Raise Youth Employment?" IFN working paper no. 1001, Research Institute of Industrial Economics, Stockholm. https://ssrn.com/abstract=2369989.

Eklund, Johan, and Johan P. Larsson. 2020. "När blir utrikes födda självförsörjande?" [When Will Foreign-Born Become Self-Sufficient?]. Rapport, Entreprenörskapsforum, Örebro University. https://entreprenorskapsforum.se/wp-content/uploads/2020/04/Rapport_Sjalvforsorjning_web.pdf.

Esaiasson, Peter. 2016. "Risk att den politiska legitimiteten försvagas" [Risk of Weakening Political Legitimacy]. Op-ed, *Dagens Nyheter*, February 25, 2016. https://www.dn.se/debatt/repliker/risk-att-den-politiska-legitimiteten-forsvagas.

Göteborgs-Posten. 2017. "Miljonbidrag – till kamelturism och mjölk" [Million Grant—For Camel Tourism and Milk]. By Michael Verdicchio, February 9, 2017. https://www.gp.se/nyheter/göteborg/miljonbidrag-till-kamelturism-och-mjölk-1.4150581.

Henrekson, Magnus, Özge Öner, and Tino Sanandaji. 2020. "The Refugee Crisis and the Reinvigoration of the Nation-State: Does the European Union Have a Common Asylum Policy?" In *The European Union and the Return of the Nation State*, edited by Antonia Bakardjieva Engelbrekt, Karin Leijon, Anna Michalski, and Lars Oxelhielm, 83–110. Cham: Palgrave Macmillan. https://doi.org/10.1007/978-3-030-35005-5_4.

Karlsson, David, ed. 2018. "Folkets främsta företrädare" [The People's Principal Main Representative]. Förvaltningshögskolan och statsvetenskapliga institutionen, Göteborgs universitet, Göteborg. https://gup.ub.gu.se/file/207522.

Kremer, Michael. 1993. "The O-Ring Theory of Economic Development." *The Quarterly Journal of Economics* 108, no. 3: 551–75. https://doi.org/10.2307/2118400.

Lazear, Edward P. 2019. "Why Are Some Immigrant Groups More Successful Than Others?" *Journal of Labour Economics*: forthcoming. https://doi.org/10.1086/706900.

Norberg, Johan, and Fredrik Segerfeldt. 2012. *Migrationens kraft: Därför behöver vi öppna gränser* [The Power of Migration: Thusly We Need Open Borders]. Stocksund: Hydra and Migro.

Norwegian Public Broadcasting. 2015. "Eksperter: Syrere kan bli vanskelig å få i jobb" [Experts: Syrians Can Be Difficult to Get into Work]. By Tormod Strand, *NRK*, October 4, 2015. https://www.nrk.no/norge/eksperter_-syrere-kan-bli-vanskelig-a-fa-i-jobb-1.12586205.

Segerfeldt, Fredrik. 2012. "Öppna våra gränser för att minska världens fattigdom" [Open Our Borders to Reduce World Poverty]. Op-ed, *SVT Nyheter*, December 1, 2012. https://www.svt.se/opinion/oppna-vara-granser-for-att-minska-varldens-fattigdom.

———. 2015. "Kåkstäder i Sverige kan visst det vara en lösning på akut fattigdom i andra länder" [Shanty Towns in Sweden May Indeed Be a Solution to Acute Poverty in Other Countries]. Twitter, September 26, 2015, 1:38 p.m. https://twitter.com/segerfeldt/status/647737113522348032.

Skedinger, Per. 2014. "Effects of Payroll Tax Cuts for Young Workers." IFN Working Paper No. 1031, Research Institute of Industrial Economics, Stockholm. https://ssrn.com/abstract=2476392.

SOU 2015:104. "Långtidsutredningen 2015: Huvudbetänkande" [Long-Term Survey: Main Report]. Betänkande av Långtidsutredningen, Statens offentliga utredningar (SOU), Wolters Kluwer, Stockholm. https://www.regeringen.se/4ae55e/contentassets/86d73b72a97345feb2a8cbc8b6700fa7/sou-2015104-langtidsutredningen-2015-huvudbetankande.

Statistics Sweden. 2010. "Svensk utbildning ger jobb" [Swedish Education Provides Jobs]. By Frida Hultgren. *Välfärd* magazine, no. 1, 2010. Statistiska centralbyrån (SCB), Stockholm.

———. 2014. "Utbildningsbakgrund bland utrikes födda" [Educational Background Among Foreign-Born]. Temarapport 2014:6. Enheten för utbildning och arbete, Statistiska centralbyrån (SCB), Örebro. https://www.scb.se/contentassets/55252e35cc1147db94245613ada36735/uf0506_2013a01_br_a40br1406.pdf.

———. 2017. "Utrikes föddas utbildningsbakgrund 2017" [Educational Background 2017 Among Foreign-Born Persons]. Avdelningen för befolkning och välfärd, Statistiska centralbyrån (SCB), Örebro. https://www.scb.se/contentassets/e9353be5b6624556a8c695c2e348a8c2/uf0506_2017a01_br_a40br1805.pdf.

Svenska Dagbladet. 2014. "Politikerna pissar på oss och vi står här utan paraply" [The Politicians Piss on Us and We Stand Here Without an Umbrella]. By Negra Efendić, SvD Näringsliv, October 4, 2014. https://www.svd.se/politikerna-pissar-pa-oss-och-vi-star-har-utan-paraply.

———. 2015. "Att vara 30 och aldrig ha haft ett jobb är inte ovanligt här" [Being 30 and Never Having Had a Job Is Not Uncommon Here]. By Yvonne Åsell and Negra Efendić, SvD Näringsliv, April 18, 2015. https://www.svd.se/att-vara-30-och-aldrig-ha-haft-ett-jobb-ar-inte-ovanligt-har.

Swedish Public Television. 2015. "Stefan Löfven (S) intervjuas av Camilla Kvartoft" [Stefan Löfven (S) Is Interviewed by Camilla Kvartoft]. *The Party Leader*, live broadcast of hearings by party leaders, April 22, 2015.

TV 2 (Denmark). 2015. "Undersøgelse: Nyankomne flygtninge har lav uddannelse" [Survey: Newly Arrived Refugees Have Low Education]. By Niels Lykke Møller and Peter Vesterlund, TV 2 Nyhederne, November 1, 2015. https://nyheder.tv2.dk/2015-11-01-undersoegelse-nyankomne-flygtninge-har-lav-uddannelse.

UNHCR. 2015. "UNHCR Says Most of Syrians Arriving in Greece Are Students." By Don Murray, December 8, 2015, UNHCR, Genève. https://www.unhcr.org/news/latest/2015/12/5666ddda6/unhcr-says-syrians-arriving-greece-students.html.

CHAPTER 18

E Pluribus Unum

> Of your safety; of your prosperity; of that very liberty which you so highly prize… Citizens, by birth or choice, of a common country, that country has a right to concentrate your affections.
>
> —George Washington's Farewell Address, 1796

The previous chapters of the book have focused on unsuccessful economic and social outcomes. This final chapter deals with the even more complex issue of cultural and national integration. Many immigrants do not perceive themselves as part of the Swedish community, including those with weak ties to their or their parents' country of origin. Instead, a common identity has developed among those of non-Western origin in the Middle East, Latin America, Africa, Central Asia, and—in some cases—the Balkans, as permanent "immigrants."

Economic and cultural exclusion are often linked, and they also amplify each other. In addition to political reforms, the solution to social exclusion would be facilitated by greater cultural integration of those with immigrant backgrounds, so that immigrants and those with Swedish background feel like parts of the same community and have stronger reciprocity toward each other. This, unlike economic policy, is not something that is directly controlled by the state, or that can be forced to happen through determined application of policy. Achieving stronger cultural integration is a matter of discourse, norm formation, and a voluntarily developed spontaneous order that facilitates the formation of a national community.

E pluribus unum is Latin for "out of many, one," or "one out of many," and was the traditional motto of the United States after the victory in the American Revolutionary War. It originally referred to the merger of the thirteen colonies into a single state. Over time, the term has come to refer to a union of immigrants from many different countries into a uniform American identity. *E pluribus unum* is thus an opposite ideal for immigration

T. Sanandaji, *Mass Challenge*,
https://doi.org/10.1007/978-3-030-46808-8_18

to multiculturalism, where different immigrant groups should maintain their particularities and separate identities while living in the same country.

The term is explained by Wikipedia (2017): "in recent years its meaning has come to suggest that out of many peoples, races, religions, languages, and ancestries has emerged a single people and nation—illustrating the concept of the melting pot." In Sweden, the American concept of a melting pot has often been misunderstood as a synonym for multiculturalism, when it actually refers to its opposite. Many cultures contribute to the mix, but the point of the allegory is that in a melting pot, metals melt together and form a final product that is uniform, homogeneous, and solid. Typical descendants of Swedes in the United States thus identify themselves as Americans, and have greater loyalty to Americans of Irish or Italian origin than to Swedes. In recent years, this ideal has also in the United States come to be questioned with the emergence of multiculturalism, which encourages immigrants to adhere to their traditional cultures and identity. An idea that has become common among both libertarians and progressives is that countries should be regarded as geographical areas with administrative institutions, and that nation-states are archaic remnants, which should eventually be abolished.

In Sweden, multiculturalism is an ideal, although there has rarely been any clear idea about what this actually entails in practice. Many have gone even further and denied that Swedish culture and Swedish values exist at all. At the same time, integration is working less well than most people would wish. As mentioned previously, a survey by Sifo in 2016 showed that three-quarters of the population do not think integration in Sweden is working well. There is also a paradox where many profess to multiculturalism as an ideal, but do not act on it in their own personal lives. Mella (2011) describes the results of a comprehensive annual survey on attitudes toward diversity. The majority of Swedes only have very few interactions with immigrants outside of school and work, and "As a rule, Swedes do not socialize with non-European immigrants. 40.9 percent never interact with non-European immigrants and 42.1 percent do so rarely."

Another example is the staffing company Proffice's survey of what employers say about diversity in the workplace in theory versus how they act. The proportion of managers who indicate that they work actively with diversity has increased to 80%; at the same time, the proportion that uses diversity as a criterion in their own recruitment has decreased to 32%. Proffice (2015) writes: "It's becoming increasingly important to work actively with diversity, but fewer considered diversity to be important in their most recent recruitment."

We saw earlier that Sweden often is ranked highest in the world when it comes to inhabitants' self-reported tolerance toward neighbors from other ethnic backgrounds in international attitude surveys. There is, again, an irony in the fact that Sweden at the same time is one of the countries where those from abroad find it the most difficult to find new friends. Integration is a social process, but Sweden is not perceived as a particularly social country.

The Expat Insider ranks the attractiveness of countries through surveys among the foreign-born (including both immigrants and people working temporarily in the country). Sweden is doing well in many respects, but is ranked among the lowest in terms of how difficult it is for those from abroad to meet friends. In the 2016 survey, Sweden ranked fourth from the bottom among 67 surveyed nations—only ahead of Denmark, Norway, and Kuwait. About 60% of those surveyed indicated that they had difficulty finding friends in Sweden. Together with other Nordic countries, Sweden also ranked lowest in terms of how welcome those from abroad felt. *The Local* newspaper (2016) interviews the founder of Expat Insider:

> The famously reserved Swedes make Sweden among the most difficult countries for foreigners to feel at home in, according to a survey ranking the quality of life for expats around the world.
>
> – – –
>
> "Expats have a hard time feeling welcome in this country; they perceive the local population as unfriendly and distant, and they have trouble finding new friends, especially Swedish ones."

In a similar survey conducted by the bank HSBC, Sweden ranked 45 out of 45 in terms of how easy expats experienced that it was to find friends.

This does not mean that Swedes are deliberately dishonest in surveys asking about tolerance. If nothing else, the generosity of Swedish taxpayers shows that an overwhelming majority actually have great goodwill toward immigrants. The explanation to the paradox is probably found at a deeper level. Sweden's exceptionally high social capital, in terms of standards and rules of behavior, makes the country well-functioning and tolerant. It also means that becoming an inside group member at the private level, such as at workplaces and in friendships, requires compliance with these norms. Many immigrants are not accepted into the group when they do not meet these implicit requirements. Simultaneously, the prevalence of multiculturalism means that Swedes are uncomfortable with demanding the same behavioral conformity from immigrants as is required by the majority group. There is a high cost for Swedes to try to enforce these rules for immigrants. It is easier to quietly isolate oneself from those immigrants who do not comply with the often unspoken behavioral rules, which Swedes have been raised with since birth.

Despite the difficulties, there are extremely strong incentives to be integrated into Sweden—in order to work, manage everyday life, and participate in popular culture—and a high proportion of Sweden's non-European immigrants have also been integrated. In some cases, it happens subconsciously over the years, despite initial reluctance. At the same time, there is a significant group that has not been integrated, often living in areas of social exclusion.

Many Swedes are not fully aware of the parallel societies that have emerged, as well as of how great the cultural distance has become. Both Swedes' stereotype of immigrants and non-integrated immigrants' stereotype of Swedes are exaggerated, but they are none the less important to be aware of. A paper by students in social work at the University of Gothenburg reproduces longer interviews with immigrant youths in Hammarkullen about their view of segregation (Ako et al. 2010):

> "Segregation can lead to crime, in turn, leading to the situation deteriorating and the problem increasing more, many immigrant guys haven't met Swedish young people, they believe that all Swedes are racists and therefore you want to pay back by committing crimes. Now I'm more mature and have met many Swedes from school or in my free time, for that reason, I've managed to get another picture of society and Swedes." … Because of segregation, us-and-them type of thinking increases, which leads to a big gap being created between different areas, which, in turn, leads to irritation and conflicts. Darin says that when he, together with his friends, visit other areas/districts, he feels that people look at them differently. He says:
>
> "Those who live there point to us and laugh too. This feels strange and you get annoyed." His friend Haval continues to explain:
>
> "You know, I think it happens because we behave differently. The others aren't used to such behavior, so they get shocked and start pointing."

The answers from the immigrant youths in the interviews highlight the distance and the mutual suspicion that often exists between immigrants and Swedes. This distance leads to both Swedes and immigrants misunderstanding each other's motives and how they are perceived by the other group. Immigrant youths who rarely or never associate with Swedes believe that Swedes are racists. This leads partly to them becoming more guarded and suspicious of Swedes, and partly to them misunderstanding the behavior of Swedes in innocent interactions. When Swedes act with reserved caution, this is misinterpreted as xenophobic aggression, which, in turn, leads to increased hostility toward Swedes. To be told to comply with Swedish behavioral rules is often misinterpreted as negative discrimination.

The deep cultural tendency of Swedes not to be socially spontaneous with their neighbors is another source of cultural misunderstandings with immigrants, who perceive it as a way to exclude, being specifically directed against them. At the same time, there is a minority of Swedes who are genuinely xenophobic and actually treat immigrants badly, which reinforces immigrants' fear of Swedes as racists.

In addition to culture clashes, young people with immigrant background quickly feel that there are negative notions of them being criminally inclined among Swedes, which many are deeply hurt by. From the Swedes' point of view, this is an inevitable statistical picture that is dependent on the fact that immigrant boys on average are more likely to commit crimes. Even if only a tenth of groups with immigrants moving around town constitute danger, it can be a reasonable strategy for others to keep a distance, since they do not know which tenth they are dealing with.

The same applies to negative beliefs about non-European immigrants as poor and low-skilled, which reduces the status of immigrants and inevitably creates discomfort for the group. The significance of low status should not be underestimated, although it is not always articulated. In everyday interactions, such as trying to get into a night club, getting to know new people, or applying for a job, both parties have a subconscious feeling about immigrants as a subordinate group. In situations where social friction inevitably occurs, such as an argument about time slots in the laundry room, or brawls among schoolchildren, there is a temptation among Swedes to resort to implying that it is their country and that immigrants should feel grateful for being there.

Exclusive High Social Capital

The concept of social capital is not precisely defined and refers—in different contexts—to norms, values, the degree of trust, or the strength of social relationships with others (cf. Bourdieu 1986; Coleman 1988; Putnam et al. 1993; Fukuyama 1995). Within social networks, an important part of social capital is reciprocity and norms for maintaining cooperation. Groups with high social capital feel mutual trust in each other, which increases group cohesion. Social capital is associated with a better functioning democracy, civil society, and economy (Rothstein 2003). The value of such "team spirit" for state and community success was emphasized already by the Medieval historian Ibn Khaldun's discussion of *asabiyya*, or group solidarity.

However, high social capital also has a dark side. Strong internal cohesion often occurs at the expense of external exclusion. Political scientist Robert Putnam (2000) distinguishes between *bridging* and *bonding* social capital. Bonding social capital has been an essential success factor for homogenous nations such as Sweden, Finland, and Japan, but has at the same time made these societies exclusionary.

When integrating strangers, the strengths of these societies turn into weaknesses. As a stranger, it is difficult to be welcomed into tightly connected networks. For several reasons, high social capital functions as a barrier to entry. Those within the group follow the same codes and trust each other, but do not necessarily trust others. Since cooperation is already working well, the members of the group are often less in need of making new connections, and—if necessary—new contacts can be found within the network by using referrals from others. Scandinavian countries are characterized by dense social networks, and in contrast to many other communities, a high level of trust—not only within the family but also between acquaintances and colleagues. Employment and business contacts often take place within informal acquaintance networks, to which immigrants are less likely to belong.

Another important reason is that high social capital has often arisen as a result of a normative process, which has created strong behavioral norms for reciprocity, compliance, communication, and cooperation. Even if the group lacks prejudices and has a benevolent attitude, outsiders who have not absorbed these behavioral norms will not fit in as well—initially, they may even risk compromising the level of collaboration and cohesion. An analogy is a well-oiled sports team that is about to bring on new players, who are not used to the group's routines.

In this and other ways, Sweden's high social capital can paradoxically make it difficult for immigrants to enter the job market as well as society in general. This is discussed by Forsander (2004), who argues that: "The homogeneity of the norm base and tight social networks lead to strong in-group loyalty that excludes outsiders who do not—from the perspective of in-group members—share the common norm base." In a similar vein, Putnam et al. (1993) write:

> Social capital, particularly social capital that bonds us with others like us, often reinforces social stratification. … Norms and networks that serve some group may obstruct others, particularly if the norms are discriminatory or the networks socially segregated.

A common example is that being told to comply with rules of order, which apply to everyone, is perceived as racist discrimination with insidious intent. Sweden is one of the world's most rules-based societies, where basically all activities are governed by explicit and implicit rules. Everyone is expected to get in line, speak quietly in public spaces, wait for the signal to cross the street, make room for others and quietly stare into space in the elevator, not arrive too late or too early to a party, and not to intrude on fellow passengers on the bus by joking with one's friends. A Swedish joke illustrates the point: "If a stranger talks to you on the street, there are two possibilities: the person is either mentally ill or an American tourist."

Visitors from Western countries such as the United States or France can also be amazed at how strictly well-regulated the Scandinavian nations are. These and thousands of other rules are rarely fully articulated and are, therefore, implemented with the help of social control, such as annoyed looks, rather than formal sanctions. Swedes themselves are often unaware of their cultural specificity, which they take for granted. Canadian philosopher Marshall McLuhan used the analogy of a fish in the water to illustrate how we may be unaware of the environments we are used to: "One thing about which fish know exactly nothing is water, since they have no anti-environment which would enable them to perceive the element they live in."

The fact that immigrants feel like strangers in Sweden is well-known, but not to what extent immigrants regard Swedes as an alien. The self-perception of Swedes is characterized by the image of an open country that has been generous to immigrants by providing asylum and welfare. The Swedes perceive themselves as being kind, soft, and tolerant. However, among many immigrants, a darker picture has been formed: The Swede is considered to be hard, frigid, hostile, and arrogant—even outright dangerous.

The reason is that immigrants feel unwelcome and experience a latent hostility in their interactions with Swedes. This is often not the effect of intentional malice on the part of the Swedes, but is still perceived as such by immigrants. Swedes interacting with immigrants in the suburb may at the same time experience a fear that is more statistically based. Power and dominance, however, are context-dependent. Swedes are, as the majority population, in many cases socially superior to immigrants, or are at least perceived in that way.

Newly arrived immigrants ultimately see Sweden as a country belonging to the Swedes, and they are therefore, for apparent reasons, easily worried and alienated when they are not invited into the community. Individual Swedes are already part of the social community. There is an asymmetrical relationship, where Swedes normally have greater power to socially exclude immigrants than the other way around. Immigrants are aware of the negative beliefs that exist about them as a group—a consciousness that has been exaggerated by constant media rhetoric about the racism of Swedes. Hence, immigrants are often particularly hurt by being negatively assessed in social interactions with Swedes.

Cultural Self-Esteem

Multiculturalism is an integration barrier. The doctrine teaches the natives that they lack the moral right to transfer their culture and values to immigrants, while immigrants are encouraged to cling to their home country's identity. This impedes integration, both into the Swedish way of life and into the Swedish economy.

Multiculturalism has harmful consequences, even though the idea behind it is well-intentioned. The doctrine morally privileges Third World cultures over Western cultures. It teaches a modern version of original sin by condemning Western civilization for historical crimes, colonialism, and racism. A large part of today's public debate is devoted to reciting lists of the historical crimes of Western nations. The problem with this discourse is not that the Western world is innocent, which it is not. The problem is that this blame-it-all-on-the-West doctrine is a one-sided interpretation of world history. To continuously and without pause repeat Western crimes against humanity, while ignoring similar crimes committed by non-Westerners, creates a dark and distorted image of Western civilization. This is done in conjunction with the Western world's contribution to humanity—such as democracy, the scientific revolution, human rights, and the industrial revolution—being toned down, or even passed over in silence.

The resentment against the West that this creates complicates integration. Immigrants learn and accept the message of victimization, which promotes aggression and contempt for the host society. Adopting the role of the victim is appealing from a psychological perspective because it confers moral superiority. Immigrants who want to integrate and embrace a Swedish identity are accused of "acting white."

In parallel with the victimization of immigrants, Sweden has developed a feeling of collective guilt. Hence, one now lacks the cultural self-esteem required to integrate immigrants into society. Former Social Democratic party leader Mona Sahlin made a statement, which perfectly illustrates this lack of cultural self-esteem during her time as Minister for Integration, when she was asked by the Turkish Youth Union's magazine *Euroturk* (2002) what Swedish culture is like:

> "I often get that question, but I can't figure out what Swedish culture is," says Mona Sahlin.
>
> "I think that's a bit what makes many Swedes so jealous of immigrant groups. You have a culture, an identity, a history, something that binds you together. And what do we have? We have Midsummer's Eve and such 'pathetic' things."

Note that this hostility toward Swedish culture does not originate from Muslim immigrants; it comes from the Swedish elite—both on the Right and the Left. This is a problem, since cultural self-esteem is important for social cohesion. Integration of immigrants requires that there is a common culture to be integrated into, at the same time as this culture must be attractive enough for someone to be tempted to embrace it. A confident and open national identity facilitates integration, since no one can be integrated into an empty nothing.

A culture whose own elite constantly communicates its deficiency and how racist its members are will inevitably have trouble attracting new recruits. Hence, Sweden today lacks a roadmap for integration of immigrants; there is no social contract whereby Swedes undertake to accept immigrants as one of their own, if certain criteria have been met. It is this contradiction between reality and ideology that is pulling Sweden apart. The political and media elite can love, or at least pretend to love, the new multicultural society, which is defined by the lack of common values. However, the Swedish public has never been particularly enthusiastic about the project.

Therefore, from the immigrants' point of view, the Swedish state is warm and generous, while Swedish society is cold and distant. Sweden has received more immigrants per capita than any other comparable country, but immigrants do not feel welcome. In response to failed integration, the establishment has doubled down on its efforts to shove multiculturalism down Sweden's throat, while non-elite Swedes and immigrants are left to take the blame for failed policy.

Again, note that Sweden has never been an easy country in which to culturally integrate. As discussed above, Swedes tend to be reserved with extensive social distance between people. The country's culture is complex and full of subtle rules as well as non-transparent norms and codes of conduct. These strong behavioral norms are maintained by social pressure. The Swedes are conformist and quite intolerant of deviations from group norms—from immigrants or Swedes. Immigrants who do not live up to the expected behavioral requirements, thus, often feel distance and negativity in their personal interactions with Swedes. Consequently, socially frigid Scandinavia is not really an ideal testing ground for the multicultural experiment.

Many immigrants are raised in Sweden but, at the same time, lack a clear path to integrating into their new homeland. The resentment that constitutes the fuel for antisocial behavior is not caused primarily by material poverty. The underlying cause is social inequality. Visible minorities often remain second-class citizens in Sweden—especially if they live in Rinkeby or Rosengård and speak with a ghetto accent.

The state can hand out welfare benefits and iPads, but it cannot force Swedes to treat immigrants as equals in daily interactions. Rebellious immigrant youths may be unable to articulate the causes of their anger, yet few of them are unaware of their place in the social hierarchy.

The Thucydidean Perspective

Lack of cultural integration degrades the prerequisites for socioeconomic integration and increases the risk of antisocial behavior. Young people who feel that they rank at the bottom of an ethnic class society get angry and easily feel that they are "fucked for life." Thus, they have nothing to lose by committing crimes, or by taking out their frustrations on established society. This attitude is clear from the tabloid *Aftonbladet*'s (2003) interview with one of the members of the Botkyrka gang "Fucked For Life" (FFL) at the Norrtälje correctional facility:

> The criminal gang FFL is behind bank heists, armed robberies, and car jackings. They have stolen several million. "We're as far outside of society as is possible. There's no turning back," says "Chico," 29. … "Chico" describes himself and his "brothers" as professional criminals. "We have no regular jobs and we can't get any either. I've never been adapted to society; I totally don't give a fuck about it."

Seeking the explanation for social exclusion and antisocial behavior in economic factors, such as public spending, has proven to be pointless. Classic materialist explanations are not adapted to the new ethnic-social reality that has emerged in Sweden and other Western countries—not least because they ignore basic human psychology. If you ask the youths of the suburbs themselves, they often say that they want "respect" more than anything else. This explanation should not be dismissed lightly. Honor and respect are not fuzzy or archaic concepts; they are key driving forces in human behavior.

The Athenian historian Thucydides—as cited at the very beginning of this book—argued that the root causes of human conflict were honor, fear, and profit. Sweden has shown great material generosity toward immigrant youths, but hardly the respect they deserve as equals. Unlike most Swedish pundits, Thucydides would not have had a problem understanding the psychological driving forces behind the riots in the suburbs. Building a society based on ethnic socioeconomic segregation inevitably leads to conflict.

The interaction between poverty, low social status, and ethnicity is explosive. Areas with many immigrants who have done well financially and have high social status do not experience these types of unrest. Moreover, ethnic Swedes with low incomes do not feel the same bitterness toward society. Swedish low-income earners have no reason to suspect that their problems are due to widespread racism.

When a person grows up, looks around in society, and observes that those who look the same as themselves tend to have lower incomes and lower social status, while those with blonde hair and blue eyes are doing well, it is easy to conclude that society is inherently racist. The result is a growing bitterness toward society. This negative view is confirmed every time a job application is denied, or every time a Swede chooses not to sit next to them in the subway.

If Sweden is to have any chance to regain the idyllic atmosphere of the good old days, it is about time that it starts practicing what it preaches. The Swedish majority population combines tolerant political values with a passive, and even passive-aggressive, attitude toward immigrants in their private lives. Paying lip service to multiculturalism and espousing empty rhetoric about "everyone's equal value" is useless when it is not matched by one's own personal actions.

Sweden has accepted a record number of immigrants spatially, but not socially. This immigration policy was designed and implemented by the Swedish elite—not by the immigrants themselves, who stand powerless in the face of the given social structures of the recipient nation. Swedish taxpayers have carried the financial burden, but it is the immigrants who have carried most of the far greater human cost. Ironically, many of those in power are well aware that the policies they themselves have implemented and still pretend to support have failed, but instead they project their failure on the immigrants.

In addition to reforms, Sweden needs a new social contract—a helping hand that gives immigrants a real path into society. It is reasonable for society to require new citizens to adhere to the country's rules and the informal institutions that make up its social bonds, if it is done in a way that is fair to all. On the other hand, it is a form of disguised racism to refuse to impose the same social demands on immigrants as on ethnic Swedes, particularly when this abdication leads to immigrants being kept out of mainstream society. Those with foreign origin, in turn, should realize that it is not racism to be expected to follow the same rules as everyone else and respect Swedish culture and values.

The immigration crisis did not end in 2015, as many shallowly believe. Current trajectories suggest that Sweden is merely at the beginning of a far dragged, long-term crisis as the problems described in this book risk growing further, since the underlying forces have not bet resolved or even acknowledged in public discourse. To avoid this and save its egalitarian and internationally admitted welfare society, Sweden needs to more sincerely confront the mass challenge the country is facing. It is not yet too late—given the will to learn from the dear-bought lessons of the past.

References

Aftonbladet. 2003. "Chico, 29: Jag skiter totalt i samhället" [Chico, 29: I Don't Give a Shit About Society]. By Andreas Harne and Camilla Norström, March 13, 2003, updated March 11, 2011. https://www.aftonbladet.se/nyheter/a/ddw59j/chico-29-jag-skiter-totalt-i-samhallet.

Ako, Sharif, Michail Timtjenko, and Wasfi Talusi. 2010. "Ungdomar och kriminalitet i Hammarkullen: En studie om ungdomarnas syn på segregation som bakomliggande riskfaktor för kriminalitet" [Youth and Crime in Hammarkullen: A Study on Young People's View of Segregation as an Underlying Risk Factor for Crime]. Bachelor's thesis. Institutionen för socialt arbete, Göteborgs universitet, Göteborg. https://gupea.ub.gu.se/bitstream/2077/23105/1/gupea_2077_23105_1.pdf.

Bourdieu, Pierre. 1986. "The Forms of Capital." In *Handbook of Theory and Research for the Sociology of Education*, edited by John G. Richardson, 241–58. New York: Greenwood Press.

Coleman, James S. 1988. "Social Capital in the Creation of Human Capital." *American Journal of Sociology* 94, S95–S120. https://doi.org/10.1086/228943.

Euroturk. 2002. "Göran & Mona" [Göran and Mona]. By Ayda Aksakal, Turkiska ungdomsförbundet, Stockholm. http://turkiskaungdomsforbundet.blogspot.se/2010/11/euroturk-pa-natet.html.

Forsander, Annika. 2004. "Social Capital in the Context of Immigration and Diversity: Economic Participation in the Nordic Welfare States." *Journal of International Migration and Integration* 5, no. 2: 207–27. https://doi.org/10.1007/s12134-004-1010-1.

Fukuyama, Francis. 1995. *Trust: The Social Virtues and the Creation of Prosperity*. New York: Free Press.

Mella, Orlando. 2011. "Mångfaldsbarometern: Sju år av attitydmätningar" [Diversity Barometer: Seven Years of Attitude Surveys]. *Sociologisk Forskning* 48, no. 4: 45–53. https://www.jstor.org/stable/41698242.

Proffice. 2015. "Mångfaldsbarometern 2015: 400 chefer svarar om mångfald" [Diversity Barometer 2015: 400 Managers Respond About Diversity]. Proffice Group, Stockholm. https://docplayer.se/2438586-Mangfaldsbarometern-400-chefer-svarar-om-mangfald.html.

Putnam, Robert D. 2000. "Bowling Alone: America's Declining Social Capital." In *Culture and Politics: A Reader*, edited by Lane Crothers and Charles Lockhart, 223–34. New York: St. Martin's Press. https://doi.org/10.1007/978-1-349-62397-6_12.

Putnam, Robert D., Robert Leonardi, and Raffaella Y. Nanetti. 1993. *Making Democracy Work: Civic Traditions in Modern Italy*. Princeton: Princeton University Press.

Rothstein, Bo. 2003. *Sociala fällor och tillitens problem* [Social Traps and Problems of Trust]. Stockholm: SNS Förlag.

The Local. 2016. "'Unfriendly' Swedes Give Expats the Cold Shoulder." By Emma Löfgren, August 29, 2016. https://www.thelocal.se/20160829/unfriendly-swedes-give-expats-the-cold-shoulder.

Wikipedia. 2017. "Talk:E pluribus unum." Last updated on June 18, 2017. https://en.wikipedia.org/wiki/Talk%3AE_pluribus_unum.

Index

T. Sanandaji, *Mass Challenge*, https://doi.org/10.1007/978-3-030-46808-8